Howard Thurman

Howard Thurman

Philosophy, Civil Rights, and the Search for Common Ground

Kipton E. Jensen

THE UNIVERSITY OF
SOUTH CAROLINA PRESS

Published by the University of South Carolina Press
Columbia, South Carolina 29208

www.sc.edu/uscpress

Manufactured in the United States of America

28 27 26 25 24 23 22 21 20 19
10 9 8 7 6 5 4 3 2 1

Library of Congress Cataloging-in-Publication Data
can be found at http://catalog.loc.gov/.

ISBN 978-1-64336-047-8 (hardback)
ISBN 978-1-64336-048-5 (ebook)

This book was printed on recycled paper with
30 percent postconsumer waste content.

To my students at Morehouse College

It is my considered judgment that the present solution is a stop-gap, a halt in the line of march toward full community or, at most, a time of bivouac on a promontory overlooking the entire landscape of American society. It is time for assessing and reassessing resources in light of the most ancient memory of the race concerning community, to hear again the clear voice of the prophet and seer calling for harmony among all the children of men. At length there will begin to be talk of plans for the new city—that has never before existed on land or sea. At the center of the common life there will be strange stirrings. Some there will be whose dreams will be haunted by forgotten events in which in a moment of insight they saw a vision of a way of life transcending all barriers alien to community. . . .

. . . One day there will stand up in their midst one who will tell of a new sickness among the children who in their delirium cry for their brothers who they have never known and from whom they have been cut off behind the self-imposed barriers of their fathers. An alarm will spread throughout the community that it is being felt and slowly realized that community cannot feed for long on itself; it can only flourish where always the boundaries are giving way to the coming of others from beyond them—unknown and undiscovered brothers [and sisters]. Then the wisest among them will say: What we have sought we have found, our own sense of identity. We have established a center out of which at last we can function and relate to other men [and women]. We have committed to heart and to nervous system a feeling of belonging and our spirits are no longer isolated and afraid.

Thurman, *Search for Common Ground* (1971)

CONTENTS

Preface

In the following chapters, I examine Thurman's thought as a philosopher: this claim constitutes both a fact about who I am—as a reader of Thurman and as someone classically trained as a philosopher, as someone attuned to the philosophical allusions and the ontological meaning of what Thurman wrote—and an expression of a modest philosophical thesis and an interpretative task, that is, demonstrating that Thurman's thought is distinctively philosophical in its scope and methods. What I have tried to do is roughly, or broadly, more analogous to what Gary Dorrien has accomplished apropos the theological or evangelical dimension in Thurman's thought, namely, to show that "Thurman called American Christianity to its best religious vision and in several ways exemplified it" (2003, 558), such that my complementary task consists in demonstrating how Thurman called—and continues to call—American philosophy, too, "to its best [philosophical] vision and in several ways exemplified it." As a revisionist reading of Thurman's thought, this text aims to better appreciate Thurman's unique genius as a philosopher of education, philosophical personalist, political pacifist, moral psychologist, social activist, identity theorist, philosopher of religion, prophetic pragmatist, social theorist, and liberation philosopher. Thurman is instructively read as an American scholar within the black philosophical tradition as well as a spiritual genius and—in the words of Sue Bailey, Thurman's wife, herself a heroine of the civil rights movement—a "tutor to the world." Although the chapters in this book oscillate between theory and practice, technical and popular, cerebral and emotive, providing a series of snapshots of Thurman's thought, I have tried to organize them in a way that—borrowing a metaphor from Thurman—"plaits the strands to create a pattern that transcends the logic of any particular strand" (1945, 94).

There is a fine distinction in Gandhi's theory of nonviolence between *ahimsa* and *satyagraha,* that is, between the "philosophy of nonviolence" and the "methods of nonviolence," which many of us conflate or overlook entirely. Howard Thurman and Martin Luther King Jr. not only took up the distinction: they understood it. Both Thurman and King saw that the philosophy and methods of nonviolence remain no less distinct, however intimate the connection. When Gandhi and Thurman finally met in 1936, they translated ahimsa as "love in the Pauline sense, yet something more." Thurman construed the philosophy of nonviolence as a "force superior to all the forces of brutality" ([1936] 2009, 335). He saw ahimsa as a spirit of love capable of keeping the world of violence at bay. For Thurman, ahimsa was at its core a deeply personal, spiritual discipline, and it is this that must serve as a platform for conciliating victims and perpetrators of violence. Thurman's distinctively African American version of ahimsa also aimed to generate a philosophy of transcendent moral purpose and self-respect among the disinherited. Via the idiom of the black church, Thurman provided an illuminating interpretation of forgiveness. On the one hand, Thurman applied the philosophy of ahimsa to racial oppression in America; on the other, he consistently adapted and extended that philosophy in an effort to promote the "unadulterated message of non-violence to the world" ([1936] 2009, 337). Thurman sought to become a true representative of this philosophy, a vital force at the growing edges of nonviolence. His writings and sermons were influential—perhaps even decisive—to Martin Luther King Jr.'s subsequent commitment to both the philosophy and the methods of nonviolence.

Gandhi's "constructive preparation programme," as implemented within his various ashrams, aimed at restoring or otherwise enhancing the spiritual as well as physical vitality of individuals who suffered from disintegrating forms of systemic discrimination. Not altogether unlike Gandhi's constructive preparation program, the philosophy of education espoused by Benjamin E. Mays and Thurman as well as King aimed at strengthening the souls of the disinherited and disenfranchised. In ways similar to Gandhi, Mays and Thurman as well as King were pedagogically preoccupied, from the pulpit and lectern, with fostering the fragile yet sacred and resilient personalities of the oppressed, as well as the oppressors, which had been abridged or otherwise distorted by the violence inherent in racism, materialism, and militarism.

Thurman's strength is as a moral psychologist and a social philosopher. Across religious traditions, the teachings of love not only command us to resist the seemingly irresistible and altogether natural tendency to become angry, to hate, to retaliate, or to exact revenge; these traditions sometimes go so far as to entreat if not demand of us that we love our enemies. As a theologian and philosopher, as a mystic and a prophet, Thurman insisted that the teachings of love in Jesus were quite simple at their core but altogether radical in their socioethical implications. "The religion of Jesus," wrote Thurman, in his early manifesto, *Jesus and the Disinherited*, "makes the love-ethic central" ([1949] 1996, 89). Elsewhere, in 1978, Thurman claims that for Jesus "love was the clue to the mystery." And yet: "The love-ethic is no ordinary achievement" (1996, 89). Thurman would have wanted us to grow in all manner of insight into this extraordinary socioethical teaching and spiritual discipline. He believed it was important to understand the roots of anger and hatred as well as the persistent temptation to resort, immediately and without further delay, to violence when dealing with those whom we perceive to be our enemies. Like many African Americans of his generation, Thurman understood the temptation to retaliate—as William James described it in 1911—"quickly, thrillingly, tragically, and by force." Thurman is quick to concede that hatred can sometimes serve the positive function of restoring or establishing for the first time the individuating core of the personality. He was a sensitive moral psychologist. What are the roots of anger? How does it arise? And how might it be overcome? His writings are replete with resources for healing ourselves and our siblings as well as our neighbors—near or far, known or unknown—and even our enemies. Like King, Thurman's response to fear and hatred as well as deception was radical because it relied on unarmed truth and unconditional love.

Thurman graduated from Morehouse College in 1923 and then taught at Morehouse from 1928 to 1931. The philosophy of education practiced at Morehouse, a historically black college in Atlanta, was personified in three luminaries of Morehouse: Benjamin E. Mays, Howard Thurman, and Martin Luther King Jr. At the centennial banquet of Morehouse College in February 1967, where he shared the rostrum with Mays and Hugh Gloster, Thurman claimed that "the educational process was only partially justified by its public results." He argued convincingly that, while "many competent voices will make a good and often dramatic case for the public results of Morehouse," there was an admittedly less tangible but nevertheless "tremendous impact of the private results of Morehouse College" ([1967] 1998, 236). Thurman emphasized, as did W. E. B. Du Bois, E. Franklin Frazier, Mays as well as King and even Cornel West, the private as opposed to public benefits of education. Indeed, each of these educators advocated a form of pedagogical personalism that stressed the sacred or otherwise inviolable character of the personality. "The creative genius of Morehouse College," as Thurman described it, consisted of an educational process that fostered a "primary intimate encounter that insisted that it was their prerogative and that it was mandatory to experience themselves as human beings." Men at Morehouse were encouraged "to get on the scent of their potential and follow it all the way" ([1967] 1998, 235). Forms of education that distort or diminish the integrity of the personality were anathema. Various philosophers contributed to a pedagogical model that enhanced or otherwise contributed to the integrity or wholeness of the person. Treating individuals as persons rather than things, as Immanuel Kant might have put it, or as a "Thou" rather than as an "it," as Martin Buber might have expressed it, was at the very heart of the pedagogical personalism as represented by philosophers of education at Morehouse, from Benjamin Mays to Howard Thurman and Martin Luther King Jr.

Thurman was preoccupied with philosophical problems of personal identity, including the paradox if not contradiction within human consciousness between the centripetal pull inward toward the "uniqueness of the private life" and the centrifugal push outward "to feel oneself as a primary part of all of life." Similar to King, who defined personalism or personal idealism as the theory that the clue to the meaning of ultimate reality is found in personality, Thurman was also convinced that the clue to the outer is the inner: "It is a truth recognized over and over again in various guises that the key to the meaning of life is found deep within each one of us" (1984, 54). Thurman formulated personalist ideals, both in his texts and spoken lectures, and the sociopolitical application of those ideals was a prescription for personal development and social transformation. Similar to Edgar S. Brightman and Walter G. Muelder, Thurman insisted that a respect for persons entails a social responsibility to create an environment conducive to freedom qua personality fulfillment. The ethic of self-realization in community is a constant theme in Thurman. As a deep-self compatibilist, Thurman thought that we are most free when we conduct ourselves in ways that are consistent with the values we associate with our deepest or most authentic self; when our behavior is caused by—if not determined by—our superficial or otherwise inauthentic self, we are unfree. Thurman's point here is more psychological than theological, but there are also philosophical implications to this aspect of Thurman's personalism. Thurman declared in *Luminous Darkness* (1965a) that "[persons] were made for one another" and that "there is a meaning in life greater than, but informing, all the immediate meanings" (1998, 258); interestingly, Thurman describes this hermeneutical center as essentially religious in character because "it embodies, however faintly, a sense of the ultimate and the divine," saying that "it is this spirit that makes for wholeness and community" (1965a, 119).

Although one hesitates to claim that Thurman is wrongly categorized as a mystic, it is misleading to suggest that Thurman was a mystic without important qualifications. In the absence of historical context, mysticism as a term of general classification simply breeds confusion in criticism and thought; similarly, general definitions of mysticism—for example, "to know God in a comprehensive sense" ([1939] 2012, 207)—achieve little more than replacing vague confusion with a quieting consensus of superficial understanding. Although he remained throughout his life "self-conscious in using the term mysticism," Thurman came to realize that that mysticism was just a word. According to Alton B. Pollard III, "Thurman was reluctant to make too much of distinctions in such subtle matters as religion and mystical experience because of the potential for reifying categories that, in the final analysis, may be artificial" (1992, 56–57). When studying Thurman's mysticism, I have tried to focus more on the quality of the experience described by Thurman than on the question of how best to label it. As I read Thurman, the closest analogue to Thurman's mysticism is that of Gandhi, whose religious mysticism entailed his philosophical creed of nonviolence as well as his sociopolitical methods of nonviolent civil disobedience. As in the case of Gandhi, Thurman was not merely a mystic, though he was indeed a mystic of a certain sort; he was also an extraordinary philosopher and a social activist. By temperament and talent, Thurman was a profound philosopher and a spiritual genius.

Thurman embodied and exemplified many if not most of the generative themes that are characteristic of the black philosophical tradition in America, and he anticipated many of the goals espoused by prophetic pragmatists along the lines of Cornel West. In *The American Evasion of Philosophy,* West describes prophetic pragmatism as a kind of cultural criticism that has "its roots in the American heritage and its hopes for the wretched of the earth" (1989, 212). By this simple definition, but also in the broader description that includes the utopian impulse of Ralph Waldo Emerson as well as John "Dewey's conception of creative democracy and Du Bois' social structural analysis of the limits of capitalist democracy" (West 1989, 212), Thurman was a prophetic pragmatist. Similar to Thurman's thought, West's own version of prophetic pragmatism is ensconced in the Christian tradition; like Thurman, West understood the "political relevance in the biblical focus on the plight of the wretched of the earth" (1989, 233). Although sharply critical of the institution of Christianity, Thurman viewed the religion of Jesus as "a rich source of existential empowerment and political engagement" (West 1989, 233). If the mark of the prophet is to bring "an urgent yet compassionate critique to bear on the evils of their day" (West 1989, 239), to speak the truth in love and courage, to allow suffering to speak, then Thurman certainly qualified as a prophet.

The trope of the beloved community was passed from Josiah Royce to Thurman and King. Thurman acknowledged an indebtedness to Royce's conception of the beloved community, especially his philosophy of loyalty. Royce also exercised an influence—directly or indirectly, through Thurman and others—on the thought of Martin Luther King Jr. The African American experience altered significantly if not decisively the socioethical trajectory of this trope—the beloved community—within the history of philosophy and theology in America. Beyond the "legal aspect of integration," which involves changes in policies and regulations, Howard Thurman emphasized in 1966 a "second meaning of integration that has to do with the quality of human relations" ([1966] 2009, 207). Although the genius of Thurman or King cannot be reduced to the ideas of their predecessors, whether Royce and Du Bois, whether intellectual or cultural, something valuable is gained by revisiting the philosophical history as well as the pragmatic meaning of this trope from Royce to Thurman and King. The influence of Royce on Thurman and King was but one of many other significant factors or variables in a complex confluence of sociohistorical and philosophical influences. Beyond our collaborative effort to gain a better understanding of the confluence of influences on King's conception of the beloved community, we must also seek to clarify in earnest what this socioethical if not theological or philosophical ideal prescribes by way of individual practices and public policies moving forward in the twenty-first century.

Mozella Mitchell compellingly claims that "first and foremost, Thurman was a philosopher of freedom" (1982, 32). Although the theme of liberation and resistance is woven into everything he wrote, and while his philosophy of freedom is on display in each of the chapters in this book, the epilogue applies his ideas to our present geopolitical moment. Thurman was a principled and tough-minded yet disarmingly tender-hearted philosopher. Thurman personified the Thoreauvian virtue of "sympathy with intelligence" and Emerson's philosophical ideal, described in his 1837 "American Scholar" address to the Phi Beta Kappa Society at Harvard, as an "active-soul" and a "man-thinking." Thurman offers us something better than, or at least something different from and more practically minded than, a philosophical system: he personified a philosophical life, one lived with courage and conviction, distinguished by service to the disinherited and downtrodden in what he understood to be a holy crusade for freedom and human dignity.

Thurman often reminded us that "we are all of us indebted to a vast host by which we are surrounded" (2018, 127). I have received sustained support and enthusiasm from several special colleagues at Morehouse, especially Preston King, Andrew Douglas, and Lawrence Carter. I wish to acknowledge the invaluable encouragement I have received from several Thurman scholars: Vincent Harding, who made me believe in this project; Luther Smith; Paul Taylor; and Peter Eisenstadt. I want to thank David Ahearn, who convinced me that Thurman's thought was both timeless and timely, as well as Ernie Freeberg and Jonathan Herman. I wish to acknowledge the initial encouragement I received from Anthony Neal, one of the few scholars I met who insisted from the outset that I should read Thurman as a philosopher. I am most especially indebted to Brenda Steele, who met with me and students, week after week, over the course of years, listening to and discussing Thurman's sermons in the Howard Thurman Meditation Room in historic Sale Hall.

I want to thank the editors as well as the reviewers at the University of South Carolina Press for their sage suggestions and patience with respect to this project as well as for their sustained commitment to Thurman scholarship. I am grateful for the kind assistance I received from numerous archivists at the Howard Gotlieb Archival Research Center at Boston University (the Howard Thurman and Sue Bailey Thurman Collections); Howard University Archives (the Benjamin E. Mays Collection); Pitts Library at Emory University; the Stuart A. Rose Library of Emory University for the image of Thurman that graces the cover of this volume; and the Morehouse College Martin Luther King Jr. Collection.

An earlier version of chapter 3, "Pedagogical Personalism at Morehouse College," was published in *Studies in Philosophy & Education* (2017); variations on chapter 7, "The Growing Edges of Beloved Community," appeared in *Transactions of the Charles S. Peirce Society* (2016) and in an article coauthored with Preston King in *Amity* (2017); and an alternative formulation of chapter 1, "An African American Philosophy of Nonviolent Resistance," can be found in *Civility, Nonviolent Resistance, and the New Struggle for Social Justice* (2019).

A Chronology of Thurman's Life and Career

1899 Thurman is born in West Palm Beach to Saul Solomon Thurman Alice Ambrose Thurman and was raised in Daytona, Florida.

1919 Thurman graduates as valedictorian from high school in St. Augustine, Florida.

1923 Thurman graduates as valedictorian of Morehouse College.

1925 Thurman is ordained as a Baptist minister.

1926 Thurman graduates as valedictorian of Rochester Theological Seminary (later Colgate Rochester Crozer Divinity School), which typically accepted only one African American student each academic year. Marries Katie Kelley and becomes pastor of Mount Zion Baptist Church in Oberlin, Ohio.

1927 The Thurmans' daughter, Olive, is born.

1928 Because Katie was suffering from tuberculosis, the Thurman family moves from Ohio to Georgia, where Thurman teaches religion at Morehouse and Spelman College as well as serves as the director of religious life at both institutions. Katie and Olive spend part of their time with the Kelley family in La Grange, Georgia.

1929 Thurman studies mysticism with Rufus Jones at Haverford College.

1930 Katie Kelley Thurman dies.

1931 Thurman travels extensively in Europe.

1932 Thurman marries Sue Bailey, and the couple moves to Washington, D.C., where Thurman teaches in the School of Religion and subsequently serves as the Dean of Rankin Chapel at Howard University.

1933 The Thurmans' daughter, Anne, is born.

1935–1936 Howard Thurman and Sue Bailey Thurman travel to India as well as Ceylon (now Sri Lanka) and Burma (now Myanmar) on a preaching tour; Thurman serves as the chairman of the "Negro Delegation" on a Pilgrimage of Friendship sponsored by the World Student Christian Movement. Howard and Sue meet with Mahatma Gandhi in 1936.

1937–1943 Thurman resumes position as dean of Rankin Chapel and professor of religion at Rankin Chapel.

1944 Thurman accepts a position as pastor of an interfaith and interracial church in San Francisco, The Church for the Fellowship of All Peoples.

Publishes *The Greatest of These* (1944); *Deep River* (1945); *The Negro Spiritual Speaks of Life and Death* (1947). *Deep Is the Hunger* (1947); *Jesus and the Disinherited* (1949); *Deep Is the Hunger: Meditations for Apostles of Sensitiveness* (1951).

1953 Thurman accepts a position as the Dean of Chapel as well as Professor of Spiritual Resources and Disciplines at Boston University.

Publishes *Meditations of the Heart* (1953); *The Creative Encounter: An Interpretation of Religion and the Social Witness* (1954); *The Growing Edge* (1956); *Footprints of a Dream: The Story of The Church for the Fellowship of All Peoples* (1959).

1960 Thurman takes a trip around the world, primarily in Pacific Asia.

Publishes *Mysticism and the Experience of Love* (1961); *The Inward Journey: Meditations on the Spiritual Quest* (1961); *Temptations of Jesus* (1962)

1963 Thurman travels to Africa, primarily Nigeria.

Publishes *Disciplines of the Spirit* (1963); *The Luminous Darkness: A Personal Interpretation of the Anatomy of Segregation and the Ground of Hope* (1965).

1965 Thurman and Sue Bailey Thurman return to San Francisco, where Thurman directs the Howard Thurman Educational Trust.

Publishes *The Centering Moment* (1969); *The Search for Common Ground: An Inquiry into the Basis of Man's Experience of Community* (1971); *The Mood of Christmas* (1973); *With Head and Heart: The Autobiography of Howard Thurman* (1979)

1981 Thurman dies on April 10.

Introduction

Howard Thurman (1899–1981) is one of the unsung heroes of the civil rights movement in America. As one of the first in a long line of African American intellectuals to meet with Mahatma Gandhi at his ashram in India, in 1936, Thurman quickly appropriated and adeptly applied the philosophy of nonviolence to the problem of racism as well as to materialism and imperialism in America. The result was a distinctively African American philosophy of nonviolent but active resistance to social injustice. Thurman, whose ideas were repeatedly put to the test during the civil rights movement, is best known as a mentor to Martin Luther King Jr. At the first meeting of the Southern Negro Leaders Conference (later called the Southern Christian L;eadership Conference) in 1957, Bayard Rustin asked King, "Do you remember what Gandhi told Howard Thurman in India, many years ago?" He then recited Gandhi's seemingly prophetic words, that "it may be through the Negroes that the unadulterated message of non-violence will be delivered to the world" ([1936] 2009, 337; see also 1975, 132). By the time he met Gandhi, and in ways similar to Gandhi, Thurman sharply distinguished the religion of Jesus from the injustices that are historically inseparable from the institution of Christianity. Thurman suggested in his 1949 *Jesus and the Disinherited* that the teachings of Jesus had a special significance for "those with their backs against the wall" ([1949] 1996, 11). Otis Moss, himself an unsung hero of the civil rights movement, suggests that while Thurman "did not march from Selma to Montgomery, or many of the other marches, [he] participated at the level that shapes the philosophy that creates the march—and without that, people don't know what to do before the march, while they march, or after they march" (quoted in Bennett 1978, 71).

Although Thurman said that he "never considered himself as any kind of leader" nor "a movement man," Albert Raboteau argues that "Thurman believed—as did another twentieth-century activist contemplative, Thomas Merton—that true social change must be grounded in spiritual experience and personal transformation" (2001, 158). Andrew Young claims that King carried Thurman's *Jesus and the Disinherited* in his briefcase almost everywhere he went (quoted in Heltzel

2015, 74). Lewis Baldwin says that "Thurman's *Jesus and the Disinherited* (1949) was as important for King as any other intellectual source he studied at Boston" (2010, 65). Makechnie relays the story that when Lerone Bennett "went to Montgomery, in the early days of the bus boycott, [he] was not at all surprised to find King not reading Gandhi but Howard Thurman" (see Makechnie 1988, 39). King was not alone in his reliance on Thurman's writings and sermons. U.S. Representative John Lewis of Georgia has said in a personal conversation with the author that he and the other freedom riders from across the country circulated Thurman's writings, especially *Deep River* (1945) and *The Negro Spiritual Speaks of Life and Death* (1947), as a "source of spiritual courage at a time when they were asked to do the impossible."

Although much of Thurman's *Search for Common Ground* (1971) was written prior to 1968, many read it as Thurman's scholarly response to King's assassination and to the looming question posed by King's final publication, *Where Do We Go from Here: Chaos or Community?* ([1968] 2010). Thurman's personal response to King's death is found elsewhere (Thurman 1998, 185–87; also 1979, 223). At a tumultuous point in the struggle for racial equality in America, some may well have been disappointed that Thurman's *Search for Common Ground* was not an impassioned political manifesto or a religious jeremiad against the hypocrisy inherent in the institutions of Christianity and democracy in America. But reconsidered from a different vantage point, Thurman's *Search for Common Ground* should be celebrated as his most impressive philosophical achievement. Mozella Mitchell claims that in his final book, *Common Ground,* Thurman "puts into the perspective of process theology the many strands of [his] keen concerns in the intense lifelong struggle for wholeness, not simply for himself but on behalf of community" (1983, 32). Thurman's *Disciplines of the Spirit* (1963) was written for philosophers of religion and theologians as well as Christian laity. For those with eyes to see, so to speak, and ears to hear, Thurman's philosophical methodology is reminiscent of William James and John Dewey, whom Thurman first read during his Morehouse years. Thurman's *Meditations of the Heart* (1953) explores the more philosophical passages to be found in Augustine's *Confessions* and Blaise Pascal's *Pensées.* Throughout Thurman's writings, there are echoes of Ralph Waldo Emerson and transcendentalists of other sorts. His *Meditations of the Heart* and *Disciplines of the Spirit* should be read as a series of parabolic reflections on the paradoxes inherent in self-examination, self-surrender, self-overcoming, self-sacrifice, self-discovery, and self-determination.

Although he taught philosophy and religion at an array of academic institutions (for example, Morehouse College, Howard University, Boston University), Thurman was neither a systematic theologian nor a professional philosopher. And yet Thurman was a systematic thinker who preached his theology and put his philosophical ideas to the test. In *Lay Bare the Heart,* James Farmer Jr., describes Thurman as "a critical scholar, but very devout" (1985, 135). Thurman was a polymath and a synesthete. One of Thurman's professors at Rochester Theological Seminary advised him saying that "it would be a terrible waste for [Thurman] to limit [his] creative energy to the solution of the race problem, however insistent its nature" and that he should give himself over instead "to the timeless issues of the human spirit" (1979, 60). In his autobiography, *With Head and Heart,* Thurman admits that he struggled to find an adequate response "to this man who did not know that a man and his black skin must face the 'timeless issues of the human spirit' together" (1979, 60). As a professor or a pastor, as a priest or a shaman, Thurman strove in earnest to create a climate of "inner unity of fellowship that went beyond the barriers of race, class, and tradition" (1979, 95). Thurman brooded over a broad spectrum of philosophical paradoxes, those allegedly "timeless issues of the human spirit," and in those matters his thought was consistent and coherent but also creative and compelling.

Although scholars often note in passing that Thurman was considered to have been philosophically profound (for example, when Philip Lenud reports that while "King loved and respected Thurman, the ontological meaning of what he said went right over many folks, including Martin" (Baldwin 1991, 300–301), few if any have taken the time to carefully examine those alleged metaphysical subtleties or prevail to plumb the depths of his profundity. Luther E. Smith claimed that "there remains a pitiful dearth of scholarship on his thought" and that there "has been little attempt to do an in-depth critical analysis of his ideas" ([1981] 2007, 3). And while the scholarship on Thurman's thought over the past decade has been substantial, most significantly in the form of the Thurman Papers Project at the Boston University School of Theology, most recently with the publication of volume 4 of Thurman's works, *The Soundless Passion of a Single Mind, June 1949–December 1962*, I agree with Smith that Thurman's thought is woefully underappreciated, but I would stress that this is doubly true of his philosophical ideas.[1] Beyond his philosophy of nonviolence, which was not only a method but also a creed for many of those who participated in the longer civil rights movement in America, Thurman should be appreciated for his seminal and original insights into the philosophy of mind, especially personal identity; theistic personalism; philosophy of education; philosophy of religion, including his exploration of mysticism; moral psychology; sociopolitical philosophy; and the philosopher of freedom.

The following pages demonstrate the serious and sustained philosophical engagement of an extraordinary man who played an essential role in laying the intellectual and spiritual foundation for the modern civil rights movement in America. Lerone Bennett, editor of *Ebony,* himself a Morehouse man and author of *What Manner of Man* (1964), went so far as to describe Thurman as "one of the greatest minds of our generation" and "perhaps the greatest storyteller in the world" (Bennett 1978, 68). But today Thurman is relatively unknown. Thurman was an exceptional individual, to be sure, but he is also representative of an entire era within the longer civil rights movement. The descriptive dimension of this book contributes to the collaborative task of documenting or otherwise acknowledging the confluence of influences that gave rise to the monumental achievements of the civil rights era. The normative aspect of this analysis consists in providing vital resources for what Vincent Harding, Thurman's friend and colleague, himself a veteran of the freedom movement, called our "continuing task of turning this wilderness nation into a land of promise for all its people" (2010a, 184). Luther Smith suggested early on that "Thurman's interpretation of the spiritual basis for social transformation may serve as the philosophy for the next generation of participants in the black struggle" ([1981] 2007, 211).

Thurman claimed that his 1936 meeting with Gandhi was but one of several monumental experiences in India. Prior to his encounter with Gandhi, up in the mountains overlooking the Khyber Pass, Thurman had an epiphany that, "at its core, confirmed the possibility of true human community" ([1959] 2009, 25). In his *Footprints of a Dream*, Thurman recalled: "All that we had seen and felt in India came miraculously into focus: we knew that we must test whether a religious fellowship could be developed in America that was capable of cutting across all racial barriers, with a carry-over into the common life, a fellowship that would alter the behavior patterns of those involved. It became imperative, now, to find out if experiences of spiritual unity among people could be more compelling than the experiences that divide them" ([1959] 2009, 24). Thurman described his ministry in 1937 as "an exploration of the problems that arise in the experience of people who attempt to be Christian in a society that is essentially un-Christian" (2012, xix). Followers of the religion of Jesus, insisted Thurman in *Deep Is the Hunger,* were "those who were willing to exercise the limit of power and moral suasion upon men in the interest of the redemption of themselves and society" and who could "against the darkness of the age see the illumined finger of God guiding in the way they should go" (1951a, 5). Whether in religious or academic institutions, Thurman decried what he perceived to be a "preening otherworldliness" and "a callow materialism." The "apocalyptic heritage of the black church," as he put it, "left it ill-equipped to deal with either the spiritual or practical realms of existence." When "some well-meaning sociologist" advised Thurman that what African Americans really needed was to "enrich themselves and learn to speak the language of economic power and control," Thurman objected that the religion of materialism was "soul-killing" and, no less than racism and materialism, was rooted in fear, deception, and hatred. Whatever distorted or warped the personality, whatever injured or killed the soul, whether segregation and poverty or imperialism and militarism, was for Thurman "not only unethical," though it was clearly unethical or immoral for those very reasons, but also "a mortal sin against God" (2009, 121). According to Walter Fluker, "Thurman's ministry of teaching and healing extended beyond the walls of the church to personal encounters with individuals who found in his presence 'a place, a moment' to declare, 'I choose!' . . . . He taught those in despair how to dream again, how to begin again, how to resurrect the crucified and forsaken symbols of life and make of them redemptive messengers in a world that conspires against faith, hope, and love" (2009, 17).

Following Luther Smith, Thurman "deserves our head as well as our heart" (2007, 5). Philosophers have tended to dismiss Thurman as a religious mystic or a theologian, as though that somehow places him outside the scope of philosophical analysis; conversely, many Christian theologians—perhaps thinking of his *Search for Common Ground*—tend to dismiss Thurman as a philosopher, maybe even a pantheist, someone inappropriately preoccupied with science and worldly utopian literature. For some, it would seem, Thurman's writings are summarily ignored as somehow too Christian in their orientation to deserve serious philosophical examination; by others, he is insufficiently Christian to merit sustained attention. To certain academics, Thurman's writings are insufficiently scholarly or inappropriately fixated on the social issues of his day rather than on the timeless issues of the human spirit; to pastors, Thurman's most substantial writings were too scholarly to recommend to their parishioners or congregants. Some scholars classify Thurman as a black liberation theologian, as a predecessor to James Cone, author of *Black Theology of Liberation* (1970) and *God of the Oppressed* (1975), while others view him as a participant in the twentieth-century American Christian liberal social gospel movement or an early advocate of a cosmopolitan ecumenicalism, perhaps even one of the grandfathers of the "new age" movement. Cornel West describes Thurman as Martin Luther King Jr.'s "most worthy theological precursor" in the sense that both Thurman and King "pulled from the rich insights of Western thinkers, yet he elevated the lived experiences of wounded, scarred, and bruised bodies of enslaved and Jim-Crowed black peoples to enact radical love" (2016, xvi). Thurman was a spiritual genius, certainly, in William James's sense of the term, but he also exemplifies all the traits of a prominent and empowering strand within the black philosophical tradition (Hord and Lee, 2016; see also Harris 2000).

Thurman has been variously characterized as a mystic-activist and a spiritual guru, as a 20th century prophet and a sophisticated modern-day shaman, as a

Lamed Vay Tzadikim (i.e., one of the thirty-six righteous ones), and as a holy man of the next millennium; theologians tend to classify Thurman as a modernistic liberal, an early African American exponent of the social gospel movement, or, most obviously, a precursor to Black liberation theology. Each of these labels sheds some light on Thurman's thought, but they also tend to obscure or ignore entirely other ways of reading Thurman. Without suggesting that the existing set of descriptive categories is either mistaken or misleading, I contend that Thurman can be creatively and instructively construed as a first-rate philosopher. In his autobiography, Thurman claims that his conclusions were "not definitive, but they point the direction in which others must go in search of the idiom of community in a strange and bewildering society in which the integrity of the individual life seems to be put under siege by the vast impersonal processes of life" (1979, 225). Thurman was interdisciplinary to the extreme: and while this poses a prima facie problem for those who wish to classify or label Thurman's thought, it is precisely Thurman's strength as a philosophical thinker.

Thurman provides vital resources for our present times. Thurman's voice, whether written or spoken, always resonant, expressed "the sound of the genuine" (1965, 38; also 1980, 14). The present generation of teachers and scholars of the civil rights movement are still discovering the broad spectrum of philosophical and spiritual or ethical and religious resources that animated or otherwise sustained what John Lewis called, in 1963, at the March on Washington, the "serious social revolution." Thurman's well-wrought words and writings, quoting what Thurman attributed to an old plantation preacher, "are seasoned with a mellowness of sustained religious insight and experience" ([1934] 2009, 205). This book also attempts to bridge the undeniable divide between, say, classical American pragmatists (for example, Charles Sanders Peirce, William James, Josiah Royce, and John Dewey) and African American philosophers (for example, W. E. B. Du Bois, Alain Locke, Howard Thurman, and Martin Luther King Jr.). Alton Pollard suggested from the outset that Thurman may well have been, and perhaps he still remains, "*too radical for us.* We have not yet caught up with him" (1992, 193).

1

An African American Philosophy of Nonviolent Resistance

And if I work for social righteousness so that every man can sit under his own fig tree and be unafraid—if I work to provide the kind of climate in which it is a reasonable thing that men may trust each other, then—then there will be the kind of atmosphere in which it becomes a possibility for nations to beat their swords into ploughshares and their spears into pruning-hooks.

Howard Thurman, *The Papers of Howard Washington Thurman,* vol. 4 ([1934] 2009)

There is a very fine distinction within Gandhi's philosophy of nonviolence, a distinction that Howard Thurman and Martin Luther King Jr. took for granted, but which the present generation of scholars tends to conflate or overlook entirely, namely, between *ahimsa* and *satyagraha*. The philosophy of nonviolence, ahimsa, or what Gandhi and Thurman agreed to translate as "agape" and "the love-ethic," as expressed by St. Paul within the Christian tradition, is distinct yet ultimately and intimately related to the success of satyagraha, which is a distinctive method of nonviolence. Thurman's creative appropriation of this distinction in Gandhi's thought, as well as a unique application of it to the problem of segregation in America, was formative to King's understanding of and sustained, albeit tested, commitment to nonviolence. Although it is sometimes assumed that the origins of philosophical or spiritual pacifism in African American history stretch back to King's veneration of Gandhi, recent scholarship suggests that the inspirational sources are to be found much earlier and extended far broader than that. Not only did Thurman meet with Gandhi in 1936, he was also a member of the Fellowship of Reconciliation from the early 1920s. King traces his conversion to pacifism back to a 1950 sermon by Mordecai Johnson in Philadelphia. In their *Black Fire* (2011), which traces the history of the "black Quaker experience," Harold

Weaver, Paul Kriese, and Stephen W. Angell suggest that the origins of African American pacifism reach back at least as far as Benjamin Banneker (1731–1806), whose annual almanacs (1792–1804) advocated directly or indirectly for religious and philosophical pacifism, the disuse of oaths, and the abolition or reduction of the death penalty. Some scholars suggest that the significance of the black Garrisonians has also been overlooked. Luther Smith claims that "the development of a philosophy of nonviolent protest for the black struggle is a foremost achievement of [Thurman's] social witness" (1992, 133).

The Thurman–King Relationship

The influence of Thurman on King remains insufficiently appreciated, if not ignored entirely, perhaps in part because the archival evidence and documentation of this influence is still emerging. But the available documents seem to confirm what many scholars have suspected all along, namely, that the influence of Thurman on King, as well as the subsequent influence of King on Thurman, was sustained and significant if not decisive to the trajectory of the civil rights movement. The extended familial relationship reaches back to the early 1920s, when Thurman was an undergraduate at Morehouse, across campus from where Martin Luther King Sr. studied theology and religion. George K. Makechnie claims that "Howard had known Martin since the latter's boyhood" because "Martin's father, 'Daddy King,' and Howard had been college mates at Morehouse" (1988, 39; also see Thurman 1979, 254). Before examining the philosophy of nonviolence in Howard Thurman and then comparing Thurman's philosophy of nonviolence to the methods of nonviolence in King and Gandhi through the lens of their respective theories or theologies of forgiveness, something must be said about the friendship that evolved between Thurman and King; for this task, I wish to hover over several archival documents, fragments really, but telling, retained by the Martin Luther King Jr. Collection at Morehouse College.

Fluker claims "several writers have made reference to the influence of Howard Thurman on his younger fellow visionary, but no scholarly treatment has demonstrated a formal tie between the two" (1990, 36). And while we may disagree concerning what would constitute an adequate demonstration or sufficient evidence of a "formal tie between the two," it seems that Fluker is himself among those scholars who have demonstrated a steady and strong influence of Thurman on King. Perhaps the most compelling demonstration of the connection is the epilogue to Quinton Dixie and Peter Eisenstadt's groundbreaking study, *Visions of a Better World* (2011). Recent scholars are also keen to emphasize the influence of King on Thurman. When discussing Thurman's role in the civil rights movement,

Albert J. Raboteau concedes that "influence is difficult to measure" (2001, 157). But the formal tie or influence will not surface by analyzing King's and Thurman's personal and professional correspondence. In 1966, for example, in response to a brief letter and donation to the Southern Christian Leadership Conference from Mr. and Mrs. Thurman, King wrote, "In the meantime, I solicit your continued prayers and support in these difficult days. These are trying times for the philosophy and method of non-violence, but I will continue to go on with the faith that this approach is right" (Martin Luther King Jr. Collection at Morehouse College: 1.1.0.46790_005). The typed letter strikes the reader as merely perfunctory. But the intellectual if not spiritual friendship between Thurman and King was deeper than one might suppose based solely on their formal correspondence, which, as we now know, was monitored by the FBI.

Thurman and King understood themselves to be allies in a nonviolent struggle against what both expressed as the triple threats of racism, materialism, and militarism. In an earlier letter to King, in 1958, Thurman wrote of their plan to "spend several hours of uninterrupted talk about these matters that are of such paramount significance for the fulfillment of the tasks to which our hands are set" (2017, 233). When it comes to demonstrating philosophical influence, the closest thing to a formal tie—perhaps better than a "formal tie" if what is meant by that is an official declaration—will consist in a scholarly comparison of their respective treatments of related philosophical material. Comparing Thurman's teachings on community with King's, as Fluker has in *They Looked for a City*, or when showing parallels or family resemblances between Thurman on King on nonviolence, as Quinton Dixie and Peter Eisenstadt begin to do in *Visions of a Better World*, has thus far provided the best evidence of influence, philosophical or otherwise. To demonstrate the reciprocal influence, scholars must "seek to unearth significant differences obscured by surface similarities," as James T. Kloppenberg puts it, but that also "yield equally valuable insights if phenomena assumed to be dissimilar can be shown to exhibit similar features when viewed from a new perspective" (1988, 8). That said, even their official correspondence—which is often thick with allusion and connotation, indicative of a shared journey shot through with meaningful encounters—provides evidence of reciprocal influence. (Surely King and Thurman knew that their correspondence was by no means confidential at that point.) Thurman's philosophical influence and spiritual genius significantly shaped what was to become a distinctively African American philosophy and method of nonviolence; beyond his influence on King, Thurman's influence extended also to James Farmer as well as James Lawson.

King's commitment to the philosophy and method of nonviolence, not altogether unlike Thurman's, was contested in 1966 by "logistical imperialists" and "black-national ideologies" such as Floyd McKissick, Huey Newton, and Stokely Carmichael, who argued for their strategies and demeaned nonviolent direct action, and other participants in the Freedom Sunday march to Chicago City Hall on July 10, 1966, and in the Chicago Freedom Movement. In May of 1966, Thurman wrote to King as if clairvoyant, as someone gifted with second sight and symbolized at his birth by the sign of the caul (Thurman 1979, 263), as someone who understood the fate of King as a "Black Christ" (Weaver et al. 2011, 22–23; also see Thurman 1971, 98), closing cryptically if not indecipherably, anticipating King's "fate and destiny," which were not the same thing for Thurman: "Those [who hunt] treasure must go alone, [at] night, and when they find it, they have to leave a little of their blood behind" (Martin Luther King Jr. Collection at Morehouse College: 1.1.0.46790_002).

Alluding to Thurman's earlier advice following the assassination attempt on King in Harlem on September 20, 1958—namely, that King withdraw for a while "from the immediate pressures of the movement to reassess himself in relation to the cause, to rest his body and mind with healing detachment, and to take a long look that only solitary brooding can provide"—King wrote that their meeting was "a great spiritual lift" that was "of inestimable value in giving me the strength and courage to face the future of that very trying period" and that he "was following your advice on the question, 'where do I go from here?'" (MLK to HT, November 8, 1958, as qtd. in Dixie and Eisenstadt 2011, 193; see also Fluker 2009, 29). After many years of collectively brooding over this question, first posed by King in the final chapter of his 1958 *Stride Toward Freedom,* which Thurman personalized in his visit to King's hospital bed in Harlem, King published a masterful set of sustained responses to Thurman's question in *Where Do We Go from Here: Chaos or Community?* Although Thurman is nowhere explicitly mentioned in these books, the Thurmanian inheritance is on rich display for those with eyes to see, that is, those familiar with Thurman's early corpus. In a similar way, Thurman's WHDH-TV reflections on loving one's enemy, delivered in a series titled "We Believe"—especially two episodes recorded in early December 1959, aired on the eleventh and the nineteenth, the transcripts of which King received and studied, as indicated by the marginalia (see Martin Luther King Jr. Collection at Morehouse College: 2.2.0.1060)—might be said to have been analogously influential on King's 1963 *Strength to Love.* At least in terms of his treatment of the "anatomy of hatred," and as a case in point, King seems to acknowledge Thurman's influence when he refers—in *Where Do We Go from Here: Chaos or Community?*—to "those psychiatrists who say, 'Love or perish'" ([1968] 2010, 67), which is the title of one of Thurman's most powerful sermons from circa 1953.

On the importance of the Gandhian philosophy, if not method, of nonviolence in Thurman and also King, and for the purposes of the human rights movement in America, there is a famous quote—one that is often rehearsed to the exclusion of the context necessary for appreciating its meaning or significance—from the initial meeting of the Southern Christian Leadership Conference in 1957: "Do you remember, Rustin asked King, what Gandhi told Howard Thurman in India, many years ago? And [then Rustin] quoted Gandhi's words [namely, 'Well if it comes true it may be through the Negroes that that unadulterated message of non-violence will be delivered to the world']" (Dixie and Eisenstadt 2011, 112). The trajectory of the movement, it should be acknowledged, was informed and shaped by the Gandhian tradition. What Dixie and Eisenstadt say of Thurman, as he and his wife departed from their meeting with Gandhi in 1936, "that the force was certainly with them," could be applied equally to the spiritual force or vitality that animated King as well as Rustin in Atlanta back in 1957. King's commitment to the "unadulterated message of non-violence" and "dangerous unselfishness," by which one gains the "capacity to project the 'I' into the 'thou,'" alluding to Buber, was reaffirmed or otherwise demonstrated on countless occasions throughout his life. The "unadulterated message of non-violence" was delivered by those who, "with their backs against the wall," were strangely liberated from the triple ills of fear, hatred, and deception by way of the love-ethic displayed on the road from Jerusalem to Jericho by the Good Samaritan in the religion of Jesus. And yet the truth of nonviolence, thought Thurman, was inherent in all the great religions of the world. The unadulterated and distinctively African American message or philosophy of nonviolence, which should have universal appeal, was expressed—in content as well as form—within the idiom of the black church. For this point, however, it is necessary to explore the grassroots pacifism in Thurman's thought prior to his encounter with Gandhi in 1936.

Howard Thurman: African American Pacifist

Thurman joined the Fellowship of Reconciliation, an international pacifist organization still in existence, as a sophomore at Morehouse College (in 1921). But prior to his formal adoption of pacifism, as expressed by his membership in the Fellowship of Reconciliation or as espoused in his philosophy of nonviolence as part of the Pilgrimage of Friendship in 1935–36, Thurman claims that he learned about the central ills or the admonitory lesson of violence from his grandmother, Nancy Ambrose, a freed slave, in Daytona Beach, Florida, where Thurman grew up. Thurman was also a pacifist because he believed that the religion of Jesus requires it and, more generally, again like Gandhi, because violence distorts the soul, which is construed as the portal of access to God. Although Thurman's "approach to social justice issues has been called 'mystical' and unresponsive to the concrete realities of oppressed peoples," argues Fluker, "this reading of Thurman is misinformed and unjustified" (2009, 31). In his encounter with Gandhi in 1936, Thurman was keen to understand the theory or philosophy of ahimsa.[1] Gandhi told Thurman that the effectiveness of the struggle depends on "the degree to which the masses of people are able to embrace such a notion [ahimsa] and have it become a working part of their total experience." Thurman claims that "it struck me with a tremendous wallop that I had never associated ethics and morality with vitality—it was a new notion trying to penetrate my mind" (qtd. in Dixie and Eisenstadt 2011, 107). According to Judith Brown, Gandhi "was convinced that the soul's strength grew in proportion to which a [person] disciplined his [or her] flesh" (1989, 187–88).

Gandhi's use of the Sanskrit "ahimsa" alludes to the ancient karmic religions, especially Jainism, for which "ahimsa stood for a commitment to refrain from harming [all] living things" (Dixie and Eisenstadt 2011, 104). While it may be relatively easy to grasp the ethical doctrine inherent in ahimsa, understood as a practical prescription for behavior, Thurman was interested in the metaphysical if not cosmological doctrine at the heart of the philosophy of nonviolence qua ahimsa. "At the center of non-violence is a force which is self-acting," Gandhi claimed, "a force more positive than electricity" and, as Dixie and Eisenstadt amend beautifully, "subtler and more pervasive than the ether" (2011, 104). With an eye turned toward the spiritual resources available within Christianity, thought Gandhi, and Thurman agreed, ahimsa was best thought of along the lines of "'love' [or 'agape'] in the Pauline sense, yet something more." Gandhi translated "ahimsa" negatively, as "nonviolence," although he stressed that nonviolence "does not express a negative force, but a force superior to all the forces put together; one person who can express Ahimsa in life exercises a force superior to all the forces of brutality" ([1936] 2009, 335). Dixie and Eisenstadt elaborate on the metaphysical strain in Gandhi's theory of ahimsa:

> For Gandhi nonviolence was not really an idea at all. It was, as he told the delegation repeatedly, a force, a physical reality, a metaphysical substrate that underlined and defined all reality, a deeper truth behind the dross and flux of the world, the truth beneath and beyond the seeming brutality that apparently confined both human life and the world of nature to endless cycles of gratuitous violence. Ahimsa was a force, as Gandhi indicated, 'the force,' in the constitution of the universe. (2011, 105)

Thurman's interdisciplinary preoccupation with deciphering this metaphysical code surfaces most prominently in his *Search for Common Ground.*

What initially appear to be distinct themes in Thurman—for example, his mysticism and his philosophical teachings on the workings of nonviolence—turn out to be united at their core in a manner analogous to Gandhian teachings on ahimsa and satyagraha. The philosophy and methods of nonviolence can be understood distinctly, even adopted separately, in some cases even mutually exclusively (for example, in certain strands of Jainism, the genuine votary of ahimsa would not deign to participate in political activism), but it was one of the distinguishing characteristics of Gandhi's teaching that one leads ineluctably to the other. The effectiveness of satyagraha as a method depends on one's vital commitment to the philosophy or metaphysics of ahimsa. Inversely, for Gandhi as well as for Thurman, ahimsa demands satyagraha: "It is not possible to be actively non-violent and not rise against social injustice no matter where it occurs" (1958, 89). Ultimately, Gandhi believed that satyagraha would succeed because "ahimsa was a force, the force, in the constitution of the universe" (Dixie and Eisenstadt 2011, 105). As Thurman expressed in a 1944 lecture, "The Cosmic Guarantee," injustice or evil is bound to fail eventually because "the source of life is alive" and because "there is a heart at the heart of the universe"; the strategy of nonviolence was animate, for Gandhi and Thurman as well as for King, by the conviction that "the cosmos is the kind of order that sustains and supports the demands that the relationships between men and between man and God be one of harmony [and] integration" ([1944] 2015, lxii). In his *Search for Common Ground,* in the context of his analysis of the "structure-functional integrity" of living organisms, Thurman suggests that "the intent [of life] is for integration, for wholeness, for community within the limits of the organism itself" (1971, 39). "It is not unreasonable, then," Thurman continues, "to assume that as he seeks community within himself, with his fellows, and with his world, he may find that what he is seeking to do deliberately is but the logic of the meaning of all that has gone into his own creation" (1971, 41).

The "art of Ahimsa," insisted Gandhi, requires courage as well as discipline and self-sacrifice. Though open to all, mastery of ahimsa is granted to very few, if any. Thurman asked Gandhi whether it is possible for an individual who had mastered or otherwise embodied ahimsa to hold violence at bay in its entirety. And while the answer admits of multiple interpretations, some specific to Gandhi and others more universal in their application, Gandhi replied, "If he cannot, you must take it that he is not a true representative of Ahimsa" ([1936] 2009, 336). (But if he were, presumably, following the implicit logic of Gandhi's reply, then he could.) Gandhi's response alludes, it seems, to what Dixie and Eisenstadt isolate as "one of the peculiarities of Gandhian nonviolence" (2011, 106). The success or failure of the struggle in India ultimately depended not only on the degree of vitality inherent in ahimsa, as embodied in a single individual—although that is also part of the teaching—but also "on the degree to which the masses of people are able to embrace such a notion and have it become a working part of their total experience" (Dixie and Eisenstadt 2011, 107). Gandhi believed ahimsa as well as satyagraha consists in an exercise in restraint not unlike fasting and chastity, which Gandhi considered to be various means by which one clings to the truth and accumulates a vitality of "soul force." Self-denial, suggests Gandhi, is always advisable and a reward unto itself, and he bemoaned the fact that the masses did not seem to have enough vitality to embrace ahimsa. In practice, the vitality of the disinherited or oppressed is diminished not only by a lack of bread but also by a profound lack of self-respect, which, claimed Gandhi, was lost to the Indian masses because of "the presence of the conqueror in their midst" (1979, 133) and the injustices within their own communities (for example, the institution of untouchability). Thurman understood all-too-well how racial oppression and the constant fear of violence undermined the self-respect of the disinherited and distorted the integrity or vitality of the personality of the oppressed as well as of the oppressor. "Both Thurman and Gandhi saw the impetus for movements of social change arising less from mass politics than from a handful of persons who had realized the proper techniques for self-mastery and could, by their example, show others the way" (Dixie and Eisenstadt 2011, 108).

Thurman's significance and role within the civil rights movement consists in what Gandhi called "constructive preparation," that is, the task of "cultivating non-violence among the brave in thought, word and deed" (2007, 36). If King represents the "Moses of the Movement," as it were, and Mays the "Schoolmaster of the Movement" (Jelks 2012), it seems fitting to characterize Thurman as the "Minister-at-Large of the Movement," that is, as someone who was personally committed to creatively intensifying "the degree to which the masses of people are able to embrace such a notion [ahimsa] and have it become a working part of their total experience" (Dixie and Eisenstadt 2011, 107). In a 1943 letter to James Farmer, Thurman recalled Gandhi's observation that civil disobedience broke down in India because "the masses of the people were not able to sustain so lofty a creative idea over a time interval of sufficient duration to be practically effective. They were unable so to do, not because they lacked in courage or in unwillingness, but rather in vitality" (2012, 328–29). In this same letter, which was a response to Farmer's Fellowship of Reconciliation Nonviolent Action Committee and CORE proposal for a civil disobedience campaign, one announced by A. Philip Randolph in December 1942, Thurman wrote that he considered Farmer's proposed nonviolence campaign in America to be a very good thing, "provided it is built upon definite disciplines so that the masses of the people will not be inspired by fear, revenge or hate." Otherwise, suggested Thurman, "civil disobedience more wide spread now [1944], is the final gesture of the human spirit before martyrdom" ([1943] 2012, 328). The campaign was subsequently and indefinitely postponed. Farmer was worried that "shootouts in the sound and bloody massacres [would] set back the non-violent movement in the US for decades" (Farmer 1985, 156; as qtd. in Thurman 2012, 328).

Not unlike Gandhi and Leo Tolstoy, Thurman and Farmer as well as King were convinced that authentic social transformation was impossible without "the quest for personal spiritual development" (Dixie and Eisenstadt 2011, 108). Thurman's bold adventure, one that he often associated with his mystical experience at the Khyber Pass overlooking Afghanistan, consisted in restoring or otherwise intensifying the spiritual vitality of the disinherited. Thurman explicitly asked Gandhi "how to train individuals or communities in this difficult art [ahimsa]" ([1936] 2009, 336). Gandhi's reply also serves as a description of Thurman's "bold adventure":

> There is no royal road, except through living the creed in your own life, which must be a living sermon. Of course, the expression in one's own life presupposes great study, tremendous perseverance, and thorough cleansing of one's self of all the impurities. If for the mastering of the physical sciences you have to devote a whole life-time, how many lifetimes may be needed for mastering the greatest spiritual force that mankind has known? But why worry even if it means several lifetimes. For if this is the only permanent thing in life, if this is the only thing that counts, then whatever effort you bestow on mastering it is well spent. Seek ye first the Kingdom of Heaven and everything else shall be added to you. The Kingdom of Heaven is Ahimsa (2009, 336).

When Sue Bailey asked about how to live the creed in practice, when one's back is really against the wall, when suffocating from injustice and trapped by the enemy, when systemically threatened and personally injured, Gandhi suggested that "it is always possible to protest in such a way as to transform injustice by severing the ties that make us complicit with evil" (2009, 336). To illustrate his point, Gandhi described the process—both literal and metaphorical—of self-immolation. The self-examination and self-purification involved in mastering ahimsa, or love, of which forgiveness could be viewed as a litmus test or a crucible, requires self-sacrifice and varying degrees of self-immolation. The philosophy of nonviolence, we might say, requires something along the lines of what Socrates called, in

Plato's *Phaedo,* the art of dying or the purification of the soul. Not altogether like Socrates, perhaps, Gandhi strove to live up to the whole truth beyond the half-truths—in thought, deed, and motive: "It is not given to man to know the whole Truth. His duty lies in living up to the Truth as he sees it and in doing so to resort to the purest means, i.e., to non-violence" (2007, 39).

Some scholars suggest that there is a good deal of common ground to be explored between what Gandhi meant by "satyagraha," as clinging to the truth, which for Gandhi was tantamount to God, and what Thurman meant, increasingly and unconventionally, by God.[2] Gandhi said he would not hesitate to say, "God is love." But when it comes to articulating an "unadulterated message of nonviolence" in the United States, between 1936 and 1966, more or less, it would distort history to reduce the sense of the "the beloved community" in Montgomery or the "Promised Land" in Memphis to Gandhi's karmic "Kingdom of Heaven" in India. "Although both [Thurman and King] were educated in leading white liberal seminaries and universities," says Fluker, "their respective understandings of community arose initially from their common experience of oppression and segregation as black Americans in the deep South" (1989, 35). Although beholden to both Gandhi's Kingdom of Heaven and the Boston personalists' kingdom of God, Thurman and King shared "the faith contained in the tradition of the black church" (Cone 1984, 413).[3] Within that tradition, claims Cone, "theology was conducted in other forms than rational reflections. We sang and preached our theology in worship and other sacred contexts. The central meaning disclosed in these non-rational sources is found in both their form and content and is identical with freedom and hope" (1984, 417).

The preached or sung theology of the black church, which Raboteau calls the "invisible institution" of antebellum south, in which "the 'real preachin' of authentic Christianity, uncompromised by the heresy of slavery, could be heard and celebrated in the land" (2001, 150). Black churches provided a structure-function of hope derived from the "the context of hundreds of years of slavery and suffering that prevented despair from becoming the defining characteristic of the lives by looking forward to God's coming, eschatological freedom" (Cone 1984, 419; also see Raboteau 1978, 251). Cone argues that "the white public and also many white scholars have misunderstood King," as well as Thurman, "because they know so little about the black church community, ignoring its effect upon his life and thought" (1984, 414). Similarly, Lewis Baldwin claims that the "failure of many scholars to recognize that King's genius was folk, black, and southern may be attributed in large measure to racism and to some extent southern bias" (1991, 3). Perhaps this is less true of Thurman's genius, but Baldwin's main contention is well taken when it comes to exploring Thurman's "particularistic" appropriation of Gandhi's "universalist" message of nonviolence: "The main contention here is that we cannot possibly understand King's interpretation and appropriation of the Bible, of Gandhian ideas and methods, of Western philosophical categories, of principles of American participatory democracy, of Reinhold Niebuhr's Christian realism, and of Personalistic and Social Gospel concepts without carefully considering how the black experience of oppression and the traditions of the black church influenced him" (1991, 2). The central themes that Baldwin explores are liberation and millennial hope, the Christian doctrine of the kingdom of God as the locus of love and forgiveness. What Baldwin claims of King—that it was his background in the black church that made him receptive to Gandhian philosophy and methods—could be said also of Thurman.

Satyagraha, Ahimsa, and Forgiveness

The technique of satyagraha, or the method of active yet nonviolent civil disobedience as a means of clinging to the truth and thus combating injustice and other forms of violence, claimed Gandhi, could be successful only if a critical mass of individuals were able to unwaveringly embody—perhaps to the point of death—the vitalizing truth of ahimsa. The success of the satyagraha campaign depends on and is justified in terms of the "means employed" rather than the "ends or goals achieved": in this case, the end is the means. Gandhi's philosophy and methods of nonviolence aim at translating ideas into action. Nonviolence, Gandhi teaches us, in its active form, is "good will toward all life" or pure love as described in the Hindu scriptures, as agape in St. Paul, but also as Sabr or Rifq in the Koran. Resist, actively but nonviolently, all forms of ill will against life—that is, conscientiously object to actions and policies as well as arguments or thoughts that are inwardly inconsistent with good will toward all life. And this is where Gandhi's philosophy of ahimsa and method of satyagraha entails a fairly counterintuitive but radical theory if not theology of forgiveness. The satyagrahi, like the votaries of Jesus, as fallible "apostles of nonviolence," are required to forgive their enemies. Although it would seem that forgiveness undermines justice, as its apparent antithesis, Gandhi and Thurman as well as King believed that the struggle against injustice and violence could only be won by wielding the weapon of nonviolence construed as the love-ethic. In his "Letter from Birmingham Jail" ([1963] 1991, 301), for example, King wrote, "The means we use must be as pure as the ends we seek." Along these lines are the words of Mahatma Gandhi: "They say, 'means are after all means.' I would say, 'means are after all everything.' As the means so the end. There is no wall of separation between the means and the end" (1958, 77). The means justifies, as it were, the ends.

For Thurman, unconditional or self-sacrificing love is both a "gift of the spirit" and a "discipline of the flesh"; it also constitutes an essential feature in the religion of Jesus as distinct from the institution of Christianity. Unconditional love and forgiveness are defense mechanisms if not an antidote for the "disinherited"—that is, for those suffering from the wounds inflicted by the system of injustice and violence, a system that operates according to fear, hatred, and deception. The system of racism destroys the integrity of the personality of the oppressed as well as the oppressor: it distorts and destroys our proprietary or otherwise wholesome relationship to ourselves (for example, self-deception, self-hatred), to one another (for example, fear, deception, hate), and to God (for example, hubris, opacity, isolation). Without forgiveness, we cannot master ahimsa; without mastering ahimsa, we cannot seriously hope to succeed in overcoming injustice or clinging to the truth. In his introductory essay to *Gandhi: Nonviolence in Peace and War*, which constitutes his description and interpretation of Gandhi's philosophy of nonviolence, Thomas Merton claims that "modern tyrannies emphasize the irreversibility of evil in order to build their power on it" (2007, 34). Merton draws on Thomas Aquinas to show that evil is not only reversible, it is also the proper motive of that mercy by which it is overcome and changed into good. Replying to the objection that moral evil is not the motive for mercy since the evil of sin or injustice deserves indignation and punishment rather than mercy and forgiveness, Aquinas says that, on the contrary, sin itself is already a punishment "and in this respect we feel sorrow and compassion for sinners" (2007, 19). In order to do this, thought Merton, we must be able to experience their sin as if it were our own. Merton mentions this as a means of explaining Gandhi's philosophy of nonviolence, in which the admission of defect and fallibility within oneself makes it possible to be merciful to others, even the enemy. The mental machinery of tyrannical oppression, Merton suggests, includes the belief in the irreversibility of sin and a resolve to wipe it out once and for all in one heroic act or purge (rather than a need to recapture it over and over again). There are more steps to the argument, of course, but what I wish to stress is the use Merton makes of Hannah Arendt's juxtaposition of the logic of violence and the logic of nonviolence:

> Nonviolence has a different logic. It recognizes that sin is an everyday occurrence which is in the very nature of action's constant establishment of new relationships within a web of relations, and it needs forgiving, dismissing, in order to make it possible for life to go on by constantly releasing men from what they have done unknowingly. Only through this constant mutual release from what they do can men remain free agents, only by their constant willingness to change their minds and start again can they be trusted with so great a power as that to begin something new. (2007, 28)

Along the lines of Gandhi and Thurman, Arendt is claiming—thinks Merton—that to punish and destroy the oppressor is merely to initiate a new cycle of violence and oppression. The only real liberation, he says, speaking of Gandhi, is that which liberates both the oppressor and the oppressed, at the same time, from the same tyrannical automatism of the violent process that contains in itself the curse of irreversibility. And then Merton cites Arendt, again; who suggests that "the freedom contained in Jesus' teaching of forgiveness is the freedom from vengeance, which encloses both doer and sufferer in the relentless automatism of the action process, which by itself need never come to an end" (2007, 240–41). In both cases, however, nonviolence may require a transcendent power or force by which to sustain one's faith and hope as well as love. Perhaps love is the greatest of these, as St. Paul claims, because faith and hope are necessary if not sufficient conditions for love. The Gandhian campaign against injustice entails a profound commitment to the philosophical principle and practice of ahimsa. Mastery of ahimsa, thought Gandhi, requires great discipline, both of flesh and spirit. This practice requires the complete removal of hatred, fear, and deception within one's own life, construed as a living sermon. Gandhi said that it took him thirty years to overcome his proclivity toward hatred and other forms of violence. Anything that stood between Gandhi and the Kingdom of Heaven, qua Ahimsa, must be removed. Thurman espouses a similar doctrine. Although he "could accept Jesus as a martyr, an embodiment of sacrifice and a divine teacher," Gandhi claimed that "philosophically there was nothing extraordinary in Christian principles" (Fischer 2010, 41). According to Thurman, who was heterodoxically ecumenical in such matters, perhaps alluding to Plato's *Euthypho,* "the things that are true in any religious experience are to be found in that religious experience precisely because they are true; they are not true simply because they are found in that religious experience" (1979, 120). As Luther Smith (2007) and Alton Pollard (1992) demonstrate, Thurman's mysticism is closely tied to his social activism.[4] Indeed, Thurman says that the mystic is required to do whatever is necessary to remove the barriers between him and his God; for Thurman, not altogether unlike King, segregation and racism, as well as materialism and militarism, are wrong because they distort the personality and create barriers between God and persons, people with one another, and distort the sound of the genuine within oneself.

The trope of the beloved community, as a symbol of faith and hope, carries with it a theology or ethic of forgiveness. As an exemplar of the disinherited, Jesus forgave the oppressor before he or she asked for forgiveness, but he also refused to the point of death, understood as an elongated form of self-immolation, to condone or otherwise cooperate with evil forces. So we might imagine that in the religion of Jesus, Christ forgave as a defense mechanism against the oppressor, as a means of sustaining the integrity of his personality, but not merely as a defense mechanism: forgiveness should also be viewed as a sacrament or mitzvah—that is, a prayer in the form of a deed—by means of which he would not be forsaken by or separated from God. Jesus forgave, recklessly, and we, like Christ, who set the example and embodied the message, where the means and end coincide, and to the point of death, ought to—and thus must be able to—forgive one another. The Boston personalists with whom King studied, namely, L. Harold DeWolf, Edgar Brightman, and Peter A. Bertocci, certainly agreed with Walter Muelder, who found in the cross of Christianity an expression of the fact that "self-sacrificing and forgiving passion are the ultimate fulfillment of person-in-community and the ultimate revelation of the character of God" (1966, 170).[5] This oversimplifies the formula, certainly, not only for liberation theologians like Thurman and King, but also for those who participated in the nonviolent civil rights campaign, those who were asked to do what many among them considered to be impossible.[6]

Prior to meeting with Gandhi, Thurman was already committed to a preached theology if not philosophy of nonviolence, one that entailed an ethical theory or theology of forgiveness. And while it oversimplifies his argument, one that was refined over the course of decades, Thurman suggested that to love and forgive one's personal enemies as well as persons who made it difficult for the disinherited to live without fear, hate, deception, and humiliation, requires "the uprooting of the bitterness of [injury and] betrayal," which in turn requires—and this is the difficult part—"some deep respect and reverence for their person" that does not require "condoning their way of life" (1996, 94–95). "The concept of the reverence of personality," Thurman explains, is "applicable between persons from whom, in the initial instance, the heavy weight of status has been sloughed off." The radical feature of Thurman's theory of forgiveness emerges in his suggestion for what comes next: "Then what? Each person meets the other where he is and there treats him as if he were where he ought to be. Here we emerge into an area where love operates, revealing a universal characteristic unbounded by special or limiting circumstances" (1996, 104–5). For Thurman, we are ethically obliged to forgive as Christ forgave, alas, seventy times seven, because—as John J. Ansbro summarizes the premises of Thurman's early argument—"God forgives us again and again for what we do intentionally or unintentionally; no evil deed represents the full intention of the person; and the evil doer will be punished" (2000, 29).[7] In Thurman's later writings, the argument in support of forgiveness relies decreasingly on the retributive premise, which even then meant something close to Immanuel Kant's moral argument for the existence of God as a regulative ideal, such that the final reckoning is removed from our hands and placed before an omniscient judge to assign praise and blame, since to believe otherwise would undermine our moral motives; increasingly, Thurman emphasized the vital if not decisive importance of agape-love and forgiveness for the growing edges of restorative or regenerative social justice and the beloved community.[8]

Although Thurman may well diverge from Gandhi as well as from King on this front, he did believe that nonviolence construed as agape-love should aim to create community. Protecting the weak from the strong or alleviating suffering and confronting injustice or speaking the truth to power was not in itself, for Thurman, the primary motive animating his adherence to nonviolence. Less like Gandhi and King, perhaps, Thurman's philosophy of nonviolence might more fruitfully be compared to Jainist teachings. It is sometimes suggested that for Gandhi the primary inducement for embracing ahimsa was less noncontamination than it was a reverence for life. For Thurman, the primary inducement toward nonviolence and social activism was his desire to remove all the barriers or obstacles that stood between him and God (Smith 2007, 45). In some sense, ahimsa is the means; in another sense, it is the end. In some sense, nonviolence is the means to truth; in another sense, the truth is nonviolence. In some sense, ahimsa refers to an ontological entity or force; in another sense, ahimsa is a practice not unlike fasting by which one asymptotically approaches the truth construed as the ontological source or ultimate reality. Though diversely devoted to the service of God or Rama rather than of Krishna, drawing on the *Bhagavad Gita* and Gandhi's own *ishtadevata*, Thurman and Gandhi, as well as King, "expressed their love in desireless and self-sacrificing action on behalf of others, especially the weak members of society" (1960, vol. 89, 125).

Reflecting on the mixed success of his earlier campaigns in South Africa, Gandhi suggested to Thurman and Bailey in 1936 that it was not necessary for all of those who participated in nonviolent civil disobedience to master, completely, ahimsa and satyagraha, and yet he believed it was necessary for a critical mass of people within the movement, and not just the leaders or the satyagrahi, to embrace—as innocently as doves if not also as wisely as serpents[9]—nonviolence completely. Not altogether unlike Gandhi, Thurman strove to purify himself as a means of confronting violence and injustice with the power of nonviolence. Thurman also sought to provide, by means of philosophical meditations and spiritual exercises as well as by means of experiments in reconciliation and community building,[10] spiritual resources and succor to the disinherited. Throughout his life, Thurman used the philosophy and methods of nonviolence to break down the barriers that separated him from his neighbors or "potential neighbors," which is how he stretched the parable of the Good Samaritan and alienated him from his

God, that is, from the voice of the genuine, which Thurman often described as the only God we'll ever know.

Conclusion

Thurman and King were separately but quite profoundly influenced by Gandhian teachings. Both Thurman and King believed, as King expressed it in 1968, that "Gandhi speaks for us: 'In the midst of death, life persists. In the midst of darkness, light persists.' We are today in the midst of death and darkness. We can strengthen life and [light] by our personal acts by saying 'no' to violence . . . by saying 'yes' to life" (Martin Luther King Jr. Collection at Morehouse College 2.6.0.180_001). This concise insight constitutes the philosophical core of King's final speech in Memphis (April 3, 1968). In that final speech, recalls Andrew Young, King focused on death. That speech culminated in those immortal lines: "I don't know what will happen now. We have got some difficult days ahead. But it really doesn't matter with me now, because I have been to the mountaintop. So I'm happy tonight. I'm not worried about anything. I'm not fearing any man. Mine eyes have seen the glory of the coming of the Lord" (1991, 286). The quote from Gandhi to which King alludes goes as follows: "And is this power benevolent or malevolent? I see it as purely benevolent, for I can see that in the midst of death life persists, in the midst of untruth truth persists, in the midst of darkness light persists. Hence I gather that God is Life, Truth, Light. He is Love. He is the supreme Good" (1962, xviii). Expressed elsewhere, Gandhi wrote:

> I have found that life persists in the midst of destruction and therefore there must be a higher law than that of destruction. Only under that law would a well-ordered society be intelligible and life worth living. And if that is the law of life, we have to work it out in daily life. Whenever there are jars, wherever you are confronted with an opponent, conquer him with love—in this crude manner I have worked it out in my life. That does not mean that all my difficulties are solved. Only I have found that this law of love has answered as the law of destruction has never done. . . . It is not that I am incapable of anger, for instance, but I succeed on almost all occasions to keep my feelings under control. Whatever may be the result, there is always in me a conscious struggle for following the law of non-violence deliberately and ceaselessly. Such a struggle leaves one stronger or fit. The more I work at this law, the more I feel the delight in life, the delight in the scheme of the universe. It gives me a peace and a meaning of the mysteries of nature that I have no power to describe. (1962, 276).

Surface differences obscure our appreciation of significant similarities between Gandhi and Thurman or King. But there are also surface similarities that tend to distort important differences between their respective theories and projects. Gandhi, Thurman, and King were committed to the philosophy and methods of nonviolence.

Baldwin argues that King "stood squarely in the tradition of William Whipper, Frederick Douglass, the National Association for the Advancement of Colored People (NAACP), and the National Urban League, all of whom had emphasized nonviolence and moral suasion as the most practical methods for achieving integration and basic constitutional rights for black Americans" (1991, 186). There were, of course, ample utilitarian grounds to animate that commitment. Nonviolence served as a useful emancipatory strategy for those who were outgunned and unable effectively to mount violent resistance. Gandhi early on referred to this "mere method" of nonviolent civil disobedience, as practiced in Europe, derogatorily, as "passive resistance." But each of these men resisted violence because they believed that their complicity, proximate or remote, perpetuated "the evils of racism, materialism and militarism," which corrupt the souls of the oppressed as well as the oppressor. Not unlike Gandhi, the means in this case is also the end. So while I agree that King and perhaps also Thurman "stood squarely in the tradition" of Whipper and Douglass as well as of the NAACP and National Urban League, Thurman and King were committed to the philosophy of nonviolence that extends well beyond the method of nonviolence espoused by, for example, the NAACP. Thurman and King as well as James Farmer and Bayard Rustin also stood squarely in the tradition of Gandhi and Tolstoy; institutionally, they also stood in the tradition of the Fellowship of Reconciliation and the Southern Christian Leadership Conference. For Thurman, our souls are initially threatened and distorted by fear and violence and are subsequently destroyed by hatred and deception as well as by self-hatred and self-deception. Although it is certainly possible to compare Thurman's philosophy of nonviolence to that of Gandhi or of King, perhaps merely as a theoretical or dialectical exercise, one that is long on conceptual or textual analysis but short on practical application, the pragmatic value of the exercise consists in translating these ideas into action.

2

On the Anatomy of Hatred and the Power of Love

"When you feel hurt, but do not hurt the other, you are truly victorious; your practice and your victory benefit both of you. When you understand the roots of anger in yourself and in the other, your mind will enjoy true peace, joy, and lightness. You become the doctor who heals himself, or herself, and who heals the other."

Thich Nhat Hanh, *Teachings of Love* (2008)

"[Hatred] cannot be exorcised by generous quotations, by wooing the love of another. It has to be understood first."

Thurman, *The Growing Edge* (1956)

When the Buddha was asked by a Brahman whether there was anything that he was willing to kill, states Thich Nhat Hanh, the Buddha replied: "Yes, anger. Killing anger removes suffering and brings peace and happiness. Anger is the single enemy that all the wise ones agree to kill" (2008, 25). Across religious traditions, the teachings of love not only command us to resist the near irresistible and altogether natural tendency to become angry, to hate, to retaliate, or to exact revenge; they also uniformly go so far as to entreat if not demand of us that we love our enemies. As a theologian and philosopher, as a mystic and a prophet, Thurman insisted that the teachings of love in Jesus were quite simple at their core but altogether radical in their socioethical implications. "The religion of Jesus," wrote Thurman, in his early manifesto, *Jesus and the Disinherited,* "makes the love-ethic central" ([1949] 1996, 89). In a mesmerizing sermon titled "Love or Perish" (1953 audio), Thurman argued that "it is unreasonable to think that a sectarian religious experience" can sustain and nourish or otherwise support a "universal morality" (that is, "anything other than a sectarian morality"). For Thurman, this insight constituted "the great and creative and radical discovery of Jesus Christ" (1953).

And yet, "the love-ethic is no ordinary achievement" ([1949] 1996, 89). Thurman would have wanted us to grow in all manner of insight into this extraordinary socioethical teaching and spiritual discipline.

Howard Thurman believed it was important for us to understand the roots of anger and hatred as well as the persistent temptation to resort, immediately and without further delay, to violence when dealing with those whom we perceive to be our enemies. Like many African Americans of his generation, Thurman understood the temptation to retaliate and exact revenge or otherwise settle the conflagration—as William James describes it—"quickly, thrillingly, tragically, and by force" (1911, 108; see also Jensen 2012). Indeed, Thurman is curiously quick to concede that hatred can sometimes serve a positive function in restoring—or establishing for the first time—the animating and individuating core of the personality. Thurman was a liberation theologian and a philosopher as well as a sensitive moral psychologist and a social philosopher. If we are to take Thurman's philosophy or theory of nonviolence seriously, if intended as a reliable guide to behavior, individually or collectively, the critic will insist that it should be at least "minimally realistic, in the sense of being in cognitive contact with the real world" (Geuss 2008, 143). Fair enough. By "minimally realistic" Raymond Geuss means that "one will demand of a candidate [political] theory that it actively encourage one to understand the ways in which power, interests, priorities, values, and forms of legitimation concretely interact in society" (2008, 143). Social transformation begins within, thought Thurman, such that the centrifugal is animated by the centripetal, paradoxically, and the near is the clue to the far. What are the roots of anger? How does it arise? And what resources are available to us for healing ourselves and our siblings or our neighbors, near or far, known or unknown, or perhaps even our enemies?

And while it may seem counterintuitive, unnatural even, this is precisely the context within which King—similar to Thurman and Gandhi or Thich—reiterated, fifty years ago, his commitment to the philosophy and method of nonviolence. This philosophy of love and reconciliation constitutes, as King expressed it, "a sword that heals" and "the solution to every problem" (1991, 526). But even if we are able to explain why it is important to love one another, even our enemies, or to overcome our hatred of those we perceive to be our enemies, perhaps even more demanding than mere justice, which some consider to be the public expression of love, we are still hard pressed to explain how it is possible. In order to love one another as we should, suggests Thurman, in a manner strikingly similar to the Buddhist sutra in the epigraph to this essay, we must seek—despite the social taboo or conspiracy of silence surrounding the issue—a deep understanding of the roots of anger in oneself and in the other. Thurman describes how hatred can "cripple a person in reverse" (1996, 88; 2006, 19), which is one reason why hatred as well as fear and deception must be overcome. Amending slightly the sutra cited by Thich, Thurman argues—as a philosopher and theologian but also as a psychiatrist, which is how King tends to characterize Thurman—that we should seek a deeper understanding of anger and hatred as well as a deeper understanding of fear and deception in order that we might become the doctor who heals himself or herself and who also heals the other. Thurman's solution, as Edward Kaplan puts it, "follows the path from fear and hatred to love and nonviolent resistance" (1982, 22).

The Anatomy of Hatred

> Often there are things on the horizon that point logically to a transformation of society, especially for the underprivileged, but he cannot cooperate with them because he is spiritually and intellectual confused. He mistakes fear for caution and caution for fear. Now, if his mind is free and his spirit unchained, he can work intelligently and courageously for a new day.
>
> Howard Thurman, "Good News for the Underprivileged" (1935)

> A man's horizon may become so completely dominated by the intense character of his hatred that there remains no creative residue in his mind and spirt to give to great ideas, to great concepts. He becomes lopsided. To use a phrase from Zarathustra, he becomes "a cripple in reverse."
>
> Howard Thurman, *Jesus and the Disinherited* (1949)

According to Thurman, hatred is one of "the hounds of hell that dog the footsteps of the disinherited in season and out of season" ([1949] 1996, 74). Hatred and deception, suggests Thurman, arise within a climate of fear, often in an environment devoid of care and mutual concern, more or less as a survival mechanism; these constitute but two ways of destroying the integrity of the personality or—as Thurman turns it, alluding to Nietzsche—"crippling a person in reverse." Thurman was convinced that as psychosocial therapists we need a deeper understanding of the anatomy of fear and hatred or deception as well as of the sources of desperation or nihilism and selfishness or naked belligerence. Although Thurman's classic analysis of "the hounds of hell" begins with a description or diagnosis of how fear distorts the personality and how subsequent survival mechanisms such as deception and hatred compound an already complicated problem, I focus here almost exclusively on Thurman's analysis of hatred. For Thurman, himself no stranger to those hounds of hell, hatred is quite distinct from merely disliking someone. It is worse than treating someone as a thing, as an exception to the golden rule, or violating the categorical imperative, worse than treating someone as an instrument to be used as we so choose, rather than as a person. Hatred, suggested Thurman, goes further than all that: "The logic of hate is to kill. It is to translate the willing of the nonexistence of another into the literal deed of his extermination" (1963, 115). Martha Nussbaum draws a similar distinction, in *Anger and Forgiveness,* when she describes hatred as a "negative emotion that focuses on the entirety of the person, rather than a single act" (2016, 50). Nussbaum elaborates: "Although anger is directed at a person, its focus is an act, and when it is disposed of somehow, anger could be expected to go away. Hatred, by contrast, is global, and if acts are involved it is simply because everything about the person is seen in a negative light. As Aristotle remarks, the only thing that will really satisfy hatred is that the person cease to exist" (2016, 50). Thurman understood this Aristotelian point about the dynamics of antipathy.

The early stages of hatred involve actively ignoring the other person, in word and deed, conspicuously, as if to underscore a pernicious prejudice, as if to add insult to injury, which—claimed Thurman—"is something that the human spirit simply cannot abide. It takes all the oxygen out of the air *and you just can't breathe*" (1953 audio, my italics). In his *Disciplines of the Spirit,* Thurman puts it this way: "When violence is met with violence, the citadel of the human heart is not invaded. . . . For this reason, the only thing that can maintain the mood of violence between men beyond the heat and excitation of direct encounter is hate. Hate is the great insulator, making it possible for one man to deny the existence of another or to will his nonexistence. Violence is the act through which such a will is implemented, and hate is its dynamic" (1963, 113). Thurman's description of hatred poses an alternative if not also a significant challenge to conventional as well as contemporary accounts of anger, for example, in Aristotle as well as Martha Nussbaum. Although she claims that contemporary philosophers "spend little time analyzing the emotion [of anger]," Nussbaum argues—drawing on Aristotle's analysis in *Rhetoric*—that "anger is normatively irrational" or at the very least "normatively problematic" (2016, 25). As for Aristotle, Nussbaum builds on the following definition of anger as "a desire accompanied by pain for an imagined retribution on account of an imagined slighting inflicted by people who have no legitimate reason to slight oneself or one's own" (2016, 17).

If we can keep the other persons outside our "magnetic field," as Thurman put it, "as somehow ethically out-of-bounds, as something else altogether, then we can deal with them as if they were not human beings." The enemy combatants must be construed as subhuman, at which point you can do anything to them you choose without destroying your sense of inner values. If I can get you out of bounds, he explains, then the normal restraints of morality and civilized behavior no longer apply. We struggle to keep certain individuals and groups out of bounds: "This is part of the madness and the immorality and the evil of segregation" (1965, 45). If I could exclude you in good conscience, if I can place you out of bounds, then I can—goes this line of thought, which is both an argument and a psychological observation—treat you as I please. Thurman captures this "cruel dilemma" by which the Christian love-ethic is occasionally restricted in *Luminous Darkness:*

> The common saying in my world was: the white man did not have religion. By implication, we did. That kept me from expecting him to act toward me as I would expect a fellow Christian to act, but curiously enough my religion did not demand of me that I act toward him as a Christian should act. At the risk of being repetitious, he was not regarded as worthy of a Christian response. It was a cruel dilemma; the price paid for a kind of inner balance that would make for some measure of peace of mind was the rigid narrowing or restricting of the Christian ethic. The struggle was to try to achieve a sense of self in a total environment that threatened the self. (1965a, 5)

Thurman reminds us, "periods of national crisis [make] it seemingly necessary to discipline men in hatred of other human beings" (1996, 89). Similarly: "During times of war, hatred becomes quite respectable, even though it has to masquerade often under the guise of patriotism" (1996, 74). We consciously or subconsciously debase and dehumanize the enemy in our minds in order to give free rein to inhumane and undignified behavior toward them. So we compartmentalize into the "we" and the "they," socioethical categories defined pragmatically in terms of a divergent set of moral responsibilities toward "us," toward our brothers, and "them," those who are not our brothers—those who are not worthy of ethical treatment. (Once we classify the enemy as subhuman, as the equivalent of zombies, say, thinking of popular video games, we feel perfectly free to annihilate them with impunity.) Our capacity to deceive ourselves about the value of our enemies poses a genuine threat to mutual recognition and reconciliation. "The first step toward love," claims Thurman, "is a common sharing of a sense of mutual worth and value" (1996, 98).

There are also seemingly less dramatic "senses of separateness," contacts or interactions of sundry sorts, but in each case they occur in a climate devoid of mutual goodwill. The are contacts, even though there is a sense of separateness. Thurman warns that "contacts without fellowship tend to express themselves in unsympathetic understanding" (1965, 39); at its core, this type of feigned understanding is hard, cruel, and impersonal yet somehow devastating, the sort of understanding and imagination that has been poisoned or otherwise malnourished, an understanding and imagination that has been distorted or otherwise diseased. "The gentle-tempered person is not vengeful," wrote Aristotle, in *Nicomachean Ethics,* "but inclined to sympathetic understanding" (1984, 1–3). Thurman then asks us to think more carefully about the anatomy of hatred in the life of the poor and the disinherited. Thurman claims "it is necessary, therefore, for the privileged and the underprivileged to work on the common environment for the purpose of providing experiences of fellowship" ([1949] 1966, 98). Stated more generally: "One of the central problems in human relations," wrote Thurman, in *Luminous Darkness,* "is applying the ethic of respect for personality in a way that is not governed by special categories" (1965a, 1).

At first, suggests Thurman, hatred is a device or survival mechanism by which the individual—those who wish—actively asserts his or her right to be in the presence of that which seeks to disrupt and demolish. In his signature "Love or Perish" sermon (1953), and overlapping in ways with his treatment of analysis of hatred in *Jesus and the Disinherited,* Thurman describes the anatomy and dynamic of hatred in an algorithm or diagram that begins its epicycle from human contact as devoid of warmth and genuine fellowship; through a psychosocial stage of "unsympathetic understanding" by which "the first step along the road of bitterness and hatred is assured" ([1949] 1996, 76; also see 1965, 40); to the crucial point at which this "penetrating, incisive, cold understanding . . . tends to express itself in the active functioning of ill will" ([1949] 1996, 76–77). This third stage of hatred is decisive, thinks Thurman, because hatred and resentment or bitterness "spreads its virus by contagion" (78). Thurman concedes that hatred can serve as a vital psychosocial function: for example, it can serve as "a source of validation for your personality" (80) or "a device for rebuilding, step by perilous step, the foundation for individual significance" (81) or the means by which "an individual seeks to protect himself against moral disintegration" (83). Thurman shifts his analysis from diagnosis to treatment with this bitter prognosis for those who hate, even when it operates within what Thurman calls "the illusion of righteousness" (82): "Despite all the positive psychological attributes of hatred we have outlined, hatred destroys finally the core of the life of the hater. While it lasts, burning in white heat, its effect seems positive and dynamic. But at last it turns to ash, for it guarantees a final isolation from one's fellows. It blinds the individual to all values of worth, even as they apply to himself and his fellows. Hatred bears deadly and bitter fruit" (86). In his 1953 sermon, Thurman says: "So this is what hate does, sometimes, to the man whose back is against the wall, when all resources are cut off, when there is a complete and radical denial of his persona, when the integrity of his existence begins to disintegrate, and when he feels that the moment of his annihilation is at hand he affirms the integrity of his life by striking out blindly by asserting his right to be." Both Thurman and King preached the good news that, as King expresses it in his "Death of Evil on the Seashore," there is "a light to guide us in the darkness of the midnight when we are thwarted and the slumbering giants of gloom and hopelessness rise in our souls. The testimony of the psalmist is that we need never walk in the darkness" (1981, 86). For Thurman and King, as for Gandhi, there was a luminous presence or guide "when the light of day vanishes, leaving us in some dark and desolate midnight—moments when our highest hopes are turned into shambles of despair or when we are the victims of some tragic injustice and some terrible exploitation" (1981, 85–86).

"Love, as critical as it is," insisted Thurman in a 1953 sermon, "must possess a deep understanding of hatred." Thurman wrote that we have been too sentimental in our attempts "to get rid of hatred by preachments, by moralizing, by platitudinous judgments" rather than by "revealing the anatomy of its development." Except for periods of serious social crisis, claims Thurman, there has been "a conspiracy of silence about hatred, its function and its meaning." But Thurman warns that "all the preaching in the world, Christian or otherwise, cannot deal with hatred in the human spirit without understanding its ground and organizational dynamic" (1953 audio). Sometimes hatred can provide the means by which life is organized. Fear and anger or hatred can galvanize the self to individuality by unifying the parts of the self. Kierkegaard captures the point in *Purity of Heart:* "For he who is not himself a unity is never really anything wholly and decisively; he only exists in an external sense—as long as he lives as a numeral within a crowd, a fraction within the earthly conglomeration" (1956, 45). Thurman claims that hatred and resentment can sometimes serve as the last line of defense in the face of annihilation, an assertion of one's right to be. Hate, then, in the life of those who have nowhere else to stand, becomes the means by which they establish—albeit fleetingly—the foundation for an integrated self. "Hating is something of which to be ashamed unless it provides us a form of validation and prestige. If either is provided, then the immoral and amoral character of the hatred is transformed into positive violence" (1996, 75). "So hate does this," claims Thurman in 1953, "it provides a ground of inner emotional security or organizational stability and announces its presence and affirms its right to be" (1953 audio). Elsewhere: "Despite all the positive psychological attributes of hatred," which operates according to the logic or organizational principles inherent in hatred, it is still hate, and—argues Thurman—"hatred destroys finally the core of the life of the hater" (1996, 86). There are positive things that hate does, sometimes, but the power of hatred is also destructive. Hatred asks few questions. Although anger and hatred are initially nourished or animated "by exercising specific discrimination," by fixating on "the persons responsible for the situations which create the reaction of resentment, bitterness, and hatred," once released, they "cannot be confined to the offenders alone" (1996, 86).

Black Radical Discourse in Wright and Thurman

I wish someone some day would get a clear and definitive insight as to the meaning and the significance of violence.

Thurman, "Quest for Peace" (1949)

In "Richard Wright and Black Radical Discourse: The Advocacy of Violence" (2013), Lawrence Jackson analyzes Richard Wright's literary and psychosocial depiction of violence, as well as perhaps a proper philosophy of violence, primarily but not exclusively in *Native Son* and *Black Boy*, which influenced and inspired following generations of advocates of sundry sorts of violence. "Wright's great leap in understanding," states Jackson, "revolved around his regular use of violence in his fictions as a means of enabling his black characters to attain their full humanity" (2013, 200). "During the 1940s and 1950s, Wright was the best-respected and most articulate black writer in the struggle to end racial segregation and inequality in the United States and Africa" as well as "the best-known advocate of physical resistance to racial and racialist subordination" (201). Wright, or at least the author of *Native Son,* says Jackson, "depicts scenes of violence and subsequent catharsis that profoundly influenced a generation of political and psychological theorists of colonial liberation, [Frantz] Fanon among them" (201). As early as *Uncle Tom's Children* (1938), Wright's protagonists display an unabashed "willingness to commit violence," and characters "betray a new level of awareness after a violent struggle" (Jackson 2013, 207). For Wright, "higher civilization" was understood as "gaining access to another plateau of consciousness. Wright pioneered not only the exploration of black working-class struggle to attain a level of heightened consciousness but also the role of physical struggle in catapulting them, ironically, upward in their search" (209). In *Native Son,* for example, "the name of the protagonist, Bigger Thomas, became synonymous for desperate black rage" and Wright "combined a genuine need with a willingness to exploit the taboo topic of black rage, fear, hatred and bitterness" (210) as well as "anger and resentment" (211).

Writing at the peak of the Great Migration (1940–1950s), Wright exposed a ripe layer of racism continuing to thwart the most basic hopes of African Americans. After murdering Mary Dalton, Bigger Thomas gets bigger—he "comes physically alive: 'Bigger Thomas felt a lessening in of the tension in his muscles; he had shed an invisible burden he had long carried.'" A "partial answer to overcoming the stranglehold of racist society lay, not in the pursuit of education advanced by the black middle class, but in simple cathartic violence" (2013, 211). Jackson elaborates: "Inevitably, the murder . . . brings to Bigger Thomas a modicum of control and internal development—a new plateau of consciousness—that had before been completely unavailable to him" (212). Wright wanted to show the destructive potential of a neurosis-inducing environment and to describe "how important violence was as a means of enabling blacks to escape degradation and fear" (212). (One thinks of Frederick Douglass: "From whence came the spirit I don't know—I resolved to fight; and suiting my action to the resolution, I seized Covey hard by the throat; and as I did so, I rose" [2010, 187]). It was for this artistic success in "racial damage imagery" (Jackson 2013, 218) that his novel was banned from most quarters, at least domestically, including by the NAACP. Even Du Bois accused Wright of egregious misrepresentations of both blacks and whites. Wright's portrayal of cathartic violence served many functions, including the outside chance of "swaying public opinion and inciting radical change" (2013, 214) or, later in the essay, the "means to be used to shift the bedrock of public sensibility in the direction of support for racial equality" (220). In terms of his influence on the trajectory of the civil rights movement, Jackson suggests that "Wright's work filled an important ideological gap by disallowing the possibility of a racial panacea in the North and by legitimizing violence as a liberating tool" (215). Slantwise, in *Black Boy,* Wright "made explicit his ideological battle against the practices and beliefs that prevented black Americans from actively resisting oppression" and, says Jackson, "*Black Boy* magnifies the fear and hatred of *Native Son*" (217); "yet again, Wright pointed to struggle, subterfuge, and violence as among the tools necessary to escape the mental stupor imposed by racist conditioning" (218). The important contribution of Wright's *Black Boy,* explains Jackson, is "its determination to show the significant role the black community plays in shaping the psyche of the young child to accept a life of injustice and deprivation" (217). George Padmore praised Wright's 1953 *Outsider* as an "attempted answer to the question of human freedom and responsibility in a world whose ideologies of power and control were obvious and failing" (222). Even if, writes Jackson, "Wright's unflagging commitment to a view of the United States as a psychologically and socially desperate nation of unfulfilled expectations was inelegant, it remains that his loud barking kept alert and vital the forces of progressive social change" (Jackson 2013, 224).

In his *Shade of Blue,* Eddie Glaude suggests that James Baldwin, in *The Fire Next Time,* reveals "the radical rage that results from the conditions of black living in the United States" (2007,12). Elaborating:

> One would expect individuals who experience systemic degradation to be angry. This is not to suggest that rage should completely define their lives. For some this may be the case. But for the majority of African Americans rage stands alongside the joys of living, and it is precisely in this intense juxtaposition that the edginess of some facets of black life can be found. Indeed, Baldwin renders intelligible the strangeness of the Nation of Islam's theodicy by translating it into the idiom of everyday black life, where rage is a constant companion: we all have our private Bigger Thomas living within our skulls. (Glaude 2007, 12).

Fanon not only believes that violence is justified, it is also effective as well as cathartic and unifying. Ultimately, wrote Fanon, following the Manichaean logic of the colonizer, "the work of the colonist is to make even dreams of liberty impossible for the colonized" (2004, 50). According to Fanon: "The colonized man liberates himself in and through violence. This praxis enlightens the militant because it shows him the means and the end" (2004, 44). Both King and Carmichael read and appreciated Fanon's *Wretched of the Earth* and, it seems, *Black Skin, White Masks.* When he refers to Fanon in his chapter on 'Black Power' in *Where Do We Go from Here?* (1968), King contends that "time is cluttered with the wreckage of individuals and communities that surrendered to hatred and violence" ([1968] 2010, 67). Although Martin Luther King Jr. and Howard Thurman as well as Frantz Fanon and Che Guevara thought that hatred and violence are interwoven such that "violence is the act through which such a will is implemented, and hate is its dynamic" (Thurman 1963, 113), it is certainly conceivable that the one might occur in the absence of the other.[1] While it may be true that King became more "militant" in the sense of being increasingly vigilant and passionately committed, he also remained committed to nonviolence. And although King acknowledged the deep insight expressed in Fanon, he beckoned us to "follow another way" ([1968] 2010, 67). King and Fanon agreed that "with every ounce of our energy we must continue to rid our nation of the incubus of racial injustice"—that is, we must be vigilant if not also militant—and yet King also believed that "we need not in the process relinquish our privilege and obligation to love" (2010, 67). King also agreed with Fanon, and this is the passage that King cites from the *Wretched of the Earth,* published the same year as Thurman's *Disciplines of the Spirit* and King's *Strength to Love*: "humanity is waiting for something other from us than such an imitation, which would be almost an obscene caricature" (King [1968] 2010, 67). Fanon elaborates: "But if we want humanity to advance a step further, if we want to bring it up to a different level than that which Europe has shown it, then we must invent and we must make discoveries. . . . For Europe, for ourselves and for humanity, comrades, we must turn over a new leaf, we must work out new concepts, and try to set afoot a new [human]" (Fanon 2004, 239; in King [1968] 2010, 67–8). King merely objects to the "willingness to imitate old concepts of violence" (2010, 68) and suggests instead:[2]

> If we want truly to advance a step further, if we want to turn over a new leaf and really set a new man afoot, we must begin to turn mankind away from the long and desolate night of violence. . . . This not only will make us new men, but will give us a new kind of power. . . . A dark, desperate, confused and sin-sick world waits for this new kind of man and this new kind of power ([1968] 2010, 68–69).

Fanon was eager earlier on, in *Black Skin, White Masks,* to find common ground for a more promising future:

> Unsure whether the white man considers him as consciousness in-itself-for-itself, he is constantly preoccupied with detecting resistance, opposition, and contestation. . . . We said in our introduction that man was an affirmation. We shall never stop repeating it. Yes to life. Yes to love. Yes to generosity. But man is also a negation. No to man's contempt. No to the indignity of man. To the exploitation of man. To the massacre of most of what is most human in man: freedom (2008, 197).

There's more to it than that, wrote Fanon in 1952, since he also asks us to remember that "Man's behavior is not only reactional. And there is always resentment in reaction. Nietzsche had already said it in *The Will to Power.* To induce man to be actional, by maintaining in his circularity the respect of the fundamental values that make the world human, that is the task of utmost urgency for he who, after careful reflection, prepares to act" (2008, 197). Contrary to Fanon's definition of cathartic violence, here's how Thurman defines violence:

> The term "violence" usually carries with it the connotation of physical force of some sort. Violence as physical force, when employed directly in face-to-face encounter, may be overwhelming and compelling. It is quick, decisive, and definite. There is a certain limited efficiency in its use. It tends to inspire fear and often makes for temporary capitulation. Its central purpose is to make it possible for one man to impose his will on another. As an instrument of national policy, its purpose is to impose one nation's will on another nation. ([1963] 2003, 112)

Thurman believed that "to confine the definition of violence to its physical expression is too restricting and limiting" ([1963] 2003, 112). "Terrible as it is, it is not violence in its worst form" (112). Alluding to an example set by Gandhi, Thurman also believed that "love itself may be a form of nonphysical violence" (112). In *Black Theology and Black Power*, James Cone argued that "the Christian does not decide between violence and nonviolence, evil and good. He decides between the less and the greater evil" (1969, 143). Cone was certainly familiar with Thurman's pacifism, and Cone respected Thurman's position, but Cone clarifies the position of the person who "decides to take the 'nonviolent' way, then he is saying that revolutionary violence is more detrimental to man in the long run than systemic violence. But if the system is evil, then revolutionary violence is both justified and necessary" (1969, 143). Luther Smith concedes that Thurman does not seem to adequately answer the counterarguments to nonviolence and inclusivity, whether Mao or Malcolm. Many of those scholar-activists who studied with Thurman were unconvinced, asking themselves: "Is it not possible that violence may at times be a better expression of love than nonviolence?" (Smith 2001, 149).

Thurman found it useful to distinguish between three ways by which one might conscientiously object to violence in general or war in particular. Perhaps Thurman's best formulation of his own brand of pacifism is found in his exposition of Olive Schreiner's statement of pacifism. While some may inherit their pacifism from their forebearers as a matter of hereditary tradition, more or less unthinkingly, a second set of conscientious objectors "may object, in all good conscience, to a particular war for some definite and limited reason" (for example, because they "believe the war to have been led up to by a false and mad diplomacy, to be based upon a mistaken judgment of the national interests" [1973, xxx]), Schreiner belongs, thinks Thurman, to a third and more radical type of pacifist who holds that "no gain inferred by war can compensate for the evils which result" (Thurman 1973, xxx). Although this radical pacifist

> may fully recognize the difference in type between one war and another; between a war for dominance, trade expansion, or the maintenance of Empire, and a war in which a class or a race struggles against a power seeking permanently to crush and subject it, or in which a man fights in the land of his birth for the soil on which he first saw light, against the stranger seeking to dispossess him (1973, xxx).

Schreiner belongs to those who, thinks Thurman, quoting Schreiner, he or she "is unable to assist not merely in the actual carnage of war, but, as far as possible, in all that leads to its success" (xxx). And while this type of "universal conscientious objector to war" is often associated with religious individuals, Thurman argues that "there is no necessity for such a man to belong to any organize religion or to base his convictions on some moral or even aesthetic teaching" (xxx). Like Schreiner, this third type of pacifism is expressive of Thurman's "total response to life and his experience of it" (xxx).

In many ways, Thurman could be fruitfully interpreted as a response to the advocacy of violence—or at least hatred—as expressed in Wright and promoted by subsequent anticolonialists and advocates of emancipatory violence. Thurman was also preoccupied with providing an antidote to fear, hatred, deception, rage, bitterness, and resentment. The power of love is also cathartic, at least potentially, in ways analogous to the power of hatred, but the power of love is uniquely creative and redemptive rather than destructive. Thurman and King also believed that love, whether in the religion of Jesus or in the philosophy of Gandhi or in the spiritual teachings of Thich, does not discriminate: we are encouraged to love one another with perfect equanimity, to love even our enemies. In each of the cases mentioned above, from Thurman and King to Gandhi and Thich, the quality of their respective religious experiences was inextricably intertwined with the vitality and intensity of their respective acts of political activism. Their political activism arose out of their respective religious experiences. In each case, their commitment to social justice required the courage of risking their lives for the sake of the disinherited. It is Gandhi who claimed, but Thurman would have concurred, that anyone "who says that religion is unrelated to politics understands neither religion nor politics." Thurman argued that hatred destroys the inner bearings of the individual and, little by little, it slowly yet ineluctably undermines the meaning of life. Nihilism comes in an array of forms, observed King in *Strength to Love,* some better suited to the "tender-minded" and others to the "hard-hearted" (2010, 495), but in each case, inevitably and tragically, warned Thurman, as a social psychiatrist, meaninglessness poses a genuine threat to our collective well-being. Hate takes on a life of its own:

> When it moves from me out this way, it doesn't know that it was created as a sense of defense. All it knows is how to reproduce itself: and the thing that it does to me, hate, when it reaches you, it bears the same fruit. If I don't want to do this, if I don't really mean to do it, then the only way I can handle the raw materials of my life is to discover another dimension of life. I am never under obligation to exchange hate for hate. My responsibility does not rest, ultimately, with the person who hates me, but rather what I do with that: return it in kind, withdraw and organize to destroy, all manner of things, but it is my responsibility, since God has snatched from us our final alibi. I must learn to hate them with a perfect hatred. But hate is hate, whether concentrated and integrated or loose, and hate is against life; and that which is against life is against God; and that which is against God cannot stand. We may choose: but if you choose hate, my God have mercy on your souls (1953, audio).

As Thurman put it in 1949, "the logic of the development of hatred is the death of spirit and disintegration of ethical and moral values." Above all else, however, "it must be borne in mind that hatred tends to dry up the springs of creative thought" and the "urgent needs of the personality for creative expression are starved to death" (1996, 88). In short, "Jesus rejected hatred. It was not because he lacked the vitality or the strength. It was not because he lacked the incentive. Jesus rejected hatred because he saw that hatred meant death to the mind, death to the spirit, death to communion with the father" (88). In *Luminous Darkness,* Thurman wrote that hate was "the thick sludge of the heart" and "a slow accumulated distillation from bitterness, resentment, frustration, and hostility" (1965, 83). In the case of Thurman,

> the imperative of social action is not merely to improve the condition of society. It is not merely to feed the hungry, not merely to relieve human suffering and human misery. If this were all, in and of itself, it would be important surely. But this is not all. The basic consideration has to do with the removal of all that prevents God from coming to himself in the life of the individual. Whatever there is that blocks this calls for action. (1970, 21)

Martin Luther King Jr. appropriated Thurman's insight into the inner logic of hate among the disinherited in his well-rehearsed sermon "Loving Your Enemies" (1963). Similar to fear and deception, argued Thurman in *Jesus and the Disinherited,* hatred distorts and also destroys the soul of the oppressed as well as of the oppressor. This belongs to what King called the "why" we refuse to hate and strain to love, which is a theoretical matter, as opposed to the practical business of "how" we might reduce hatred and increase the power of love. Thurman asks us to consider the sociohistorical context of Christ's command that we love our enemies: "Is it reasonable to assume that Jesus did not understand the anatomy of hatred?" ([1949] 1996, 86). Thurman believes that "every battle you win, you must win it over and over again, for as long as you are living and growing and experiencing and developing" ([1962] 1978, 50). Amending slightly King's use of Emerson, replacing "his fear" with "his anger or hatred": "He has not learned the lesson of life who does not every day surmount [his anger or hatred]" (1912, 276). Cornel West makes a similar observation: "Nihilism is not overcome by arguments or analysis; it is tamed by love and care. And disease of the soul must be conquered by a turning of one's soul. This turning is done through one's own affirmation of one's worth—an affirmation fueled by the concern of others. A love ethic must be at the center of a politics of conversion" (1993, 29).

Although Thurman and King bore heavy burdens in their respective efforts to "achieve full status as citizens and human beings" for African Americans, "all-here-now" (King 2010, 154), they firmly believed that—as King put it in *Where Do We Go from Here: Chaos or Community?*—"Hate is too great a burden to bear" ([1968] 2010, 67). In what I take to be an allusion to Thurman, King wrote:

> Like an unchecked cancer, hate corrodes the personality and eats away its vital unity. Many of our inner conflicts are rooted in hate. This why the psychiatrists say, "Love or Perish." I have seen that expressed in the countenances of too many Mississippi and Alabama sheriffs to advise the Negro to sink to this miserable level. Hate is too great a burden to bear. . . . For the salvation of our nation and the salvation of mankind, we must follow another way. This does not mean that we abandon our militant efforts. With every ounce of our energy we must continue to rid our nation of the incubus of racial injustice. But we need not in the process relinquish our privilege and obligation to love. ([1968] 2010, 67; also see Thurman 2012, 158)

King goes on to quote from Frantz Fanon, who wrote in his *Wretched of the Earth* that "humanity is waiting for something other from us than such an imitation [of Europe]," saying that "we must turn over a new leaf, we must work out new concepts, and try to set afoot a new man" ([1968] 2010, 67–68; Fanon 2004, 255). King's critique of Fanon, as filtered through the Black Power movement—that is, the "belief that violence is the only thing that will bring about liberation" and "that violence is a psychologically healthy and tactically sound method for the oppressed" ([1968] 2010, 56)—consists in pointing out the contradiction involved in "seeking 'to work out new concepts' and 'set afoot a new man' with a willingness to imitate old concepts of violence" ([1968] 2010, 69). This was a consistent message in King's teachings; this was also a consistent message in Thurman. And it seems clear that King had Thurman in mind, whom he identifies not by name but by the title of one of Thurman's signature sermons ("Love or Perish," 1953) in both of these texts by King.

Although Thurman concedes that hatred can play a relatively positive role in consolidating or galvanizing the disparate or disintegrated parts of personal identity, it remains essentially and ultimately destructive. The essential message of Jesus for the disinherited is that, claimed Thurman, "you must abandon your fear of each other and fear only God. You must not indulge in any deception and dishonesty, even to save your lives. . . . Hatred is destructive to hated and hater alike. Love your enemy that you may be children of your father who is in heaven." "While it lasts," Thurman warned, "burning in white heat, its effect seems positive and dynamic; but at last it turns to ash, for it guarantees a final isolation from one's fellows" ([1949] 1996, 86). Thurman understood how, as he put on several occasions, "resentment simmers and simmers and simmers until at last it settles into something that is heat—and it is a kind of heat that temporarily gives a reinforcement and a validation to the personality" (1968). Hatred "blinds the individual to all values of worth, even as they apply to himself and his fellows," and "bears a deadly and bitter fruit" (ibid.). Like a poisonous contagion, observes Thurman, "hatred cannot be controlled once it is set in motion" ([1949] 1996, 87). Love, on the other hand, which is something well beyond charity in the conventional sense, says Thurman, is both positive and creative (that is, capable of generating the kinetic energy that can "reinforce and validate" the personality). Not altogether unlike normal fear, anger and hatred can protect us, thinks Thurman. "Normal fears protect us," wrote King, but "abnormal fear constantly poisons and distorts our inner lives. Our problem is not to be rid of fear but rather to harness and master it" (1991, 511). In ways analogous to fear, anger and hatred—wrote Thurman in 1949—warp or otherwise distort the personality. In his eulogy to King, Thurman encouraged his audience to look honestly at their anger and hatred, to understand their nature, but more than that, "to harness the energy of our bitterness and make it available to the unfinished work which Martin has left behind" (1979, 224). In *Strength to Love,* King encouraged us to "discover that there is another light that shines even in the darkness, and the 'spear of frustration' is transformed 'into a shaft of light'" (2010, 85).

"During the lifetime of the Buddha," states Thich Nhat Hanh,

> those of the Brahmanic faith prayed that after death they would go to Heaven to dwell eternally with Brahma, the universal God. One day a Brahman asked the Buddha, "What can I do to be sure that I will be with Brahma after I die?" The Buddha replied, "As Brahma is the source of Love, to dwell with him you must practice Brahmaviharas: love, compassion, joy, and equanimity." Vihara means abode or dwelling place, so a brahmavihara is the dwelling place of Brahma (2007, 1).

Gandhi says something similar: Love, said the Mahatma, or ahimsa, is the soul force that animates one's political activism construed as a way of clinging to the truth, or satyagraha. The distinction in Gandhi's theory of nonviolence between ahimsa and satyagraha—between the "philosophy of nonviolence" and the "methods of nonviolence"—is one that many observers conflate or overlook. Thurman and King understood that the philosophy and methods of nonviolence remain no less distinct however intimate the connection in practice and theory. Gandhi and Thurman agreed to translate ahimsa as "love in the Pauline sense, yet something more." Not unlike Thurman, King believed that "nonviolence not only calls upon its adherents to avoid external physical violence, but it calls upon them to avoid internal violence of spirit" (2014, 157–58).

Thurman sought to become a true representative of this philosophy, a vital force at the growing edges of nonviolence. Interestingly, Gandhi's theory of satyagraha was influenced while in South Africa by sundry teachings on *jihad* within Islam; in each case, "clinging to the truth" becomes more important than whether one lives or dies. Thurman also construed the philosophy of nonviolence as a "force superior to all the forces of brutality." He saw ahimsa as a spirit of love capable of keeping the world of violence at bay. He believed ahimsa is at its core a deeply personal spiritual discipline that must serve as a platform for conciliating victims and perpetrators of violence. Thurman's distinctively African American version of ahimsa also aimed to generate a philosophy of transcendent moral purpose and self-respect among the disinherited. Via the idiom of the black church, Thurman provided an illuminating interpretation of forgiveness. On the one hand, Thurman applied the philosophy of ahimsa to racial oppression in America; on the other, he consistently adapted and extended that philosophy in an effort to deliver "the unadulterated message of non-violence to the world" (1979, 132).

Redefining the Notion of Brotherhood: "Love or Perish"

> But far from being an impractical idealist, Jesus has become the practical realist. The words of this text ["Love your enemies, bless them that curse you, do good to those who hate you, and pray for them that despitefully use you, that ye may be the children of your Father which is in heaven" (Matt. 5:44–45)] glitter in our eyes with a new urgency. Far from being the pious injunction of a utopian dreamer, this command is an absolute necessity for our civilization. Yes, it is love that will save the world and our civilization, love even for enemies (King [1963] 2010).

Without ignoring the "theological and metaphysical interpretation of the Christian doctrine of salvation," as he put it back in 1949, which the oppressed have long dismissed as relevant to the "the crucial issues by which their days are turned into despair without consolation" (1996, 29), Thurman insists:

> The basic fact is that Christianity as it was born in the mind of this Jewish teacher and thinker appears as a technique of survival for the oppressed. That it became, through the intervening years, a religion of the powerful and the dominant, used sometimes as an instrument of oppression, must not tempt us into believing that it was thus in the mind and life of Jesus. "In him was life; and the life was the light of men." Wherever his spirit appears,

> the oppressed gather fresh courage; for he announced the good news that fear, hypocrisy, and hatred, the three hounds of hell that track the trail of the disinherited, need have no dominion over them. ([1949] 1996, 29)

Although Thurman was ecumenical to the extreme, he also acknowledged that he was steeped in the religion of Jesus and that he "preached his theology" in the idiom of the black church; and because a person "must be at home somewhere before he can feel at home everywhere" (1965, x), Thurman acknowledged that his own "roots [were] deep in the throbbing reality of the Negro idiom, from which [he drew] a full measure of inspiration and vitality" (1965, 30; also see Pollard 1992, 58). For those familiar with Thurman's writings on the topic of love and nonviolence, King's *Strength to Love* ([1963] 2010) demonstrates an intimate familiarity with Thurman. One of the sermons in that collection, "Loving Your Enemy," which King originally delivered at Dexter Avenue Baptist Church (November 17, 1957), was revised while King was in jail and subsequently delivered at Ebenezer in 1962. King claimed that this subject—"the whole idea of love, the whole philosophy of love"—was part of his "basic philosophical and theological orientation" (1998, 39).

For Thurman, the ultimate antidote to hatred is the creative and redemptive energy generated by the spiritual disciplines of love and reconciliation or, if those terms are irretrievably damaged, what Thich calls loving kindness and compassion but also joy and equanimity. The problem, both practical and theoretical, and what worried Thurman most, was that we have not learned how to creatively harness the power of love in a way that others have harnessed the power of hatred. Drawing on the resources inherent in love as opposed to hatred, Thurman sought a neutralizing if not ultimately redemptive quantum of "conatic energy," as it were, which seems to be contagious, together with an organizing principle of identity by which to fortify or otherwise promote the integrity of the personality and the dignity of persons. Thurman worried that we had become complacent: "There is something about goodness that causes us to believe that it can good itself through the world" (1953, audio). But, like King, Thurman knew that time is not neutral.

Thurman acknowledges the obvious: "The term 'brother' is a very exclusive term." The unique ethical contribution of the Master, wrote Thurman, was to appropriate or otherwise transform the exclusivity of the term "brother" into a universal term of inclusivity. And when Jesus put this principle into practice, when he practiced what he preached, to treat the other, or non-brother, as a brother, to collapse the distinction and transcend or transgress the barrier between us and them, Thurman emphasized, "it cost him his life" (1953, audio). Jesus could have restricted or retained the notion of brother to the tight inner circle of the Jewish faith, claims Thurman, "but He kept insisting, always insisting, that you have to redefine the term brother—and if it costs you your life, well, then it costs your life." The early church saw this, claims Thurman, but the modern church had forgotten it altogether. "It is through our experience of the father that I understand my relationship to my brother. I enter into the brotherhood through the God who is the father of all" (1953, audio). "If I define brother on the basis of any other category," claims Thurman, "then I can't love." Moreover, Thurman adds, after a sustained silence: "Sometimes I wish this wasn't true. It just worries a man to death" (1953, audio). As Thurman understands the problem, the solution has less to do with a limitation of intelligence than with a deficit of desire and imagination. "Every man is potentially every other man's neighbor" (1996, 89; see also 2018, 124). After a long yet cadenced silence, Thurman prays: "Help us, oh, God, to want to want to love. Create in me the desire to desire to love" (1953, audio). For King: "All humanity is involved in a single process and all men are brothers" (1991, 20). For Thurman, in an article published in 1957, "The Christian Minister and the Desegregation Decision," for each and all of us who wish to "live under the rule of Christ," for us, "all forms of anti-brotherliness would be sin" (2017, 170).

But how might we love our neighbor, really, even our enemies? There's no such thing as "humanity in general." We don't love "in general," claims Thurman, we love in particular. As Thurman puts it: "To love means dealing with persons in the concrete rather than the abstract." This poses a genuine challenge to our limited because underexercised imaginations. In order to find common ground, to meet you at your center, claimed Thurman, "I must be able, somehow, to strip you of your classification. Oh how the Master must have worked at this" (1953, audio sermon). To illustrate his point, Thurman rehearses what happened when Jesus interacted with the prostitute and the tax collector, who betrayed the idiom of his people, as well as with a Roman centurion, all of whom constitute variations on the enemy among us: How could Jesus have gone home with a man like that? What must have happened inside the Master to enable him to go home with a Roman? What sort of panic must have run through his disciples when he spoke with the centurion or the prostitute? Is he selling us out? When asked who thy neighbor is, Jesus rehearsed "with sheer artistry and great power," in the parable of the Good Samaritan, "what happens when a man responds directly to human need across the barriers of class, race, and condition" (1996, 89). In *To Make the Wounded Whole*, Lewis Baldwin states: "Love takes off masks that we fear we cannot live without and know we cannot live within. I use the word 'love' here not merely in the personal sense but as a state of being, or a state of grace—not in the infantile

American sense of being made happy but in the tough and universal sense of quest and daring and growth" ([1962] 1992, 95).

As a working definition, Thurman suggests that "love is the experience of dealing with a person at a point in him or her that is beyond all his faults and all his virtues. Love means to deal totally with a person. And you can't do this without a disciplined and sensitized imagination" (1984, 191). Thurman says that I must find some way of getting past the wall or block so that I might see myself through your eyes, at which point all other barriers melts. "To love means to love a person from the other side." And Thurman also admits: "I can't do this of myself, regardless of my best intentions; and if I think that I can, I deceive myself" (1953 sermon). King, in his "Loving Your Enemies," which merits comparison with Thurman's 1954 sermon "Love Your Enemies," defines love as a "creative, understanding good will for all [persons]" ([1963] 2010, 20; 2014, 158). This sort of love, claims King, "refuses to defeat any individual. When you rise to the level of love, of its great beauty and power, you seek only to defeat evil systems. Individuals who happen to be caught up in that system, you love, but you seek to defeat the system" (1993, 42). As Thurman expresses it in *Disciplines of the Spirit:*

> Behold the miracle! Love has no awareness of merit or demerit; it has no scale by which its portion may be weighed or measured. It does not seek to balance giving and receiving. Love loves; this is its nature. This does not mean that it is blind, naïve, or pretentious, but rather that love holds its object securely in its grasp, calling all that it sees by its true name but surrounding all with a wisdom born both of its passion and its understanding. Here is no traffic in sentimentality, no catering either to weakness or to strength. Instead, there is robust vitality that quickens the roots of personality, creating an unfolding of the self that redefines, reshapes, and makes all things new. Such an experience is so fundamental that an individual knows that what is happening to him can outlast all things without itself being lost" (1963, 123).

Thurman and King teach us how it's done as well as why it's done. For King, the way it begins is by looking inward, deeply and honestly, by discovering the evil principle within ourselves, by discovering the good in the enemy—that is, by finding the center of goodness within them and placing your attention there, and by refusing to defeat our enemy whenever the occasion arises. Thurman describes it as a process involving self-projection, half centripetal and half centrifugal, and some type of "soundings." Nonviolence is more than hatred sublimated or violence postponed.Thurman understood the sort of pessimism expressed by José Ortega y Gasset, who claimed in *The Revolt of the Masses* that

> violence is always present, in fact or threat, in all human relations. The thing that distinguishes the barbarian from the civilized man is the priority given to the use of it. The civilized man postpones violence until all other methods are exhausted; while the barbarian resorts to it as soon as his will is thwarted. It is well to remember that the violent act is the desperate act. It is the imperious demand of a person to force another to honor his desire and need to be cared for, to be understood. ([1963] 2003, 112)

In *Disciplines of the Spirit,* Thurman states: "The spirit of retaliation must be relaxed and overcome. Here again the reconciliation must go on in a man's [or a woman's] spirit before he [or she] can be at one with the technique of nonviolence he [or she] employs as an instrument for social change" (1963, 117).

The logic of nonviolence is reconciliation. Thurman captures the confusion nicely when he says, in *Jesus and the Disinherited,* that "love of enemy means that a fundamental attack must first be made on the enemy status" (1996, 97). How can this be done? Does it mean merely ignoring the fact that he belongs to the enemy class? Hardly. However, insists Thurman: "A person's fact includes more than his plight, predicament, or need at a particular moment in time. It is something total which must include awareness of the person's potential. This, too, is part of the person's fact. This is why love always sees more than is in evidence at any moment of viewing" (1984, 192). For lack of a better term, claims Thurman, "an 'unscrambling' process is required" ([1949] 1996, 97). Thurman claimed that we can always find—or that we should never quit seeking—our own center somewhere toward the center of the other, where our two centers can meet (Harding 2009, 99). An intrinsic interest in another person, which is part of what Thurman means by love, is impossible "apart from a sense of fact where other persons are concerned—this sense of fact means that the other person is dealt with as he is in the light of the details of his life" (1984, 192). Thurman advises us quite simply to "meet them where they are, mean, distorted, sometimes vicious, full of hate, and to deal with them there, so as to free them and yourself as well as others affected by hate" (1953, "Love or Perish"). We may fail again and again. We might be mistaken. Our only responsibility is to love, to earnestly work at it, and to never give up; whether reciprocated or not, whether productive or not, that is not our task. Thurman expresses his point this way: "And if you work at it—*really,* work at it, despite all the things that we know about the psychology of relations—if you really work at it, you can depend upon this: That there will open up to you, more and more, the strength to keep on working at it. Not to achieve it—that is beside the point—but that is the *assignment of man,* and the degree to which he stays in school and works at it, to that degree is it a reasonable thing to dream about a time when this world will be a decent place for friendly men underneath a friendly sky" (2018, 56). Elsewhere, Thurman suggests that "the unfortunate servant" in the parable of the talents was cast out not because he failed to turn a profit, but rather "because he did not work at it" (1963, 61).[3] The discipline that love provides, claims Thurman, in *Disciplines of the Spirit,* is that "it is something that I must quite deliberately want to do" (1963, 124) and also because "an increased understanding of the other person is arrived at by a discipline use of imagination" (125).

Conclusion

Analogous to the "audacious leap of the mind of the scientist when it soars far out beyond what is known to fix a beachhead on distant [and] unexplored shores," suggests Thurman,

> the imagination shows its greatest powers as the angelos of God in the miracle it creates when one man, standing on his own ground, is able while there to put himself in another man's place. To send his imagination forth to establish a point of focus in another man's spirit, and from that vantage point so to blend with the other's landscape that what he sees and feels is authentic—this is the great adventure in human relations." (1963, 125; 1984, 187)

We discover ourselves in the other: in this sense, personhood is an achievement. Perhaps not altogether unlike Buber, Thurman also believed that God was to be encountered as persons are to be encountered, that is, "upon the narrow ridge, where I and Thou meet," or "in the realm of the between" (Buber 1958, 25; see also Thurman 1998, 298). These genuine encounters, which are "neither individualistic nor collectivistic, neither inner nor outer, nor the sum of the two" will "help to bring about the genuine person again and to establish genuine community" (Buber 1958, 34). "Community cannot for long feed on itself," says Thurman, "it can only flourish with the coming of others from beyond, their unknown and undiscovered brothers" (1971, 104). The tender edges of the beloved community grow, creatively, by means of genuine encounters with and a sympathetic understanding of our unknown brothers and sisters. Love is by no means a sentimental thing: at its core, it is a demanding "discipline of the spirit" (Thurman 1963, 121; King [1963] 2010, 45).

This discipline or practice of love and reconciliation is not for the faint of heart. Throughout his life, Thurman believed that "the experiences of unity in human relations are more compelling than the concepts, the fears, and the prejudices, which divide" (1959, 24). What is the process, what is the logic of it, what is its ground and dynamic, asks Thurman incessantly, by which both individuality and community emerge? Again Thurman: "If one is moved from within one's own spirit to do the deed of ministering to the need of another, and if the need of another is the point at which the spirit is most highly sensitized to communication, then it follows that the good deed is a meeting place of one life with another" (1973, 38). One discovers oneself in the process of sacrificing oneself to the needs of others: this disclosure constitutes "a genuine alternative," thought Thurman, perhaps the only viable alternative, to alienation and violence if not mutual annihilation. Thurman claims that "the experience of love is either a necessity or a luxury. If it be a luxury, it is expendable; if it be a necessity, then to deny it is to perish. So simple is the reality, and so terrifying. Ultimately there is only one place of refuge on this planet for any man or woman—that is in another person's heart. To love is to make of one's heart a swinging door" ([1963] 2003, 127; 1984, 188).

3

Pedagogical Personalism at Morehouse College

Dark copies of dying whiteness are no longer needed. New Black models claim the day.

Vincent Harding, "Toward the Black University" (1970).

Howard Thurman was the beneficiary of a visionary philosophy of education at Morehouse College. The educational process at Morehouse, which I construe here as a form of pedagogical personalism, is personified or exemplified in three luminaries of Morehouse College: Benjamin Elijah Mays, Howard Washington Thurman, and Martin Luther King Jr. Colleges like Morehouse, states Mark Giles, "helped to shape the spiritual blueprint of the civil rights movement" (2006, 107). Historically black colleges and universities (HBCUs) served, claimed Mays, as "ongoing experiments in democratic education" (1962, 32). The pedagogical personalism practiced at Morehouse College constitutes a significant contribution to the history of higher education in America.

Morehouse College

The educational process at Morehouse College, which is a private historically black liberal arts college for men, founded in 1867, should be interpreted as an ambivalent response to segregation and discrimination in Jim Crow America. Like all of the black institutions in the South, Morehouse was subject to racist constraints. Morehouse was created and existed in large part due to just such constraints. But not all HBCUs can be conceived to cope in any one identical way. More attention should be paid to the historical significance and contemporary relevance of Morehouse College as well as other HBCUs "to America's educational and religious life"

(Giles 2006, 106; also see Pollard 1992). Morehouse was an incubator, but it was also a crucible. Giles puts it this way:

> HBCUs offered a different training ground for resistance to the racial hate and segregation that was commonplace across the country. The year Thurman enrolled into Morehouse is known as the "Red Summer" of 1919 because of the approximately two dozen race riots. The earning of a college degree in 1923 placed Thurman in a small but growing group of Blacks earning college degrees in America and stood in critical contrast to what many other Southern Blacks experienced that year. For example, 1923 was also the year of the Rosewood, Florida massacre. The opportunity for Blacks to attend school and college and contribute to their communities during this time period should be understood within the context of Jim Crow America. (2006, 106)

For Benjamin Mays, states Edward A. Jones, in *Candle in the Dark,* the objective inherent in desegregation and integration was "to unshackle the minds of Negro youth, loose the chain from the Negro's soul, and free his heart from fear and intimidation so that he will be able to develop whatever gifts God has given him and share the fruits of his mind and soul with humanity around the globe in the arts and sciences, in the professions and sports, in business and industry, in medicine and law, in music and dance, and in painting and sculpture" (1967, 306). By the time that Thurman arrived at Morehouse College, which had already "established its reputation as a builder of men under the institutional leadership of President John Hope," notes Pollard (1992, 30),

> the faculty was undergoing change, wrestling with an admixture of old and new philosophies concerning the education of African Americans. Newcomers such as E. Franklin Frazier and Benjamin Mays were young graduates of eastern and northern colleges, whose penetrating and disciplined approaches to academic investigation often brought them in conflict with the prevailing 'exceptionist' pedagogical tradition so insightfully delineated by Cornel West [see below]. The older generation of African Americans [was] sometimes seen as placing the development of moral character above the development of the intellect. At other times, they reportedly repressed progressive or liberal educational values in order to ensure continued white fiscal support, tenuous and meager that it was. The young professor of sociology, E. Franklin Frazier, dourly summed up the situation thus [in his "A Note on Negro Education" (in *Opportunity,* 1924, 76; also see Frazier's *The Negro in the United States,* 1957b)]: "Negro

> education in the past, to characterize it briefly, has been too much inspiration and too little information."

Almost twenty-five years ago, Cornel West dealt with the HBCU in broad and sweeping terms. In this, nonetheless, he opens a helpful window onto the discussion, and subsequent approaches to this question must start from his initiative. West describes four "distinct traditions within the African American response to racism in America" (1982, 69). His revisionary topology views African Americans as "active subjects" rather than as "passive objects of history." He deftly identifies a "black counter discourse to modern European racist discourse" (69), which becomes a story of a "gallantly persistent struggle" for dignity and self-determination. West is not content merely to recount the conventional story of exclusion and "severe discrimination reinforced by naked violence within a nascent industrial capitalist order" (1982, 69). The picture he paints is more complex. In *Prophesy Deliverance! An Afro-American Revolutionary Christianity* (1982), West describes or otherwise stipulates four distinct varieties of African American response to racism. These traditions he identifies as the assimilationist, marginalist, exceptionalist, and humanist.[1] These four categories or ideal types are not altogether satisfactory nor perfectly pellucid: one might well object to them on the grounds that they are both falsely bounded and exceptionally porous, or one could quibble with West's criteria for inclusion and exclusion or with the integrity of this supposed tradition or that one or even with the proper placement of figures under one head or another. Nonetheless, West's working "theoretical reconstruction" of "the black counter discourse" (1982, 69) has its uses and is recalled here as a possibly instructive grid against which to document and survey resistance to oppression within HBCUs. Not unlike other HBCUs, states Gary Dorrien, "Morehouse walked a tightrope, refusing to teach or exemplify submission but also refraining from challenging the system" (2018a, 106).

Whether he was teaching at Morehouse College or at Howard University, Frazier consistently complained that

> instead of filling the Negro's mind with knowledge and training him in the fundamental habits of civilization, his teachers have quite often led him from one emotional debauch to another. Surfeited with emotional appeals never resulting in action, the product of Negro education has become a spectator of civilization incapable of participation. He has been a spectator mainly because he has maintained the attitude of one enjoying rather than one helping to create. . . . In this case the type of education given the Negro has produced a sentimental rather than rational attitude towards life." (1924, 76)

Frazier argued that Negro education was already confronted, back in the 1920s, with a severe crisis. "The older ideals were inadequate," wrote Frazier, and while "missionary education might have prepared the Negro to live in heaven, it did not fit him for the cultural context within which he finds himself" (1924, 78). For Frazier, similar in certain ways to pedagogical progressivists from Charles Beard to Carter G. Woodson, a successful education for African Americans would be one that adequately prepared them for the cultural context within which they found themselves, that is, an education that would empower African Americans to participate more effectively in democratic processes and cosmopolitan citizenry; Frazier also suggests the pedagogical objective of training African Americans "in the fundamental habits of civilization." The progressivist educational ideals that Frazier proposes "make the Negro the center of their aims," which was rarely the case under the earlier regime of white missionaries and philanthropists, "educate him for his own sake as a constituent member of American civilization," and "develop the Negro into full manhood and afford ample development for a personality that has been abridged" (1924, 77). In all of this, Frazier's progressivist critique anticipates many if not most of the shortcomings catalogued in Carter G. Woodson's "The Miseducation of the Negro" 1931 or in his *Mis-Education of the Negro* in 1933.[2] Jeffrey Snyder claims that Woodson's "*Miseducation* demonstrated that while black and white educators might be equally invested in the progressive ideal of social reconstruction, they could advance very different ideas about what exactly needed restructuring" (2015, 276).[3] For educators such as Woodson and Frazier, and perhaps also Mays, the most relevant and immediate concern was less about "a volatile and ruthless capitalist system" than the "vicious regime of Jim Crow segregation" (Woodson 1931, 345); on this front, Thurman and Du Bois may well serve as the exceptions that prove the rule.

The new education, insisted Frazier, "must be built upon the sure foundation of sound scholarship" and "represent an attitude determined by possession of the most advanced knowledge extant." Book learning is not enough, of course, and Frazier believed that the "new educational model" would include "a sound moral education," by which he meant "an education that subjects [the student] to situations where desirable motor responses will be elicited so as to build up habits valuable for the civilization in which he is placed" (1924, 76). Although their relationship was complicated, Thurman admitted that Frazier was one of the most influential of his teachers at Morehouse. Back in 1924 Frazier was already worried that the next generation was "either revolting against the old ideals or adopting a narrow and selfish individualism; hence the large number of students who are preparing themselves for the professions as a means to wealth and enjoyment, and not as a means for deeper and more responsible participation in our civilization"

(1924, 76; also see Alridge 2007).[4] And while Mays and Thurman were themselves critical of Frazier's assimilationalist critique of the Afro-American exceptionalist tradition, they certainly shared Frazier's concern that African American men at Morehouse were "adopting a narrow and selfish individualism" that prioritized personal wealth or bourgeois prestige over community service and social activism.[5] Indeed, both Thurman and Mays were powerfully influenced by Frazier as well as John Hope (see Davis 1998, 85–89).[6] I call this strand of the educational philosophy at Morehouse "pedagogical personalism."

Pedagogical Personalism

Pedagogical personalism is not only one strand among others within the Morehouse philosophy: rather, it constitutes the vital core of what Carter calls "a responsible ethical pedagogy of poetic rebellion" (1998, 10). Philosophical personalism is a fairly elaborate and occasionally slightly esoteric theory of personal identity, one traditionally associated with a coterie of American philosophers and theologians from Edgar S. Brightman to L. Harold DeWolf and Peter A. Bertocci or Walter G. Muelder, all of whom taught at Boston University, where King did his graduate studies and where Thurman was dean of Marsh Chapel. According to Bertocci, King "demonstrated the significance of understanding persons with capacities for striving toward authentic identity in an unprecedented philosophical personalist activism through the Civil and Human Rights Nonviolent Movement" (1970, 95). Personalists are variously committed to a philosophical or theological conception of the person "as a sacred personality." King expresses it succinctly when he says that "souls are of infinite metaphysical value" (2010, 191). Warren E. Steinkraus suggests that "this means that there is no higher principle than the person. All other values are subordinate. Abstract laws, the state, property, and other institutions are all to be judged in the light of their effect on persons. This is, of course, the moral base of democracy" (1973, 103).

Recent scholars are keen to locate the roots of certain personalistic principles, such as "God is personal, and persons are sacred," in Africana religiocultural traditions (Baldwin 2011, 3; Burrow and Kirby 1999, 286); indeed, Rufus Burrow maintains that "strands of personalism can be traced to African thought" (2006, xiii). Although there is a good deal disagreement among personalists about how best to describe and interpret these "effects on persons," such that philosophical personalists are often subcategorized as theistic personalists or communitarian personalists or even countercultural personalists, the pedagogical personalism practiced at Morehouse traditionally stressed the sacred or otherwise inviolable dignity of persons, certainly, but it also promoted an educational process that activated the potential of individuals within and across diverse communities. This is not to say that all members of the faculty agreed about the best pedagogical strategies for achieving this personalist ideal, but they did seem to be collectively committed to a shared mission. But beyond this admitted broad personalist or humanist ideal, the faculty and administrators at Morehouse also emphasized, typically, but to varying degrees, the social benefit of awakening the power of the person's individual potential; the centrality of the oppressed and poor persons, using their conditions as an index of health and justice; the harmony of means and ends in pursuing social justice; and the importance of negotiating through institutions and acting politically for social and structural change. And while some faculty did not participate in the religious life of the college, most of the faculty, men and women alike, seem to have fostered the view of a personal God who is the liberator of the oppressed and to have promoted the harmony of means and ends in the pursuit of the beloved community (Carter 2008).

Back in 1924 E. Franklin Frazier argued that a liberal arts education in general and an HBCU education in particular must, among other things, "afford ample development for a personality that has been abridged" (1924, 76). The new education, insisted Frazier, one that would be suitable to the new Negro (Giles 2006, 109), "must be built upon the sure foundation of sound scholarship" and "represent an attitude determined by possession of the most advanced knowledge extant" (1924, 77). (It should be noted that participation in civilization was for Frazier essential to the vital growth of the personality.) So while it is true that Frazier objected to certain forms of exceptionalism at Morehouse—namely, those forms of superficial and thus dishonest edification—he might well be classified in other ways as a weak exceptionalist, in deference to West's topology, in that he considered it part of his vocation to stimulate—by means of "the most advanced knowledge extant and sound scholarship"—the compensatory development or growth of his students' personality; as a realist, he knew that his students' personalities had been "abridged" or otherwise circumscribed. Similar to Frazier as well as Mays and King, Woodson argued that it was mere common sense rather than a capitulation to racist theories of black inferiority to insist that "people who have been oppressed and exploited . . . require special attention" (1931, 345; also see Snyder 2015, 282–85). Whether Frazier should be classified as a weak or strong assimilationalist or whether he contributed more to the marginalist or humanist traditions is perhaps less important than recognizing the pedagogical personalism that animated his critique of exceptionalism and the rationale implicit in his assimilationist-sounding corrective and rhetorically charged counterpolemic. Although Frazier and Mays could in some ways both be viewed as assimilationists or meliorists, if not accommodationists, to use West's topology, or as divergent positions along the spectrum of black educational progressivism in the 1920s and 1930s, which is the period during which Frazier and Mays taught at Morehouse, what from one perspective may appear as appropriation can from another appear to be subversive (Gaither 2003).

Mays's Educational Philosophy: "House-Spun" Personalism

In *Born to Rebel,* Mays recalls that back in 1921, when he taught mathematics and coached the legendary debate team, Thurman among them, he discovered at Morehouse "a special, intangible something . . . which sent men out into life with a sense of mission, believing that they could accomplish whatever they set out to do. This priceless quality was still alive when I returned [as president] in 1940," namely, "instilling in Morehouse students the idea that despite crippling circumstances the sky was the limit" (1987, 172). The Morehouse philosophy, together with its accompanying pedagogical mission, was purpose-driven but politically complicated to the extreme: certain strands of the philosophy of education at Morehouse were implicit yet subversive, radical even; others were explicit but conservative. "For twenty-seven out of a 100 years," Carter says of what Samuel DuBois Cook has called "the golden age" (Cook 2009, 55), that is, between 1940 and 1967, "Mays and Morehouse had tried to develop a free man in a racially circumscribed nation" (Carter 1998, 25). In 1967, as part of his Centennial Convocation statement, "*Et Facta Est Lux,*" Mays claimed:

> The Morehouse philosophy was and is that a man does not have to accept the view that because he is a Negro certain things were not meant for him. He can be free in a highly segregated society. Long before demonstrations and Supreme Court decisions abolished segregation, the Morehouse students were taught to accept no segregated situation except that which was absolutely necessary; and that though their bodies were segregated, their minds could be free. . . . The philosophy drilled into them is that the Morehouse man can succeed in the world despite crippling circumstances under which he had to live. (*The Alumnus*, Morehouse College Bulletin 36 (Spring 1967): 60; also in Carter 1998, 26)

But as early as 1928, it should be noted, Mays and his YMCA colleagues were "impressed with the truth of Dr. Mordecai W. Johnson's statement: 'Negroes must do a contradictory thing; they must work with all their might against segregation, and at the same time strengthen their so-called segregated institutions as if they expected them to last forever. They must insist that the doors of Harvard and Yale be kept open to Negroes and at the same time build up Howard and

Lincoln as if there were no Harvard or Yale'" (Mays, 1928; quoted in Jelks 2012, 75). This "contradictory thing" is captured nicely by Woodson, who claimed, several years later, in the *Mis-Education of the Negro,* that "our minds must become sufficiently developed to use segregation to kill segregation" ([1933] 2000, 54). So while E. Franklin Frazier may well serve as the "unchallenged theoretician of the weak assimilationist tradition," as West turns it (1982, 78), it should be noted that African American educators from Frazier and Mays to Thurman and King were working simultaneously, if not contradictorily, on multiple fronts. This conundrum is complicated in all directions. In an essay titled "The Dilemma of the Negro Author," James Weldon Johnson described the difficulty posed by African Americans, who must write for "a double audience; it is a divided audience made up of two elements with differing and often quite opposite and antagonistic points of view" (1928, 12). Adolf Reed claims that "although Johnson focused primarily on creative writing, his observation that the white audience's biases dispose black authors toward a 'defensive and exculpatory literature' applies more generally" (1995, 81).

"The educational philosophy of Benjamin Mays has a religious base that began early in his youth," says Barbara Lewinson, and "it is from a particular conception of what it is to be a Christian that his thinking evolves" (1998, 215). King's writings and speeches seem to suggest that King was theologically and philosophically more similar to Mays than he was to either Frazier or Thurman. Indeed, Orville Vernon Burton goes so far as to suggest—in his foreword to Mays's *Born to Rebel*—"there could not have been a Martin Luther King Jr. if there had been no Benjamin Elijah Mays" (Mays 1987, xli). Although Mays's philosophy of education evolved from 1921, when he initially taught at Morehouse, until 1967, when he retired as the sixth president of Morehouse, he often reiterated a fairly simple yet visionary philosophy, expressed quite concisely and addressed to a religious audience: "Education was designed to glorify God and serve humanity" (1964:5). Perhaps unlike Frazier, Mays thought—in the words of Lucius Tobin, professor and Mays's pastor at Providence Baptist Church—that fidelity to religion in general and Christianity in particular "did not require surrender of critical intelligence" (1967, 36).[7] The threefold purpose of education for Mays, says Lewinson, was "to train the mind to think clearly, logically and constructively; to train the heart to understand and sympathize with the aspirations, the sufferings and injustices of mankind; and to strengthen the will to act in the interest of the common good" (1998, 218).

By the time he took the helm at Morehouse, in May of 1940, Mays was already "directing [his] students to be agents of social change" (Jelks 2012, 122). Characterized by an Atlanta reporter in 1939 as a "notorious modernist," which is to say that that he was trained in biblical criticism and social gospel theology, Mays was sometimes quite critical of the black church, which he described in *The Negro's God* ([1938] 1968, 19) as "an otherworldly religion" that was animated by "a merely compensatory idea of God."[8] Thurman disagreed with Mays on this point: "The view that the traditional attitude of the religion of black people was, or is, otherworldly is superficial and misguided" (1979, 17). Although Mays emphasized character development, community-mindedness, citizen-mindedness, and historical-mindedness, he also thought that "Negro liberal arts colleges should instill in [their students] a faith equivalent to that of their enslaved ancestors," by which he meant that "religion at its best is a faith in God which gives one poise and stability and the strength and courage to carry on in the midst of chaos and insecurity" (1942, 410–11). By the time he was offered the position as president of Morehouse, and while still serving as the dean of the School of Religion at Howard University, Mays insisted that "a college must be judged not only by excellent teachers, but by the spirit and philosophy which permeates it from top to bottom" (Mays, quoted in Jelks 2012, 138). Although Mordecai Johnson and Benjamin Mays recruited excellent teachers during their years at Morehouse, perhaps it was Mays who best articulated or otherwise personified the "spirit and philosophy" that permeated Morehouse College between 1921 and 1967 "from top to bottom."

In ways analogous to Thurman and King, Mays sometimes discussed "racial uplift," or occasionally "Black internationalism"; but Mays more often than not spoke quite simply of helping the man further down, regardless of race or nationality. As pastors and ministers or chaplains, Mays and King as well as Thurman were committed to feeding, literally and figuratively, the hungry and protecting those among us with the least. For Mays, claims Jelks, "Black Americans had to be the guardians of democracy and faithful to their Christianity if justice were to be equitably served in America" (2012, 247). In this sense, Mays is analogous to Richard Wright, classified by West as a weak exceptionalist, who claimed that "African Methodism will carry the Christian message of brotherhood to the white man" (West 1982, 74; also see Savage 2007, 801). Similarly, Du Bois advocated for HBCUs that would "emancipate not simply the Black folk of the United States, but those White folk who in their effort to suppress Negroes have killed their own culture—men who in their desperate effort to replace equality with caste and to build inordinate wealth on a foundation of abject poverty have succeeded in killing democracy" (1933, 129).[9]

Analogous to Frazier, Mays objected to the sort of exceptionalism that traffics in platitudes and other forms of banal instruction. "Pride and dignity must be developed and upheld," states Lewinson, but "it is only through individual striving for the best, Mays felt, that this would happen" (1998, 225). The pedagogical mission at Morehouse College, from the beginning, aimed at shaping the whole person and included the task of spiritually uplifting or otherwise edifying their students by turning their minds toward noble ends (Jelks 2012, 146–47; Lewinson 1998, 223). So while Mays was also quite dismissive of the sort of shallow or hollow edification described so derisively by Frazier, it is true that Mays believed that the development of character was as important as intellectual development. "The circumference of life cannot be rightly drawn," counseled Mays, "until the center is set" (1942, 26). In most ways, Benjamin Elijah Mays represents—perhaps even as an exemplar of the type—what West describes as an "Afro-American humanist." And while this tradition "accents the universal human content of Afro-American cultural forms, it makes no ontological or sociological claims about Afro-American superiority or inferiority. Rather, it focuses on the ways in which creative Afro-American cultural modes of expression embody themes and motifs analogous to the vigorous cultural forms of other racial, ethnic, or national groups" (West 1982, 71). West argues: "These norms of individuality and democratic control of the political and productive processes are acceptable [to Afro-American philosophers and educators] because they promote personal development, cultural growth, and human freedom. They foster the fulfillment of the potentialities and capacities of all individuals, encourage innovation and originality in Afro-American culture, and expand people's control over those institutions which deeply affect their lives." Following Lerone Bennett, in "The Last of the Great Schoolmasters," Mays "conceived education broadly as an instrument of social and personal renewal, and he anticipated Paulo Freire's conception of education as the 'practice of freedom'" (1998, 335).

These humanist norms, which "neither romanticize nor reject Afro-American culture" (1982, 91), are integral also to pedagogical personalism from Frazier and Mays as well as from Thurman and King. The pedagogical personalism espoused at Morehouse includes but also extends beyond these humanist norms. Mays was convinced in 1966 that the "great need within higher education," one that should be compelling not merely to leaders in education or religion at HBCUs but at all institutions of higher learning, regardless of racial and ethnic or national identity, consisted in providing "an education with a social conscience, a social concern; science has made the world a neighborhood, it is up to us—leaders in education and religion—to make it a brotherhood. There is no guarantee that education alone can do this job. It may be that religion and education cannot do it. But it must be done if mankind is to survive" (Mays, in Morehouse *Alumnus,* May 7,

1966, 685). Maurice Jelks suggests that Mays's "educational philosophy struck a middle ground between that of Booker T. Washington, who advocated industrial training, and W. E. B. Du Bois, who promoted classical or liberal arts education" (2012, 145). Without denying the importance of technical skills, industrial or otherwise, Mays insists that "the Negro student needs other skills—skills in how to remain poised and hopeful and jubilant in an environment that is not always friendly to his ambitions and strivings. He needs the mind of the scientist, the wisdom of a philosopher, and the religious faith of the Negro slave" (Mays, quoted in Jelks 2012, 148). In the same recruitment pamphlet, Mays claims that it was his personal duty as well as the responsibility of his faculty to shape Morehouse men into "democratic citizens." Education consists in more than "producing clever graduates," insisted Mays, in a 1943 pamphlet titled "What We Seek to Achieve at Morehouse," it must also seek to nuture "honest men, men who can be trusted both in public and private life—men who are sensitive to the wrongs, the sufferings, the injustices of society and who are willing to share the responsibility for correcting them" (1943). Mays's educational philosophy was "rooted in his principled democratic beliefs and an ethical theological vision" (Jelks 2012, 145), to be sure, but it should be noted also that his democratic beliefs and theological vision as well as his commitment to nonviolence and opposition to communism (see Berg 2007) were ultimately justified in terms of philosophical or theological personalism.

Although Negro colleges had been segregated, argued Mays, they were not segregating institutions: "Unhindered by the traditional customs of the past," wrote Mays in 1962, "they [that is, HBCUs, especially private historically black colleges] are free to become ongoing experiments in democratic education. . . . They meet the special needs resulting from three centuries of disability and they are demonstrating their ability to serve all society" (1962, 32–33). The democratic ideals for which Americans fought abroad, viz., the four freedoms of speech and worship as well as freedom from fear and want, were still denied to African Americans when they returned home from war (see Thurman 1965, 51). In 1942, Mays suggested that "the Negro liberal arts college should be experiment stations in democratic living. It should be a living protest against the undemocratic practices which the Negro experiences on every hand in his environment. . . . If it is true that scholars develop best in a free atmosphere, the Negro liberal arts colleges should produce scholars of the first magnitude" (Benjamin E. Mays, "Negro Higher Education in the War and Post-War Reconstruction"). Because segregation diminished or denied the basic idea of the worth of each person, because it branded as inferior the person who was segregated, thus penalizing a person for something over which he had no control, reasoned Mays, segregation was both undemocratic and un-Christian. Barbara Lewinson put it this way:

> Mays believed that the formerly all-black schools cannot be justified just because they fill a special need. They must be willing to strive for academic excellence while at the same time remaining aware of the disabilities peculiar to deprived students. They must prepare their graduates to compete successfully in every area of life at the same time that they are developing a larger role. These black colleges are changing and, according to Mays, will very definitely survive but in a different form. The form of these schools will change as will the former primarily white university. (1998, 229)

As a Christian personalist, Mays argued that "the chief sin of segregation is the distortion of human personality; it damages the soul of both the segregator and the segregated" (1948, 225). More recently, but along similar lines, Cone says that "racism is a disease that perverts one's moral sensitivity and distorts the intellect" (1986, xviii). For Mays in particular, but also for Thurman and King, the ideal of democratic politics, religion, and education was the same: freedom and solidarity. Mays's philosophy of education, which could well be classified as a form of pedagogical personalism, constitutes a consistent and conscientious application of his overarching philosophical or theological position, which, similar to King, displays "a fundamental commitment to the essence of personalism" (Carter 2008, 219).

As early as 1928, in "Earmarks of an Educated Man," Mays suggested that an educated man is someone who "thinks for himself by getting at the root of an issue," who maintains an "open mind," who demonstrates the "courage of his convictions," who cultivates an active impatience with "social and economic injustices," who exhibits "an appreciation for all values and all knowledge," and who displays a sensitivity to the needs of the most vulnerable (quoted in Jelks 2012, 145). For Mays, as Jelks puts it, in his splendid biography of Mays, *Schoolmaster of the Movement,* the privilege of education implies "the practice of altruism and self-sacrifice" (2012, 145). Mays elaborates or otherwise embellishes this "visionary philosophy of education," which is "rooted in his principled democratic beliefs and an ethical theological vision" (Jelks 2012, 145), in his delineated "objectives for the School of Religion" at Howard University in 1934; with minor revisions in the form of a pamphlet describing the mission of Morehouse College back in 1940; under the auspices of "Five Abiding Values" in 1957; and, as a swan song, in the Crown Forum Address to Students in 1967. Throughout his years at Morehouse, Mays insisted that an educated person was a radical. Mays did not mean "radical" in the politically charged sense often associated with the radical left or the radical right; rather, and at least primarily, he meant radical in the mathematical and etymological sense of "getting at the root of an issue, and in the case of the black man, radicalism prompts him to acknowledge that 'the Negro is not inferior'" (Jelks 2012, 145).

Thurman's "Religious and Pedagogical Personalism"

Thurman should be esteemed as an exemplary "apostle of sensitiveness," who, as the Reverend Jesse Jackson put it, "sowed the seeds that bred a generation of activists who tore down ancient walls of oppression" (quoted in Makechnie 1988, 82) and—together with Mays and Johnson—"blew away the philosophical underpinnings of racism and segregation" in his "emphasis on the spiritual dimensions of social transformation" (Jackson 1982, 83). But Thurman was also a "transformational educational leader" (Giles 2010, 362). The educational process at Morehouse was intentional in its development of the personality within the climate of mutual concern and what Thurman called sympathetic understanding. As a young seminarian, in an essay titled "College and Color," Thurman wrote:

> By sympathetic understanding I do not mean a patronizing attitude or anything that is cheap and sentimental. Nor do I mean an attitude that is so swollen with condescending pride that its stench is intolerable. But I do mean an attitude which says that a man of another race is essentially myself, and that I feel toward him fundamentally as if he were myself. His [or her] needs and craving and the drives which lie behind his [or her] actions are similar to mine in their essentials. (2009, 37)

Thurman loved philosophy from the beginning, something nurtured and encouraged by Mays at Morehouse. In his autobiography, *Head and Heart,* Thurman says that E. Franklin Frazier and Benjamin Mays, among other younger and older faculty at Morehouse, "placed over our heads a crown that for the rest of our lives we would be trying to grow tall enough to wear. This was a gift far greater than the imparting of information and facts" (1979, 41). With respect to the study of philosophy, Thurman goes on to say that in 1921

> Morehouse offered [and Mays taught] a course in logic and a course in ethics, neither of which was strictly in the field, and no courses whatever in formal philosophy. I do not think this was accidental. In the missionary colleges of the South, few (if any) courses were offered in the formal study of philosophy. I believe that the shapers of our minds, with clear but limited insight into the nature of our struggle for survival and development in American life, particularly in the South, recognize the real possibility

> that to be disciplined in the origins and development of ideas would ultimately bring under critical judgment the society and our predicament in it. This, in turn, would contribute to our unease and restlessness, which would be disastrous, they felt, for us and for our people. (1979, 42–43)

During the summer between his junior and senior year at Morehouse, Thurman took philosophy courses at Columbia University. When Thurman studied with Rufus Jones at Haverford, he attended every course they offered in philosophy. Before he was asked to join the faculty at Boston University, during the time that King was finishing his course work, Thurman corresponded with philosophical personalists from Brightman to DeWolf.[10]

"All in all," suggests Alton Pollard, "Thurman attempted to direct the exceptionalist position into a closer relation with the empiricism and causal imputation of the new social sciences" (1992, 31). Although Thurman supplied his students at Morehouse and Spelman as well as those he encountered at Howard University and Boston University with a steady stream of empirical facts and a wide array of progressive methods of analysis or interpretation of those "facts" (for example, psychoanalysis, feminism, socioeconomic theories, philosophical pragmatism, and historical criticism), he was legendary also for providing his students with spiritual succor and ethical inspiration. As a pedagogical habit, Thurman would begin his lectures or meditation sessions with an interesting display of "cold hard facts," as he called them, but would culminate in a crescendo of philosophical or religious if not mystical insight. Thurman insisted that his best teaching took place outside the classroom. James Farmer Jr., whose father "could have been a star anywhere" but who dropped everything to join the faculty of religion at Howard in 1938, describes—in his *Lay Bare the Heart*—the faculty at the School of Religion as "critical scholars, but very devout" (1985, 135). And not altogether unlike Mays, Thurman's philosophy of education combines pedagogical personalism with spiritual cosmopolitanism; these two strands of the "Morehouse philosophy" are also on display, it should be obvious, in King's socioethical philosophy of peace and justice within the beloved community.[11] While at Morehouse, from "the very beginning," and throughout his life, Mays was a trusted mentor if not a "senior consigliore" (Jelks 2012, 245) to King; while at Boston University, at Marsh Chapel, King would, according to Philip Lenud, "shake his head in amazement at Thurman's deep wisdom" (quoted in Baldwin 1991, 300–301; Dixie and Eisenstadt 2011, 245). Thurman's unique form of pedagogical personalism—perhaps also his brand of ecumenical liberalism and philosophical cosmopolitanism—was indebted to E. Franklin Frazier and Benjamin Mays, to be sure, but was also inspired by W. E. B. Du Bois and Alain Locke as well as Mordecai Johnson and John Dewey.[12]

In ways analogous to King, who defined personalism or personal idealism as "the theory that the clue to the meaning of ultimate reality is found in personality" (King 1958, 8), Thurman was convinced that "the beyond is within" (1956, 34; also see 1971, 80). Perhaps not unlike King, Thurman's theology and social activism was subordinate to his philosophical personalism and religious experience. Thurman's personalism was influenced by the black church, certainly, but also by Rufus Jones, the Quaker and scholar of mysticism, whom Thurman described as a revelation, as well as by William James on religious experience and John Dewey on communitarian individuality. The focus here is on Thurman's own formulation of personalist ideals as a prescription for social transformation. "Personality is something more than mere individuality," wrote Thurman, "it is the fulfillment of the logic of individuality in community" ([1978] 1998, 116).

At the Centennial Banquet of Morehouse College in February 1967, where he shared the rostrum with Mays and Hugh Gloster, Thurman argued that "while the educational process is justified, in part, by its public outcomes, the most significant measure of higher education among African Americans has been its private results" (1998, 233). On this occasion, but consistent with the pedagogical personalism he promoted on countless occasions, Thurman emphasized "the ways Morehouse College, since its humble beginnings during Reconstruction, has instilled in young black men core values of self-validation and self-respect against the onslaught of an often violent, segregated culture" (233). Speaking in the voice of the ancestors, as it were, and as a tribute "to those men [and women] during the past hundred years who are no longer living in the flesh" (233), Thurman declared, drawing on a line from Hermann Hagedorn's 1917 "Lines from an Unknown Soldier": "We died but you who live must do a harder thing than dying is, for you must think and ghosts shall drive you on. Amen" (233). Thurman claimed that "the educational process was only partially justified by its public result" (1998, 234); and while "many competent voices will make a good and often dramatic case for the public results of Morehouse," Thurman argued rather convincing for the admittedly less tangible but nevertheless "tremendous impact of the private results of Morehouse College" (1998, 236). Thurman suggested that

> the educational process that was set in motion a hundred years ago in Augusta, Georgia, as the creative genius of a school for Negro men, is justified by its private result—that is, by its result in the lives of the generations of men who have been touched by its glow. The most important thing in life

> for any man at any time is the development of his own best self, the incentive to actualize his own potentials. The central emphasis of the past was on the intrinsic worth of the individual student, the necessity to experience himself as a human being in a climate in which he had no standing. (234–35)

The "creative genius" of Morehouse College, as Thurman described it, consisted in an educational process that fostered a "primary intimate encounter that insisted that it was their prerogative and that it was mandatory to experience themselves as human beings," that is, not only to recognize their potential but also "to get on the scent of their potential and follow it all the way" (235). And while it may be more difficult to measure or otherwise assess this private result, Thurman asks us to keep in mind "the overwhelming impact down in the quiet places where the ultimate decisions as to self-validation and affirmation remain" (237).[13]

Baldwin thinks that Burrow is correct in suggesting that "King was probably first introduced to the term personalism and personal idealism during his undergraduate years at Morehouse College in Atlanta, Georgia, in the mid- to late 1940s" (2011, 5; also see Burrow 1999, 2006); indirectly, through Mays and Johnson but also because he was reading Thurman at the time, King must have been familiar with Thurman's type of personalism that emphasized, at bottom, that persons are sacred and that the human heart requires a personal God and, as a working hypothesis of personal idealism, that "the beyond is within" (Thurman 1956, 34). It seems quite likely that King was introduced to philosophical personalism by Samuel Williams, who taught philosophy at Morehouse from 1947 to 1970. (In 1962 King taught a course in social philosophy at Morehouse with Williams.) While King was a student at Morehouse, Thurman was leading an interracial and interfaith church in San Francisco, where "the core of [his] preaching always concerned itself with the development of the inner resources needed for the creation of a friendly world of friendly men [and women]" (1979, 160); for Thurman, "it was important that individuals who were in the thick of the struggle for social change would be able to find renewal and fresh courage in the spiritual resources of the church" (1979, 160).

The Gandhian tradition of nonviolent activism was strong at Morehouse College: Thurman, together with his wife, Sue Bailey, was but the first in a long line of African American leaders to visit Gandhi at his ashram in India; Thurman was followed by Mays, Mordecai Johnson, A. Philip Randolph, and, finally, twenty years later, King, who visited "the land of Gandhi" in 1959. Thurman and Mays as well as King were impacted by their respective encounters with Gandhi. By the time King visited the land of Gandhi, the teachings of satyagraha and ahimsa were built into "the civil rights movement's carefully crafted theological platform that tied Christianity to democracy and governance" (Jelks 2012, 244). Not altogether unlike Gandhi, or even Jesus, at least as portrayed in Thurman's *Jesus and the Disinherited,* Mays and Thurman as well as King were pedagogically preoccupied, from the pulpit and lectern, with developing the sacred and resilient personalities of the oppressed as well as the oppressors, which had been abridged or otherwise distorted by the violence inherent in racism, materialism, and militarism.

Conclusion

It is my simple faith that this is the kind of universe that sustains that kind of adventure, and what we see dimly now in the churning confusion and chaos of our tempestuous times will someday be the common experience of all children of men [and women] everywhere

Thurman, *The Creative Encounter: An Interpretation of Religion and the Social Witness* (1954)

"The legacy of what a Morehouse Man was and is might best be understood," believes Mark Giles, "in the transformative power of teaching and mentoring the next generation of Black Men who fully values that legacy and implicitly commits to passing on the spirit of high expectations, achievement, and commitment to the beloved community" (2006, 110). When it comes to justifying HBCUs in the twenty-first century, there will always be—as Thurman said there were back in 1967—those prepared to "make a good and often dramatic case for the public results of [the educational process that Thurman was calling for at] Morehouse," but let us pause also to consider "tremendous impact of the private results of Morehouse College." One of the goals of a liberal arts education, one could argue, and not merely at an HBCU liberal arts institution but consistent with the African American humanist tradition, is the "promotion of an individuality strengthened by an honest encounter with [his or her] past and the expansion of democratic control over the major institutions that regulate lives in America and abroad" (West 1982, 90).[14] Morehouse College, which one should construe as a distinctive strand of educational progressivism in America still serves as an ongoing experiment in democratic education and an incubator if not crucible for self-actualization and social transformation. Within that broader if not parallel tradition of educational humanism or progressivism, the pedagogical personalism as embodied in representative educators at Morehouse College from Frazier and Mays or Thurman and King constitutes a unique contribution to higher education in America. Their respective responses are still relevant, poignant even, not only to the pedagogical objectives inherent in colleges proximately analogous to Morehouse but also in more remotely analogous educational institutions; thus, their responses should be included in the ongoing discussion of the value of liberal arts in general and HBCUs in particular for the collective progress of America as well as the "World House."[15]

4

Reading Thurman as a Philosophical Personalist

I am aware of the national span of racial prejudice and the virus of segregation that undermines the vitality of American life. Nevertheless, a strange necessity has been laid upon me to devote my life to the central concern that transcends the walls that divide and would achieve in literal fact what is experienced as literal truth: human life is one and all [people] are members of another. And this insight is spiritual, and it is the hard core of religious experience.

Thurman, *Luminous Darkness*

Although fascinated by the question of whether Thurman could be correctly classified as an African American personalist, perhaps even as uniquely important in the Boston personalist tradition, the concern here is less with accurately locating Thurman within the topology of American personalism—in Boston or elsewhere—than it is with showing that Thurman's philosophical writings display many of the characteristic features of philosophical personalism broadly construed.[1] As a prophetic civil rights personalist, perhaps not altogether unlike contemporary prophetic pragmatists, Thurman placed special emphasis on the spiritual dimensions of social transformation (Raboteau 2001, 158; Smith 2007, 211).[2] Borrowing a pragmatic formula in Dewey (that is, transforming the noun into an adjective as well as adverb by which one converts the essentialist categories of being into the sphere of the pragmatic event), I want to move beyond the complex if not occasionally tedious task of classifying Thurman's type of personalism to the more rewarding enterprise of exploring various ways that Thurman's thought shares common ground with theistic and philosophical personalism. It seems useful to read Thurman as a philosophical personalist.

Although Muelder does not explicitly label Thurman as a personalist, for example, when he says that "there is a profound affinity between the evangelical social ethic of Thurman and that of his younger personalistic contemporary" (1983, 9), Muelder does think that "from a philosophical perspective the writings of Thurman are seen to be coherent with a personalistic and communitarian ethic" (1983, 13). While relying heavily on Muelder's analysis of Thurman in 1983, I want also to describe the confluence of mutual influences between Muelder and Thurman but also King over the course of almost forty years. As a way of illustrating the general affinity that exists between Muelder and Thurman, I compare their thought along the lines of those adumbrated by Muelder in *The Idea of the Responsible Society* (1955). More specifically, I wish to point out several similarities between their respective systems of thought on the communal character of personal identity. By way of conclusion, I suggest that Thurman is a rich resource for the next generation philosophical personalists or prophetic pragmatists and social critics as well as liberation theologians and conscientious ethicists or identity theorists.

Personalism: King and Thurman

Although King would have been proud to say that he studied with most of the "third-generation personalists" at Boston University (that is, Bertocci, DeWolf, and Muelder) as well as with Brightman, briefly, and Knudson, both "second-generation Personalists," some scholars suggest that King was a "home-spun personalist" by the time he entered Morehouse (Burrow, 1999, 77; Baldwin 2011, 3; Carter 2008, 49); increasingly, scholars are emphasizing the "familial and cultural influences" on King's personalism, theology, and ethics (Burrow 1999, 2006; Baldwin 1991; Carter 2006, 211). Lawrence Carter argues that King appropriated academic or formal personalism in a way that inspired personalists to look beyond "the social and economic implications of Personalism" and to follow Muelder as well as Gandhi in their loyal and "unyielding devotion to non-violence and radical social and economic justice." And yet, claims Baldwin, "it is not excessive to contend that King contributed essentially as much to personalism as personalism gave to him" (2011, 4). (I think that the same could be said also of Thurman's relationship to the Boston personalists.) Burrow claims that "King's most original and creative contribution to the personalist tradition was his persistence in translating it into social action by applying it to the trilogy of social problems—racism, poverty/economic exploitation, and militarism" (2006, 86; also see 1999, 76–78). Back in 1943, in "Personality and Christian Ethics," Muelder put it this way:

> Personality is the most concrete category of existence and value. This means that the richest synoptic grasp of existential wholes and the highest value in the axiological hierarchy are both apprehended in personality. Since

> personality refers to both the quality of ultimate reality and to real finite selfhood, the problems of ethics are circumscribed by the finite person's relation to himself, to other finite persons, and to ultimate personality. What is given is a society of persons human and divine together with the ends of conduct and the problems of their realization. The ideal ends as aspects of ideal personality. (1983, 85)

According to Steinkraus, "King's wedding of Personalism and nonviolence in both theory and practice is virtually original in the development of American Personalism, and it seems a natural union, not a marriage of convenience" (1973, 103). The ethic of nonviolence, or satyagraha, following Gandhi and King as well as Thurman and Mays or Mordecai Johnson, is implicit in the guiding principle of personalism because "souls are of infinite metaphysical value" (2010, 191). King demonstrates this ethical principle throughout his writings but perhaps most dramatically in his "Letter from Birmingham Jail" (1991, 293), where he proclaims that "any law that uplifts human personality is just" and that "any law that degrades human personality is unjust," that is, that injustice inheres in whatever "distorts the soul and damages the personality." Similarly, in 1965, "segregation stands diametrically opposed to the principle of the sacredness of human personality. It debases personality" (1965, 237–38). In his *Where Do We Go from Here,* King claimed "the immorality of segregation is that it treats men as means rather than ends, and thereby reduces them to things rather than persons" ([1968] 2010, 97); this rather doctrinaire Kantian formulation of the golden rule was also something that King as well as Mays and Thurman could preach from the pulpit. The life and thought of King, believes Lewis V. Baldwin, displays an "intense loyalty to the essence of the personalist tradition" (2011, 2). "In studying the Gandhian nonviolent method of nonviolent resistance," suggests Carter, "King discovered in his philosophically based activism a consistency between the principles of personalism and the inherent respect for the person in the method of nonviolence as a strategy and a way of life" (2008, 220).

Thurman's theology and social activism was seemingly subordinate to his personalism and religious experience. Indeed, Thurman put this thesis to the test in his most philosophically ambitious work, *In Search of Common Ground,* which he composed in response to the assassination of King; Thurman's response constitutes a careful if not stoic argument for believing that nonviolent resistance to whatever obstructs justice and community or the flourishing of individuals is consistent with the goals of nature as disclosed in all aspects (for example, biological phenomena, consciousness, religion or myth, and political arrangements). Steeped in Christianity and active in shaping the ideals of the social gospel movement of the time, Thurman is probably rightly or fruitfully categorized as a "theistic personalist": and yet, like many philosophers of his day, Thurman offers a revisionist conception of God and Jesus or, as he puts it, the transformative religion or God of Jesus. Thurman's personalism was influenced by the black church, certainly, but also by Rufus Jones, the Quaker and scholar of mysticism, as well as William James on religious experience and John Dewey's "communitarian theory of self-realization" (Shook, Good, and Dewey, 2010, 24). There are other important influences as well, including Gandhi and Buber or Abraham Heschel and Alain Locke, but for the present purposes, it is best to focus on Thurman's own formulation of personalist ideals in his texts and the application of those ideals as a prescription for positive and nonviolent as well as deliberative but participatory if not also democratic social transformation.

Although Thurman was a precursor to King, and while I believe that Thurman's religious personalism was influential on King's brand of personalism, I wish to start with King's personalism and then trace it back to Thurman's personalism. I trust that there is something valuable to be gained by rediscovering the origins and reassessing the significance of personalism in Thurman and King. Beyond the secondary literature examining the points of contact between the Boston school of personalists, which routinely suggests that King beautifully appropriated the central tenants of Boston personalism but that he also advanced the school in demonstrating the active application of personalism to social transformation, it is sometimes suggested that King's exposure to personalism predates his arrival in Boston (Baldwin, 2011; Burrow 1999, 2006). Already in his youth, and as a matter of course for those who grew up in the black church at the time, but not just those within the church, King was a crypto-personalist who, claims Baldwin, gained in Boston the conceptual vocabulary by which to formally articulate or profess his social activist personalism. Baldwin suggests that King was most probably exposed to personalism, construed in religious if not also distinctively philosophical terms, "during his years at Morehouse" (2011, 2). Lawrence Carter has argued that King displays a unique form of philosophical personalism; like Baldwin, Carter extends King's personalism beyond the affiliation with the doctrine at Boston University (2007). King's first philosophy courses with Williams were replete with the kind of Christian personalism and philosophical pragmatism professed by Thurman during his years at Morehouse and Spelman.

While King was at Morehouse, Thurman was leading an interracial and interfaith church in San Francisco, The Church for the Fellowship of All People, where "the core of [his] preaching always concerned itself with the development of the inner resources needed for the creation of a friendly world of friendly men [and women]" (1979, 160). Thurman saw quite clearly that "it was important that individuals who were in the thick of the struggle for social change would be able to find renewal and fresh courage in the spiritual resources of the church" (1979, 160). Thurman's philosophical ideas were "born of struggle," borrowing a phrase from Leonard Harris. As part of a Festschrift dedicated to Thurman, who died prior to its publication, Ricardo Millet and Hughes wrote that "the roots of Dr. Thurman's thought go deeper than the sands of traditional scholarship. They were embedded in the tradition of a people who, like himself, found discipline and respite in a creative center, born of an unalterable religious experience" (1982, iii).

Rather than losing the forest for the trees, so to speak, or getting bogged down in the philistinism inherent in topologizing Thurman's unique form of personalism, or classifying King's personalism, or assessing its kinship to Brightman or Bowen and Muelder, I wish simply to describe here what might be viewed as Thurman's unique contribution to American personalism. Thurman espoused what might be called a theistic personalist interpretation of the sanctity of persons, as the first dynamic principle of his philosophical system, one that emphasized the role of community in the formation of persons as well as the vital importance of a personal God. Thurman was also one of the pioneers in applying Gandhi's principles of nonviolence to race issues in America, but for Thurman, following Gandhi's satyagraha teachings, nonviolence was more than a mere strategy or means to an end: Satyagraha believes that nonviolence is a way of being in the world. Reinhold Niebuhr considered nonviolence to be unrealistic if not ultimately also counterproductive, although he viewed it as a "particularly strategic instrument for an oppressed group that was hopelessly in the minority" (1932, 252); Niebuhr withdrew his membership from the Fellowship of Reconciliation in 1936. For Thurman, perhaps distinctively, violence should be viewed as a form of hate, which, similar to fear and deception, distorts the integrity of the soul and obstructs communion with other people and distorts one's capacity for encountering God. The fundamental issue involved in the experience of segregation, Thurman believed—although there are analogues to be found in the practices associated with materialism and militarism—"is the attack it makes on his dignity and integrity." In ways that resonate with African communalism, wherein "I am because we are," *ubuntu*-like, Thurman claims in *Luminous Darkness* that "we become persons by an-other-than-self reference which is other persons" (1965a, 6). Similar to Brightman and Muelder, Thurman insists that a respect for persons entails a social responsibility to create a nonviolent climate or environment conducive to freedom and the fulfillment of personality. The ethic of self-realization in community is a constant theme in Thurman.

Beyond Personalism in the "Minimalist Sense"

Similar to King, Thurman was a personalist in the minimalist sense well before he started corresponding with Brightman in 1936. (Brightman became an associate member of The Church for the Fellowship of all Peoples, Thurman's congregation in San Francisco, in 1946.) Burrow says that "King was actually a personalist (in the minimalist sense) long before he first read books on Brightman's personalism at Morehouse College" (1999, 77). By personalism in the minimalist sense, Burrow means that King was already committed to or believed in "the existence of a personal God and the dignity and sanctity of persons" (1999, 77). As a corrective to those who might otherwise reduce King's philosophical and theological development to the academic influences, Burrow and others argue (for example, James Cone, Garth Baker-Fletcher, Lewis V. Baldwin, and Garrow 2004) that "what Crozer and Boston University actually did was to give King a name and a theoretical framework for what he already believed as a result of this family upbringing and his training in the black church in Atlanta, Georgia" (Burrow 1999, 77). But Thurman is also a personalist in the sense that he (not unlike King, and using Burrow's concise formulation of the principles) placed emphasis—variably but consistently—on the existence of a personal God, the dignity or sacredness of all persons, and "the existence of an objective moral order and corresponding moral laws, freedom, and moral agency" (1999, 78).

"According to King," writes Carter, "not only is the person what Bertocci would later refer to as a 'unitas multiplex,' but what Walter George Muelder would call 'a center of autonomous value' worthy of unconditional love" (2006, 219).[3] Bertocci defines a person as "a unique, telic, indivisible, but complex self-identifying unity of activity-potentials best characterized in consciousness as sensing, feeling, desiring, remembering, imagining, thinking, willing, oughting, allotting, anticipating, and appreciating, and the activities we distinguish as aesthetic and religious, that is, able to develop reason and values" (1988, 9; 2002, 35). Buford elaborates: "We call these activity potentials a complex unity because rarely is one potential developed without involving others. Persons do not simply see; they also think about what they see, appreciate what they see, and remember what they see. And we must remember that, as agents with activity potentials, those potentials actualize in a suggestive and limiting context" (2015, 22). The argument is more or less transcendental in the Kantian sense, which means that emphasis is place on the conditions necessary for the possibility of some phenomenon. Bertocci defines the personality as something that is "learned as a person interacts with other persons; more exactly, a person's personality is his more or less systematic mode of response to himself, to others, and to his total environment in the light of what he believes them to be, and what they actually are" (1970, 95). In *The Way of Chuang Tzu,* Thomas Merton argues that "a personalism that has nothing to offer but evasion will not be a genuine personalism at all, since it destroys the relationships without which the person cannot truly develop" (1995, 17).[4] "For King," argues Lawrence Carter, "the person's structure is shaped, at least in part, by the value conferred upon him or her. Thus, there is no separation between the structure, or how a person is defined, and the value, or how the person might be viewed in light of that definition" (1998, 219ff.).

Warren E. Steinkraus suggests that "this means that there is no higher principle than the person. All other values are subordinate. Abstract laws, the state, property, and other institutions are all to be judged in the light of their effect on persons. *This is, of course, the moral base of democracy*" (1973, 103; emphasis added). Although there is a good deal disagreement among personalists about how best to describe and interpret these "effects on persons," such that philosophical personalists are often subcategorized as theistic personalists or communitarian personalists or even countercultural personalists, the pedagogical personalism practiced at Morehouse traditionally stressed the sacred or otherwise inviolable dignity of persons, certainly, but it also promoted an educational process that activated the potential of individuals within and across diverse communities. In his *Philosophy of Personalism,* Knudson observes that "personalism lays more stress on the will than the intellect and inclines to the view that life is deeper than logic" (1969, 67). Thurman's philosophical if not prophetic personalism operates at the growing edges of the beloved community, where the I and the Thou interact, where the common ground sought is found in compassionate acts and loyalty to interwoven causes conducted in a climate of spiritual solidarity, acts of self-sacrifice and loyalty. Sometimes the sacrifice is monumental, other times it may seem mundane, and sometimes it is forced, times when action is urgently required but the way forward—amid live but divergent options—is unclear. Sometimes the acts of self-sacrifice for others—past, present, or future—may seem quite mundane and voluntarily undertaken, perhaps as an act of supererogation. Thurman is quite pragmatic, in the philosophical sense of the term, in tracing and anticipating the consequences of various world formulas that constitute or reintegrate the core elements in of one's diachronic identity. Segregation as well as imperialism and materialism undermine the integrity of the socioethical or communal self. Thurman puts it quite beautifully in his *Luminous Darkness:* "It is clear that for the Negro the fundamental issue involved in the experience of segregation is the attack that it makes on his dignity and integrity. We become persons by an 'other-than-self' reference which is other persons. We become human in a human situation" (1965a, 5).

This communalist strand in Thurman's personalism is born of the "struggle to try to achieve a sense of self in a total environment that threatened the self" (Thurman 1965a, 5). For Thurman, argued Smith, the "crucial of relationship" provides "the hermeneutical key to ultimate reality" (1988, 95, 98). So while the damage done by social isolation is displayed most acutely in settings of racism or poverty and militarism, Thurman believes that there is a "built-in resistance in all human being against the threat of isolation. It is a major safeguard against the disintegration of the self" (1971, 82). Thurman's communalist notion of personal identity attends to the necessary and sufficient conditions or requisite resources for "the constant renewing and sustaining of the private life of the individual." Elsewhere, Thurman says: "Here the raw materials are provided for establishing an inner climate for growth of personality and for giving full scope to the inner urge for whole-making that in turn increases the possibility for actualizing the potential of the individual. For in such a setting the individual not only has an awareness of being cared for, but also the way is opened for him to emerge as a person in an enlarged relationship of persons" (1971, 82).

Ultimately, Thurman's personalism entails a working hypothesis concerning identity formation and ethical agency, something along the lines of "deep-self compatibilism" understood as the coincidence of behavioral determinism and volitional agency. Culpability or responsibility assumes freedom, construed quite simply as a live set of options, as William James might have described it in his "Dilemma of Determinism," but perhaps also in a legal sense; rather than James, however, the better guide to Thurman's thoughts on freedom and determinism, although Thurman was well versed in James, especially his *Varieties of Religious Experience*, is the theological personalism of Augustine and Aquinas as well as the philosophical personalism of Plotinus and Emerson. For Thurman, this constitutes a vast paradox: "It must be true, then, that there is something in every [person] that remains intact, inviolate, regardless of what he [or she] does. I wonder! Is this true? Is there an integrity of the person, so intrinsic in its value and significance that no deed, however evil, can ultimately undermine this given thing" (1956, 17–18)? The free act and the rational act, the real and the rational, in each of these models of personal identity and moral agency ultimately coincide. Anything that disturbs that optimal growth of the self is violent, sinful even, whereas those things that contribute to the maximal or optimal maturation of the self are considered to be good and just. Segregation disturbs the integrity or optimal growth of the personality of both the oppressed and the oppressor: it disturbs our relationship to others and to God, but it also undermines the integrity of the self because it survives by means of hatred and deception. In short, thought Thurman, "it is against God, it is against life, and if it is against life, it cannot abide" (1978, 42). Elsewhere, Thurman writes: "What is against life will be destroyed by life, for what is against life is against God" (1963, 18).

> It is the intent of God that man shall live in community. Now when I violate this, or when my community or civilization violates this, then I am caught in the kind of conflict that can never be resolved until I accept this necessity of my nature. If, however, I am under the necessity to accept the purpose of God, how can I be free? If I am free, then I must be able to accept it or reject it. Granted. But if I reject it, then my life becomes self-defeating, and self-destructive; so, if I accept it, then it means that I move into one of the most fundamental dimensions of the meaning of freedom. What is that? When I am faced with what seems to me to be a necessity that reduces all of my effective options to zero, then the only way I can guarantee the integrity of my freedom is to make as my self-conscious deliberate act, that which is my necessity. The moment I do that, I become free.

Thurman's interpretation of personal identity, which suggests that an act is free to the extent that it not coerced or caused by another, goes well beyond mere negative freedom in Isaiah Berlin's sense of the absence of obstacles to the exercise of my agency: autonomous acts admit of degrees, of course, but an important part of the equation includes the extent to which the action under consideration is representative of whatever one construes as one's deepest or most authentic self, for example, the self that we claim to be the truest part of our identity.

Thurman lived in an age of psychoanalysis, certainly, but his early thinking on personal identity was influenced more by James or Dewey and Olive Schreiner than Sigmund Freud or Carl Jung. King sometimes refers, e.g., in his allusion to "Love or Perish," to Thurman as a psychiatrist (2010, 67). According to Gandhi, one's power and energy or soul force is enhanced by denying the appetites, the lower or baser desires—fasting from food or sex, for example—but also daily acts of self-sacrifice or psychological immolation undergone on behalf of others and for purposes that extend beyond our immediate sphere of consequence. Thurman found an analogue within the Christian tradition, one beholden in part to Nikolai Berdyaev. Thurman thunders: "We appear to be face to face with a principle of mechanics" (1963, 16). Thurman thought that this conatic principle was characteristic of many, if not most, of the classical ascetics and mystics: "The German mystic, Meister Eckhart, implied in his teachings that the conditions upon which

God enters a [person's] life are automatic . . . [and that] to the extent that a man rids himself of creatureliness, to that extent God must enter his life" (1963, 16). As a deep-self compatibilist, or something along those lines, Thurman suggested that we are most free when our individual will is attuned to and directed by our deepest self, variously expressed as "the apex of the soul" or "the uncreated element in the soul" (1963, 96; also 1970 and 1975a), construed as the divine within, the voice of the genuine, and "the citadel of encounter." Personal identity is socially constructed, surely, in Thurman's sense that "human beings become human in a human situation" (1971, 83), that individuality and personality is conferred within the context of communities, both proximate and remote, and is thus perhaps amenable to creative and dynamic reconfiguration or conversion.

Reading Thurman as an Identity Theorist

Thurman's philosophical thoughts on personal identity should be placed within the context of his most sustained treatment of the topic in *Search for Common Ground,* where he is so bold as to suggest that our socioethical and political dream of dynamic integration is ultimately "rooted in the life process itself" (1971, xiii).

Thurman thinks or otherwise senses that "all life is engaged in goal-seeking" and that

> the degree to which the potential in any expression of life is actualized marks the extent to which such an expression of life experiences wholeness, integration, community. The clue to community can be found in the inner creative activity of living substances. The more highly developed the organism, the more pronounced seems to be the manifestation of the clue. . . . In human society, the experience of community, or realized potential, is rooted in life itself because the intuitive human urge for community reflects a characteristic of all life. (1971, 6–7)

Thurman argues that the same impulse expressed in the dreams of our prophets as well as in our creation stories and utopian literature "is universal and is not unique to any particular cultural, religious, or ethnic origin" (1971, xiv). Thurman found intimations of this cosmic yearning in Olive Schreiner as well as George Bernard Shaw. Thurman was also familiar with the teleological thought associated with Aristotle and the natural law theory of St. Thomas Aquinas. But on a more visceral level, something closer than a thought or theory, Thurman claimed that he was "on the scent of the tie that binds life at a level so deep that the final privacy of the individual would be reinforced rather than threatened. I have always wanted to be me without making it difficult for you to be you" (1971, xiii). Thurman puts it this way:

> The paradox of conscious life is the ultimate issue here. On the one hand is the necessity for the declaration that states unequivocally the uniqueness of the private life, the awful sense of being an isolate, independent and alone, the great urgency to savor one's personal flavor—to stand over against all the rest of life in contained affirmation. While on the other hand is the necessity to feel oneself as a primary part of all of life, sharing at every level of awareness a dependence upon the same elements in nature, caught up in the ceaseless rhythm of living and dying, with no finally immunity against a common fate that finds and holds all living things. (1971, xiv)

Elsewhere, Thurman claims:

> I have had to discover, after the pattern of the grain in my wood, the difference between solitariness and loneliness. I have had to wrestle with many spiritual crises growing out of what seemed to be the contradictory demands of love and hate, of vengeance and mercy, and of retaliation and reconciliation. In all of these experiences there is a part of me that seeks ever for harmony, for community, for unity and creative synthesis in conflicting relations; and an equally articulate urgency within me for withdrawal, for separateness, for isolation, and for aggression. . . . But more and more the makings of such a thoroughgoing dualism seemed not only intolerable but also the constructing of an essentially false dichotomy. (1971, 77)

Twenty years earlier, in his *Deep Is the Hunger,* Thurman claims that "all of life is one, and yet life moves in such intimate circles of individuality. The power of life, perhaps, is its aloneness" (1951a, 175; also see Mitchell 1992). In his preface to *The Search for Common Ground,* Thurman wrote: "Over and over again I have asked myself: What is the common ground that floats the private adventure of the individual or solitary life? Is it merely conceptual, is it only the great idea, the hunger of the heart rationalized into a transcendent God-idea, concept, or notion? Or are these but the scent of the eternal in all living things, perhaps reaching its apotheosis in [person], and in the religious [person] in particular" (1971, xiv). Such questions, Thurman reminds us, are by no means merely academic; rather, these questions constitute an existential "crisis for a black man living in American society in the last decades of the twentieth century" (xiv).

Thurman claims that his *Search for Common Ground* manuscript, which was written at a time when "the lines of separation between black and white [were] seen psychologically as being absolute," constituted his "lifelong working paper," since he had been "from his early childhood on the scent of the tie that binds life at a level so deep that the final privacy of the individual would be reinforced rather than threatened" (1971, xiii). Whereas philosophers along the lines of René Descartes adopt a form of centripetal introspection that leads to solipsism or egocentrism, Thurman believed that it was possible to go deep within oneself in a way that actually strengthened one's interconnectedness with others. For Thurman, there is a centripetal motion that culminates in a centrifugal achievement. Vincent Harding considers this movement as spiritual genius and general drift of Thurman's "own God-intoxicating pilgrimage": "He moved deep into the heart of his own spiritual idiom and came up inside all peoples, cultures, and faiths" (qtd. in Makechnie 1988, 54).

When he asks whether we are on the scent of eternal in all living things, or when he suggests that "the goal of fulfillment appears on the far horizon and persists as the pull of the long-timed emotion of the ideal" (1971, 81), Thurman harkens back to Plato, whether in the *Phaedrus* or the *Symposium,* where desire implies a previous unity, thus desire construed as a lack, as a foretaste or aftertaste of something better, maybe along the lines of Plotinus, but then one discovers that there are better philosophical analogues to be found in Augustine's *mihi quaestio factus sum* (I have become a question to myself) and Pascal as well as Kierkegaard and Emerson.[5] In the *Confessions,* in the throes of grieving the death of a friend but in a way that foreshadows his subsequent existential plight (*quia fecisti nos ad te et inquietum est cor nostrum donec requiescat in te* [because thou hast made us toward thyself and our heart is restless until it rests in thee]), Augustine wrote:

> Everything I had shared with my friend turned into hideous anguish without him. My eyes sought him everywhere, but he was missing; I hated all things because they held him not, and could no more say to me, "Look, here he comes!" as they had been wont to do in his lifetime when he had been away. I had become a great enigma to myself [*mihi quaestio factus sum*], and I questioned my soul, demanding why it was sorrowful and why it so disquieted me, but I had no idea how to respond [*nihil noverat respondere mihi*] (1997, 97).

And while one could classify Augustine and Kierkegaard as personal identity theorists of a certain sort, religious in general and Christian in particular, one could also view them—as well as Pascal and Emerson—as religious critics: the same holds for Thurman. But it is also true that Thurman cannot be reduced to his predecessors. Although there are certain resonances between Kierkegaard's critical enterprise of what it meant to become a Christian in any society ostensibly Christian and Thurman's conundrum of becoming a Christian within an institution and society that was decidedly un-Christian in deed if not also in word, the differences deserve as much attention as the similarities.

Thurman provides us with a theory of personal identity, something akin to deep-self compatibilism, but he is also interested "in the meaning of search for identity." That part of our identity is to seek our identity as well as to assert or establish our identity through intentional or purposeful actions, for example, resisting exclusionary social classifications. (In this, Thurman agrees not only with Muelder but also Borden Parker Bowne in treating purpose as integral to—if not constitutive of—personal identity and volitional agency.) Thurman strikes me as especially insightful when it comes to the role of feelings and reflective thought in shaping personal identity. Indeed, Thurman considered this to be one of the "seminal concepts that nourished both [his] mind and [his] spirit over many years" (1979, 226). And while this certainly constitutes a classical philosophical problem, perhaps even a paradox, which is how Thurman views it, a question staged dramatically in Aescelius's *Medea,* Thurman claims that the question of how best to relate one's feelings to reflective thought was also "a recurring challenge of [his] life" (1979, 226). Elaborating:

> It is a misreading of the role of feelings to separate them from the function of mind at work! No matter how clear and penetrating and detached may be the vast reaches of creative thoughts at their best, they are but lifeless forms until they are energized by the continuum of emotion that is always present and antedates the emergence of the mind. After all, it may be true that what is called "thought" is a function of feeling, reduced to slow motion. (1979, 226)

Thurman explores this idea in both the *Creative Encounter* and *Search for Common Ground.* Thurman explores a different philosophical question of personal identity in reference to the story of Legion, the disintegrated soul who was redeemed or otherwise restored to his right mind when Jesus asked for his name. Theories of personal identity are often tightly interwoven with questions of whether—and if so, in what sense—human actions are free as opposed to determined. Authentic freedom for Thurman was neither anonymity nor freedom from interference, for example, "to go nameless up and down the streets of other minds" (1961, 38): rather, freedom is "a core of discipline and an inner structure" (1961, 63). As he put it in his *Inward Journey:*

> There is a medley of confusion as to the meaning of personal freedom. For some it means to function without limitations at any point, to be able to do what one wants to do and without hindrance. This is the fantasy of many

> minds, particularly those that are young. For others, personal freedom is to be let alone, to be protected against any force that may move into their life with a swift and decisive imperative. For still others, it means to be limited in one's power over others only by one's own strength, energy, and perseverance. At the very center personal freedom is a discipline of the mind and of the emotions. The mind must be centered upon a goal, a purpose, a plan (1961, 63).

In *The Inward Journey,* Thurman was convinced that "freedom is a discipline" and that "there can be no personal freedom where there is not an initial personal surrender" (1961, 63), that orders, organizes, and empowers. Similarly, and as he expressed this point in *Meditations of the Heart,* "the central element in communion with God is the act of self-surrender" (1953, 174). Much later in life, Thurman would come to say that "the experience of community based on innocence obtains so long as elements of disharmony are not apparent. There is present the freedom and abandonment of innocence, and yet the freedom is not absolute. Freedom has meaning only with reference to limitations in some form" (1971, 25).

Similar to Muelder, who wrote that "the ethic of respect for personality must also be one of personality fulfillment" (1955, 13), Thurman thought that "when a person actualizes his own potential he becomes whole, harmonized, or fulfilled" (1971, 80). Thurman encouraged us to think of this potential as something "dynamic and without measure." Thurman seems to have read Berdyaev, who suggests, in *Slavery and Freedom,* that "the realization of personality in man is this continuous transcending of self" (1944, 29). The goal of fulfillment, or the ideal of integration and harmony, of a unity that lies beneath the disorder, constitutes a "built-in demand of the mind, the insistence of the organism, the upward push of the racial memory, the glow of the prophet's demand and the dream of the seer; it is what in religion is often called the will of God as touching the life of [human beings]" (1971, 81). Without taking the extreme position that whatever impedes the development of the personality is prima facie wrong, perhaps even evil, Thurman wants us to think more carefully about "the essential building blocks" for growth construed as the actualization or fulfillment of human potential. "It has often been said that that a child is not born human but becomes human in a human situation or context" (81). Thurman says that the family, as the primary social unit, provided, ideally, the "raw materials for establishing an inner climate for the growth of personality and for giving full scope to the inner urge for whole-making that in turn increases the possibility for actualizing the potential of the individual" (82). In the absence of these conditions, claims Thurman, "the child is apt to become permanently crippled" (81); elaborating, he suggests that "if the child is forced by the circumstances of his life to cope with his environment as if he were an adult, his very nervous system becomes enraged and an utter sense of alienation is apt to become the style of his life" (82). Thurman then reminds us that "the family group is a part of a larger social unity in an ever-widening circle of belonging" (83). This "ever-widening circle of belonging" is the clue to Thurman's social philosophy. Within the inner circles of familial domain but extending outward toward "a larger social unity," one encounter at a time, an individual should receive, both in the ethical and in the developmental sense of what an individual deserves and requires, "an awareness of being cared for" and a way by which "to emerge in an enlarged relationship of persons" (82). Thurman states: "the frustration of this tendency to wholeness in [human life] is the withering blight that is making so much of modern life a wasteland" (83).

Insider–Outsider Complexes

Although he identifies a wide array of ways by which individuals become disintegrated and persons become alienated, whether because one forgets one's rootedness in nature or through experiences of violence of various types, Thurman seems to be especially insightful when it comes to a series of "inside–outside dilemmas" (1971, 84; also [1966] 2009, 204) that distort the personality and disintegrate one's sense of self or damage the soul.[6] What are the conditions for actualizing the potential of the human personality? Similar to Thurman, Johan Galtung defines violence quite simply, almost mathematically, as "the absence of peace" and argues that "violence is present when human beings are influenced so that their actual somatic and mental realizations are below their potential realizations" (1969, 168).[7] As a social scientist, Thurman would have considered this to be an empirical question. He also directs our attention to utopian literature as replete with this sort of speculation (1971, 46–55). As a bold hypothesis, Thurman thought that one of the essential conditions was a "recognition of the continuing sense of belonging" (1971, 83). The development of the personality requires a nurturing environment, of course, but what constitutes a climate conducive to self-actualization? "Man has to feel at home if he is to be nurtured," explains Thurman, because "home means place and place means territory" (1971, 84). As a symbol of homeland, especially in the absence of a state religion, claims Thurman, the sovereign state "formally defines an outsider and establishes rites and rituals for belonging" (1971, 84). Thurman thinks that secular states take on a transcendent role, thereby fulfilling one of the basic requirements of religion.[8] Civic religion can inspire "a sense of participating in a collective or communal destiny, thus reaffirming in crisis a sense of belonging to a transcendent entity in which the individual life is somehow transformed into something so much more than itself" (1971, 85). And this notion of citizenship and civic character serves as a basis for self-sacrifice. "It becomes clear that if there are any citizens within the state who by definition, stated or implied, are denied freedom of access to the resources of the community as established within the state, such persons are assailed at the very foundation of their sense of belonging" (86). As second-class citizens, Thurman reiterates, "such persons are 'outsiders' living in the midst of 'insiders,' required to honor the same demands of sovereignty but denied the basic rewards of sovereignty" (87).

Thurman claims that "wherever citizens are denied the freedom of access to the resources that make for a sense of belonging, a sense of being totally dealt with, the environment closes in around them, resulting in the schizophrenic dilemma of being inside and outside at one and the same time. Or worse still, they are subject to the acute trauma of not knowing at any given moment whether they are outsiders or insiders" (1971, 88). Such is the terrifying fate of many minorities in America and "all those ethnic strands that make up the so-called Third World" (1971, 88). Thurman made this point, more or less, back in 1956, in *The Growing Edge,* when he wrote: "There is an inner need that is a permanent part of our life and my life, for belonging, for feeling and knowing and being assured that we are included in, as it were" (1956, 65). "The search for community on the part of the Afro-American minority within the larger American community," Thurman believed, "reveals still another facet of the inside–outside dilemma" (1971, 89). Victor Anderson, in his analysis of black heroic genius, contends that "Thurman described African American presence in America as an epic search for identity in a nation where blacks are bound by [this insider–outsider] dilemma" (1999, 80). In *Search for Common Ground,* Thurman reminds us: "Many tried to keep before their view heroes and heroines of the past to bolster a sagging self-estimate in the present. But there was ever the insinuating circumstance, the heroes failed where they themselves had failed—they were outsiders—the walls, sometimes bold and direct, often soft-spoken and indirect, were ever present" (1971, 95; qtd. in Anderson 1999, 80).

"Aggression," Thurman believes, "cannot be separated from the urge for and to community" (1971, 90). Thurman uses an example from cellular biology to explain his point. The disgruntled youth of the civil rights movement, suggests Thurman, were expressing "their disenchantment with the society in which they were born. The result is that more and more they regard themselves as outsiders in the midst of the land of their roots and culture" (1971, 91). The quest for a sense of self, or personhood, is the quest for "the magic circle within which one stands in a kind of splendid and austere isolation" (1962), but it is also the center from which one relates to ever-encircling world. The emergence of a "sense of self" is rooted in what seems to Thurman to be a "sense of one's own embodiment" (1962). Yet the sense of self is not only rooted in one's own physical persona—it also expresses

> one's own idiom, one's own flavor, this . . . is the underside or the inside of every outside that you manifest . . . it is the unique tang that belongs to you . . . it is your idiom. It is this sense of private flavor or awareness of the grain in your wood, it is with this that you relate to the style of your society . . . and it is the degree to which this relatedness is worked out, your sense of self and identity is enlarged . . . ever-outward . . . sufficient vitality and vigor to reject the social style of this or that group or when he identifies with an age yet to come or an age long gone. Often one finds the most meaningful aspect of one's idiom, the "you-ness of you," as expressed within a lifestyle that undertakes to provide ultimate answers about the meaning of life and existence. (1962)

What remains standing after and through the storms? What ties continue to bind? And how might the next larger circle come to be drawn? There is an array of causes for the breakdown or disintegration of the self. "The struggle for persona or selfhood is one of the most critical struggles of the human spirit" (1962a). The quests of the human spirit comingle such that whenever one of these quests is discussed, there is always an overtone of other. As a case in point, Thurman believes the quest for identity will comingle with the quest for community and the quest for God: "I have only one basic statement to make about the love of God and that is that it is always concerned with breaking the sense of isolation that the individual human spirit feels as it lives its way into life" (1956, 65). For Thurman, it is within "the primary experience of the family that the stage is set for the constant renewing and sustaining of the private life of the individual" (82), and personal identity oscillates between the inside and the outside, between the centripetal and centrifugal forces.

The Communitarian Dimension of Personality

Although Thurman expresses his insight concerning the role of the community in the formation of the personality in various ways at different times in his life, as if putting his bold hypothesis or mystical insight to the test, looking at it from this angle and then the other, it seems that his philosophical position on personal identity took its final form during the Boston years. In *Disciplines of the Spirit,* Thurman wrote that "any structure of society, any arrangement under which human beings live, that does not provide maximum of opportunities for free-flowing circulation among one another, works against social and individual health" (1963, 127). Put differently:

> Any attitudes, private or group, which prohibit people from coming into "across-the-board" contact with each other, works against the implementation of the love ethic. So considered, segregation, prescriptions of separation, are a disease of the human spirit and the body politic. It does not matter how meaningful the tight circle of isolated security may be in which individuals or groups move. The very existence of such circles, whether regarded as a necessity of religious faith, political ideology, or social purity, precludes the possibility of the experience of love as a part of the necessity of a [person's] life. (127)

Thurman returned to the question of how best to facilitate, whether as a pastor or an activist, a creative "free-flowing circulation" or sense of community between individuals and groups that was more compelling than the differences that separate them. Thurman wrestled throughout his life to "make sense out of [his] concern for community and to honor intelligently its profound urgency in the human spirit" (1971, 77). Perhaps, says Thurman, "it may not seem too far-fetched to examine a person's need to be loved, to be understood, to be cared for, as the essential building blocks for the actualizing of [their] potential and the essential stuff of community" (80). Thurman reiterates here the thesis that animates "the search" for common ground and community, that is, that those who seek community are "not going against life but will be sustained and supported by life" or, put differently, that "there is a spirit in [persons] and in the world working against the things that destroys and lays waste" (6). Thurman is careful to distinguish conformity from harmony or uniformity for synthesis. The synthesis or harmony that Thurman has in mind is one that "transcends all diversities and in which diversity finds its richness and significance" (1971, 6).

Thurman believed that one's sense of self is rooted in one's embodiment, something that explains why those who "wish to break the will, the inner entity of others, they resort to direct and violent cruelty upon their bodies" (1971, 79). Similar perhaps to identity or unity as the underlying assumption of all mathematical systems, Thurman says "the necessity that all experience makes sense and the feel for harmony is sui generis or given. The clue is to be found in the nature of mind itself" (80). Thurman suggests that the "body shares with all living things the urgency to actualize its potential as a body" (79) and, as a bold philosophical hypothesis, that the "tendency of the mind for whole-making or 'seeing whole,' for seeking harmony, for community, is rooted in the experience of the body that in turn is grounded in all of life" (79). Indeed, Thurman suggests that "it was helpful to [him] in [his] search to think of a time when mind as a separate and conscious entity did not formally exist in the body," that is, a time when "the mind was hidebound but mind as such was not" (79). Taken together with his claims about a "racial memory," mentioned earlier, and what he says in his chapter on common consciousness (see 56–68), Thurman's allusion to a "hidebound mind" starts to resonate with Muelder's equally puzzling theory of the social mind as a means of explaining the metaphysics of intersubjective continuity and individual totalities. "The self is not an individual center of experience that is merely influenced by its social environment, as Bowne imagined," says Dorrien, describing Muelder's unique contributions to personalism, "it is its social experience and unique individual experience" (2009, 310). In a way that distinguished him from his predecessors, whether Bowne or Brightman, Muelder insisted that the self—construed as "a socius with a private center" (1983, 6)—is historical and social through and through. "With Bowne and Brightman, Muelder affirmed that each person acts from a creative center, personality means freedom, and the highest virtue of personality is love" (Dorrien 2009, 310).

Although he did not describe Thurman as a personalist per se, Muelder does claim—in 1982, as part of a special issue of *Debate & Understanding* dedicated to Thurman's thought—that "there is a profound affinity between the evangelical social ethic of Thurman and that of his younger personalistic contemporary [King]" (1982, 9) and that "from a philosophical perspective the writings of Thurman are seen to be coherent with a personalistic and communitarian ethic" (1982, 13). Muelder shows a familiarity with and an appreciation for Thurman's main ideas; he also provides, as usual, a useful grid and a working set of categories with which to assess the structural coherence of a philosophical position. When Muelder turns his attention to "the rational structure of personalistic moral law," which he further adumbrates into fourteen principles, Muelder claims that "Thurman's theory conforms to the formal, the axiological, the personalistic, and the communitarian levels of the principles" (1982, 10). Drawing on the system of regulatory moral laws formulated by Edgar S. Brightman, which Muelder modified together with DeWolf, Muelder suggests that Thurman's "ethical theory is neither heteronomous, nor autonomous, but is [instead] theonomous":

> What this means is that the imperatives are not imposed from external sources, nor completely devised by inner personal mandates, but expressed at the deepest level a metaphysical divine moral order which is also the rational laws of a person's own being. There is a meeting place for the communication between God and the person, a place of yielding private,

> personal will to transcending purposes that are at the same time common ground. Here revelation and intuition meet, a place rich with the sense of the ultimate worth of the individual as a private and social person. (1982, 9)

Thurman read Muelder, but Muelder also read Thurman. It was an unlikely philosophical friendship, given the times, such that they constituted for one another both a colleague and a datum, but they somehow found a way to one another. Muelder's relationship to Thurman is disclosed in their shared relationship to and influence on Martin Luther King Jr.: mutual recognition and respect as well as the common ground of shared concerns for freedom and equality in America. As a case in point, Walter G. Muelder, who was the dean of the School of Theology and professor of social ethics while King attended Boston University and while Thurman was dean of Marsh Chapel, delivered a prestigious set of lectures in 1954 and 1955 that were subsequently published as *The Idea of the Responsible Society* (1955; also see Bowne 1905, 1910). It seems instructive to compare Muelder's *Idea of the Responsible Society* (1955) with Thurman's *Creative Encounter* (1954) and *Search for Common Ground* (1971). Thurman no doubt attended Muelder's "Responsible Society" lectures when they were delivered in Boston. And yet, it seems to me—at least once we come to the "The Religious Component in the Idea" lecture, followed by discussions of "Respect for Persons" and "the Meaning of Freedom" as well as the lengthy chapter "Justice and Equality"—Muelder demonstrates a certain philosophical indebtedness to Thurman's sermons and writings, especially *Jesus and the Disinherited.* Although there is always the axiological dimension of personalism in Thurman or Muelder, personalism also constitutes an epistemological method and a metaphysical orientation. "The idea of personal worth," Muelder maintains, "is not a monopoly of Western religious groups" (1955, 12). The responsible society is constituted by free and responsible persons who "not only make claims, but they accept their duties" (Muelder 1955, 13). In 1959, in his *Foundations of the Responsible Society,* Muelder expanded his earlier socioethical statement about the ethic of self-realization in community by appropriating DeWolf's communitarian principles. Following DeWolf, who, "while stressing the value of sacrificial love, [was] equally emphatic that agape in its sacrifice should aim to create community" (Ansbro 2000, 24), the Boston personalists seemed to agree that "life under the reign of God is not an individualistic affair. Since love is its dominant principle, it is communal to the very core. This communal life of the kingdom has already begun in some groups and relationships. So far as that love and life are present, the kingdom of God is here" (DeWolf 2011, 303).

This communalist strand in Muelder's theological and philosophical worldview, something he inherited from his father but later adopted as his own, was on display in his 1947 essay "Essential Elements in the Christian Conception of Man," in which he claimed from the outset that humans are "nurtured physically and spiritually through a group, and he [or she] comes to self-realization as a participant in group life. The end for which God has created [humans] is communion; thus the perfection of community, or the Kingdom of God, is the goal of [humanity]" (117). In short: "Community is written into the nature of [human beings] in such a way that it is proper to think of [humans] as persons-in-community" (117). Thurman makes this point in an unpublished 1956 sermon titled "Freedom" (Gotlieb Archives, BU):

> For in the thought of Jesus what a man most deeply desires, what a man most deeply wants when he is stripped to the literal substance of himself is precisely what God wants. So when I work against community, when my intent is to separate, when my intent is to introduce into the structure of my relationships that which is divisive, that which alienates, that which compounds hatred, and misery and meanness, that which closes the door against my fellows, when I do these things even in response to what seems to me to be the imperative of an insistent historic moment, or in response to what seems to me to be the necessities for my own physical survival, when I act against community, I become a house divided against itself, and a house divided against itself cannot stand. . . . It is the intent of God that man shall live in community.

Beyond their resonate ideas with respect to various conceptions of freedom and purposiveness, it seems that Thurman and Muelder were working in parallel trenches, as well as when, more or less, it came to notions of justice and equality.

By the time he arrived at Boston University in 1927, after graduating from Knox College, Muelder "was already a full-fledged social gospeler, personalist, pacifist, and [a] socialist" (Dorrien 2009, 308); with minor qualifications, we could say the same of Thurman when he arrived in Boston in 1953. There is, of course, a conceptual relationship between various conceptions of freedom or liberty and notions of justice and equality; both Thurman and Muelder were keen to understand these conceptual relationships as a means to changing them. According to Muelder, "[s]ocial justice includes distributive justice but is a dynamic idea which embraces also sound goals, social well-being, democratic control of power in industry and business, and the fulfillment of a wide range of needs and rights" (1959, 27). The task of social justice, suggests Muelder, "is to define the rightful place and privilege which each life must have in the harmony of the whole and to assign the duty of each to each. In such a view justice has both a negative and a positive significance. Negatively justice delineates principles to restrain each and the evildoer. Positively justice formulates the political and the economical skeletal structure of society which carried the organic element of the community" (1959, 31). Here justice serves and extends the work of love, which is something that Muelder discovers in Thurman's 1954 *Creative Encounter,* which was published shortly after Thurman arrived on the scene at Boston University. Muelder elaborates: "Purpose and responsibility are both emphasized by Thurman, as self-realization is combined with the demands of duty, integrity, and universal community. However, both the ethics of purpose and of duty (the horizontal and the vertical) are transcended and included in an ethic of relation. Love is a relationship as well as a goal and an obligation" (1982, 10). Muelder claims that this feature of Thurman's thought is on display in *Luminous Darkness* (1965a), which Thurman published shortly following his retirement from Boston University. Muelder draws our attention to Thurman's declaration that persons "were made for one another" as well as that "there is a meaning in life greater than, but informing, all the immediate meanings," which Thurman describes as essentially religious in character because "it embodies, however faintly, a sense of the ultimate and the divine," and "it is this spirit that makes for wholeness and community" (Thurman 1965a, 112). Perhaps Muelder understood as well as anyone the deep ontology implicit in Thurman's final and most philosophically ambitious manuscript, *Common Ground* (1971). Muelder recognized how, if we know where to look in Thurman's work, "there is a metaphysical foundation for an ethic of wholeness" (11) and that "the validity of the whole-making tendency in human life rests finally upon empirical sanction" (1971, 78). Thurman's point here is perhaps more psychological than theological, but there are also philosophical implications to this aspect of Thurman's personalism.

Thurman wrote that a person's "horizon may become so completely dominated by the intense character of his [or her] hatred that there remains no creative residue in his [or her] mind and spirt to give to great ideas, to great concepts. He [or she] becomes lopsided. To use a phrase from Zarathustra, he [or she] becomes 'a cripple in reverse'" (1996, 88). For Thurman, hatred constitutes one of "the hounds of hell that dog the footsteps of the disinherited in season and out of season" (1996, 74). Hatred and deception, suggests Thurman, which arise within a climate of fear or in an environment devoid of care and mutual concern, more or less as a survival mechanism, constitute but two among the many ways of destroying the integrity of the personality or—as Thurman put it, drawing on an aphorism from Nietzsche—"crippling a person in reverse." Even if we already suspect that Thurman and King will prescribe the love-ethic as "an antidote" to fear and hopelessness as well as to self-hatred and self-deception, as "the solution to every problem" (1991, 526), as King turned it, individually and collectively, Thurman was convinced as a therapist that we needed a deeper understanding of the anatomy of fear and hatred or deception as well as of the sources of desperation or nihilism and selfishness or sheer belligerence. Commenting on this complex "interplay of the moral laws of the personality and of community" in Thurman, Muelder suggests that "the future may well belong to that power" that—articulating Thurman's communitarian personalism all at once—"makes available to all its citizens freedom of access to a social ecology in which persons not only have authentic sense of belonging, but in which they have a reasonable hope to actualize their potential, thereby experiencing community within themselves as part and parcel of the experience of community and state" (1982, 12; see also Thurman, 1971, 87–88).

Muelder also stresses that in Thurman, as elsewhere, "the dialectical arrow flies not only from a community of persons but also from the private person to the social whole" and that "the realm of the ethical is personal and private, but never exclusively so" (1982, 11–12). In this respect, Thurman probably subscribed to L. Harold DeWolf's principles of community as articulated in *Responsible Freedom*, which was published in the same year as Thurman's *Common Ground*. DeWolf's later formulation in which he distinguished three basic laws is the most concise: the principle of cooperation (that is, that "every person ought, when possible, to cooperate with others in the production and enjoyment of shared values"), the principle of social devotion (that is, "every person ought to devote himself to serving the best interests of the group and to subordinate personal gain to social gain"), and the principle of the ideal of community (that is, "every person ought to form all of his ideals and values in loyalty to his ideal of what the whole community ought to become; and when possible to participate responsibly in groups to help them similarly form and choose all their ideals and values") (1971, 166–71).

Conclusion

Thurman has been undervalued as philosophical and religious resource for King and the civil rights movement, but I also believe he is undervalued as a resource for the movement going forward into the twenty-first century. Thurman's personalist vocation and prophetic spirituality emerged in the sociohistorical and existential context of a man who understood all-too-well that "a man and his black skin must face the timeless issues of the human spirit' together" (1979, 60); for Thurman, addressing questions of social justice were integral to the life of the spirit. And perhaps it would be correct to say that Thurman's life and thought, not unlike the life and thought of King, display an "intense loyalty to the essence of the personalist tradition" (Baldwin 2011, 2). Perhaps one could go so far as to characterize Thurman's philosophical theology, in ways analogous to King, as profoundly personalistic. It is tempting to think of Thurman as an African American Muelder in his theological or philosophical orientation, although his thought also harkens back to Emerson, at least in terms of his implicit gnosticism and his conception of freedom as self-enlargement, though creatively embellished and applied to a different and more pernicious type of double-consciousness but amending Emerson's "nothing sweeter than the sound of the next larger circle being drawn" with Thurman's metaphor of the growing edge: "All around us worlds are dying and new worlds are being born; all around us life is dying and life is being born. The birth of the child—life's most dramatic answer to death—this is the growing edge incarnate. Look well to the growing edge" (1956, 180). But it is important for us to recognize that personalism has often carried with it a small set of metaphysical commitments: personalism is at once, at least from the inside, an ethical theory and cosmology as well as an epistemological orientation. Philosophical personalism would seem to provide the best framework for describing what Thurman has in mind here, but it also serves as a prism through which to explore the scope and subtlety of philosophical enterprise.

5

Reading Thurman as a Social Activist Mystic

Perhaps there is no word in our language that has been as completely misunderstood and as freely interpreted with unintelligent sympathy as "mysticism."

Thurman, "Mysticism and Social Change," 1939

Although hesitant to claim that Thurman is wrongly categorized as a mystic, which is how most people classify him, I think it is misleading to suggest that Thurman was a mystic without important qualifications or without providing the context of his unique form of mysticism. Classifying Thurman as a mystic has also obscured alternative interpretations of Thurman's intellectual vocation. Thurman was most certainly one of those "seekers," as Rufus Jones called them, "who are keen and eager for fresh truth and new light on mysticism" (1931, x). In the absence of historical context, mysticism as a term of general classification merely generates confusion. William James wrote that "mysticism" was merely "used as a term of reproach to throw at any opinion which we regard as vague and vast and sentimental and without a base in either facts or logic" (1987, 342). In 1960, Thurman suggested that there was "a medley of confusion as to the meaning of mysticism" (1973, 5). When studying Thurman's mysticism, I have tried to focus more on the quality of the experience described by Thurman than on the question of how best to label it. Still, it matters how we go about classifying individuals and labeling patterns as well as defining concepts and categorizing experiences. And while I want to understand what Thurman meant by mysticism, and how Thurman's mysticism fits within the larger topology of mysticism, I am especially keen to explore what Pollard calls "Thurman's radical understanding of mysticism as personally transforming and socially transformative" (1992, 2). We can build on the work of Luther Smith and Alton Pollard to explore the most prominent concepts, images, symbols, and values that shaped or otherwise determined Thurman's own mystical experience and his interpretation of mysticism.

According to some of those who participated in the civil rights movement, it was sometimes said of Thurman, derogatorily, as early as the 1940s, that "we thought that we had found our Moses, but alas, he turned out to be a mystic instead" (Harding 2010a). Because his thought cuts across conventional boundaries of form and content, Thurman is admittedly difficult to classify: Philosophers tend to dismiss Thurman as a religious mystic, or a theologian, as though that places him outside the scope of philosophical analysis; conversely, many Christian theologians tend to dismiss Thurman as a philosopher, maybe even a pantheist, and as someone inappropriately preoccupied with science and worldly utopian literature. (For some, Thurman's writings are dismissed as too Christian in their orientation; by others, he is insufficiently Christian to merit sustained attention.) Thurman's writings—similar to King's—could be seen as insufficiently scholarly or inappropriately fixated on the social issues of his day. Although many in the black church are eager to claim him as one of their own, Thurman's theology was and perhaps continues to be unsettling to evangelical Christians who study him carefully. The ambivalent compromise has been to venerate Thurman—perhaps like King—from afar, that is, drawing on him for inspiration or pressing him into service for their causes without subjecting him to in-depth or systematic analysis; in this, however, we have done Thurman an injustice. Thurman's mysticism should be understood as both the center and the circumference of his philosophy of religion if not also the metaphysical foundation to his social ethics.

Beyond the Traditional Topologies of Mysticism

Although he was "self-conscious in using the term mysticism," Thurman came to realize rather early on that "that term [mysticism] was just a term," and "the important thing about it was the quality of the experience" (2015, 3). Pollard argues quite convincingly that Thurman's reflections on mysticism "convey a logic of their own that is at once powerfully creative and strikingly consistent" (1992, 56). Mozella Mitchell makes a similar point: "The ideas of [Thurman's] earlier books are fitted into a kind of system that was in the making all along" (1982, 32). Thurman wrote that his "reflections on mystical experiences were reflections after the fact, dealing with meaningful dimensions of the raw materials of my experience with being able to designate them in any particular category" (2015, 4–5); elsewhere he claimed that the term or label of mysticism came into his life "long after the experience." Indeed, Thurman says that his formal study of "mysticism and its categories and so forth and so on" (2015, 3), which began in earnest during his work with Rufus Jones in Haverford in 1929 (although he was already reading about the mystics from Meister Eckhart and Jakob Boehme to Olive Schreiner during his studies in Rochester), distracted him from his "own inner familiar alter." According to Pollard, "Thurman was reluctant to make too much of distinctions in such subtle matters as religion and mystical experience because of the potential for reifying categories that, in the final analysis, may be artificial" (1992, 56–57). Thurman was well versed in the traditional topologies of mysticism (for example, William James's traits of ineffability, noetic insight, transiency, and passivity), but he was also conversant with classification matrices in Evelyn Underhill, Rufus Jones, Mary Ann Ewer, Charles Bennett, Thomas Hywel Hughes, and Rudolf Otto. In many ways, Thurman's descriptions of mystical experience extend well beyond the traditional Jamesian topology (see Katz 1989, 752). Luther Smith draws on other topologies, including Douglas C. Macintosh and Walter Stace, to classify Thurman's type of mysticism.[1]

Thurman's discussion of mysticism should be understood within the context of his more general definition of religious experience: "The religious experience is defined as a dynamic encounter between man and God through the experience of prayer and human suffering. All of this has to do with the inwardness of religion. The outwardness of religion is examined in terms of the impact of the religious experience itself on the individual nervous system, thus altering ingrained behavior patterns as the new life takes hold and spreads its influence through all of living" (1979, 226–27). In mystical experience, as a subspecies of religious experience, claimed Thurman, "the individual is seen as being exposed to direct knowledge of ultimate meaning, *ne plus ultra* being, in which all that the individual is becomes clear as immediate and often distinct revelation" ([1954] 1972, 24). The quality of Thurman's religious experience, whether it is called mystical or not, was by all accounts quite contagious. Both early and late, Thurman thought of mysticism as including "the response of the individual to a personal encounter with God within their own spirit. Such a response is total, affecting the inner quality of the life and its outward expression and manifestation" (1970, 6; [1954] 1972, 20). The oscillation that Thurman describes between the *inwardness* and the *outwardness* of religious experience, whether centripetal or centrifugal, alternating rhythmically, constitutes the heartbeat of his social activist mysticism. Thurman defines mystical experience as "the conscious and direct exposure of the individual to God. Such an exposure seems to the individual to be inclusive of all the meaning of his [or her] life—*there is nothing that is not involved*" (1972, 20; my italics). In his "Mysticism and the Experience of Love," Thurman defined mysticism "as the response of the individual to a personal encounter with God within his or her own spirit" (1961, 6). Thurman suggests that "such a response is total, affecting the inner quality of life and its outward expression and manifestation" (1961, 6). In this respect, Thurman is reminiscent of Kierkegaard: "The operative principle informing appropriation is that, where a relationship with God is concerned, knowing entails doing, a doing in response to God's call. For Kierkegaard, your response to that call matters more than anything else in life" (Barrett and Stewart 2010, 244).

Similar to Thurman, but sixty years later, Leigh Eric Schmidt suggests that "there is hardly a more beleaguered category than 'mysticism' in the current academic study of religion" (2003, 273). The surface similarity between Thurman in 1939 and Schmidt in 2003 betrays vast changes within the academic study of religion. The study of mysticism, both in terms of the methods used and the information available, has blossomed over the past century. William James and Evelyn Underhill as well as Rufus Jones constituted the cutting edge of religious studies at the time that Thurman began studying the mystics. Jones once claimed to be living in an age distinguished by "a profound interest in mysticism" as opposed to "a distinct revival of mysticism itself" (1915, 156). Perhaps the same could be said of our own times. In ways that he could not have anticipated one hundred years ago, we could say with Jones—as quoted in Schmidt—that while the earlier revivals were "led by 'luminous mystics' and 'first-hand prophets of mystical religion,' this one was led by secondhand historians and psychologists, self-confessed (if reluctant) outsiders like William James" (2003, 294). But when it comes to contemporary research on mysticism, most scholars agree with Jess Byron Hollenback that "both Underhill's and James's studies of mysticism suffer from ethnocentricity and a lack of comparative breadth" (1996, 3).[2] Other scholars have summarily dismissed mysticism as "a false category" and "an essentialist illusion" (Penner 1983, 89; see also Katz 1978; Jantzen 1995). So while it may be true, as William James suggests, that mystical experiences are the "mother sea and foundation head of all religions" (1985, 434), recent scholars of religion are keen to demonstrate that it is a serious mistake to treat "all mystical experiences are the same or that such experiences are contextually undetermined or under-determined" (Katz 1978, 46). On the contrary, the contemporary consensus is that "mystical experience is 'over-determined' by its socio-religious milieu: as a result of his process of intellectual acculturation in its broadest sense, the mystic brings to his experience a world of concepts, images, symbols, and values which shape as well as color the experience he eventually and actually has" (Katz 1978, 46).

The first misunderstanding of earlier analyses of mysticism, according to recent critiques, one prominent among those who worked on mysticism during Thurman's lifetime, is the essentialist fallacy—that is, the idea that mysticism is "hardly altered by differences of clime or creed" (James 1985, 419). Mysticism is never essentially this or that, argue cultural historians of religion, but rather "a constantly shifting social and historical construction" (Jantzen 1995, 24).[3] The editors of *The Papers of Howard Washington Thurman* concede that Thurman's "essentialist rendering of self, God, and history, however, becomes problematic when tested against postmodernist readings" (2012, xxi). Schmidt observes that past postmodern scholars of mysticism are beginning to experience "the reverse of nostalgia for Enlightenment skepticism" (2003, 293):

> Leaning too heavily on recent critiques may only do historians more harm than good, for it effectively diverts attention from existential intensity of the liberal religious worlds that invested so much in mysticism. The construct mattered to its Jamesian devotees because of the despair it potentially assuaged, the questions of meaning it hoped to answer, the divided selves it tried to make whole, and the epiphanies it occasionally wrought. It requires neither protectiveness nor nostalgia to insist that the crises in belief and personal identity that haunted James and his wider circle deserve intensive historical engagement. (2003, 294)

Alternatively, and drawing on Rufus Jones, Schmidt says that mysticism marks "an emptied space of longing for 'a heightened, intensified way of life,' a search for an 'undivided whole of experience' in an increasingly fragmented world of serialized and alienated selves" (2003, 294). Thurman was for various reasons less susceptible to this alleged essentialist fallacy than many of his contemporaries. But perhaps we concede too much. Even James was circumspect in his generalizations: "As there appears to be no one elementary religious emotion, but only a common storehouse of emotions upon which religious objects may draw, so there might conceivably also prove to be no one specific and essential kind of religious object, and no one specific and essential kind of religious act" (1985, 30–31). Thurman insisted that "creative encounters" or mystical experiences "must somehow be achieved in a framework of experiences native to his own life which his life 'for instances' in a rich variety of details" ([1939] 2012, 213). For Thurman, not unlike Jones, all experiences are produced within "a social and intellectual environment"; indeed, in mystical experience, thought Thurman, "there is nothing that is not involved" (1919, xxxiv).

Thurman argues that "the mystics sense of union with God is the ground of the creative synthesis which he achieves in his experience" (1970, 23). The mystic "finds that the two worlds must in some sense be one because he participates actively in both at the same moment but he is convinced that the meaning of the below is in the above" (29). Thurman argues against a similar misnomer that mysticism is life denying: Although the spiritual disciplines often involve a "retreat within, to disentangle his life from those things that make for fragmentation, divisiveness, and attachment" (1961, 7), although ascetic practices involve "self-denial, even of self-annihilation, or of utter and complete absorption in the experience of union with God" (7), the movement is to be understood as an alternating two-stage process that is ultimately and "in its most profound sense life affirming" (11). "Thurman's primary identity was that of mystic," says Luther Smith, but he "was a mystic who recognized the necessity of social activism for enabling and responding to religious experience" (Smith 2007, 15). Muelder wrote with usual concision that "Thurman's social ethics begins and ends in religious experience" (1982, 7). As early as 1939, in his essay on "Mysticism and Social Change," Thurman follows Jones in noting the mission of "affirmation mystics to apply to those who are concerned with working out in a social frame of reference the realism of their mystic experience." He says that the mystic is always more than any finite task declares, and "yet he accepts this task because he has discovered that only through the finite is the Infinite to be found" (2012, 213).

We can safely say of Thurman what Barnard says of James, namely, that mystical experiences extend beyond "systems of logically concatenated adjectives" and they were "more than simply an amalgam of physiological, psychological, and sociological factors" (1997, 133); instead, they open windows into "unseen worlds." Although Thurman typically cited Jones's 1919 definition of mysticism, namely, "the type of religion which puts the emphasis on the immediate awareness of a relationship with God" (Jones 1919, xv; Thurman 1961, 6), Jones's later definitions resonate with James's characterization of mystics as individuals with special organs of perception into unseen worlds: "The mystic, as I was saying, carries his range of acquaintance a little further than the common sense-experiencer does, through his increase of range does not make the situation any more mysterious than it already was in the field of sense" (Jones 1930, 16). Thurman suggests that "the mystic experiences [constitute] unity—not identity" (1970, 24). Although this experience of unity "penetrates through all the levels of consciousness," claims Thurman, and this corresponds to James's topology, it cannot be maintained "over long-time intervals." The memory of these events or encounters, even when aided by symbolism, "fades away even though it leaves a deposit in the personality" (24). Thurman also thought it was a common misunderstanding of mysticism to think that encounters with divinity were reserved for gurus or saints. That said, it should be noted that Jones wrote extensively on "mysticism for everyone" and the need for its democratization. The insight of the mystic anticipates the hunger of every heart for "deliverance from things that divide, which bind and render us impotent and purposeless" (28) and for the discovery of "some controlling purpose for our lives" and "a way to live with dignity and courage in our world" (28). Indeed, Thurman believed that mystical experiences "may be a common experience for everyone" (1978, 4). Thurman was also fond of Sheldon Cheney's 1945 *Men Who Have Walked with God.*

Brightman's Four Questions

When it comes to the writings of mystics, wrote Walter Muelder, Thurman's colleague and King's professor at Boston University, Edgar Sheffield Brightman dispelled vagueness and confusion by posing four questions: "(a) what was the preparation for the experience? (b) how was the experience described? (c) what was the mystic's interpretation of the experience? And (d) what were the practical fruits?" (1982, 7–8). The following paragraphs explore these questions.

Thurman explores a wide array of spiritual disciplines, from meditation and asceticism to social activism, as means of preparation for creative encounters and mystical experiences: for example, "the basic consideration [of social activism] has to do with the removal of all that prevents God from coming to himself in the life of the individual" (1978, 5–6). Thurman argued in 1970 that as the glow of mystical experience is dimmed, "discipline of some sort becomes necessary and inevitable" (24). One discovers "the fact that deep within the structure of his own personality and life are the things which obscure and blot out his vision" (24). The ascetic or disciplinary practices, what Thurman sometimes calls the "psychopathology of the mystics," demonstrate a recognition among mystics "of the reality of evil and the profound conviction that it can be overcome" (1978, 9). So while Thurman knows that mystical experience has involved elaborate modes of preparation, some inspiring and some bewildering, any number of things may "place the individual in candidacy for spiritual awareness and insight" (1963, 9). In "Mysticism and the Experience of Love" (1961), Thurman discusses spiritual exercises of sundry sorts that "are meant to 'ready' the spirit for an awareness of the Presence of God dwelling in the core of the individual's being. . . . The insistence is not so much that something invade the life of man from without but rather that, through quietness and inner solitariness, the individual becomes conscious of what is there all the time" (1961, 7). Thurman uses the analogy of an underground river (1961, 8). Quoting Charles Bennett, but thinking back to Gandhi, Thurman stresses that "the mystic insight is not to be won without a certain preparation of the will, above all the moral will" (Thurman 1961, 8; Bennett 1923, 72).

How was the experience described? Similar to Olive Schreiner and to Albert Schweitzer, Thurman possessed throughout his life, even as a small child an "instinctual sense of the unity of life" (1979, 225; also see Mitchell 1985, 29–30).[4]

> As a boy in Florida, I walked along the beach of the Atlantic in the quiet stillness that can only be completely felt when the murmur of the ocean is stilled, and the tides move stealthily along the shore. I held my breath

> against the night and watched the stars etch their brightness on the face of the darkened canopy of the heavens. I have the sense that all things, the sand, the sea, the stars, the night, and I were one lung through which all of life breathed. Not only was I aware of a vast rhythm enveloping all, but I was a part of it and it was a part of me (1979, 225–26).

It was only after reading Schreiner, Thurman recalls in his autobiography, that he "was able to establish sufficient psychological distance between me and the totality of such experiences to make the experience itself an object of thought" (1979, 226; 1973, xxviii). In "Mysticism and the Experience of Love," Thurman wrote: "The mystic cannot escape the necessity for giving some kind of 'data content' to his experience. How he speaks of this content reflects the religious, cultural, and social heritage in which he finds meaning and in which he is rooted" ([1961] 1973, 9). As part of his 1934 "Review of Mary Anita Ewer, *A Survey of Mystical Symbolism,*" Thurman wrote: "Much of the confusion as to the meaning of mysticism is due to the fact that the language of the mystic is itself very often shrouded in much that is vague and misleading. The reality of the mystic's experience is much more clear cut to the mystic than the symbolism he employs in communication" (2009, 203). Thurman emphasizes Ewer's "methods of symbolic expression" that progress developmentally from analogies "between simple sensory experience and a spiritual experience" or "a physical process to a spiritual process" to attempting to "express the relationship of the human soul to God in terms of some familiar physical or human relationship" (2009, 203).

Thurman thought that the primary religious experience was always denser than the subsequent description or conceptualization was able to express. Steven Katz is useful as a corrective to Walter Stace on the function of language within mysticism:

> By assuming the distinction between subjectivity and objectivity and trying to locate the mystical reality in one or the other realm on the basis of a descriptive function of mystical language, Stace has undercut his analysis of the trans-subjective reality affirmed by the mystic. An alternative way to understand the function of language . . . is to analyze their effort either to reinforce or to avoid the attachment to terms, common assumptions about the descriptive function of concepts, or habitual expectations regarding the attributes about a class of things (1978, 153).

As early as 1934, Thurman claimed that "it is a very precarious business to attempt to get behind the thought forms and imagery with which any experience cloths itself" (2009, 204). Similarly, in *Deep River* (1945), which explored "the ground of hope and self-respect in the idiom of the Spirituals" (1945, 6), something he initially developed as a series of chapel addresses for students at Morehouse and Spelman in 1929–30, Thurman claimed: "The living context of experience is always richer than the articulation of experience. This is one of the reasons why the language of any people is rich in meaning and overtone. Again and again mankind tries to put into words and symbols the meaning of the experience that can never quite be implied by any words or symbols, however great and strategic such words and symbols may be" (1975, 83). Thurman sometimes quoted Augustine when describing the inwardness of his religious experience: "After saying all that, what have we said, my God, my life, my holy sweetness? What does anyone who speaks of you really say? Yet woe betide those who fail to speak, while the chatterboxes go on saying nothing" (1997, 41).

Thurman thought that attempts to "establish empirical verification of [one's] experience, if by empirical verification we mean a body of separate evidence" (1961, 10), often detract attention away from the pragmatic meaning of one's "response of the individual to a personal encounter with God within [one's] own spirit" (1961, 6). It seems that something important is still to be gained by rehearsing Thurman's varied definitions and efforts to express the insight to be gleaned from mystical experience. Robert Richardson claims that Friedrich Schleiermacher "insisted that no religious experience was complete until it was communicated to another person" (2006, 393). As an example of how the mystic interprets his or her experience, Thurman says that "certain experiences entail specific cosmological insights" (1961, 9).

Thurman claims that

> the mystic's concern with the imperative of social action is not merely to improve the condition of society. It is not merely to feed the hungry, not merely to relieve human suffering and human misery. If this was all, in and of itself, it would be important surely. But this is not all. The basic consideration has to do with the removal of all that prevents God from coming to himself in the life of the individual. Whatever there is that blocks this, calls for action. (1978, 23)

Muelder claims that Thurman's ethics is metaphysically grounded in an ultimate event, involving the nature of personality and the being of reality" (1982, 7). Muelder elaborates: "Metaphysical grounding indicates more than first principles. Its source and fruition is religious experience" (1982, 8).

Thurman provides a case in point:

> For instance, if central to [the mystic's] experience is the recognition of God as being the Creator of life and existence, then God must, in a very definite

> manner, stand over against creation. God is the subject and all existences of whatever form are predicates. What then is the relationship between God and his creatures? [God] cannot be wholly transcendent because this would not satisfy the demands of the mystic's experience, which is a personal response to God. Here we are face to face with what is claimed to be a form of personal communion between two principals, man and God. This means that either the soul of man must be regarded as a very part of God or else some other means must be devised to make authentic communication in the mystic sense between man and God possible. The mystic claims that some connection does take place (1961, 9–10).

Thurman quotes approvingly Charles Bennett's maxim that the "truth was not to be won by violence" (1923, 72; Thurman 1961, 9). The practical fruits of Thurman's mystical experience were twofold: "On the one hand, the debilitating effects of racial discrimination were transcended. On the other hand, self-centeredness was transformed to God-centeredness" (Pollard 1992, 36). William James put it this way in his *Varieties of Religious Experience:* "There is a state of mind known to religious men, but to no others, in which the will to assert ourselves and hold our own has been displaced by a willingness to close our mouths and be as nothing in the floods and waterspouts of God" (1985, 46; also see Richardson 2006, 394). Luther Smith cites Segundo Galilea, who, in "Liberation as an Encounter with Politics and Contemplation," claims that "authentic contemplation, through the encounter with the absolute of God, leads to the absolute of one's neighbor" (Smith 2007, 17).

Radical Theories of Personal and Societal Transformation

Beyond the traditional topologies of mysticism is what Hollenback calls "a common but largely ignored accompaniment of recollective practice and mystical experience," namely, the metamorphosis or radical empowerment (*enthymemis*) of the imagination (1996, 196–97). Thurman's prayers or meditations illustrate this ancient recollective practice. In Mozella Mitchell's initial essay on the topic, "'The Shaman's Doorway': Technique of Myth and Ritual in Thurman," she observes that "Thurman shares much in common with the shaman of archaic societies" (1982, 28; also see 1985, 88). Mitchell argues that Thurman "consciously appropriated techniques of the shamanistic tradition" as a means of healing communities and addressing the "hunger of the human spirit." Mitchell explains: "This hunger [Thurman] sees as having to do with the quest for wholeness, conversion, commitment, and community. To execute this task he cultivates the shaman's ability to participate in the sacred more completely and fully than others and to communicate that experience to others or even lead others into such a participation. The result of the venture both ways is healing" (1982, 29).

Thurman understood the hunger of the heart. "The psychosocial function of the shaman," says Stephen Larson, and Mitchell takes this as applicable at least analogously to Thurman, consisted in "awakening the awareness of the sacred in members of the community" and "renew contact between the mythic and the human worlds" (1998, 11).[5] "In the shamanic role as community healer," says Mitchell, "Thurman here [in his 1971 *Search for Common Ground*] more systematically than elsewhere assumes an 'essential role in defense of the psychic integrity of the community'" (1982, 32). Thurman exercised his powers of stretching his mythic imagination to induce, in his sermons and his writings, in himself but also in others, "an alternative mode of consciousness" and a "sacred mode of comprehension" (Mitchell 1982, 12).

The shaman on this model provides "a gateway that lures man from his waking, three-dimensional consciousness to a contemplation of what has been called the *mysterium tremendum et fascinans,* the universe seen in its sacred aspect" (Larson 1998, 30; also see Mitchell 1985, 80). Recall James's suggestion that "Our normal waking consciousness, rational consciousness as we call it, is but one special type of consciousness, whilst all about it, parted from it by the flimsiest of screens, there lie potential forms of consciousness entirely different. We may go through life without suspecting their existence; but apply the requisite stimulus, and at a touch they are there" (James 1985, 388). Thurman used ritual and mythic consciousness as a guide and a measure. Mitchell finds parallels between "the healing, ecstatic nature of these rituals" and African religious functions; she claims that Thurman "uses myth to measure his experience and finds that experience in turn must be the measure of the myth" (1985, 86). In this sense, exercising our mythic imagination leads to political resistance: "These modes of valuation and resistance are rooted in subversive memory—the best of one's past without romantic nostalgia—and guided by a universal ethic of love" (Cornel West 2001, 19).

In *Disciplines of the Spirit,* Thurman describes the "disciplined use of the imagination" as the singular means by which to increase our "sympathetic understanding" of another person.

> The imagination shows its greatest powers as the angelos of God in the miracle it creates when one man, standing on his own ground, is able while there to put himself in another man's place. To send his imagination forth to establish a point of focus in another man's spirit, and from that vantage point so to blend with the other's landscape that what he sees and feels is authentic—this is the great adventure in human relations. Yet this is not enough. The imagination must report its findings accurately, without regard

> for all previous prejudgments and private or collective fears. And even this is not enough. There must be both a spontaneous and a deliberate response to such knowledge which will result in the sharing of resources at their deepest level (1963, 125).

Although Thurman may not have become a shaman "in every sense of the archaic tradition," Mitchell says "the use of the word in reference to him may be considered analogical" (1982, 28). Hollenback believes "the supernormal phenomena that sometimes accompany mystical experience deepens our understanding of mysticism" (1996, 20–21). One such supernormal or paranormal phenomenon is what Hollenback denominates the "metamorphosis" or "empowerment" of the imagination, which, in ways analogous to Mitchell's description of Thurman as a "sophisticated modern-day shaman" (1985, 88), is animated by recollective if not ritualistic acts.

Along similar lines, Henry Corbin claims in *Creative Imagination in the Sufism of Ibn 'Arabi* that mystical imagination has "a noetic value" and serves as "an organ of knowledge" (1969, 180). This fits nicely with Rufus Jones's claim that "the word mystic stands for a person who insists on a somewhat wider range of first-hand acquaintance with reality or of direct experience than that which is confined to the operation of the five or more special senses" (1930, 15). Hollenback describes a broad spectrum of recollective practices or techniques by which to quiet the mind and awaken latent paranormal sensitivities, many of them reminiscent of the shamanistic methods described by Mozella Mitchell. Whether active or passive in their approach, the practitioner involved in the recollective practice must possess "a peculiar kind of empathetic identification with the images and emotional states that come into his awareness." The role of the modern-day shaman as described by Mitchell overlaps in interesting ways with what others have called "the prophetic ministry" (Brueggemann 1979; Smith 2007). At other times, however, Thurman ministry harks back to the more archaic function of relieving the pain and suffering of those who are ailing:

> Sometimes there is a moment of complete and utter identity with the pain of a loved one—all the intensity and anguish is felt. One enters through a single door of suffering into the misery of the whole human race with no margin left to mark the place which is one's own. What is felt belongs nowhere but is everywhere binding and holding in a title circle of agony until all of life is gathered into a single timeless gasp. (1961, 51)

The "sophisticated modern-day shaman" nurtures and conveys a sense of mystery and enlarged perception but also experiences of reconciliation and spiritual alertness: these things, thought James, "may determine attitudes though they cannot provide formulas, and open a region though they fail to give a map" (1985, 307–8).

Similar to Kierkegaard, Thurman "takes delight in leading his readers along a path, only to arrive at an unexpected junction where he suddenly leaves them to make a decision about a set of events" (Oden 1978, xi). Since, for Kierkegaard, "the truth exists only in the process of becoming, in the process of appropriation," then the communication of truth must be indirect, unlike the "objective presentation of data or information." Such indirect communication requires what Kierkegaard calls "double reflection," because indirect communication presents alternative possibilities, an "either/or" decision in the "appropriation process," where human beings grasp their own human possibilities. "If anyone is to profit by this sort of communication," Kierkegaard wrote, "he must himself undo the knot for himself" ([1850] 2004, 117–118):

> Each man himself, as an individual, should render his account to God. No third person dares venture to intrude upon this accounting between God and the individual. Yet the talk, by putting the question, dares and ought to dare, to remind man, in a way never to be forgotten, that the most ruinous evasion of all is to be hidden in the crowd in an attempt to escape God's supervision of him as an individual, in an attempt to hear God's voice as an individual. ([1850] 2004, 118)

What Kierkegaard is saying about parables could be applied also to Thurman's techniques of recollective empowerment and indirect communication.

"Mysticism in the modern age," argues Grace Jantzen, "became a way of keeping politics, materiality, embodiment, power relations, and social ethics off the scholarly table" (1995, 274). This depoliticization of religious experience may be considered by some to be a relative gain since it would appear to cut through seemingly minor differences that separate us and draw us into a shared core of experience. But in case after case, and using Thurman as a case in point, mystical experience has had profound and radical if not subversive consequences for each of these: that is, "politics, materiality, embodiment, power relations, and social ethics" (Jantzen, 274). Schmidt says that this depoliticization thesis doesn't hold up: "Time and again, social gospel Protestants were adamant about the inseparability of mysticism and political activism, religious experience and arduous saintliness, contemplation and efficiency, prayers and pickets" (2003, 293).

In *Luminous Darkness,* Thurman wrote, "A strange necessity has been laid upon me to devote my life to the central concern that transcends the walls that divide and would achieve in literal fact what is experienced as literal truth: human life is one and all men are members of one another. And this insight is spiritual, and it is the hard core of religious experience" (1965, x). Charles C. Everett wrote that mysticism refers to "the fact that all lives, however distinct they may appear, however varied may be their conditions and their ends, are at heart one" (Quoted in Schmidt 2012, 55). Abraham Heschel describes the importance of divine encounters—of "being taken up into the heart of the divine pathos"—to the prophetic ministry (Heschel 1962, 26; also see Brueggemann 1978). "The makers of the new mysticism," explains Schmidt, "were enabled as well to negotiate the intensification of religious diversity and to see it not as a threat to the solidity of Christian identity but as an opportunity for self-exploration and cross-cultural understanding" (2003, 289).

Mozella Mitchell claims that the "concept of conversion was the dynamic force of Howard Thurman's life" (1985, 174). Thurman's centripetal movement or inward journey recoils or unfolds into a centrifugal force that animates and sustains social change. Luther Smith suggested early on that Thurman "was a mystic who recognized the necessity of social activism for enabling and responding to religious experience" (2007, 15). As a supporting text, Smith cites Thurman's earlier statement (see p. 97). Thurman believed, claims Albert Raboteau, "that true social change must be grounded in spiritual experience and personal transformation" (2001, 158). Similarly, Luther Smith describes the significance of personal transformation to social change in this way: "Thurman's prophetic mysticism stresses the formation of community through a liberation process that includes inner freedom; inward liberation is not only a prerequisite for social transformation, it preserves the revolutionary sense of purpose after social transformation" (2007, 208). Moreover, the mystical vision includes a sense of community—a unity not only with God but a unity with all of life, particularly human life. In the mystical experience, Thurman believed, one discovers that "personality is something more than mere individuality—it is a fulfillment of the logic of individuality in community" (1998, 116). This brings us back to Alton Pollard's claim that Thurman maintained a "radical understanding of mysticism as personally transforming and socially transformative" (1992, 2).

William James encouraged philosophers and psychologists of religion to focus on mysticism as the wellspring of all religions. The mystics or religious geniuses that James examines "owed their power originally to the fact of the direct personal communication with the divine" (1985, 133) For James, the divine, is "not a deity *in concreto,* not a superhuman person, but the immanent divinity in things, the essentially spiritual structure of the universe" (1985, 34). James sought out the "pattern setters," that is, "individuals for whom religion exists not as a dull habit, but as an acute fever" (1985, 15).[6] For our present purposes, exploring the "dynamics of conversion" in Thurman, it is James who makes the connection between mystical experience and individual transformation.

James provides us with a "uniquely individualistic reading of mystical experience," claims Barnard (1997, 70), but he tries nevertheless to demonstrate that "mystical states of awareness have the capacity to revitalize life" and "provide standards by which a meaningful and valuable life is measured" as well as "serve the function of questioning a culture's encrusted assumptions" (1997, 73). James was interested early on in subliminal if not subconscious influences on "new birth" or "conversion" construed as the shifting of the habitual center of one's personal energy (Richardson 2006, 402): "The truth is that in the metaphysical and the religious sphere," suggests James, "articulate reasons are cogent for us only when our inarticulate feelings of reality have already been impressed in favor of the same conclusion" (1985, 73). "Freedom," writes Mitchell, "is found in conversion, for this is what conversion means in Thurman's thinking—the surrendering of the core of one's self to God, the rule of God within the person, enabling the person to achieve his or her unlimited potential" (1985, 174). Alas: "There can be no personal freedom where there is not an initial personal surrender" (Thurman 1961, 63).

Conclusion

> On his road to freedom, Frederick Douglass experiences religion as a reinforcement and justification for his desire to be free. Out of Christian doctrine, he deduces the equality of all men before God. . . . Freedom, the abolition of slavery, liberation, the destruction of alienation—these notions receive a metaphysical justification and impetus through religion.
>
> Davis ([1969] 2010)

Although it stretches the analogy, Thurman experienced religion in ways similar to Douglass: both positive and negative. As a philosopher of religion, Thurman was interested in the psychosocial role that religion played in restoring dignity to disinherited and transforming society. Religion provided a rocky road to freedom. Similar to Douglass, Thurman's enthusiasm for the institution of Christianity was dampened by the hypocrisy he detected in those who claimed to be Christian. "By some amazing but vastly creative spiritual insight," claimed Thurman, "the slave undertook the redemption of the religion that the master had profaned in his midst" (1945, 36). Like Angela Davis, Thurman understood that "religion can play both a positive and a negative role in that road to self-knowledge" in the sense that "it can thwart liberation" or "it can provide powerful assistance" (2010, 67). Unlike

Davis, Thurman believed that religion was more than "a much-needed medicine that helps to ally suffering" and at the same time provides "an inverted consciousness of the world" as a "projection of real needs and desires into [a] supernatural domain" (2010, 68). Thurman's teachings were never meant, and neither was the religion of Jesus, "merely as a defense mechanism and a substitute for action that would relieve the pressure" (1975, 63). And while Davis concurs with Marx that "one must overcome religion in order to regain one's reason," she concedes that "to a certain extent, the illusory nature of religion may well be transcended" (2010, 73) and that, on occasion, there are those who—and I believe that Thurman belongs to this religious and philosophical tradition—"turned Christianity against the missionaries" (63).

6

Reading Thurman as a Prophetic Pragmatist

To be sure, the political philosophy of W. E. B. Du Bois carries the imprint of pragmatism, and Alain Locke's theory of value and critical theory of race reflects pragmatic commitments. Both take up the pressing issues of American democracy in light of the history and political economy of white supremacy, which gives their pragmatism a timbre and tone different from that of Dewey and Rorty.

Eddie S. Glaude, *In a Shade of Blue* (2007)

In the *American Evasion of Philosophy*, Cornel West describes prophetic pragmatism as a kind of cultural criticism that has "its roots in the American heritage and its hopes for the wretched of the earth" (1989, 212). On this simple definition, Thurman was a prophetic pragmatist. But he was a prophetic pragmatist also in a broader sense that includes the utopian impulse of Emerson as well as "Dewey's conception of creative democracy and Du Bois' social structural analysis of the limits of capitalist democracy." Not altogether unlike Thurman, West's version of prophetic pragmatism is steeped in the Judeo-Christian tradition. Similar to Thurman, West wishes to emphasize the "political relevance in the biblical focus on the dispossessed" and reject the "static dogmas and decrepit doctrines" (West, 1989, 233) associated with the institution of Christianity in America. And like Thurman, West believes that the religion of Jesus provides "a rich source of existential empowerment and political engagement" (1989, 233).

If we accept West's characterization of the prophet as someone who brings an "urgent and compassionate critique to bear on the evils of their day" or who "speak the truth in love and courage" (1989, 233), then Thurman certainly displayed the propensities of a prophet. And West claims that "the social movement led by Martin Luther King, Jr., represents the best of what the political dimension of prophetic pragmatism is all about" (1989, 234). Because West construes prophetic pragmatism as a unique response to "the postmodern moment" (1989, 239), however, neither King nor Thurman qualifies, technically, as a prophetic pragmatist. It is nevertheless instructive to examine Thurman's philosophical position and political activism through the lens of prophetic pragmatism.

Although Cornel West "inserted Du Bois into the pantheon of pragmatist thinkers," says Eddie Glaude, "this insertion is much like the use of gender-specific pronouns to draw attention to feminist concerns in philosophical writing" (2007, 2). The question is more complicated than it seems: even if we can show that Du Bois and Locke or even Julia Cooper display commitments to—as Appiah puts it in his recent *Lines of Descent*—identities or labels as "nominal, normative, and subjective" (2014, 151) such that we can recognize philosophical similarities and patterns of interpersonal relationships, this is not to say that these philosophers were active participants in shaping the pragmatist tradition. On this criterion, West and Glaude are pragmatists in ways that Du Bois and Locke were not. Such a claim may be unduly optimistic since it may create the illusory impression that pragmatism has made progress in redeeming itself from what some consider to be the unforgivable.[1]

West claims that he "was grounded in and nourished by American pragmatism." He also claims that Du Bois "looks at the United States through a different lens from those of Emerson, Peirce, James, Dewey, Hook and Mills." Although Du Bois concedes that he was "blithely European and imperialist in outlook," (1989, 139), it is also true that he "allied himself in word and deed with the wretched of the earth" (1989, 138). After Fisk, Du Bois attended Harvard, where he "became a devoted follower of James at the time that he was developing his pragmatic philosophy." West believes that part of the attraction to James's thought was Du Bois's "sense of pragmatism's relevance to the Afro-American predicament" (1989, 139). Luther Smith suggests that Thurman's life "provides a modern case study of the nexus between religious experience, prophetic response, and social transformation" (2007, 197). "Prophetic pragmatism," says West, "calls for the reinvigoration of a sane, sober, and sophisticated intellectual life in America and for the regeneration of a social forces empowering the disadvantaged, degraded, and the dejected" (1989, 239).

Charles Mills says that "West's own prophetic pragmatism seeks to combine the pragmatist tradition with Black liberation theology" (2001, 198). In his preface to the 1986 edition of *A Black Theology of Liberation,* James Cone states: "Theology is not only rational discourse about ultimate reality; it is also a prophetic word about the righteousness of God that must be spoken in clear, strong, and uncompromising language" (1986, xvi). Thurman was prophetic in all aspects of his vocational ministry. Thurman felt compelled throughout his life "to act against the spirit of the times," as prophets do, but he also seemed "to anticipate a spirit which is in the making" (1959, 7). Thurman seemed to see so much further than his contemporaries.

Early and late, in causes big and small, global and local, Thurman answered the voice of conscience in word as well as in deed. He understood the courage required to speak truth to power. By the time he returned from the Pilgrimage of Friendship, in 1937, to his teaching responsibilities at Howard University, Thurman described his ministry as "an exploration of the problems that arise in the experience of people who attempt to be Christian in a society that is essentially un-Christian" (2012, xix). The "apocalyptic heritage of the black church," wrote Thurman, "left it ill-equipped to deal with either the spiritual or practical realms of existence" (2009, 121). As a religious and social critic, Thurman was capable of expressing his intense impatience with injustice and hypocrisy: "We are clothed and fed," wrote Thurman to his mentor, Mordecai Johnson, president of Howard, "by a vast system built upon deceit and adulteration" (2009, 117–18). The task of African American religious leaders, thought Thurman already in 1928, was "to encourage the cultivation of spiritual power over the demand for things, to draw practical meaning out of personal piety, and to ensure that the spirit of Jesus is not overshadowed by Christian institutions" (2009, 141). King made a similar distinction while still at Crozer Theological Seminary.

Glaude clarifies the significance of pragmatism to our present geopolitical moment and what is gained by adopting West's refinement of the pragmatist tradition:

> In this pragmatic view, then, history is understood quite differently. Not only its subject matter changes but also the role it plays in our lives. To begin with, historical actors are not seen as stable, continuous subjects. We are constantly changing because our environments are changing, for better or for worse. Any kind of stability depends upon actions chosen intelligently with the aim of securing the values we cherish. Moreover, history is not a dispassionate detailing of past facts or a mere elaboration of different points of view, history helps us by illuminating our present predicament (2007, 35).

West drew a certain amount of criticism for his appropriation of Deweyan pragmatism (see Tunstall 2008; Garrison 1997) as well as for the value of labels such as "prophetic pragmatism." Dwayne Tunstall suggests that "what most distinguishes West's prophetic pragmatism from Dewey's pragmatism (and by extension Deweyan pragmatism) is how West's pragmatism thinks that pragmatism, as a philosophic method, prescribes democratic norms for persons to follow while Deweyan pragmatism does not and how West's pragmatism roots itself in a prophetic religious tradition (i.e., prophetic Protestant Christianity) while Deweyan pragmatism does not" (2008, 112).

Others have gone further in suggesting that Dewey leads us in an oppositional direction to West's prophetic pragmatism. Deweyan pragmatism does not count as prophetic pragmatism because it does not root itself in any particular prophetic religious tradition. As a case in point, Steven C. Rockefeller notes: "[Dewey] left the church in the name of human community [and] abandoned the idea of special revelation in the name of truth and morality" (1991, 216). Cornel West has his own inimitable way of characterizing classical American pragmatism: "American pragmatism is a diverse and heterogeneous tradition. But its common denominator consists of a future-oriented instrumentalism that tries to deploy thought as a weapon to enable more effective action. Its basic impulse is a plebeian radicalism that fuels an anti-patrician rebelliousness for the moral aim of enriching individuals and expanding democracy" (1989, 5). West has also projected his preferred notion of philosophy, which regards it as the "cultural expression generated from and existentially grounded in the moods and sensibilities of a writer entrenched in the life-worlds of a people" (1982, 24).

West's views have changed, perhaps significantly, since 1989.[2] In recent years, West has resisted the characterization of his philosophic thought as a form of pragmatism, prophetic or otherwise, without serious caveats and provisos. He has occasionally characterized himself as someone who rummages through many diverse intellectual traditions, classical American philosophy among them, in the fond hope of unearthing resources that can sustain radical democracy and human possibilities for self-transcendence. This is certainly how West characterizes his relationship to American pragmatism in *Cornel West: A Critical Reader:*

> Prophetic pragmatism is a particular historicist interpretation of American pragmatism put forward after such developments as the decolonization of Third World peoples, the second wave of feminism, and the collapse of American apartheid; it is a specific historicist philosophic intervention into our postmodern moment after the rise of analytic philosophy, structuralism, deconstruction, and Western Marxism. The "prophetic" in prophetic pragmatism refers to both the Protestant sources of the philosophical movement and my own attempt to be true to the blue notes in American history (its own forms of evil and death and its wrestling with tragicomic darkness). . . . The prophetic has little or nothing to do with prediction. Instead, it has to do with identifying, analyzing, and condemning forms of evil and forging vision, hope, and courage for selves and communities to overcome them. Radical democracy is visionary *plebodicy*—the grand expression of the dignity of the *doxa* of the suffering *demos* (2001, 350–51).

West is correct to note that Deweyan pragmatism "promotes a critical intelligence that defers to no authority other than the enrichment of human experience and the alleviation of . . . human plight" (1989, 99). This interpretation of Deweyan pragmatism, says Tunstall, is "inspirational, interesting, and maybe the most suitable and worthwhile version of it in our current socio-historical milieu, but West's interpretation of Deweyan pragmatism runs contrary to how Dewey characterizes not only pragmatism, but philosophy in general" (2008, 112). Moreover: "What West does not seem to realize is that the normative stances of Deweyan pragmatism—e.g., the pursuit of a radical democracy and the cultivation of critical intelligence in its citizenry—is something that Dewey, the social activist and democrat, adds to pragmatism, the philosophic method. Said another way, Dewey's democratic sensibilities and commitments provide the normativity for Dewey's own philosophical project and for the philosophical projects of Deweyan pragmatists" (2008, 110).

Philosophy is not an autonomous discipline. It is dependent on the social institutions and cultural practices in which we engage. It is the metacriticism of our cultural and social institutions and products, including politics, art, religion, and previous philosophical projects. For Thurman, Dewey's pragmatism consists largely in his account of reflective thought in *How We Think*. Thurman took a course on reflective thinking at Columbia University in 1922, while he was still at Morehouse. Thurman described Dewey's model this way:

> It examined a basic methodological approach to problem solving in all fields of investigation, from simple decision-making to the understanding and treatment of disease and the most confused patterns of human behavior. This course ["Reflective Thinking"] established for me a basic approach that I would use not only in my subsequent work as a counselor but also in thinking through the complex and complicated problems I would encounter in my personal life and as a social being. As a tool of the mind, there is no way by which the value of this course can be measured or assessed. (1979, 44)

Thurman sets reflective thought within the context of Deweyan pragmatism. Following Dewey's model, Thurman suggests that "only in the experience of commitment is an authentic sense of self born" (1963, 26). For Dewey, "philosophy as a critical organ becomes in effect a messenger, a liaison officer, making reciprocally intelligible voices speaking provincial tongues, and thereby enlarging as well as rectifying the meanings with which they are charged" (1988, 306). "Deweyan pragmatism, by itself," again Tunstall, "cannot tell anyone how to alleviate human suffering because it is simply a philosophic method of inquiry. It can only enable us to clarify the alternative courses of action available to us in a given circumstance more effectively, to articulate a problematic situation in a larger historical context, and to render our deliberations more systematic and intelligent" (2008, 110). What Dewey stated in the revised edition of *Ethics* about moral theory applies equally to philosophy in general:

> Moral theory can (i) generalize the types of moral conflicts which arise, thus enabling a perplexed and doubtful individual to clarify his own particular problem by placing it in a larger context; it can (ii) state the leading ways in which such problems have been intellectually dealt with by those who have thought upon such matters; it can (iii) render personal reflection more systematic and enlightened, suggesting alternatives that might otherwise be overlooked, and stimulating greater consistency in judgment. But it does not offer a table of commandments in a catechism in which answers are as definite as are the questions which are asked. It can render personal choice more intelligent, but it cannot take the place of personal decision, which must be made in every case of moral perplexity (Dewey and Tufts 1932, 175–76).

Dewey's pragmatism does not have a normative thrust beyond the realm of method. It is parasitic on the normative interests of the given pragmatist and the sociocultural exigencies that the pragmatist must contend with when conducting philosophical inquiry. Dewey's normative commitment to existential democracy—that is, democracy not only as a social institution but also as a way of life—is antecedent to his allegiance to the American pragmatist tradition. His pragmatism is a conduit for his critique of the Western philosophic tradition. This strand in Dewey is echoed in Angela Davis, who, in her 1969 "Lectures on Liberation," wrote: "Philosophy is supposed to perform the task of generalizing aspects of experience, and not just for the sake of formulating generalizations, of discovering formulas, as some of my colleagues in the discipline believe. My idea of philosophy is that if it is not relevant to human problems, if it does not tell us how we can go about eradicating some of the misery in this world, then it is not worth the name of philosophy" (2010, 66).

If we accept prophetic pragmatism on a political level, then we accept the Judeo-Christian-Islamic concern and preference for "the wretched of the earth" and that this concern acquires an increased political relevance in today's age once we add to it "modern interpretations of racial and gender equality, tolerance, and democracy" (1989, 233). Assuming that one has accepted prophetic pragmatism on a political level, one would be under a binding obligation to assist those who need material, psychological, and even spiritual assistance. Moreover, one would be obligated to gear one's ameliorative actions to the specific interests and needs articulated by those in need. For that reason one would listen to the testimony and witness of those persons who are less fortunate regardless of where they live and help them acquire control over the resources they need to adequately address their respective problems and predicaments. It also would oblige one to work with one's local and regional grassroots organizations, both religious and secular, to improve the social circumstances of the less fortunate and economically disadvantaged.

Although it makes sense to read W. E. B. Du Bois and Alain Locke as African American pragmatists, explains Glaude, their willingness to "take up the pressing issues of American democracy in light of the history and political economy of white supremacy . . . gives their pragmatism a timbre and tone different from that of Dewey and Rorty" (2007, 3). Along similar lines, it is useful to think of Thurman and King as African American pragmatists. At the political level, prophetic pragmatism demands that one act on the norms of individuality and democracy that West articulates in his first published book, *Prophesy Deliverance!* (1982). These norms are ones that originate not in a secular ethos or in secular practices but out of the prophetic Protestant Christian tradition. Indeed, West derives his norm of democracy from the prophetic Christian tradition. He even separates the norm of individuality from the norm of democracy, saying that democracy is the best means of upholding the dignity owed to every human person as a creature created *imago Dei* in a fallen if not radically evil world. This only reinforces the view that the normative dimension of West's prophetic pragmatism is religious in nature and is dependent on his theological (and ontological) commitments to the prophetic Christian tradition, particularly the black prophetic Christian tradition.

In *Cornel West and the Politics of Prophetic Pragmatism,* Mark David Wood claims that "prophetic pragmatism, like other theologies of liberation, uses theological categories to represent the conflict between private control over labor and its fruits and the potential to create a society based on democratic control" (2000, 37). In *Cornel West: The Politics of Redemption,* Rosemary Cowan contends that "no matter how much West insists that he is not a liberation theologian, it is impossible to fully understand his work without grounding it in a liberationist theological perspective" (2003, 15). Cowan adds: "What West labels as non-theological 'prophetic Christianity' is simply another name for his African-American liberation theology" (15). An important aspect of this work, and one of the challenges of post-soul politics, consists in "galvanizing black constituencies to address effectively their circumstances" (Glaude 2007, 133). Whatever one calls this sort of work, whether prophetic pragmatism or African American liberation philosophy, it still needs to be done.

West is—and Thurman was—relentlessly yet lovingly engaged in the difficult work entailed by prophetic pragmatism: the dynamic project and liberatory process of prophetic pragmatism entails a broad spectrum of what Du Bois called "impossible musts." In "The Revelation of Saint Orgne the Damned," Du Bois wrote:

> In some way, as all intelligent men acknowledge, we must in the end, produce for the satisfaction of human needs and distribute in accordance with human want. To contend that this cannot be done is to face the Impossible Must. The blind cry of reaction on the one hand, which says that we cannot have a planned economy and, therefore, must not try; and the cry of blood which says that only by force can selfishness be curbed, are equally wrong. It is not a question of deliberate guilt but of selfish stupidity. (2001, 111)

One such requirement is "to do philosophy in a way that engages a world" (Hord and Lee 2016, xiv).

There is also the question of whether Thurman might serve as a prototypical representative of the African American tradition that led to prophetic pragmatism. At the very least, let it be said of Thurman what West attributes to Sojourner Truth, Walter Rauschenbusch, Elizabeth Cady Stanton, Dorothy Day, and Martin Luther King, Jr.: viz., that "like them he was a prophet, in which role he contributed mightily to the political project of prophetic pragmatism" (1989, 235). Even if the term "prophetic pragmatism" has outworn it initial purpose, there are other ways to describe or label the critical work it performs. West and Glaude, among others, insist that "pragmatism must be made to sing the blues" (Glaude 2007, 8). West wanted to do more than merely synthesize or otherwise combine the American pragmatist tradition with black liberation theology, even though black liberation theology does advocate most, if not all, of what West demands of his prophetic pragmatism. West yearns for the American pragmatist tradition to take religious sensibilities, traditions, and practices seriously as a means of advancing radical democracy and betterment for all persons. Granted, West does focus a lot of his critical attention on the social plight of urban African Americans, but his main intent is to "negate what is and transform prevailing realities against the backdrop of the present historical limits" (1982, 19–20) in such a way that more and more human persons are able to live out their existential freedom in this world and have others recognize their social freedom.

Victor Anderson argues that "both Thurman and West hold open the possibility that the apparently binary oppositions that characterize racial discourse can be transcended. But transcendence requires a cause or loyalty that is sufficiently categorical to include within itself both the cultural aspects of group life and personality. For Thurman, the dialectics of race is transcended in the idea of the beloved community. For West, radical democracy serves the function of transcendence" (1999, 49). Jim Garrison argues that poetry plays a transcendent function and "prominent place in Dewey's prophetic pragmatism" (1997, 57). Poetry, says Garrison, "in the classical sense of poiesis, or calling into existence, is about constructing, deconstructing, and reconstructing the world" (1997, 57). This explains, suggests Garrison, why Dewey thought that "the chief instrument . . . more poetry than morality" (58). And while it may be true that prophetic pragmatists are poets of a certain sort, since they "perceive beyond the limits of the actual into the possibility of unifying ideals that could heal our wounds" (58), it should also be noted that, following Santayana, "poetry is religion when it intervenes in the affairs of life, and religion, when it merely supervenes, is nothing but poetry" (1922, v). Commenting on this fine phrase from Santayana, Dewey writes: "The difference between intervening *in* and supervening *upon* is as important as is the identity set forth" (1986, 13). For Thurman, "the imagination shows its greatest powers as the angelos of God in the miracle it creates when one man, standing on his own ground, is able while there to put himself in another man's place" (1963, 125). Burrow argues in *Martin Luther King, Jr., and the Theology of Resistance* that the prophetic traditions "placed less emphasis on theories of justice, for example, than actually doing justice in the world" (2015, 6). Like the Hebrew prophets of old, the role of the prophetic pragmatist consists in transforming systems of injustice. In *Prophetic Reflections,* West describes the vocation of the intellectual as "trying to turn easy answers into critical questions and putting those critical questions to people in power" because the "quest for truth, the quest for the good, the quest for the beautiful, require us to let suffering speak" (1993, 103).

Anderson claims that both Thurman and West, "each in his own way and under different contexts displays the dual dimensions of cultural and religious criticism" (1999, 22). Anderson elaborates: "Each critic names and unmasks demonic powers that vitiate cultural fulfillment among African Americans. Each does so in the name of some transcendent cause and loyalty (beloved community or radical democracy) around which African Americans may center their hopes of cultural fulfillment" (1999, 22). This pairing seems instructive. Thurman and West "display the dual intensions (iconoclastic rigor and utopian hope) of religious criticism" (38). Anderson argues that "Thurman's philosophy exhibits pragmatic sensibilities grounded on his evolutionary theory of consciousness" and that "there is a religious pragmatism operative in his estimate of human life and actions" (40). Although it may be helpful to read Thurman as a pragmatist of a certain sort, Anderson's real insight comes in reading Thurman as a religious and social critic:

"Thurman believed that the dialectic of race and citizenship is not so total as to foreclose on the possibility of internal mediation or transcendence" (42).

Luther Smith, in his groundbreaking *Howard Thurman: The Mystic as Prophet,* thought it useful to speak of Thurman as "an American prophet." And while there are those who viewed Thurman as a prophet in the literal sense, what Smith meant by "prophet" is quite close to what West means by the term "prophetic pragmatism." Like West, Smith thinks that "prophets are products of their culture, speaking to specific traditions, problems" and whose "warning and urgings deal with particular crises of their particular age" (2007, 19). In a similar sense, Thurman portrays Jesus as bearing prophetic witness in a manner not altogether unlike the prophets of old: "It is my sense and profound conviction that [Jesus] is the great enemy of our civilization and out culture. And if his will, as he experienced it, becomes operative in our society, not a single stone will be left upon another" (1959, 7). Just as "prophetic pragmatism" was designed as a rhetorical space or sphere of discourse in response to a unique geopolitical moment such that it is an anachronistic to think of Thurman as a prophetic pragmatist, Thurman's prophetic witness must be understood within the context of what some have called the longer civil rights movement. What Thurman proclaimed, says Smith, is "that the mistreatment of the nation's disinherited and acceptance of the will to segregate are betrayals of American and Christian ideals" (2007, 19). Thurman's prophetic witness is not unrelated to West's conception of prophetic pragmatism and radical democracy. "Prophetic witness has an impact beyond particular contexts, and Thurman's thought should prove relevant wherever humanity is involved with the meaning and formation of community" (Smith 2007, 20).

Reading Thurman as an African American Liberation Philosopher

> Truth is always connected with freedom and is bestowed upon freedom only. Slavery is always the denial of truth, and the dread of truth. Love for the truth is triumph over enslaving fear.
>
> Nikolai Berdyaev (1944)

There are affinities to be found between classical American pragmatism and the prophetic aspect of the black experience of slavery and disenfranchisement in America—for example, between the sort of pragmatism or instrumentalism espoused by William James or John Dewey, which is perhaps as good as it gets within the Anglo-American philosophical tradition, and the black philosophical tradition that includes W. E. B. Du Bois and Alain Locke as well as Howard Thurman and Martin Luther King Jr. There are also vast differences. But the differences are a good place to start when reading Thurman as, *in nuce*, a prophetic pragmatist. To argue that Thurman was a philosopher, though, involves revisioning the philosophical tradition in America. Thurman belongs to a black philosophical tradition on display in Hord and Lee's *I Am Because We Are: Readings in Black Philosophy* (2016), one that stretches back to ancient Egyptian-Kemetic thought. "More than any other theologian of his time," Alonzo Johnson believes, "Thurman brought the black experience into the forefront of his theological project" (1997, 121). Thurman was convinced that "there was a truth in black religion that needed to be unfolded to the world" (123). For those with eyes to see and ears to hear, Thurman was really in lockstep with many of the thinkers that we now consider to be "liberation philosophers," including Kwame Nkrumah, Julius Nyerere, and Kwame Gyekye.[3]

For Hord and Lee, there are three seminal or "generative themes" that constitute the black philosophical tradition: "the idea that the identity of the individual is never separable from the sociocultural environment"; "a relational conception of reality" that "provides the metaphysical foundation for much of the philosophical reflection of this black philosophical tradition"; and "the central importance of religion and religion-based ethics as dominant forms for the fundamentally social expression of core philosophical ideas" (2016, 17). Hord and Lee "do not intend these generative themes to serve as reductionist specifications of the 'essence' of black philosophy; [they] recognize in them, rather, the seeds from which an astonishing number of different gardens have grown" (2016, 15). Thurman is one such garden. Thurman belonged to what Hord and Lee describe as "a tradition of doing philosophy that engages the world in order to change it" and a "conception of philosophical activity as essentially a matter of building bridges between diverse cultures and individuals, between individuals and their multiple communities" (2016, 16). Hord and Lee are cognizant of Appiah's concern, expressed in *My Father's House,* that to identify "a philosophical tradition in terms of race runs the double risk of tying this tradition to false theories of race and of homogenizing the remarkable variety of beliefs, attitudes, and values characteristic of thinkers of African descent" (1995, 2; see also Appiah 1993, 3–46).

As discussed in the previous chapters on personalism, Thurman was convinced that the development of the personality was an intrapersonal as well as an interpersonal accomplishment. Thurman sometimes suggested that the ancient meaning of know thyself was to know thy brother, writing: "It is not unreasonable, then, to assume that as he seeks community within himself, with his fellows, and with his world, he may find that what he is seeking to do deliberately is but the logic of the meaning of all that has gone into his own creation" (1971, 41). The black philosophical tradition tends to emphasize "a relational conception of reality" that "provides the metaphysical foundation for much of the philosophical reflection of this black philosophical tradition" (2016, 16). In *Search for Common Ground,* in the context of his analysis of the "structure-functional integrity" of living organisms, Thurman explains: "In the whole panorama of the external world of nature, there seems to be a pattern of structural dependency and continuity, or what may be called an inner logic, which manifests itself in forms, organizational schemes, and in a wide variety of time-space arrangements" (1971, 5). Thurman was convinced that "the intent [of life] is for integration, for wholeness, for community within the limits of the organism itself" (1971, 39). "For many," notes Eddie Glaude, "invocations of the black freedom movement and its exemplars situate our efforts in a tradition of struggle and sacrifice. That traditions, to the extent that the trope of the black freedom movement carries with it a certain conception of character, also encourages to act justly toward our fellows as we struggle for a more inclusive democracy" (2007, 133). Thurman is an exemplar of the black freedom movement.

The black philosophical tradition, suggest Hord and Lee, stresses "the central importance of religion and religion-based ethics as dominant forms for the fundamentally social expression of core philosophical ideas" (2016, 16). (Although it is true that we reduce Thurman by restricting him to the "black philosophical tradition," he does deserve to be considered as someone who contributed to that important philosophical movement.) Thurman was adept at using religious language and metaphors to convey philosophical and ethical as well as political and economic insights, but he ought to be placed within the larger sociohistorical context. Angela Davis's luminous "Lectures on Liberation" (Douglass 1910) assist in this task. Thurman addresses the issue of Black Power in his chapter titled "Search for Identity" in *Common Ground* (1971). Black Power was as an ideological trope that traveled the circuit through Richard Wright and Stokely Carmichael as well as Martin Luther King Jr. (in the second chapter of *Where Do We Go from Here* [1968]) and Huey Newton. Anthony Neal has demonstrated an uncanny similarity between Thurman and Newton, for example, in their respective doctrines of revolutionary consciousness and social transformation. Neal suggests in *Common Ground* that Thurman and Newton, although different in many other ways, shared more than a sense of social urgency: they shared analogous diagnoses if not also prognoses and prescriptions as cultural critics (2015).

By 1969 Angela Davis similarly insisted that philosophy, if worthy of the name, must aim at "eradicating some of the misery in this world" (Douglass 2010, 66). Black liberation theologians, for example, James H. Cone, also in 1969, were increasingly convinced that "what [was] needed [was] not integration but a sense of worth in being black" (1969, 19). Hord and Lee encourage us to "construe the discipline of philosophy in a way that brings social and ethical questions into the foreground, along with issues about the nature of human identity" (2016, 13). As a philosopher, Thurman engaged the world in order to change it. Parabolically, perhaps, but Thurman clearly and courageously addresses ethical and social questions as well as the nature of human identity.

In her "Lectures on Liberation" Davis notes, alluding to Marx and Nietzsche, that religion can be "the cruelest thing" when "used for the purposes of brainwashing, indoctrinating, and pacifying" (Douglass 2010, 61; also see Bloom 1992, 23).[4] And while she mentions Marx's claim that religion "teaches men to be satisfied with their condition in this world—with their oppression—by directing their hopes and desires into a supernatural domain" (60), Davis would have us think instead of Herbert Marcuse's reading of Marx, especially the notion that "religion is the wish-dream of an oppressed humanity" (60). Davis also thinks that religion can play a positive role in overcoming alienation, reinforcing the resolve to resist and struggling toward liberation. Davis claims that "what is crucial is that those dreams are always on the verge of reverting to their original status—the real wishes and needs here on earth" (61). Further:

> There is always the possibility of redirecting those wish-dreams to the here-and-now. Frederick Douglass redirected those dreams. Nat Turner placed them within the framework of the real world. So there can be a positive function of religion because its very nature is to satisfy very urgent needs of people who are oppressed. . . . All that needs to be done is to say: let's begin to create that eternity of bliss for human society here in this world. Let's convert eternity into history. (61)

Thurman belongs to those religious geniuses who "redirected the wish-dreams of an oppressed people" and strove to "convert eternity into history." Thurman certainly belongs to a powerful remnant of those who, following Davis, "turned Christianity against the missionaries" (63). Among others, Davis mentions Frederick Douglass, Gabriel Prosser, Denmark Vesey, and Nat Turner. Rather than "passages that emphasized obedience, humility, pacifism, patience" (62), Douglass and others discovered more agonistic themes of equality, freedom, and resistance: "Resistance," Davis says, "was the lesson learned from the Bible. Christian spirituals created and sung by the masses of slaves were also powerful songs of freedom that demonstrate the extent to which Christianity could be rescued from the ideological context forged by the slaveholders and imbued with a revolutionary content of liberation" (63). Thurman's work on the spirituals, published as *Deep River* (1945) and *The Negro Spiritual Speaks of Life and Death* (1947), in addition to its value to ethnomusicologists, are chock full of philosophical insights on freedom and personal identity. Harold Bloom puts it like this: "The black Jesus of the great spirituals is an immediacy, and he is a rhetorician who teaches how to transmute survival into liberation" (1992, 244).

Thurman explains:

> He [the black Jesus of the spirituals] picks up the searching words of Jeremiah and sings his affirmation, "There is a balm in Gilead!" Of course there are those who may say that this is merely a defense mechanism, likened unto the mood of a man in prison who thanks God that he is there; for if he were not, he might be hit by a stray bullet. Such reflections regard this mood as a defense mechanism, which becomes a substitute for action that would relieve the pressure. The only answer to this is that there would have been no survival in this philosophy for the Negro if it were merely a mechanism of sheer defense (1975, 66).

Although they disagreed on other fronts, Benjamin Mays and E. Franklin Frazier were similarly critical of the "otherworldliness" of the Negro religion. So was Thurman, but he focused on those things that were in Christianity because they were true. Followers of the religion of Jesus, contested Thurman, were "those who were willing to exercise the limit of power and moral suasion upon men in the interest of the redemption of themselves and society" and who could, "against the darkness of the age see the illumined finger of God guiding in the way they should go" (2012, 111). Thurman claimed in *The Negro Spiritual Speaks of Life and Death* that religion gave expression to "a very searching insight" as well as a "most daring and revolutionary concept" (1975, 95):

> God is not only the creative mind and spirit at the core of the universe but . . . He—and mark you, I say He—is love. . . . There are no completely satisfying ways by which this conclusion may be arrived at by mere or sheer rational reflective processes. This is the great disclosure: that there is at the heart of life a Heart. When such an insight is possessed by the human spirit and possesses the human spirit, a vast and awe-inspiring tranquility irradiates the life. This is the message of the spiritual. (95)

Thurman's "philosophy of freedom," as Mitchell puts, should be viewed through the lens of Davis's 1969 "Lectures on Liberation." In her conclusion to the *Spiritual Dynamics of Howard Thurman's Theology,* Mitchell states that Thurman's "only fixation was freedom itself—more rightly called flux" (1985, 171). Davis's course explored "the idea of freedom as it unfolded in the literary understanding of Black people" (Douglass 2010, 46), which included "the crucial transformation of the concept of freedom as a static, given principle into the concept of liberation, the dynamic, active struggle for freedom" (47). In this "concretized notion of freedom, resistance, rejection, on every level, on every front, are integral elements of the voyage toward freedom" (56).

Following Davis, it makes sense to think of Thurman as a liberation philosopher rather than a philosopher of freedom. A liberation philosopher does not construe freedom as something abstract and static nor as anonymity qua freedom from interference. For Thurman, as also for Mitchell, personal freedom would be a delusion without the "core of discipline and inner structure" (1985, 174). Davis claims that "the collective consciousness of an oppressed people entails an understanding of the conditions of oppression and the possibility of abolishing those conditions" (Douglass 2010, 49). Thurman would have appreciated Davis's refusal to accept a "pseudo-concept of freedom" by which the master is a slave of . . . his own brutality" (Davis 2010, 49). Nikolai Berdyaev captures this notion brilliantly in *Slavery and Freedom:* "The free man [or woman] cannot even desire to be a master, since that would indicate the loss of freedom" (1944, 71).

Thurman always placed his concept of freedom within the serious struggle—the philosophical yet physical voyage—from slavery to freedom, from disintegration to wholeness, from despair to hope. Thurman also held out hope for something better than struggle:

> It is time for assessing and reassessing resources in the light of the most ancient memory of the race concerning community, to hear again the clear voice of prophet and seer calling for harmony among all the children of men. At length there will begin to be talk of plans for the new city—that has never before existed on land or sea. At the center of the common life there will be strange stirrings. Some there will be whose dreams will be haunted by forgotten events in which in a moment of insight they saw a vision of a way of life transcending all barriers alien to community. (1971, 103)

In "The Politics of Conversion," Walter Fluker puts it this way: "Thurman understood this quest for personal space to involve defiant activity, for it presupposes that one's liberative quest in society cannot ultimately be divorced from one's wrestling with the internal issues of power and dominance" (1999, 116).

Conclusion

Billie Holiday's artistic sensibilities and Howard Thurman's sentiments are exemplary New World African expressions of the personal aspects of existential democracy. Prophetic criticism suffers from a kind of Du

Boisian double-consciousness—of being deeply shaped by Euro-American modernity but not feeling fully a part of it.

West (1993)

In what ways are the artistic sensibilities of Billie Holiday, for example, in her rendition of "Strange Fruit," analogous to Howard Thurman's "sentiments"? And in which ways are they "exemplary expressions of the personal aspects of existential democracy"? (1993, xii). Cornel West is not alone in comparing Thurman to Holiday. James Cone treats "Strange Fruit" as "a prophetic call for blacks to take up the cross of black freedom because nobody was going to carry it for them" (2011, 139). For Cone, Thurman and Holiday found ways to address "the deep-down hurt that blacks felt and gave them a way to deal with it" (2011, 138). Thurman claims that his craft and his gift was the spoken word: the sound of the genuine and a haunting voice of resistance. Citing Ralph Ellison's claim that "the art—the blues, the spirituals, the jazz, the dance—was what we had in place of freedom" (2011, 139), Cone believes that "the blues and the spirituals spoke about the tragic and the comic, sorrow and joy simultaneously" (2011, 139).

Thurman's interpretation of Jesus, says Cone in *God of the Oppressed,* is "consistent with the black struggle for liberation" (1975, 31). Cones suggests that "without Billie's voice, "Strange Fruit" would hardly be remembered" (138). Perhaps the same could be said of Thurman's protest songs and sermons. Cone cites Max Roach, Holiday's drummer, who said that her "styling of the song was incomparable" and "more than revolutionary" (2011, 137). Her shamanic voice conveyed a degree of bitterness and sorrow that "could jolt an audience out of its complacency anywhere" (ibid.). Thurman contributes this to what Cornel West calls the "enabling tradition" (1989, 233). "Like Thurman before him," says Anderson, "West proposes a form of cultural criticism that is both iconoclastic and utopian" (1999, 48). But there's also the existential strand and the undeniable blue note in both Thurman and West. "While consciously aware of the pervasive existential influences of white racism on black life, neither thinker regards racist influences as so pervasive as to render black life totalized by its demonic consequences" (Anderson 1999, 48).

Whether or not Thurman represents an early version of prophetic pragmatism is less important than showing that Thurman provides valuable resources for the sociopolitical project that animates prophetic pragmatism. At the very least, prophetic pragmatists will find solidarity and precedence in Thurman for their call for—in West's words once more—"the reinvigoration of a sane, sober, and sophisticated intellectual life in America and for regeneration of social forces empowering the disadvantaged, degraded, and dejected" (1989, 239). "In the tradition of the Hebrew prophets," says Smith, "Thurman calls America and Christianity to recall the sources of their identity" (Luther Smith, 2007, 20–21). In *The Cornel West Reader*, looking back at his *American Evasion of Philosophy*, West said that what he was attempting to do was "to argue that there are fundamental themes like experimentation and improvisation that can be found in the works of Ralph Waldo Emerson, for example, that are thoroughly continuous with the great art form that Afro-Americans have given the modern world, which is jazz" (1999, 542). Emerson's self-trust and willingness to go it alone, as an apotheosis of strength and self-reliance, is the root and branch of American philosophy as well as poetry.

In his *Negro Spiritual Speaks of Life and Death,* Thurman claims that "the notion that life is its own restraint sustained the slave in his darkest days and gave him an elemental vigor that expressed itself in a deep optimism arising out of the pessimism of life" (1975, 62–63). Brilliantly, James Cone places "Strange Fruit" in the tradition of Negro spirituals and protest songs: "Just as the old slave spiritual 'Were You There?' placed black Christians at the foot of Jesus' cross, 'Strange Fruit' put them at the foot of the lynching tree. Both songs created a dark and somber mood. One was sung in church and the other in a night-club, but both addressed the deep-down hurt that blacks felt and gave them a way to deal with it" (2011, 138). Rosemary Cowan suggests that "West's liberatory enterprise is inherently problemic given the conflicting ideas in it. Most significant is the dialectic of hope and despair at the center of his thought" (2003, 173). Howard Thurman and Angela Davis as well as Cornel West and Eddie Glaude strike a similar blue note when it comes to questions of social hope and political progress. Hord and Lee claim that, within the black philosophical tradition they plait together, "philosophy is here called upon to evaluate and counter the dehumanization to which people and ideas of African descent have been subjected through the history of colonialism and of European racism" (2016, 13–14). Philosophers serve a wide array of "mediating" roles. Thurman was a mediator as well as a religious and cultural iconoclast, but he was also a principled meliorist if not pragmatic in his philosophical loyalties and allegiances. Throughout his life, claims Luther Smith, "Thurman proved the inclusive genius of Christianity" (2007, 144).

7

The Growing Edges of Beloved Community

"The term [viz., the beloved community] has a soft and sentimental ring. It conjures an image of tranquility, peace, and the utter absence of struggle and of all things that irritate and disturb. But my thought is far from such a utopian surmise. . . . Disagreements will be real and germane to the vast undertaking of man's becoming at home in his world and under the eaves of his brother's house"

Thurman, "Desegregation, Integration, and the Beloved Community" ([1966] 2009)

Not altogether unlike King, Thurman acknowledged an intellectual indebtedness to Josiah Royce. The influence of Royce on King's conception of the beloved community is contested, of course, but scholars readily concede that Royce's ideas exerted, as Rufus Burrow puts it, "at least an indirect influence on King's socioethical thought" (2015, 132). The African American experience altered significantly if not decisively the socioethical trajectory of this trope—"the beloved community"—within the history of philosophy and theology in America. Admittedly, the influence of Royce's philosophical speculations on "the beloved community" and "loyalty to loyalty" can sometimes seem quite remote from, for example, Thurman's work with The Church for the Fellowship of All Peoples in San Francisco or King's activist-advocacy work with the civil rights movement from Montgomery to Memphis. The influence of Royce on Thurman and King was but one of many significant factors or variables in a complex confluence of sociohistorical and philosophical influences; still, I think that the philosophical influence or impact of Royce's teachings on Thurman and King was nontrivial. And while the genius of Thurman or King cannot be reduced to the ideas of their predecessors, whether Royce and Du Bois or even Mays, whether intellectual or cultural, I believe that something valuable is gained by revisiting the philosophical history as well as the pragmatic meaning of this trope from Royce to Thurman and King.

As an exercise in comparative analysis or search for common ground, I show how surface differences have obscured our appreciation of significant similarities between Royce and Thurman or King, but I also want to suggest that several surface similarities tend to distort important differences between their respective theories and projects. And while the focus here is almost exclusively on "the beloved community" in Royce and Thurman, worth noting briefly is the contested influence of Royce and Thurman on King's iconic vision of the beloved community. "Since the beloved community nomenclature is traceable to Royce," says Rufus Burrow, "and was later picked up by King and essentially made the chief regulative principle of his theological social ethics, it makes sense that we should know better than we have previously known, just how King came to know and appropriate the term" (2015, 130). Royce's thought exercised an influence on Thurman and King, although the nature of that influence is contested, and influence is notoriously difficult to measure. But beyond our collaborative effort to gain a better understanding of the confluence of influences on King's conception of the beloved community, we must also seek to clarify in earnest what this socioethical if not theological or philosophical ideal prescribes by way of individual practices and public policies moving forward in the twenty-first century.

Royce and the Beloved Community

For the sake of comparison, let us begin with Royce's distinctively religious if not uniquely Christian interpretation of the beloved community.[1] In general, historians have underestimated both the philosophical novelty and the social impact of Royce's formulation of the beloved community: "the principle of all principles in all Christian morals remains this: 'Since you cannot find the universal and beloved community, create it'" (2001, 359). And while it may be true that his philosophy of loyalty sometimes "shimmers with liberal hopes of human progress and perfectibility," as Charles Marsh puts it, it would be a mistake to imagine Royce as endorsing the view that "most of what one needs to know of God is discovered in ethical religion, slightly adjusted for churchgoers in capitalist economies" (2005, 49). In particular, I want to understand the role or function of the beloved community as it relates to what Royce calls the "saving absolute" and an "infinite atonement." For Royce, one's loyalty to the beloved community constituted a "transfiguring experience" (2001, 18). Marsh refers in this passage to Royce's *The Problems of Christianity,* where Royce speaks of the beloved community as "a perfectly lived unity of individual men joined in one divine chorus" (2001, 350). Perhaps Royce was thinking of Kant, who suggested that fundamental changes to the "foundation of maxims" could not be "effected through gradual reform but must rather be effected through a revolution in the disposition of the human being" (1996, 92).

For Royce, the beloved community "does not consist simply in making a transition from an individual to a social level, but in the establishment of that special community which does not breed individualism because it embodies some higher and therefore super-human form of love powerful enough to transform the individual and at the same time do away with the fatal outcome of natural social cultivation which is based on nothing higher than human talents and potentials" (1950, Smith 76; qtd. in Nagl 2012, 110). Royce understood in his own way that participating in a community united by love transforms the individual. This transfiguring relationship, this "mystery of loving membership in a community whose meaning seems divine" ([1913] 1967, 140), is for Royce the "specific condition" of that particular genuineness or authenticity that constitutes "the graced or beloved community." Similar to Thurman, Royce thought that religious communities allow us "to carry on, even after serious defeat and loss, and to believe that our experience of finitude will not be the last word" (Nagl 2012, 110). I wish to begin my examination of Royce's use of the trope "the beloved community" where Ludwig Nagl ends his compelling reading of Royce in "Loyalty: Royce's Post-Kantian, Pragmaticist Conception of Ethics," in *Josiah Royce for the Twenty-First Century* (2012). Royce "begins to elucidate his community-oriented ethics in explicitly religious terms," which constitutes what might be viewed as "a third definition," one that extends beyond "loyalty to loyalty" and that appropriates the language of William James and the semiotics of Charles Sanders Peirce, with a permanent deposit of the Hegelian dialect of the identity of identity and nonidentity, namely, that "loyalty is the will to manifest, so far as possible, the Eternal, that is, the conscious and superhuman unity of life, the form of the acts of an individual Self" or, alternatively, "the Will to Believe in something eternal, and to express that belief in the practical life of a human being" (Royce, *The Philosophy of Loyalty*; qtd. in Nagl 2012, 109). This third definition is increasingly expressed in terms of distinct if not unique communities, such that religious communities are pragmatically distinct from communities of scientific inquiry along the lines of Peirce or even communities of interpretation as expressed in Royce's second definition of loyalty since, suggests Nagl, authentic or vital communities "operate (as finite and situated communities) always in view of their specific infinity" (Nagl 2012, 110). In his analysis of religion, Royce "elucidates the special structure of those specific communities that operate on the limits of our private and political actions: communities that allow us, even after serious defeat and loss, to carry on, and to believe that our experience of finiteness . . . will not be the last word" (Nagl 2012, 110). The invisible but at the same time pluralistically and imperfectly instantiated community, which Royce calls the "beloved community," has a special quality and unique type of infinity or conception of the absolute.

Religious communities are constituted at their core, suggests Nagl's reading of Royce, "by an internal loving interrelation, and by a trustful [or loyal] relationship —not towards an immanent infinity (cognitive truth, e.g., or institutional reform) but towards a saving absolute" (Nagl 2012, 110). This relationship, namely, "the mystery of loving membership in a community whose meaning seems divine" (Royce 2001, 140), is—rounding off Nagl's analysis—"the specific condition of that particular 'genuineness' which constitutes the 'graced or beloved community' (Nagl 2012, 110)." Like Thurman and King, Royce was loyal to the growing edges of a beloved community. Royce suffered from various blindnesses, certainly, which is all too human, as his friend William James never tired of reminding us (for example, in "On a Certain Blindness in Human Beings"), but it doesn't seem to me to be disloyal to Royce or to the procedural ideals that Royce espoused and practiced to suggest that the spirit of his philosophy of loyalty implies a degree of inclusivity that extends beyond what he—or we, perhaps what any of us—can see or imagine. The philosophers considered here are undeniably diverse, certainly, but I believe that the philosophical or religious trope of the beloved community, diversely envisioned, is an informative if not also inspiring lens through which—as Thurman put it—"to perceive a harmony that transcends all diversities and in which diversity finds its richness and significance" (1971, 6). On a personal level, Royce and James as well as Thurman and King were committed to building a more beloved community—that is, a human community built on love—because they were each convinced that "their help was needed." The sort of help that was needed, as they perceived it, sympathetically yet intelligently, was diverse, certainly, but there is a shared yet growing edge inherent in "provincialism" that stretches if not strives toward increasingly nonexclusionistic loyalties. In this sense, Royce's philosophy of loyalty constitutes a socioethical *summum bonum:* "Reverberating all through you, stirring you to your depths, loyalty first unifies your plan of life, and thereby gives you what nothing else can give—viz., your Self as a life lived in accordance with a plan, your conscience as your plan interpreted for you through your ideal, your cause as your personal purpose in living" (2005a, 1008). But loyal to whom and to what? As a socioethical imperative or maxim: Act in such a way, choose your loyalties in such a manner, that the rule of your behavior advances or increases the cause of loyalty itself: "Find your own cause, your interesting, fascinating, personally engrossing cause; serve it with all your might and soul and strength; but so choose your cause and so serve it, that thereby you show forth your loyalty to loyalty such that the practical work or cause in question contributes to "the furtherance of universal loyalty" (2005, 916; also see Clendenning 1999,

301). So while it is true that there is an ethical aspect of Royce's philosophy of loyalty such that a cause is good in that "it is an aid and furtherance of loyalty in my fellows" (2005a, 56), there is also a metaphysical if not ultimately theological or religious dimension, including a theory of personal identity, to his thought during the final ten years of his life.

Acts of loyalty and devotion, which express voluntary acts of self-renunciation, constitute something along the lines of a conversion experience: an individual is transformed from an individual to a person, suggests Royce, similar to Kant, at that moment when one renounces one's selfishness. If loyalty consists in a "willing and practical and thoroughgoing devotion of a person to a cause," as Royce expresses it in the opening lecture of his *Philosophy of Loyalty*, and if "commitment requires self-sacrifice, for no cause is loyal which seeks to gain a purely personal advantage" (2005a, 874), selfhood as opposed to mere individuation is attained or accomplished through a voluntary renunciation of selfishness as an act of devotion. As John Clendenning puts it, "The principle that defines the ego also shows the emptiness of egoism" (1999, 299). For Royce, "If you wholly decline to devote yourself to any cause whatever, your assertion of moral independence will remain but an empty proclaiming of a moral sovereignty over your life, without any definite life over which to be sovereign" (2005a, 891). Royce entreats us to recover our sovereignty for the sake of the causes for which we are willing to make personal sacrifices. Drawing on a different tradition in American thought, communitarian personalism, Walter Muelder argued in 1947 that persons "grow through decision and commitment, through facing and overcoming crises, through reciprocity and mutuality" (125). As an idealist, Royce argued that personal identity is composed of the interwoven and contested if not also occasionally divided loyalties to which we are genuinely committed; as a pragmatist, the significance of those loyalties is disclosed in the way we live our lives.

Before his years at Boston University, Thurman was a colleague of Alain Locke at Howard University. Judith Green suggests that Alain Locke's "pragmatist critical relativism" could be read as "a culture-transforming version of James's metaphysical and ethical pluralism" (2008, 150). But Green would also have read Locke as beholden to Royce's thoughts on the great and beloved community: "Building on these insights, Royce's and James's student, the great 'critical pragmatist' Alain Locke, expanded this insight by suggesting the possibility and the importance of relationally reframing our rival histories of harms though face-to-face experiences of collaboration in hope-building, world-healing practical projects" (2008, 150). Alain Locke's ideal of "unity amid diversity" is a collaborative achievement and a dynamic epiphenomenon. Similar to Locke, Thurman thought that there must be a mechanism or a process by which experiences of unity, incrementally and over a protracted period of time or in one fell swoop, overpower, whether temporarily or with a lasting residue, the barriers that separate us. For Thurman, experiences of worship and the spiritual disciplines served the function of Locke's "collaboration in hope-building" and "world-healing practical projects." Like Locke, Thurman believed that the whole is greater than the sum of its parts. Thurman may be alluding to Locke when he describes a "harmony that transcends all diversities and in which diversity finds its richness and significance" (1971, 6). Beyond the influence of Royce's notion of the beloved community, Locke and Thurman were also familiar with Royce's thoughts on the role of love in transforming society.

Clendenning is quite masterful in describing the "social motive" in what might be called the last phase in the epicycle of Royce's life and thought: "Love had always been central to his philosophy: the principle of harmony, the world of appreciation, the theory of individuation, the philosophy of loyalty are all variations on the same theme—that love gives meaning to life" (1999, 322). What is required by the love-ethic in Royce? What, according to Royce, was the pragmatic meaning of love? What habits does love require of us? In the earliest phase of Royce's academic career, for example, in his 1893–95 essays for the *Archiv der systematische Philosophie,* when discussing the ethical significance of the doctrine of progress, of the "perfectibility of [persons]" and the "evolution of humanity," Royce argues that "there is an ultimate goal, to which, by simple self-knowledge, by immanent criticism of human desire, all the various and conflicting goals of action can be reduced"—namely,

> the goal of rendering as full and as definite as possible all the conscious life that at any moment comes within the circle of our influence. Devotion, then, to universal conscious life, is the goal of conscious life itself; or the goal is the self-reference or self-surrender of each conscious moment to the great whole of life, in so far as that whole is within reach. Separation from other conscious life means failure. Conscious union with other conscious life means for every conscious being success in proportion to the fullness, clearness, and definiteness of that union. This union is the highest goal, not for itself logically demonstrable as such, but deducible from the other actual goals of mankind when they are analyzed in their true meaning (2005b, 270).

Construed in terms of psychological or sociological geography, as a spiritual community, the telos implicit in all other teloi, and thinking also of Peirce's description of thought as an activity of mind by which one moves from irritation to rest, from doubt to belief, from paralysis to action, it makes sense to think of the beloved community as the outward sign or symbol of an internal reality, which is a standard definition of a sacrament. Royce suggests that we can feel, intermittently, on certain occasions, this perfect harmony and union with the whole of conscious life. But when it comes to describing the conditions and occasion for this feeling of harmony and union, Royce extends beyond experiences of religious worship to acts of "self-sacrifice, chief of all, and in the next rank hard work for any impersonal end, or the mere contemplation of active life, the union with others for the doing of work that involves no warring with an opposite party, even warfare when carried on for the good of the whole of conscious life" (2005b, 270). And yet, Royce concedes that "such union is perfected only in moments—for the rest of the time selfishness, self-conceit, struggle with hated equals, in a word, unrest, are predominant" (2005b, 270).

The socioethical dimension of Royce's philosophy of loyalty is important, certainly, but it also contains a "metaphysical aspect" in its attempt "to conceive human life in an essentially superhuman way, to view our social organizations as actual personal unities of consciousness, unities wherein there exists an actual experience of the good which, in our loyalty, we only partially apprehend" (2005a, 978). By the conclusion of his *Philosophy of Loyalty,* Royce defines loyalty as "the will to manifest, so far as is possible, the Eternal, that is, the conscious and superhuman unity of life, in the form of the acts of an individual self" or, alluding to James, "the will to believe in something eternal, and to express that belief in the practical life of a human being" (2005a, 996). In this sense, I suppose, one could agree with Clendenning that Royce "wished his audience to understand that loyalty is primarily a practical guide to action, a guide that, in its merely pragmatic usefulness, can stand apart from the philosopher's speculative system" (1999, 301). But perhaps Royce was still closer to James than even Clendenning concedes: I agree that loyalty to the beloved community serves as a regulative ideal, but I think that the (absolute) pragmatic point is that ideas—for example, the idea of loyalty to loyalty—are best construed as working plans of action and tentative prescriptions for behavior.

In *Pragmatism and Social Hope: Deepening Democracy in Global Contexts,* Judith M. Green states:

> Even if we have become fully convinced, contra Rorty, that a careful, truth-seeking historical memory is necessary for moral and practical guidance in a dangerous but not possibility-closed world, we must face with him the reality of rival memories sometimes linked to narrow loyalties that seem to license terrible things: murder and war, famines and epidemics, religious intolerance, ethnic cleansing and cultural erasure, exclusion of women and ethnic minority groups from participation rights and educational opportunities, cruelty to other species, devastation of our shared habitat. (2008, 151–52)

The socioethical ideal of the beloved community served for Royce as "the central principle of the moral life" (2005a, 859). Dwayne Tunstall suggests that the "Roycean metaphysics of community enables King to say that we are able to actualize the Beloved Community, however partially we may do so" (2008, 106). Between Royce's original formulation of the principle and King's iconic formulation of the phrase was Walter Rauschenbusch and Edgar Brightman, certainly, but also Alain Locke and Howard Thurman. (There were also broader cultural influences at work when it comes to the beloved community trope.)[2]

The Influence of Royce on Thurman

As part of a lecture series devoted to the philosophy of loyalty and delivered in San Francisco in 1951, Thurman describes Royce as "that great, winsome, and sometimes devastating philosopher who stated for the first time in the English language, and definitively, the philosophy of loyalty" (1951a). Like G. W. F. Hegel before him—not the British Hegelians but the French and American Hegelians—Royce expresses the philosophy of loyalty in terms of a submission or sublimation process that resolves the thesis of internal singularity and its antithesis for supplying a dynamic synthesis and source of inner strength. Thurman claims that "the ghost of Royce had been moving in and out of his mind for many years" (1951a, audio; 1951b).[3] Although he acknowledged an indebtedness to Royce on the philosophy of loyalty, Thurman spoke, as he put it, "on his own authority." Thurman emphasizes the transformative process that occurs when one submits or surrenders one's will, construed as the "fluid nerve center of consent," to either an abstract socioethical ideal (for example, loyalty to loyalty, universal good will toward all, nonviolence, nondiscrimination) as well as very specific acts of solidarity (for example, how one votes in local elections, the charities we support, the projects we undertake, whether feeding the hungry or clothing the naked or advocating on behalf of the disenfranchised neighbor). Thurman is interested in the "politics of conversion," borrowing a phrase from Cornel West and Walter Fluker, and the psychosocial or spiritual process by which one becomes a living "for-instance" of the cause to which he or she is loyal (West 2001, 19; Fluker 1999, 103). Thurman describes loyalty as "a willing and thoroughgoing devotion of the person to a cause" (1951a, audio). Thurman also suggests that "our loyalty to the individual is derivate because the thing that is primary is my devotion to the tie that unites me to you and you and you and you" (1951a, audio). In a separate sermon series on the parables of Jesus, also in 1951, he claimed that "the kingdom of God is a way of life under the rule of God" (1951a, audio). In the *Temptations of Jesus,* Thurman construes Jesus as "the living embodiment of the Kingdom of God" ([1962] 1978, 52).

Thurman thought that both Royce and James, despite their differences, were instructive when it came to describing the broad spectrum of psychosocial dynamics at work within religion. Beyond his writings on religion, psychology, and philosophy, Thurman was exposed to Royce and James through his colleagues at Morehouse College and Howard University, especially W. E. B. Du Bois in Atlanta and Alain Locke in Washington, both of whom studied at Harvard with James and Royce. Locke's earliest musings on multiculturalism and pluralism were stimulated, at least in part, by the work of one of his mentors, William James's *The Pluralistic Universe.* As colleagues at Howard University, Locke and Thurman envisioned the beloved community as exemplifying a "harmony that transcends all diversities and in which diversity finds its richness and significance" (Thurman 1971, 6). And Du Bois, who influenced Thurman during the Morehouse years, first as a student and later as a colleague, was at least initially considered to be a pragmatist of a certain type. (The first course that Thurman taught at Morehouse was guided by Dewey's pragmatism and philosophy of education.) So while there were philosophical influences, including Royce and James, at least through Locke and Du Bois, but also through the Boston personalists, Thurman's unique formulation of the "beloved community" expresses what he considered to be the logic of non-exclusionism "inherent in the genius of the Christian faith itself" (1959, 21). Perhaps his work with The Church for the Fellowship of All Peoples in San Francisco (1944–1953) serves as a pragmatic lens through which to clarify the ideal of the beloved community at work in Thurman. "For Thurman," says Walter E. Fluker, "community refers to integration, mutuality, and harmony" (1990, 39). Elsewhere Fluker suggests that "suffering and community are defining motifs of the social environments from which twentieth-century black leaders in the Deep South emerged and from which they took their primary discursive cues" (2013, 156).

Beyond the "legal aspect of integration," which involves changes in policies and regulations and is understood as a mechanical movement from segregation to desegregation to integration, Thurman emphasizes a "second meaning of integration that has to do with the quality of human relations" (2009, 205). Thurman describes the "dynamic meaning of integration" this way:

> During the years when the Church for the Fellowship of All Peoples in San Francisco was being developed, it became increasingly clear that the mere presence of people of different ethnic or cultural backgrounds in the membership did not mean that the church itself was integrated. The coming together of people in such institutions must be rooted in natural communal association. They must be able to participate meaningfully in the various phases of their living if their relationship is to be positive and creative. Meaningful experiences of integration between people are more compelling

> than the fears, the inhibitions, the dogmas, or the prejudices that divide. If such unifying experiences can be multiplied over an extended time, they will be able to restructure the fabric of the social context (2009, 206).

Thurman sought to build a beloved community as "a living confirmation" or "empirical validation" of what he considered to be "a profound religious and ethical insight concerning the genius of the church as a religious fellowship" (1959, 21). Thurman explained that he "had to find out for [himself] whether or not it is true that experiences of spiritual unity and fellowship are not more compelling than the fears and dogmas and prejudices that separate [people]" (21). So while Thurman's vision of the beloved community was born out of his struggle to understand and to subsequently resolve to dedicate his life to breaking down the exclusionary barriers that segregated, de facto if not de jure, white from black Christian churches, the situation in San Francisco in 1944 broadened his vision of or glimpse into a radically nonexclusionary spiritual community. "Community cannot for long feed on itself," wrote Thurman, "it can only flourish with the coming of others from beyond, their unknown and undiscovered brothers and sisters" (1971, 104). Thurman's *Footprints of a Dream* recounts the origins and results of his experiment in community building, which put to the test his working hypothesis that "a way could be found to unite people of great ideological and religious diversity through experiences which were more compelling than the concepts that separated and divided" (1959, 28). The spiritual disciplines must comingle when it comes to the work of reconciliation. The clue to the communal is the individual, and the clue to the individual is the communal. But for Thurman and King as well as Royce, the sphere of the communal also includes a "third dimension." In our struggle for community, thought all three thinkers, we have a "cosmic companion" (see Mikelson 1990, 5). Although it is possible to adopt their socioethical perspective without adopting comparable ideas when it comes to their respective views of God, it certainly seems worthwhile to notice that, in each case, their image of God reflects their socioethical teachings: for example, Thurman's audacious assertion that he had "only one basic statement to make about the love of God and that is that it is always concerned with breaking the sense of isolation that the individual human spirit feels as it lives its way into life" (1956, 65).

King scholars from Lawrence N. Jones to Rufus Burrow have suggested that "blacks have been searching for the beloved community for as long as they have been in this country" (Jones 1981, 12; also see Burrow 2015, 134). In ways analogous to Royce, Thurman believed that individuation consisted in expressions of sincere loyalty to some communal cause. In *Disciplines of the Spirit*, Thurman claims that "commitment means that possible for a [person] to yield the nerve center of [his or her] consent to a purpose or a cause, a movement or an ideal, which may be more important to him [or her] than whether he [or she] lives or dies" (1963, 17). And similar to Royce, looking backward, and King, looking ahead, Thurman insists: "If love is not operative, then community is impossible" (1963, 17). In Thurman, those who are loyal to the beloved community are required—in ways not altogether unlike Royce's ambivalent response—to take evil seriously but also to believe that it does not have the last word. Luther Smith explains Thurman's position this way: "Even as evil is active in the lives of men and women, it becomes an ingredient for personal growth. It tests the moral fiber of the person, and by stretching and straining makes the fiber stronger" (2007, 60). Indeed, without trying to explain away or otherwise dismiss the jolting reality of radical evil, suffering "can be instrumental in shaping community." In *Luminous Darkness,* Thurman suggests that "the degree to which [one's] suffering is shared by others marks the potential that such suffering may itself become redemptive" (1965a, 55). In ways similar to King and Royce, looking forward and then back in time, although it all seems to bend temporal markers, Thurman brooded long and hard over the problem of evil. Neither Thurman nor King believed that all suffering was redemptive. This is a delicate idea in all three of the thinkers under consideration here. Rufus Burrow captures it beautifully in *Martin Luther King, Jr., and the Theology of Resistance:* "According to King, unearned suffering must be made to be redemptive by sustained and determined nonviolent struggle against it" (2015, 133). In his autobiography, *With Head and Heart,* Thurman says of the Fellowship Church:

> There are times when guidance as to techniques and strategy is urgent, when counsel, support, and collective direct action are mandatory. But there can never be a substitute for taking personal responsibility for social change. The word "personal" applies both to the individual and the organization—in this instance, the church. The true genius of the church was revealed by what it symbolized as a beachhead in our society in terms of community, and as an inspiration to the solitary individual to put his weight on the side of a society in which no man need be afraid. (1979, 161)

In his *Search for Common Ground,* in which he argues that "directiveness and creativeness are inherent in life" and that "there is a unity of life across kingdoms or species," Thurman claimed that "it is not unreasonable, then, to assume that as [one] seeks community, with [one's] fellows, and with [one's] world, he [or she] may find that what he [or she] is seeking to do deliberately is but the logic of the meaning of all that has gone into his [or her] own creation" (1971, 41). It is sometimes suggested that freedom and community are the two great philosophical themes in Thurman's thought: at bottom, freedom and community are of one cloth.[4] In a sermon from 1955 Thurman said, "It is not chauvinistic to affirm that our total life as a nation has been a schooling in the meaning of human freedom against a time when the only thing that serves the collective life of man is a dynamic faith in the worth of the individual and the freedom that it inspires." ("Freedom," unpublished sermon).

When an individual surrenders his or her will to a cause, Thurman thought that "the cause then gives him back his will in order that he might put at the disposal of the cause all that he is, worthily or unworthily" (1951a). In this respect, thought Thurman, the dynamic principles inherent in acts of loyalty resemble the pretzel logic of love and reconciliation. Freedom often means finding community or integration within oneself for Thurman. In *The Luminous Darkness,* Thurman explains:

> The burden of being black and the burden of being white is so heavy that it is rare in our society to experience oneself as a human being. It may be, I don't know, that to experience oneself as a human being is one with experiencing one's fellows as human beings. It means that the individual must have a sense of kinship to life that transcends and goes beyond the immediate kinship of family or the organic kinship that binds him [or her] ethnically or "racially" or nationally. He has a sense of being an essential part of the structural relationship that exists between him and all other men [and women], and between him, all other men [and women], and the total external environment. As a human being, then, he belongs to life and the whole kingdom of life that includes all that lives and perhaps, also, all that has ever lived. In other words, he sees himself as a part of a continuing, breathing, living existence. To be a human being, then, is to be essentially alive in a living world. (1965a, 94)

In reply to this passage, Vincent Harding, who was close to both Thurman and King, claims: "What more could one ask from a spirituality? To show us the way to be alive with God's life in God's world. That's what the father was about. That's what the brother was about" (1999, 3). Rufus Burrow claims that, despite recent scholarship on the "black American cultural, family, and religious influences on King" (2015, 121), especially but not exclusively by Lewis Baldwin and Clayborne Carson, a coterie to which Burrow himself belongs, "much remains to be done" (2015, 121). Burrow claims that, among others (namely, Delia King, A. D. Williams, Martin Luther King, Sr., Benjamin E. Mays, George Kelsey, William Holmes Borders), "we do not know nearly enough about the influence of . . . Howard Thurman" (2015, 122). I agree, although I recognize that in my effort to learn more about the influence of Thurman on King, or of Mays on King, the point of the exercise extends beyond the confluence of influences to the question of their collective influence on how we choose to live our own lives. In Thurman, King encountered both "a man of ideas and theologian of nonviolent resistance" (Burrow 2015, 14), as Burrow puts it, and all of it was expressed within the idiom of the African American spiritual experience. "To understand this kind of interaction between the forces of oppression, on the one side, and the spark of redemptive possibility, on the other," claims Fluker, "is to discover a clue to Thurman's early conceptualizations of the central concern of is life: the search for common ground" (2013, 156).[5]

Although the most elaborate presentation of his radically nonexclusiveness thesis is in his 1971 *Search for Common Ground,* the most succinct formulation of his theory of the beloved community is found in an essay that Thurman wrote in 1966 but was only recently published, in 2009 in *Benjamin E. Mays: His Life, Contributions, and Legacy,* titled "Desegregation, Integration, and the Beloved Community." In that essay, Thurman attempts "to analyze the significance of desegregation against the background of segregation in American society, to interpret integration in the social context created by segregation, [and] to assess the meaning of the 'beloved community' against such a total background" ([1966] 2009, 197). And while Thurman suggests that his theme had been, already in 1966, prior to the assassination of his colleague associated with the phrase, "well-nigh exhaustively mined," his thoughts on the beloved community in particular seem—more than fifty years later—poignant and profound if not more than a little bit prophetic. For our present purposes, I wish to focus primarily on the distinction Thurman draws, one of many helpful distinctions drawn in this essay, between integration and community.[6] According to Thurman, genuine integration cannot be achieved "by any kind of mechanical arrangement of persons or rules or regulations" (204). Rather,

> it may be facilitated by changes in policies and regulations—it may be provided for in the structure of the organized life of the community or an institution; but integration can never be achieved as an end in itself. It must emerge as an experience after the fact of coming together. The damage to the body politic growing out of ancient patterns of segregation in our society is so profound that the meaning of integration is most often limited to the superficial and mechanical juggling of different kinds of belonging. (204)

As an interesting case in point, Thurman quipped that "unless some other forces are at work which disturb power and controls, then power and social controls use the ballot as a viable instrument in their hands" (201). Thurman is working with two distinct meanings of integration. The legal aspect of integration, as Thurman calls it, by which he means that "there must be no closed systems which operate automatically with reference to any members of society" (204), is expressed in a formula describing an oversimplified process "from segregation to desegregation to integration" (205). This legal aspect of integration—which is a necessary yet insufficient condition for "dynamic integration," something that should be guaranteed by our political contract—suggests Thurman, "can never be achieved as an end in itself"; although enactments of legislation are necessary, "they cannot determine or guarantee the quality of the personal adjustment within the broad range of open privilege" (205). Dynamic integration and wholeness can only emerge out of a "natural communal association" sustained by meaningful experiences of togetherness that are "multiplied over an extended time" (206).

Thurman maintained his conviction, which had been confirmed in India thirty years earlier, that "meaningful experiences of integration between people are more compelling than the fears, the inhibitions, the dogmas, or the prejudices that divide. If such unifying experiences can be multiplied over an extended time, they will be able to restructure the entire fabric of the social context" ([1966] 2009, 205). This "unscrambling process," as he refers to it elsewhere ([1949] 1996, 97), by which legal integration is qualitatively transformed over time into something more dynamic and dependable, gets us a little closer but not quite yet to what Thurman means by the beloved community.

> The Beloved Community is created by the quality of the human relations experienced by the people who live within it. The term itself is an abstraction and becomes concrete in a given time and place in the midst of living human beings. It cannot be brought into being by fiat or by order; it is an achievement of the human spirit as men [and women] seek to fulfill their high destiny as children of God. As a dream of the race, it has moved in and out on the horizon of human strivings like some fleeting ghost. And yet, it remains to haunt and inspire [human beings] in all ages and all conditions. In some sense, it is always vague, and the blueprint for it is often outmoded before it can be translated into living texture ([1966] 2009, 206).

As early as 1963, in *Disciplines of the Spirit*, Thurman speculated that "what is taking place at the level of the physical organism may find its counterpart in the life of the mind and the spirit" (39). In *Search for Common Ground* (1971), Thurman expanded his thesis apropos community as simultaneously "a natural fact" and "a moral truth," in deference to a beautiful line in Emerson's 1836 essay *Nature*. The beloved community, for Thurman, and for others who were at that time in the throes of "the civil rights revolution," served as both a here-and-now experience of freedom, always within a "social climate," the residue of which one retains even in solitude, and a "radical moral imperative" that "steadfastly refused to separate the means open to revolution from the ends to be achieved by revolution" (2009, 206). Although some contemporary scholars may scoff at questions associated with whether it is really possible to usher in the beloved community, literally, figuratively, partially, here but not yet, in principle, or "within the vast decay of our diseased, prejudiced-ridden society" (2009, 206), but not Thurman: "The presence of the Beloved Community is always manifesting itself in the lives of people in the very midst of the social decay which surrounds them. It begins in the human spirit and it moves into the open independence of society" (2009, 206). Thurman claims that each of us is somehow personally responsible to bring it to pass within the "society in which he [or she] lives and functions" (2009, 206). Thurman reminds his readers that "the whole point of the attack on the evils of segregation for the individual, as well as the total society, is that the system renders healthy human relations impossible" (2009, 206).

> This essential point can be very easily overlooked, forgotten, or ignored in the white heat of the long, hot summer, the angry violence of a suburban Cicero or the unbelievable Mississippi sadism of Grenada. The issue at stake is only incidentally, though crucially so, the pattern of the civil rights, open occupancy, destruction of ghettos, desegregation of schools, churches, etc. What is being sought is a way of life that is worth living and a faith in one's self, in others, and the society that can be honestly and intelligently sustained. This is what the Beloved Community is all about. (2009, 206)

Thurman appropriated and applied or otherwise adapted the dynamic sociological principle articulated—seminally, winsomely, though perhaps not altogether originally nor definitively—in Royce's theory of individuation as well as his doctrine of loyalty and an early conception of the beloved community. Although he wrote extensively about the search for community after 1966, and while he remained preoccupied throughout his life with what he later called "the tie that binds life at a level so deep that the final privacy of the individual would be reinforced rather than threatened" (1971, xiii), Thurman rarely used the phrase "beloved community" following the assassination of King.

From Royce and Thurman to King

"Like Thurman," says Walter Fluker, "community is the single, organizing principle of King's life and thought" (1989, 159; 1990, 43). In his December 1956 address to the Montgomery Improvement Association at the Holt Street Baptist Church in Montgomery, King claimed that the boycott and its achievements did not in themselves represent the goal of the struggle: "The end is reconciliation, the end is redemption," King said, "the end is the creation of the beloved community" (King 1984, 12). In his 1966 "Non-Violence: The Only Road to Freedom," which he intended as a defense of the SCLS's position on nonviolent resistance, King claimed that "only a refusal to hate or kill can put an end to the chain of violence in the world and lead us toward a community where men can live together without fear. Our goal is to create a beloved community, and this will require a qualitative change in our souls as well as a quantitative change in our lives" (1984, 58; also see Burrow 1997, 442). Although it may seem that King's 1966 argument in defense of nonviolent resistance and his reference to the beloved community is perfectly consistent with his earlier pronouncements apropos the logic of the beloved community, things had changed considerably between 1956 and 1966. Whereas the young pastor in Montgomery initially wished merely to incrementally adjust the systems and institutions of racial inequality from within, minor improvements here and there, Harding claims in *Martin Luther King Jr.: Inconvenient Hero* (2008) that by 1966 King had begun to struggle against the distinct and thus disheartening possibility that the entire system was beyond repair or redemption. King's minimalist description of the beloved community refers to a psychic state or quality of experience if not a geographical home within which persons might simply "live together without fear." But Charles Marsh seems correct to insist that "the logic of King's dream was theologically specific: beloved community as the realization of divine love in lived social relation" (2005, 3). Fluker agrees that "the theological dimension of the 'beloved community' is primary for King" (1989, 159). "The beloved community concept was for King more than an operative or regulative principle, although it was also this," says Rufus Burrow. "King was of man of the Christian faith" (2015, 124).[7] In his essay "They Looked for a City," Walter Fluker put it this way: "King's vision of the beloved community, like Thurman's, however, was also bred and nurtured in the black church tradition, which has historically seen its particular struggle for the liberation of black people through the prism of universal liberation of all peoples" (1990, 37).

"The universal themes of forgiveness, reconciliation, and hope which characterized King's and Thurman's vision of community," per Fluker, "have always been fundamental to the black community in general and the black church in particular" (1990, 37; also see Cone, 1984, 416). Similar to King, Thurman actively but nonviolently resisted the injustices inherent in materialism, militarism, and racism. In December 1961 King proclaimed: "We have before us the glorious opportunity to inject a new dimension of love into the veins of our civilization. There is still a voice crying out in terms that echo across the generations, saying: 'Love your enemies, bless them that curse you, and pray for them that despitefully use you, that you may be the children of your Father which is in Heaven'" In his *To Make the Wounded Whole,* Lewis Baldwin claims that "King's vision of world community was parallel to, and largely derived from, the vision of Mays and Thurman" ([1962] 1992, 257). For Martin Luther King Jr., says Fluker, "all human life is interrelated and must be seen as a single process culminating in the beloved community" (1990, 39).

In one of his final speeches in Atlanta, as the peroration of his paean "Honoring Du Bois," King recommended "a committed empathy with all of the oppressed" and a "divine dissatisfaction with all forms of injustice" (1970, 19). In a similar spirit, King claimed, in one of his final speeches (February 23, 1968), as the peroration of his paean to Du Bois, that we are "still challenged to be dissatisfied":

> Let us be dissatisfied until every [person] can have food and material necessities for his body, culture and education for his mind, freedom and human dignity for his spirit. Let us be dissatisfied until rat-infested, vermin-filled slums will be a thing of a dark past and every family will have a decent, sanitary house in which to live. . . . Let us be dissatisfied until brotherhood is no longer a meaningless word at the end of a prayer but the first order of business on every legislative agenda. Let us be dissatisfied until our brother of the Third World—Asia, Africa, and Latin America—will no longer be the victim of imperialist exploitation, but will be lifted from the long night of poverty, illiteracy, and disease ([1968] 2010, 110).

But as an "applied personalist," to borrow Lewis Baldwin's useful description, King's dream of a beloved community or world house extended well beyond this minimal but by no means trivial condition. For Thurman, we might add that the beloved community includes not only freedom from fear, as he discusses it in *Jesus and the Disinherited,* but also freedom from hatred and deception. Similar to Gandhi, Thurman and King believed that love, whether construed as ahimsa or agape, provides the vital resources requisite for breaking down the barriers that separate us from one another. Kenneth Smith and Ira Zepp argue that "King could not envision the Beloved Community apart from the alleviation of economic inequality and the achievement of economic justice" (1998, 136). Citing Cicero's dictum that "freedom is participation in power," King claimed in *Where Do We Go from Here* that "America must be a nation in which its multiracial people are partners in power" since "this is the essence of democracy toward which all Negro struggles have been directed since the distant past when he was transplanted here in chains" ([1986] 2010, 55). The depth and breadth of the beloved community is extended, ultimately, for Thurman and King but also for Royce and Gandhi, by the transformative strength of love. The radical Royce, if that makes sense, and I think it does, as well as the radical Thurman and the radical King were committed to an ethic of radical love—that is, a love that goes beyond simplistic notions of justice. "Although King's conception of the 'beloved community' represents a synthesis from a wide range of thinkers," suggests Fluker, "a simple working definition is a community ordered by love" (1990, 39).

Perhaps the best treatment of the wide array of philosophical and theological influences on King's theory of agape and beloved community, on both sides of the Charles River but also down South in Atlanta and Montgomery, is to be found in Rufus Burrow's *Martin Luther King, Jr., and the Theology of Resistance* (2015). Although there has been a tendency among King scholars to focus on either the formal or informal influences on King's development, for example, between the technical language of Boston personalism or the theological fineries of Paul Tillich, on the one hand, or "the religion of Ebenezer Church," on the other, Burrow argues that "both are important for one who seeks a fuller, more thorough understanding of King and his work" (2015, 122). Black churches provided a structure-function of hope derived from the "the context of hundreds of years of slavery and suffering that prevented despair from becoming the defining characteristic of the lives by looking forward to God's coming, eschatological freedom" (Cone 1984, 419; also see Raboteau 1978, 251). Cone argues that "the white public and also many white scholars have misunderstood King," as well as Thurman, "because they know so little about the black church community, ignoring its effect upon his life and thought" (1984, 414). Similarly, Lewis Baldwin claims that the "failure of many scholars to recognize that King's genius was folk, black, and southern may be attributed in large measure to racism and to some extent southern bias" (1991, 3). Perhaps this is less true of Thurman's genius, but Baldwin's main contention is well taken when it comes to exploring Thurman's thought. Although he generally agrees with Gary Herstein that "most of the philosophical aspects of King's beloved community ethic already existed in Royce" (2009, 8), Burrow insists that "King went well beyond Royce in characterizing the actual concrete nature of such a community, as well as proposing and consistently applying a method—nonviolent direct action—for achieving it" (2015, 125). King made a similar contribution to the American personalist tradition. But Burrow also contends that "even before his arrival at Crozer Theological Seminary and later at Boston University, King was already quite family with the idea expressed by the beloved community, even if he did not then know the term" (2015, 130).

The best comparative study of Thurman and King on the beloved community ideal is certainly Walter E. Fluker's meticulously researched *They Looked for a City* (1989; also see 1990). Similar to Burrow, Fluker insists that beyond the question of influence of Royce or Thurman, formal or informal, intellectual or experiential, we must also attend to "the normative and empirical dimensions of the problem" within their respective conceptions of community as well as to "each thinker's recommendations for overcoming the barriers to community" and "the actualization of community" (1989, xiii–xiv). Fluker argues that Thurman's personal pilgrimage, which he called "the search for common ground," culminated in a theocentric vision of reality which emphasized the nature and role of the committed individual in the actualization of community. King's personal odyssey toward "the beloved community" resulted in a Christocentric conception of community that stressed the nature and the role of society in the actualization of individual potential within community. Future scholars may find that the discontinuities that exist between Thurman and King are perhaps more important than the continuities. They reveal different dimensions of the common problems that their conceptualizations and recommendations address and provide new insights and directions in the creation of a model for the work of community in the world (1990, 49).

Conclusion

For King and Thurman, certainly, but also for Royce, although each expressed it in his own way, the notion of the beloved community signaled a loyal commitment to unconditional love, social justice, and an acknowledgement of the inviolable dignity of persons. Royce as well as Thurman and King were responding to the voice of their own conscience. Each of these philosophers was willing to make sacrifices in order to serve the needs of "those with their backs against the wall," as Thurman put it, because they believed, each in their own way, that—as King expressed it—"we are caught in an inescapable network of mutuality, tied in a single garment of destiny" (1986, 290). In his earliest extant correspondence, which he wrote to Mordecai Johnson, Thurman wrote: "I feel the needs of my people, I see their distressing condition, and have offered myself upon the altar as a living sacrifice, in order that I might help the 'skinned and flung down' as you interpret. God wants me and His precious love urges me to take up the cross and follow Him" ([1918] 2009, 2). The edges of the beloved community grow, creatively, by means of discovering our unknown brothers and sisters. Near the conclusion of *Common Ground,* Thurman proclaims:

> One day there will stand up in their midst one who will tell of a new sickness among the children who in their delirium cry for their brothers who they have never known and from whom they have been cut off behind the self-imposed barriers of their fathers. An alarm will spread throughout the community that it is being felt and slowly realized that community cannot

> feed for long on itself; it can only flourish where always the boundaries are giving way to the coming of others from beyond them—unknown and undiscovered brothers. Then the wisest among them will say: What we have sought we have found, our own sense of identity. We have established a center out of which at last we can function and relate to other men. We have committed to heart and to nervous system a feeling of belonging and our spirits are no longer isolated and afraid (1971, 104).

What is the dynamic process by which genuine community emerges? Thurman's response: "If one is moved from within one's own spirit to do the deed of ministering to the need of another, and if the need of another is the point at which the spirit is most highly sensitized to communication, then it follows that the good deed is a meeting place of one life with another" (Thurman, quoted in Fluker 1989, 193). Like Buber, Thurman also believed that God is encountered as persons are to be encountered, that is, as Buber put it, "upon the narrow ridge, where I and Thou meet," or "in the realm of the between" (Buber 1958, 25; also see Thurman 1998, 298): these genuine encounters are "neither individualistic nor collectivistic, neither inner nor outer, nor the sum of the two" but rather an interpersonal realm that is something more, "something common to each but reaching beyond their separateness" (Kramer 2003, 204). Like his sermons, Thurman's philosophical writings aim at "the illumination of the imagination, the stirring of the heart, and challenge us to live life meaningfully" ([1962] 1978, 5). The doctrine of the beloved community, whether theological or philosophical construed, constitutes for King and Thurman as well as Royce a philosophical theory of social freedom and a call to service. Until the very end, argues Fluker, "King maintained the belief that authentic community would come to America through the redemptive struggles of black Americans and others who dared to follow their glorious example" (1989, 187).

Epilogue

The time and place of a man's life on earth are the time and place of his body, but the meaning and significance of his life are as vast and as far-reaching as his gifts, his times, and the passionate commitment of all his powers can make it.

Thurman, *With Head and Heart* (1979)

Thurman was both gifted and committed. Although he lived through troubled times and in precarious places, the meaning and significance of his life was both vast and far-reaching. Thurman is one of those rare philosophers who satisfies the demands of the head as well as the needs of the heart and is often said to be timeless but always timely: but the always timely makes sense, tragically, because the social upheaval to which he was responding—what King dubbed the "giant triplets of racism, materialism and imperialism"—is still with us (2010, 196–197). Thurman was an insightful philosopher, and he contained multitudes. In fact, Thurman was an exemplary American scholar, in Emerson's sense of the term; a spiritual genius, in the way that James described it; a profound philosopher; and—as his wife described him—a "tutor to the world."[1]

Although Thurman's thought was first and foremost fixated on ministering to those "who needed profound succor and strength to enable them to live in the present with dignity and creativity" (1996, 11), his teachings were never meant "merely as a defense mechanism and a substitute for action that would relieve the pressure" (1975, 63). Any form of philosophy worthy of the name, thought Thurman, must aim—as Angela Davis puts it—at "eradicating some of the misery in this world" (2010, 66). As a philosopher and as a theologian, Thurman attempted to understand the world in order to improve it.

Thurman wrote for his contemporaries, to be sure, for those who were in the throes of the civil rights struggle of his era, but one also gets the distinct impression that he wrote to a distant progeny. Although Alton Pollard suggests that Thurman might have been—and perhaps he still remains—"too radical for us" and that "we have not yet caught up with him" (1992, 193), perhaps Thurman's time really has come. Although Thurman constitutes a rich resource when it comes to addressing contemporary geopolitical crises, which in many ways are merely later stages of the earlier injustices, Victor Anderson is surely right when he observes—in *Beyond Ontological Blackness*—that "Thurman's thought breeds an optimism about the possibility of human reconciliation that is hard to sustain in light of our postmodern conditions of cultural fragility, the threat of urban and rural nihilism, and the often tragic qualities of daily life" (1999, 43).

When we consider the way he lived his life, the decisions he made, it is clear that "the bias, the emphasis, the prejudice, the slant of his life," as Thurman expressed it in his *Temptations of Jesus,* "was on the side of the hungers of his mind and his spirit" (1978, 20). "All his life," wrote Thurman, he had "been on the scent of the tie that binds life at a level so deep that the final privacy of the individual would be reinforced rather than threatened" (1971, xiii). Thurman's chiseled yet gentle face represents for me an exemplar and unique ideal of what it means to be a man—as a father, husband, widower, and a free thinker. Thurman was remarkably self-actualized: he dedicated his life to growing the edges of beloved community. One could say of Thurman what he said of Jesus: "Wherever his spirit appeared, the oppressed gathered fresh courage, for he announced the good news that fear, hypocrisy, and hatred, the three hounds of hell that tract the trail of the disinherited, need have no dominion over them" (1996, 29).

Thurman played an essential yet still largely unappreciated role in the early civil rights movement in America. It is tempting to say of Thurman what Larson says of the shaman: "He is the prototype of the artist, the priest, the dramatist, the physician, all rolled into one" (1976, 10). When one encounters the breadth and depth of Thurman's thought, his luminous darkness, the sweep of his interests and the creativity of his imagination, one recognizes that one has come in contact with an exceptional individual and an extraordinary personality. Thurman sometimes advised his students as well as his congregants to search carefully, patiently, intentionally, inwardly as well as outwardly, for the voice or sound of the genuine. Thurman's voice was one such voice. (In the epigraph with which this book began, Thurman would have been one of the wise ones.) "Rather than asking what the world needs," advised Thurman, "ask rather what makes you come alive, and go do that, because what the world needs is people who have come alive." Philosophy made Thurman come alive. He was simultaneously tough-minded and tender-hearted. That said, Thurman was a thinking man from the outset. In *Search for Common Ground,* Thurman confesses that when he was a small boy, back in Daytona Beach, he was "so enamored of [the imagine of Rodin's "Thinker"] that [he] tried to reproduce the pose, the stance, the furrowed brow, the chin resting on the flat side of the fist—these became for [him] the hallmarks of thought and profundity" (1971, 9).

One could also say of Thurman what he wrote of Rabindranath Tagore: namely, that "his tremendous spiritual insight created a mood unique among the voices of the world. He moved deep into the heart of his own spiritual idiom and came up inside all peoples, all cultures, and all faiths" (1979, 129). Thurman was a transformative leader, despite the fact that—as Luther Smith puts it in *Mystic as Prophet*—he "was not interested in forming a social action organization that embodied his ideas, or in becoming the leader of a mass movement, he has drawn a following which attests to the significance of his witness. Thurman devotees speak of his radical effect upon their lives, his gift for enabling peak experiences, guiding one to the presence of God and sharpening the vision of reality" (2007, 2). Smith suggests that "Thurman's interpretation of the spiritual basis for social transformation may serve as the philosophy for the next generation of participants in the black struggle" (2007, 211). Although I appreciate Martin E. Marty's observation that "locating Thurman in older contexts is not as productive as is the effort to take him from his time and place and apply his ideas to our own" (1998, xiii), I have belabored the sociohistorical context and conceptual landscape as a means of providing the present generation with a model of philosophical courage. Eulogizing King but in terms that describe his own life, Thurman wrote: "His thinking, his feeling, and his deeds must transcend all that separates and divides. He must know hate and conquer it with love; he must know fear and conquer it with a strange new courage" (1971, 95). Thurman personified precisely these qualities. In *Search for Common Ground,* Thurman describes the hero or heroine as a person "of courage, possessing the acumen of mind and the discipline of training that could stand up under the scrutiny of the sharpest critics who guarded the citadels of power" as well as "one whose sense of community was deep in the throb of Negro life so that between his heart and theirs there would be a swinging door that no man could shut" (1971, 94).

Inside the Thurman obelisk at Morehouse College, engraved in black marble, and to the left of their burial niche where Howard Thurman's and Sue Bailey's ashes are interred, there is a redolent quote from Sue in which she describes her husband as a "seeker and finder of genuine existence—a tutor to the world." The philosophical dimension in Thurman's thought often consists more in the seeking than finding. Thurman brooded over an astonishingly wide array of philosophical and sociopolitical problems and theological paradoxes. Although it is sometimes said that the philosopher one chooses depends on the sort of person one is, I think that it is also true that the sort of person one becomes depends on the philosopher one chooses. At least in part, I was initially drawn to Thurman because of a shared theological or philosophical training and a kindred spiritual temperament, but I continue to study Thurman because the more I seek, in him, in what he was seeking, the more I find. Thurman's thought evolved constantly, sometimes incrementally, sometimes by leaps and bounds, for example, between 1954, when he wrote *Creative Encounter,* which displayed "many indications of seeking but perhaps little evidence of finding" ([1954] 1972, 12), and 1963, when he wrote *Disciplines of the Spirit,* which provided ample evidence of philosophical insight or spiritual discovery, or in 1971, when he wrote his resplendent *Search for Common Ground.* Thurman would also want us to recognize, however, that "seeking and finding are so united that failure and frustration, real though they are, are no longer felt to be ultimately real" (1961, 112).

Notes

Introduction

1. For more on the Howard Thurman Papers Project, see the Boston University School of Theology page, http://www.bu.edu/htpp/.

1. An African American Philosophy of Nonviolent Resistance

1. Thurman discusses the doctrine of ahimsa as an ethical doctrine with a spiritual foundation as means of dealing with their poverty, of which the spinning-wheel was the symbol in his 1953 lecture on Gandhi, which was part of a series called *Men Who've Walked with God*, part 7, "Gandhi," available from the Expanding Common Ground, Howard Thurman & Sue Bailey Thurman Collections at Boston University, http://hgar-srv3.bu.edu/web/howard-thurman/virtual-listening-room/detail?id=367489.

2. Makechnie claims that Thurman's "intimate knowledge and appreciation of religions went well beyond the Christian and Judaic traditions. Amiya Chakraverty, a one-time academic secretary to Rabindranath Tagore, in conversation with [Makechnie] in 1971, stated that he considered Howard's knowledge about Hinduism to be 'creative and insightful'" (1988, 22).

3. Following L. Harold DeWolf, who, "while stressing the value of sacrificial love, [was] equally emphatic that agape in its sacrifice should aim to create community" (Ansbro 2000, 24), the Boston personalists seemed to agree that "life under the reign of God is not an individualistic affair. Since love is its dominant principle, it is communal to the very core. This communal life of the kingdom has already begun in some groups and relationships. So far as that love and life are present, the kingdom of God is here" (DeWolf 2011, 303).

4. Fischer suggests that "God preoccupied Gandhi but he never had a mystic experience. . . . He argued instead that '[God] reveals himself daily to every human being, but we shut our ears to the small voice.' . . . God never appears to you in person but in action" (2010, 118); also see Ansbro (2000, 33). The distinction is telling: depending on how one defines mysticism, perhaps Thurman was and Gandhi wasn't a mystic. Then again, for many, perhaps even for Thurman, using Rufus Jones's description of mysticism as a direct encounter with the Divine, Gandhi's description of the voice of God and ahimsa might well qualify him as a mystic. If one is, and the other isn't, we

need to identify what distinguishes the voice of God in Gandhi from a direct encounter with God for Thurman. Oddly, Thurman is perhaps closer to Gandhi on the voice of God or sound of the genuine within than he was to most of his contemporaneous Christians in America.

5. Rudolf Steiner:

> For the majority, one suspects, of 'practicing' Christians—and what does 'practicing' entail in this context?—the Crucifixion remains an unexamined inheritance, a symbolic marker of familiar but vestigial recognitions. This marker is revered and involved in conventional idiom and gestures. Its concrete status, the enormity of suffering and injustice it incarnates, would appear to have faded from felt immediacy. How many educated men and women now hear Pascal's cry that humanity must not sleep because Christ hangs on his Cross till the end of the world? (qtd. in Dixie and West 1999, 224).

6. In the same year as his "Letter from Birmingham Jail," 1963, during the Birmingham campaign, King and the Birmingham affiliate of SCLC developed the following commitment card:

> I hereby pledge myself—my person and body—to the nonviolent movement. Therefore, I will keep the following ten commandments: (1) Meditate daily on the teachings and life of Jesus. (2) Remember always that the nonviolent movement seeks justice and reconciliation—not victory. (3) Walk and talk in the manner of love, for God is love. (4) Pray daily to be used by God in order that all men might be free. (5) Sacrifice personal wishes in order that all men might be free. (6) Observe with both friend and foe the ordinary rules of courtesy. (7) Seek to perform regular service for others and for the world. (8) Refrain from the violence of fist, tongue, or heart. (9) Strive to be in good spiritual and bodily health. (10) Follow the directions of the movement and of the captain on a demonstration" (Young 1996, 238).

7. Following Ansbro's reading of Thurman, who associates this "punishment or retribution clause" with Thurman's claim—reminiscent of Parker and anticipating King's 1963 reference to the long arc of history—that "in the wide sweep of the ebb and flow of moral law our deeds track us down, and doer and deed meet" (1996, 108), King offers a "more consistent . . . presentation of the reasons for forgiveness" (Ansbro 2000, 29). According to Ansbro, King's reformulation of Thurman's argument emphasizes "the eventual defeat of injustice rather than punishment of the persons who perpetuated injustice and were its victims" (29). And while it may be true that King's reformulation of this retributionist doctrine will still appeal to those who do not believe in yonder heaven or a fiery hell, Thurman's statement employs the trope inherent in the black church as the most powerful way to avoid retributionary violence.

8. In his *Strength to Love,* King wrote, "Agape is love seeking to preserve and create community" ([1963] 2010, 87). According to Paul Ramsey's description of agape, which influenced King in significant ways, "while appeals to self-love, enlightened self-interest, and mutual love for common values can preserve community, only Christian love [qua agape] performs the 'work of reconciliation' and enters the 'no man's land' where dwell the desperate and the despised outcasts from every human community and brings community with them into existence" (Ramsey, qtd. in Ansbro 2000, 27). Bertocci, alternatively, defined love as "the total orientation of a person's thinking, feeling, and willing insofar as his controlling commitment is the ideal growth of the personality in himself and in all other persons" (1962, 403). As a working definition, Thurman suggests that "love is the experience of dealing with a person at a point in him or her that is beyond all his faults and all his virtues. Love means to deal totally with a person. And you can't do this without a disciplined and sensitized imagination." Only on this basis, can forgiveness really take place—I must get past the thing that created the wall in the first place. Thurman says that we must find some way of getting past the wall or block so that I might see myself through your eyes, at which point the wall melts. "To love means to love at a person from the other side. I can't do this of myself, regardless of my best intentions; and if I think that I can, I deceive myself" (1953, "Love or Perish" audio). In "Loving Your Enemies," King defines love as a "creative, understanding good will for all [persons]." This sort of love, claims King, "is the refusal to defeat any individual. When you rise to the level of love, of its great beauty and power, you seek only to defeat evil systems. Individuals who happen to be caught up in that system, you love, but you seek to defeat the system" (2010, 20).

9. Political moralists part ways with politics, however, whenever politicians begin to treat morality as if it were "a universal *doctrine of prudence,* that is, a theory of maxims by which to choose the most efficient means of furthering one's own interests, which is to deny that morality exists at all. Politics says, 'Be ye wise as serpents,' to which morality adds (as a limiting condition) 'and as innocent as doves'" (Kant 2009, 94).

10. Analogous to Gandhi's experiments with *satyagraha,* Thurman's creative experiments with ahimsa sought to build rather than merely preserve community: Thurman's work with the Church for the Fellowship of All Peoples aimed at providing empirical evidence in support of his guiding thesis—namely, that we have spiritual resources available to us that are sufficiently compelling to break down the ideological barriers that separate people. Although he initially resisted the idea of a formal pledge or commitment card or membership statement, Thurman and Fisk did develop a commitment card in 1945.

2. On the Anatomy of Hatred and the Power of Love

1. In "Black Power," Stokely Carmichael cites Guevara as someone who "clearly understood the savagery of white America, and who was ready to meet with armed

resistance. It is the young bloods especially who contain the hatred Che Guevara speaks of: Hatred as an element of the struggle, relentless hatred of the enemy that impels us over and beyond the natural limitations of man, and transforms us into effective, violent, selected and cold killing machines" ([1967] 2007, 88).

2. In *Black Power: A Basic Understanding,* Walter Rodney sizes up the situation this way: "Violence in the American situation Is inescapable. White society is violent, white American society is particularly violent, and white American society is especially violent towards blacks" ([1969]2014, 58). Rodney would also object to King's equivocation on the violence perpetrated by the oppressor with the response of those who are oppressed: "By what standard of moral can the violence used by a slave to break his chains be considered the same as the violence of a slave master? By what standards can we equate the violence of blacks who have been oppressed, suppressed, depressed, and repressed for four centuries with the violence of white fascists? Violence aimed at the recovery of human dignity and at equality cannot be judged by the same yardstick as violence aimed at maintenance of discrimination and oppression" (ibid). Similarly, Steve Biko insists: "Not only have [whites] kicked the black but they have also told him how to react to the kick. For a long time the black has been listening with patience to the advice he has been receiving on how best to respond to the kick. With painful slowness he is now beginning to show signs that it is his right and duty to respond to the kick in the way he sees fit" (2002, 65).

3. In a series of lectures delivered at the behest of the Student Christian Movement of Canada, "The Significance of Jesus," Thurman writes: "I must exhaust all possible means, and this is important, that do not conflict with my ends, for defeating the kingdom of evil. And this means that I must put my creative mind to work at the devising of strategies, personal strategies and group strategies for the achievement of these ends. . . . Moral suasion, yes, but it is important to point out that moral suasion is limited by the amount of moral atrophy that has taken place in a man. I may be patient; I may keep working and trying to keep appealing and appealing and appealing on the assumption, of course, that all men are children of God—those instruments of evil, as well as those who are suffering because of evil. I shall endure, hoping that moral suasion will finally cause dead things to come to life" (2012, 87).

3. Pedagogical Personalism at Morehouse College

1. The first tradition or representative response described by West is that of the assimilationist. He says the assimilationist, "unlike the exceptionalist tradition, does not romanticize Afro-American culture; instead, it deprecates this culture" (1982, 80). West classifies E. Franklin Frazier as ultimately "the unchallenged theoretician of the weak assimilationist tradition in Afro-American history" (78). Although many if not most scholars would disagree with him on this point, West thinks that Carter G. Woodson, who wrote the *Miseducation of the Negro,* is similarly classified as an assimilationist.

West views both exceptionalist and assimilationist stances as pathologies, configuring the second as an inversion of the first. Viewing it as a pathology, West infers that "Afro-American critical thought must hold the assimilationalist response to be unacceptable" (80). Both traditions constitute for West "a rash reaction against a hostile white society rather than a responsible response to particular challenges. Both traditions represent the peculiar predicament of the Afro-American middle class" (80).

West's second tradition has to do with marginality: He cites Richard Wright as the marginal man par excellence. James Baldwin is similarly classified; old-style church leaders, those who rounded upon the inadequacies of their members, are likewise culpable and complicit. These religious leaders were notoriously critical of "their own church members and American society" (1982, 80). These marginalists, though constantly revolting against American society, represented—suggests West—a "conscious embodiment and rejection of [Afro-American culture]," they "maintain a distance and express a denial of Afro-American culture," they emphasize a "rejection and distrust of American society," and they are all—perhaps Baldwin to a lesser degree than Wright—perennially "uprooted" and "vindictive" (1982, 81).

West's third tradition, the "exceptionalist response to the challenges of self-image and self-determination, is this: a romanticization of Afro-American culture that conceals the social mobility of an emerging opportunistic Afro-American petite bourgeoisie. . . . It generates cathartic and amorphous feelings of Afro-American pride, self-congratulation, and heroism that contain little substance" (1982, 70–78). West considers King to be a "weak exceptionalist" (74) for rather interesting reasons, reasons that take us some distance in the direction of understanding the conceptual context of "an emerging Black theology, whether Islamic or Christian" (78).

West's final category is that of the humanist: the Afro-American humanist tradition is best captured "in [Afro-American] music" (85), but it is represented also in such authors as Jean Toomer and Ralph Ellison and in such political activists or philosophers as "the later Du Bois" and "post-Mecca Malcolm X" (89).

2. Woodson's "caustic and uncompromising litany [of inconsistencies, shortcomings, and abject failures of 'Negro education'] seemed to go on forever" (Snyder 2015, 273). "Negro education, Woodson charged, clung to a defunct 'machine-method' based on the misguided assumption that 'education is merely a process of imparting information.' It failed to inspire black students and did not 'bring their minds into harmony with life as they must face it.' . . . And the more education blacks received, the more 'estranged from the masses' they became" (Snyder 2015, 273).

3. Ronald K. Goodenow suggested long ago that "historians of progressivism have totally ignored . . . black progressives" (1978, 60); Snyder, who suggests that the same could be said forty years later, also suggests that "progressive education has been effectively coded as a white movement (2015, 276; also see Alridge 2007; Chennault 2013).

4. At about the same time, circa 1925, Alain Locke quipped that African Americans were less in need of a missionary education "for the Negro" (what Woodson would later call an "education under outside control") than an education "by the Negro" (qtd. in Snyder 2015, 277). Du Bois had been arguing along similar lines that "the function of the university is not simply to teach bread winning, or to furnish teachers for public schools or to be a center of polite society. It is, above all, to be the organ of that fine adjustment between real life and the growing knowledge of life, an adjustment which forms the secret of civilization" ([1903] 2007, 60).

5. As for West, the exceptionalist response is "undesirable" because it fosters "a romanticization of Afro-American culture that conceals the social mobility of an emerging opportunistic Afro-American petite bourgeoisie" and also because it "generates cathartic and amorphous feelings of Afro-American pride, self-congratulation, and heroism that contain little substance" (1982, 75–76).

6. John Hope Franklin has remained, according to Leroy Davis, "the least known major figure in the annals of African American history between Booker T. Washington and Martin Luther King" (1998, xxiv). In his foreword to Davis's *Clashing of the Soul,* Franklin says that "Hope consistently fought on the civil rights front as well as on the educational front" (1998, xi).

7. "We were admonished," claimed Tobin, who taught philosophy, "to maintain the dialectic between the community of faith and the community of learning. Dr. Mays knew how easily teachers and professors became 'prisoners of procedures; victims of arteriosclerosis.' Nothing is worse [for Mays] than the 'hardening of the categories'" (Tobin, quoted in Carter 1998, 27).

8. Mays argued that a compensatory idea of God encouraged "a shallow pragmatism," by which a "belief or idea may be accredited as true if it satisfies our desire, if it uplifts and consoles; or if it makes us happier to believe it even though the belief or idea does not fit observed fact" (Mays 1968, 14; also see Jelks 2012, 95–96.

9. Commenting on Du Bois's provocative belief that the university, if it is to be firm, must hark back to the original idea of the [West African] bush school" (2001, 117), Andrew Douglas suggests that, "especially in his later work, Du Bois conceives of the Black college as a kind of counsel of universality, an institution uniquely attendant to the struggle for a more sustainable and publicly oriented society distinctly situated to expose the particularity of the White world" (2015, 34).

10. Beyond these outward signs of Thurman's keen interest in philosophy, the student of philosophy will recognize throughout Thurman's written corpus numerous allusions to perennial philosophical paradoxes, for example, the structural similarity of Thurman's insistence that a specific religious doctrine that "the things that are true in any religious experience are to be found in that religious experience precisely because they are true; they are not true simply because they are found in that religious experience" (1979, 144) with Socrates' poignant question *Euthyphro,* or the problem "one and

the many" or references to Theseus's ship on questions of personal identity) and great dexterity with the philosophical terminology of the time (for example, his use of the "principle of alteration" in Hocking or the "process of individuation" as articulated in Royce or the "notion of self-overcoming" in Goethe's *Faust* and Nietzsche's "will-to-power" or the "master-slave dialectic" in Hegel and the "coincidence of opposites" in Boehme.)

11. In 1957, in an essay titled "The New Heaven and the New Earth," Thurman wrote:

> The curriculum provided for no such [courses in philosophy]. There was logic for a half year and a wonderful course in ethics, so called, which gave the president the opportunity to become acquainted intimately with the seniors and to expose them to his working philosophy, but it didn't teach you anything about ethics as a discipline. This was not an accident, and in this regard, Morehouse was not unique. For if students are exposed to the creative process which causes them to raise profound questions about meanings and to seek answers, they may go on to raise questions about the structure of the institution which made it possible for them to get their college education. (2017, 201)

12. Jelks suggests that Mays's philosophy of education "struck a middle ground between that of Booker T. Washington, who advocated industrial training, and W.E.B. Du Bois, who promoted classical or liberal arts education. What Mays found appealing about Washington was that he gave black people pride in the accomplishments and building of Tuskegee Institute. . . . On the other hand, he agreed with DuBois on the virtue of liberal arts education, especially in training leaders for the freedom struggles of black people" (2012, 145–146). Orville Vernon Burton, who wrote the foreword to Mays's *Born to Rebel,* says "Mays's life provides insight into the transitional years from Booker T. Washington's accommodationist philosophy to the Black Power radicalism of the late 1960s and early 1970s" (Mays 1987, xiii). For more on the influence of Dewey on Mays, during the years that they overlapped at the University of Chicago (1936–1940), see Jelks 2012, 158.

13. In an essay titled "The New Heaven and the New Earth," Thurman wrote: "The great contribution made to my generation by men like 'Bennie' Mays, Lorimer Milton, 'Smokey Joe' Caroll was this: They heightened our morale. Morale by simple definition is belief in one's own cause" ([1958] 2017, 201). Thurman thought that the pedagogical emphasis at Morehouse had shifted by 1967, not fundamentally, "but a shift that is a radical and creative derivative from the original emphasis [namely, a shift from the competition with one's self to competition with others]" (1998, 237). Without diminishing the importance of entering into "active competition in the whole arena of ideas," Thurman insisted that "it is mandatory for us to try to discover an 'other-than-self'

reference for the validation of our own experience of one's mind" (238). Thurman would preach this philosophical point. In 1956, in a sermon titled "Freedom," which was part of series on the religion of Jesus, Thurman said:

> I grow in favor with man when I recognize first of all that I must understand myself. Now the sociologists tell us that the child is not born human. A child is born in a human situation and the degree to which he establishes a primary set of other than self references in a human situation, to that degree he becomes a human being. It is in the primary social unit that he has it conferred upon him, so that he may grasp as part of his awareness, his persona, his person, his self. I'm not saying tha the social situation creates the core of his self, but I'm saying that the primary social unit defines the self so that the self can become aware of the self. (1956b)

14. Pedagogical personalists also believe that individuality is strengthened by a genuine encounter with one's own past. In the case of African Americans, Du Bois's concern with cultural sustainability constitutes an auxiliary argument in defense of HBCUs. As early as the 1930s, claims Carley M. Shinault, Du Bois "began to note the benefits of remaining in segregated institutions" (2014, 4), and "in his 1940 work, *Dusk of Dawn,* Du Bois reminded the educated elite that race forever tied their fate to that of the Black masses, and that no degree of economic, social or political success could alter that" (4). Even after *Brown v. Board of Education* in 1954, Du Bois was convinced that "racial integration without cultural integration in the schools would deprive Blacks of the tools necessary for true racial uplift" (4). Although Du Bois believed that discrimination within the educational system would be reduced, that there would be increased opportunities for African Americans to study at historically white colleges and universities, he warned—as late as 1960, in "Whither Now and Why?"—that "the deficiency in knowledge of Negro history and culture, however, will remain and this danger must be met or else American Negroes will disappear" (2001, 152).

15. See *Where Do We Go from Here: Community or Chaos* ([1968] 2010), especially the final chapter, titled "The World House," 234–89.

4. Reading Thurman as a Philosophical Personalist

1. What Albert Knudson conceded back in 1927 is in large part still true today: Personalism

> cannot yet be said to be a popular term. Many who might be classed as personalistic in their philosophy or at least as near-personalists, still avoid the term so far as they themselves are concerned. But it is nevertheless steadily gaining in favor, and bids fair before long to have a well-established place in philosophical usage. . . . The very word, it is true, implies that a philosophy so named must make the idea of personality central and basal,

> and must interpret reality in personal terms. . . . There are wildly divergent types of personalism. It thus becomes our task to determine, if possible, the true or normal type. (1969, 20–21)

Although he conceded that there were already more than "fifty different definitions of personality" in 1937, in reference to Gordon W. Allport's 1937 report in *Personality,* and "great differences of opinion among authorities," Brightman claimed that "different definitions are not always contradictory" and suggested that many if not all of them may constitute "correction definitions of various aspects of the personality" (1945, 52–53). Brightman then suggests that a "philosophical definition, such as we are trying to formulate, must be consistent with all the truths about personality which are necessarily present in all contexts" (ibid., 52).

2. On prophetic pragmatists, see West (1999, 141 and 558) for evidence that West has distanced himself from the American pragmatist tradition. For more on West's prophetic pragmatism, see chapter 6 of this volume.

3. Stated differently, Bertocci defines personality as something that is "learned as a person interacts with other persons; more exactly, a person's personality is his more or less systematic mode of response to himself, to others, and to his total environment in the light of what he believes them to be, and what they actually are" (1970, 95). Lawrence Carter, who studied with Bertocci, says that "for King, the person's structure is shaped, at least in part, by the value conferred upon him or her. Thus, there is no separation between the structure, or how a person is defined, and the value, or how the person might be viewed in light of that definition" (1998, 219). In Brightman, *Nature and Values,* the condensed definition reads: "A person is a unity of complex conscious changes [that is, a *unitas multiplex*], including all its experiences—its memories, its purposes, its values, its powers, its activities, and its experienced interactions with its environment" (1945, 56). Muelder puts it most concisely: "Personality is the most concrete category of existence and value. This means that the richest synoptic grasp of existential wholes and the highest value in axiological hierarchy are both apprehended in personality" ([1943] 1983, 85).

4. Merton continues: "After all, the idea that one can seriously cultivate his own personal freedom merely by discarding inhibitions and obligations, to live in self-centered spontaneity, results in the complete decay of the true self and of its capacity for freedom. Personalism and individualism must not be confused. Personalism gives priority to the person means respective the unique and inalienable value of the other person, as well as one's own, for a respect that is centered only on one's individual self to the exclusion of others proves itself to be fraudulent" (1995, 17).

5. Luther Smith suggests that "Thurman's theology resembles that of Ralph Waldo Emerson. The rejection of dogma in order to discover truth in nature, the belief in humanity's divinity, the emphasis upon the individual, the commitment to

mysticism, and the certainty regarding the possibility for community are primary in their thought" (1991, 100)—taken together, these things could, says Smith, "lead one to characterize [Thurman] as the Emerson of the twentieth century" (100).

6. On "rootedness in nature," Thurman would seem to anticipate a personalist environmental ethic:

> One of the deceptive aspects of mind in man is to give him the illusion of being distinct from and over against but not a part of nature. It is but a single leap thus to regard nature as being so completely other than himself that he may exploit it, plunder it, and rape it with impunity. This we see all around us in the modern world. Our atmosphere is polluted, our streams are poisoned, our hills are denuded, and wild life is increasingly exterminated, while more and more man becomes an alien on earth and a fouler of his own nest. The price that is being extracted for this is a deep sense of isolation, of being rootless and a vagabond. Often I have surmised that this condition is more responsible for what seems to be the phenomenal increase in mental and emotional disturbances in modern life than the pressures—economic, social, and political—that abound on every hand. The collective psyche shrieks with the agony that it feels as a part of the death cry of a pillaged nature. (1971, 83–84)

7. Although Galtung defines violence as "the cause [or conditions] of the difference between the potential and the actual, between what could have been and what is," he also claims that "it is not so important to arrive at anything like the definition, or the topology—for there are obviously many types of violence," as it is "to indicate theoretically significant dimensions of violence that can lead thinking, research and, potentially, action towards the most important problems" (1969, 168).

8. Moreover: "It seeks to answer three basic needs of the human spirit: for a supreme object of devotion and therefore worship, for a way of thinking about and believing in the object of devotion, and for a way of life in which the spirit of the object of devotion is expressed—the assumption is that the citizen who is loyal to sovereignty experiences community" (1998, 84). This is important because the state is trying to provide "a climate in which it is reasonable to assume that his potential can be actualized" (84), but it also serves as "a socially accepted judgment that can determine for him when he [or she] is lost, when he has missed the way—i.e., when he is out of community" (85).

5. Reading Thurman as a Social Activist Mystic

1. Smith considers it helpful to differentiate Thurman's brand of mysticism from that of others as distinct from extroverted or introverted mysticism as discussed in Stace: "The extrovertive way looks outward through the physical senses into the external world and finds the One there. The introvertive way turns inward introspectively,

and finds the One at the bottom of the self, at the bottom of the personality" (1960, 15). Smith's point apropos of Stace's topology is that Thurman makes use of both movements, the centripetal and the centrifugal, thus "ambivertive" ([1991] 2007, 79).

2. In *Mysticism and Philosophical Analysis,* Katz examines both Jones and Underhill. Rufus Jones has pointed out that "the essence of mysticism is the soul's communion with god. He explains that in the mystical experience one finds oneself in direct relationship with the Over-World of reality of the same nature as his own inmost self and with which he feels akin" (1978, 148). Although Jones does discuss the essence of mysticism, he also insists that all experiences are produced within "a social and intellectual environment" (1909, xxxiv). Thurman goes further than that in suggesting that in the throes of mystical experience, "there is nothing that is not involved." As a parallel text, Katz cites Underhill's "summary statement": "Mysticism, in its pure form, is the science of ultimates, the science of union with the Absolute, and nothing else, and . . . the mystic is the person who attains to this union, not the person who talks about it. Not the know about, but to Be, is the mark of the real initiate" (Katz 1978, 148).

3. Indeed, Schmidt suggests that the "mystical tradition," understood as a distinct classification of religious texts, emerged only in the early seventeenth century; the second frame of reference emerges at the turn of the twentieth century, which includes James, Underhill, Rufus Jones (with whom Thurman studied in Haverford), and Rudolf Otto. Between the first and the second frame of reference, that is, in the interim period of the eighteenth and nineteenth centuries, there was only—at least until relatively recently—Friedrich Schleiermacher to consider (see Schmidt 2003, 275).

4. Thurman maintained a lifelong fascination with Albert Schweitzer, who, thought Thurman, was animated by a profound reverence for life. In an unpublished essay from 1949, Thurman wrote: "And this to me is the most significant thing about Dr. Schweitzer. And this reveals the character of his spiritual genius. The interpretation he gives—or shall I say the interpretation that was given to him—of the concept of the 'reverence for life'—for this concept is at once one of the central, ethical problems of man. For there can be no ethics if the individual does not affirm life" (07/17/1949 [B11/F35] Howard Gotlieb Archival Research Center. Boston University). At the center of the reverence for life, concludes Thurman, lies compassion and spiritual insight.

5. Stephen Larson embellishes: "There is a continuum, it seems, between the most primitive forms of mythic consciousness and the highest forms of mysticism, The meaning that motivates primitive magic and ritual is another aspect of the truth sought by the mystic: that the universe is—beneath the illusion of separateness—interconnected" (1976, 28).

6. The mystics or religious geniuses that James examines "owed their power originally to the fact of the direct personal communication with the divine" (1985, 133). Thurman would have appreciated but perhaps amended William James's definition of divinity as "not a deity *in concreto,* not a superhuman person, but the immanent divinity in things, the essentially spiritual structure of the universe" (34). James sought out

the "pattern setters," that is, "individuals for whom religion exists not as a dull habit, but as an acute fever" (15). Thurman was a spiritual genius and a real pattern setter in the sense described by James. Elaborating on James's description of religious genius, Barnard claims that "it is their religious mysticism, their powerfully felt, transforming, personally interpreted experiences of an unseen spiritual reality that can rejuvenate a religion, that can instill within different individuals the strong, unshakable faith in the reality and goodness of that unseen world" (1997, 39). So while I believe that Thurman would serve us well as a philosophical tutor, perhaps even as a philosophical prism, he was also a spiritual genius, in Einstein's sense of the phrase, as someone distinguished by a religious if not spiritual sensibility—what might be called a cosmic intuition for wholeness and purposiveness—that is "difficult to elucidate . . . to anyone who does not experience it" (1930, quoted in Tippet 2010, 33). Einstein elaborates:

> The individual feels the vanity of human desires and aims and the nobility and marvelous order which are revealed in nature and in the world of thought. Individual existence strikes him [or her] as a kind of prison, and he [or she] wants to experience the universe as a single, significant whole. The religious geniuses of all ages have been distinguished by this kind of religious feeling. In my view, it is the most important function of art and science to awaken this feeling and keep it alive in those who are receptive to it. (1930, quoted in Tippet 2010, 33)

Einstein described his own spiritual sensibilities in these terms. Thurman exhibited waves of religious sensibility similar to the type characterized by Einstein, certainly, but he was most masterful in his capacity to "awaken this feeling and keep it alive in those who [were] receptive to it." "Despite tremendous differences," says Winifred Gallagher, "spiritual geniuses affect us" primarily, though not exclusively, by focusing "our attention on a reality that's more than meets the eye" and by how they "compassionately teach us by words or example how to find and develop our own special roles in the great sacred scheme of things" or in how they "inspire us by demonstrating the ultimate expression of our human potential" (2001, xv). Thurman fits that description.

6. Reading Thurman as a Prophetic Pragmatist

1. Glaude is convinced "that the failure [of the classical American pragmatists] to address white supremacy philosophically constitutes an unforgivable moral failing" (2007, xv); even Thurman, who stresses the spiritual importance of forgiveness, claims that the evils of racism are beyond forgiveness if not also redemption. West suggests that while "none of the pragmatists were fervent racists themselves—and most of them took public stands against racist practices—not one viewed racism as contributing greatly to the impediments for both individuality and democracy" (1999, 147).

2. See West (1999, 141 and 558) for evidence that West has distanced himself from the American pragmatist tradition.

3. Thurman's thought resonates with Nkrumah on various levels, including the "cardinal ethical principle of philosophical consciencism" and the "monistic thesis of materialism" (Nkrumah 1964, 78–79). Thurman would also agree with Nyerere that "ujamaa, or familyhood," should serve as "the basis of African socialism" and a much-needed corrective to "parasitic capitalism" (1968, 163–64) as well as with Kwame Gyekye about the need for something along the lines of "moderate communitarianism" (1997, 36–47).

4. "Christianity," says Harold Bloom, "gives suffering a meaning not so much to relieve suffering as to allow meaning to get started. The suffering of Jesus gives Christianity its supposed truth and its supposed meaning, since the Christ or God-man does not come so much that we can share God's joy, but rather that God can share our suffering. We perish of this truth, in Nietzsche, and we perish without it, in Kierkegaard" (Bloom 1992, 23). Bloom claims in his *American Religion* that Nietzsche's darkest insight is that "all religions are at the deepest level systems of cruelties" (1992, 23).

7. The Growing Edges of Beloved Community

1. Royce suggests—in "The Hope of the Great Community"—that both Christianity and Buddhism agree that there is no salvation for an individual who is detached.

> for the detached individual there is no salvation, but between the Buddhist and the Pauline solution "there exists a significant difference"—Buddha sought the salvation of the detached individual through an act of resignation whereby all desires are finally abandoned. Paul describes what is essentially salvation through loyalty, salvation through the willing service of a community, and the salvation of those whom he characterizes by the words "They are in Jesus Christ, and walk not after the flesh, but after the spirit." (2005, 1154.)

Royce appropriates this Christian solution in the following way: "But for Paul the being whom he called Jesus Christ was in essence the spirit of the universal community" (2005, 1154).

2. There is an entire body of literature among Anglicans on the beloved community in the 1920 and 1930s. Thurman would have gotten a good dose of Rauschenbusch, himself influenced by Royce, maybe even filtered through Benjamin Elijah Mays's selections in *A Gospel for the Social Awakening: Selections from Rauschenbusch* (1950, with Hopkins), while at Rochester Seminar, although Rauschenbusch died several years prior to Thurman's arrival. There is also a good deal of talk about the beloved community "in the broader currency" among the socialists and communists of the time as well as a host of American liberal Protestants, and people associated with the Fellowship of Reconciliation, especially among pacifists like Horace M Kallen, plus some social critics at Columbia University, for example, Randolph Bourne's writings in *The Radical Will* (1918) and Dewey's early writings about the Great Community, to

which Thurman must have been exposed, at least peripherally, during the summer of 1922. Bourne refers to "the good life of the personality lived in the environment of the beloved community" (1977, 264). Roger Lloyd wrote *The Beloved Community* in 1937. Lewis Mumford's *Golden Day* uses the trope. In an essay on the philosophy of religion at Boston University taught by Brightman, King cited Brightman's *Religious Values*, where Brightman wrote that "the supreme consummation of worship as well as the very soul and purpose of the universe is the Community of Love, or, as Royce calls it, the Beloved Community" (1925, 221). Brightman and Royce corresponded. Thurman and Brightman corresponded from 1936 to 1946, when Brightman became an associate member of the Church for the Fellowship of All People, and afterward, although intermittently, until Brightman's death in 1953, the very year that Thurman formally joined the faculty at Boston University School of Theology and the Marsh Chapel. So it seems to me that Thurman really must have been fairly familiar with beloved community, both in Royce and as used within the Boston University community, as Carmichael suggested in 1977, in "Foundations of the Beloved Community." I think we should take Thurman at his word when he says in May of 1951 that he had been thinking for a long time about Royce's philosophy of loyalty and his seminal formulation of the beloved community. Thurman would have been familiar also with various counter formulations from Rauschenbusch and William James as well as John Dewey and Walter Muelder. Special thanks to Peter Eisenstadt for pointing me in the direction of this material.

3. In examining Royce's doctrine of loyalty and the beloved community, Thurman says that we have our hands on something that is at the very structure of the universe. When the individual surrenders or yields his or her will to a cause, the cause to which someone is loyal reciprocates somehow by returning that person's transformed will in such a way that the will becomes the servant of the cause. One can do that unworthily. The cause serves as the crucible within which the conflicting elements are integrated or galvanized into an individuated self and unified personality. In this sense, it is the "choosing" or "willing" and "abiding" that constitutes personhood. This process occurs, it seems, even if the cause to which one pledges one's loyalty is unworthy of one's devotion: for Thurman, the universe is dynamic in this way. Loyalty, then, is a word to describe what is essentially a spiritual phenomenon derived from the nature of the universe. It means that it is the fusing of the inner and the outer, between my will and thy will. Loyal to whom? Loyal to the tie that binds me to the person. And my loyalty to that person operates through the tie that binds me to that person. Thurman suggests that our loyalty to an individual is derivative since my primary devotion is to the tie that binds each of us one to another. As an illustration of the principle, Thurman claimed that Paul felt that he could be loyal to himself only he was being loyal to the one who had put Paul's parts together. Elsewhere, and often, Thurman uses the story of Legion to explain his philosophical point.

4. In *Luminous Darkness*, he put it this way:

> One may lose fear also by a sense of being a part of a company of people who share the same concerns and are conscious of participating in the same collective destiny. This is an additional form that the feeling of community inspires. A strange and wonderful courage often comes into a man's life when he [or she] shares a commitment to something that is more important than whether he [or she] lives or dies. It is the discovery of the dynamic character of life itself. This may not be a conscious act as far as the rationale for it is concerned. It is a discovery of the conditions under which fresh resources of energy. (1965a, 58)

5. Thurman, "Reflections on the Black Experience" and the *The Search for Common Ground.* http://hgar-srv3.bu.edu/web/howard-thurman/virtual-listening-room/detail?id=360484.

6. Thurman also thought that it is was important to "delineate the difference" between segregation in "the closed system of the South," which he described as "formal, deliberate, open declaration" ([1966] 2009, 201), and the "basic immorality and dishonesty of the systems of power" disclosed within the "de facto segregation in the North" (202). Along similar lines, Thurman recognized that certain forms of token integration could inadvertently provide "protection to the pattern of segregation by which the character of such a group is determined" (204). These distinctions are still instructive today.

7. According to Walter Fluker: "These final years of King's life and ministry, though beleaguered with controversy and sabotage, are the most crucial in understanding the maturation of his personal and intellectual growth in respect to community. It is in this period that one sees most clearly King's wrestling with nonviolence as a means of achieving human community, his increased realization of the international implications of his vision, and his understanding of the nature and role of conflict in the realization of human community" (1990, 39).

Epilogue

1. Thurman exemplifies the philosophical ideal of which Emerson foretold in his iconic address, "American Scholar," considered by many to be the declaration of independence for American philosophy:

> It is one of those fables, which, out of an unknown antiquity, convey an unlooked-for wisdom, that the gods, in the beginning, divided Man into men, that he might be more helpful to himself; just as the hand was divided into fingers, the better to answer its end.
>
> The old fable covers a doctrine ever new and sublime; that there is One Man—present to all particular men only partially, or through one faculty;

and that you must take the whole society to find the whole man. Man is not a farmer, or a professor, or an engineer, but he is all. Man is priest, and scholar, and statesman, and producer, and soldier. In the divided or social state, these functions are parceled out to individuals, each of whom aims to do his stint of the joint work, whilst each other performs his. The fable implies that the individual, to possess himself, must sometimes return from his own labor to embrace all the other laborers. But unfortunately, this original unit, this fountain of power, has been so distributed to multitudes, has been so minutely subdivided and peddled out, that it is spilled into drops, and cannot be gathered. The state of society is one in which the members have suffered amputation from the trunk, and strut about so many walking monsters,—a good finger, a neck, a stomach, an elbow, but never a man.

Man is thus metamorphosed into a thing, into many things. The planter, who is Man sent out into the field to gather food, is seldom cheered by any idea of the true dignity of his ministry. He sees his bushel and his cart, and nothing beyond, and sinks into the farmer, instead of Man on the farm. The tradesman scarcely ever gives an ideal worth to his work, but is ridden by the routine of his craft, and the soul is subject to dollars. The priest becomes a form; the attorney, a statute-book; the mechanic, a machine; the sailor, a rope of a ship.

In this distribution of functions, the scholar is the delegated intellect. In the right state, he is, Man Thinking. In the degenerate state, when the victim of society, he tends to become a mere thinker, or, still worse, the parrot of other men's thinking.

In this view of him, as Man Thinking, the theory of his office is contained. Him nature solicits with all her placid, all her monitory pictures; him the past instructs; him the future invites (1837).

References

Alridge, Derrick P. 2007. "Of Victorianism, Civilizationism, and Progressivism: The Educational Ideals of Anna Julia Cooper and W. E. B. Du Bois, 1892–1940." *History of Education Quarterly* 47, no. 4: 416–46.

Anderson, Victor. 1999. *Beyond Ontological Blackness: An Essay on African American Religious and Cultural Criticism*. New York: Continuum.

Ansbro, John J. 2000. *Martin Luther King, Jr.: Nonviolent Strategies and Tactics for Social Change*. Lanham, Md.: Madison Books.

Appiah, Anthony. 1993. *In My Father's House: Africa in the Philosophy of Culture*. Oxford Paperbacks. New York: Oxford University Press.

———. 2014. *Lines of Descent: W. E. B. Du Bois and the Emergence of Identity*. W.E.B. Du Bois Lectures. Cambridge, Massachusetts: Harvard University Press.

Aristotle. Translated by Jonathan Barnes. 1984. *The Complete Works of Aristotle: The Revised Oxford Translation*. Bollingen Series, 71:2. Princeton, NJ: Princeton University Press.

Augustine. 1997. *The Confessions*. Translated by Maria Boulding. Edited by John E. Rotelle. New York: New City Press.

Baldwin, Lewis V. 1991. *There Is a Balm in Gilead: The Cultural Roots of Martin Luther King, Jr.* Minneapolis: Fortress.

———. (1962) 1992. *To Make the Wounded Whole: The Cultural Legacy of Martin Luther King, Jr.* Minneapolis: Fortress.

———. 2010. *The Voice of Conscience: The Church in the Mind of Martin Luther King, Jr.* Oxford: Oxford University Press.

———. 2011. "The Unfolding of the Moral Order: Rufus Burrow, Jr., Personal Idealism, and the Life and Thought of Martin Luther King, Jr. in *Pluralist*, 6, no. 1, pp. 1–13.

———. 2014. *Lines of Descent: W. E. B. DuBois and the Emergence of Identity*. Cambridge, Mass.: Harvard University Press.

Barnard, G. William. 1997. *Exploring Unseen Worlds: William James and the Philosophy of Mysticism*. Albany: State University of New York Press.

Barrett, Lee C., and Jon Bartley Stewart. 2010. *Kierkegaard and the Bible*, vol. 1, book 2, *The New Testament*. Burlington, Vt.: Ashgate.

Bennett, Charles A., and Irl Goldwin. 1924. "A Philosophical Study of Mysticism." *Philosophical Review* 33, no. 4: 406–19.

Bennett, Lerone. 1978. "Howard Thurman." *Ebony*, February, 68–85.

———. 1998. "The Last of the Great Schoolmasters" (333–44). In *Walking Integrity. Edited* by Lawrence Carter.

Berdiaev Nikolaĭ, and Donald A. Lowrie. 1965. *Christian Existentialism: A Berdyaev Anthology*. Harper Torchbooks. The Cloister Library. New York: Harper.

Berg, Manfred. 2007. "Black Civil Rights and Liberal Anti-Communism: The NAACP in the Early Cold War." *Journal of American History* 94, no. 1 (June): 71–96.

Berlin, Isaiah, and Ian Harris. 2013. *Liberty*. Edited by Henry Hardy. Oxford: Oxford University Press.

Bertocci, Peter A. 1970. *The Person God Is*. London: Allen and Unwinn.

———. 1988. *The Person and Primary Emotions. Recent Research in Psychology*. New York: Springer.

Bertocci, Peter A., and Richard M. Millard. 1962. *Personality and the Good: Psychological and Ethical Perspectives*. New York: David McKay.

Biko, Steve, Aelred Stubbs, Desmond Tutu, Thoko Mpumlwana, and Lewis R Gordon. 2002. *I Write What I Like: Selected Writings*. Chicago: University of Chicago Press.

Bloom, Harold. 1992. *The American Religion: The Emergence of the Post-Christian Nation*. New York: Simon & Schuster.

Bourne, Randolph Silliman. 1977. *The Radical Will: Randolph Bourne 1911–1918*. New York: Urizen Books.

Bowne, Borden Parker. 1905. *The Immanence of God*. Boston: Houghton, Mifflin.

———. 1910. *The Essence of Religion*. Boston: Houghton, Mifflin.

Brightman, Edgar S. 1925. *Religious Values*. New York: Abingdon.

———. 1945. *Nature and Values: The Fondren Lectures for 1945, Southern Methodist University*. New York: Abingdon-Cokesbury Press.

Brown, Judith M. 1989. *Gandhi: Prisoner of Hope*. New Haven: Yale University Press.

Brueggemann, Walter. 1978. *The Prophetic Imagination*. Philadelphia: Fortress Press.

Buber, Martin. 1958. *I And Thou*. 2d ed. Scribner Library. New York: Scribner.

Buford, Thomas O. 2015. "Be the Change You Wish to See: An Essay on Personalism and Education." In *In the Beginning: The Martin Luther King, Jr. International Chapel at Morehouse College; a Festschrift in Honor of Lawrence Edward Carter, Sr.* Edited by Echol Lee Nix. Macon, Ga.: Mercer University Press.

Burrow, Rufus, Jr. 1997. "King's Beloved Community Ideal: Making the Connections." *Journal of Religion* 77, no. 3: 442–48.

———. 1999. *Personalism: A Critical Introduction*. St. Louis: Chalice.

———. 2006. *God and Human Dignity: The Personalism, Theology, and Ethics of Martin Luther King, Jr.* Notre Dame, Ind.: University of Notre Dame Press.

———. 2015. *Martin Luther King, Jr., and the Theology of Resistance.* Jefferson, N.C.: McFarland.

Burrow, Rufus, Jr., and Jimmy L. Kirby. 1999. "Conceptions of a God in the Thinking of Martin Luther King, Jr., and Edgar S. Brightman." *Encounter* 60, no. 3: 283–305.

Carmichael, Stokely, and Mumia Abu-Jamal. 2007. *Stokely Speaks: From Black Power to Pan-Africanism.* Chicago, Ill.: Lawrence Hill Books.

Carter, Lawrence Edward. 1998. *Walking Integrity: Benjamin Elijah Mays, Mentor to Martin Luther King, Jr.* Macon, Ga.: Mercer University Press.

———. 2008. "The African American Personalist Perspective on Person as Embodied in the Life and Thought of Martin Luther King Jr." *Speculative Journal of Philosophy* 20, no. 3: 219–23.

Cheney, Sheldon. 1945. *Men Who Have Walked with God: Being the Story of Mysticism through the Ages Told in the Biographies of Representative Seers and Saints.* New York: Knopf.

Chennault, Ronald E. 2013. "Pragmatism and Progressivism in the Educational Thought and Practices of Booker T. Washington." *Philosophical Studies in Education* 44 (January): 121–31.

Clendenning, John. 1999. *The Life and Thought of Josiah Royce.* Nashville: Vanderbilt University Press.

Cone, James H. 1969. *Black Theology and Black Power.* Maryknoll, N.Y.: Orbis Books.

———. 1975. *God of the Oppressed.* San Francisco: Harper & Row.

———. 1984. "Martin Luther King, Jr., Black Theology—Black Church." *Theology Today* 40, no. 4: 409–20.

———. 1986. *A Black Theology of Liberation.* 2nd ed. Maryknoll, N.Y.: Orbis.

———. 2011. *The Cross and the Lynching Tree.* Maryknoll, N.Y.: Orbis Books.

Cook, Samuel DuBois. 2009. *Benjamin E. Mays: His Life, Contributions, and Legacy.* Franklin, Tenn.: Providence House.

Corbin, Henry. 1969. *Creative Imagination in the Sufism of Ibn 'Arabi.* Princeton, N.J.: Princeton University Press.

Cowan, Rosemary. 2003. *Cornel West: The Politics of Redemption.* Cambridge: Polity.

Davis, Angela Y. 2016. *Freedom Is a Constant Struggle: Ferguson, Palestine, and the Foundations of a Movement.* Edited by Frank Barat. Chicago: Haymarket.

Davis, Leroy. 1998. *A Clashing of the Soul: John Hope and the Dilemma of African American Leadership and Black Higher Education in the Early Twentieth Century.* Athens: University of Georgia Press.

Dewey, John, and James Hayden Tufts. 1932. *Ethics.* New York: H. Holt and Company.

———. 1986. *The Later Works, 1925–1953.* Edited by Jo Ann Boydston. Carbondale, Ill.: Southern Illinois university Press.

———. 1986. *The Later Works, 1925–1953.* Edited by Jo Ann Boydston. Carbondale, Ill.: Southern Illinois University Press.

———. 1988. *Later Works of John Dewey*, vol. 1, *Experience and Nature*. Edited by Jo Ann Boydston. Carbondale and Edwardsville: Southern Illinois University Press.
DeWolf, L. Harold. 1971. *Responsible Freedom*. New York: Harper and Row.
———. 1986. "Ethical Implications for Criminal Justice." *Boston Personalist Tradition in Philosophy, Social Ethics, and Theology*. Macon, Ga.: Mercer University Press.
———. 2011. *Theology of the Living Church*. Charleston, S.C.: Nabu.
Dixie, Quinton, and Cornel West, eds. 1999. *Courage to Hope: From Black Suffering to Human Redemption*. Boston: Beacon.
Dixie, Quinton, and Peter Eisenstadt. 2011. *Visions of a Better World: Howard Thurman's Pilgrimage to India and the Origins of African American Nonviolence*. Boston: Beacon.
Dorrien, Gary. 2003. *The Making of American Liberal Theology: Idealism, Realism, and Modernity*, 1900–1950. Louisville, Ky.: Westminster John Knox.
———. 2009. *Social Ethics in the Making: Interpreting an American Tradition*. Chichester: Wiley-Blackwell.
Douglas, Andrew. 2015. "W. E. B. Du Bois and the Critique of Competitive Society." *Du Bois Review* 12, no. 1: 25–40.
Douglass, Frederick. 2010. *Narrative of the Life of Frederick Douglass, an American Slave, Written by Himself: A New Critical Edition*. Edited by Angela Y. Davis. Open Media Series. San Francisco: City Lights Books.
Du Bois, W. E. B. (1903) 2007. *The Souls of Black Folk*. New York: Oxford University Press.
Du Bois, W. E. B, and Herbert Aptheker. 2001. *The Education of Black People: Ten Critiques 1906–1960*. New York: Monthly Review Press.Emerson, Ralph Waldo. 1914. *Complete Works of Ralph Waldo Emerson*. Boston: Houghton Mifflin.
———. 1983. *Essays & Lectures*. Edited by Joel Porte. New York: Literary Classics of the U.S.
Emerson, Ralph Waldo. 1837. "The American Scholar." https://emersoncentral.com/texts/nature-addresses-lectures/addresses/the-american-scholar/#complete-essay.
Fanon, Frantz, and Anthony Appiah. 2008. *Black Skin, White Masks*. Translated by Richard Philcox. New York: Grove Press.
Fanon, Frantz, Jean-Paul Sartre, Homi K Bhabha, and Richard Philcox. 2004. *The Wretched of the Earth*. Translated by Richard Philcox. New York: Grove Press.
Farmer, James. 1985. *Lay Bare the Heart*. New York: Arbor House.
Fischer, Louis. (1945) 2010. *Gandhi: His Life and His Message for the World*. New York: Signet.
Fluker, Walter E. 1989. *They Looked for a City: A Comparative Analysis of the Ideal of Community in the Thought of Howard Thurman and Martin Luther King, Jr.* Lanham, Md.: University Press of America.
———. 1990. "They Looked for a City: A Comparison of the Ideal of Community in

Howard Thurman and Martin Luther King, Jr." *Journal of Religious Ethics*, Spring, 33–55.

———. 1999. "Howard Thurman and the Politics of Conversion." In Dixie, Quinton Hosford, Cornel West, and James Melvin Washington. *The Courage to Hope: From Black Suffering to Human Redemption—Essays in Honor of James Melvin Washington.* Boston, Mass.: Beacon Press. 103–19.

———. 1999. "The Politics of Conversion and the Civilization of Friday." In *The Courage to Hope: From Black Suffering to Human Redemption; Essays in Honor of James Melvin Washington*. Edited by Quinton Hosford Dixie and Cornel West, 103–117. Boston: Beacon.

———. 2009. *Ethical Leadership: The Quest for Character, Civility, and Community.* Prisms. Minneapolis: Fortress Press.

———. 2013. "Dangerous Memories and Redemptive Possibilities: Reflections on the Life and Work of Howard Thurman." In *Black Leaders and Ideologies in the South: Resistance and Non-Violence.* Edited by Preston King and Walter Earl Fluker. Hoboken: Taylor and Francis.

Frazier, E. Franklin. 1924. "A Note on Negro Education." *Opportunity* 2 (March): 75–77.

———. 1957. *The Negro in the United States.* Revised ed. New York: Macmillan.

Freire, Paulo. 1958. *All Men Are Brothers: Life and Thoughts of Mahatma Gandhi.* New York: Columbia University Press.

———. 1993. *Pedagogy of the Oppressed.* 20th anniversary edition. New York: Continuum.

Gandhi. 1960. *The Collected Works of Mahatma Gandhi.* New Delhi: Publications Division, Ministry of Information and Broadcasting, Government of India.

———. 1962. *The Essential Gandhi: An Anthology.* Edited by Louis Fischer. New York: Random House.

———. 2007. *Gandhi on Non-Violence: Selected Texts from Mohandas K. Gandhi's Non-Violence in Peace and War.* Edited by Thomas Merton. New York: New Directions Pub.

Gaither, Milton. 2003. *American Educational History Revisited: A Critique of Progress.* New York: Teacher's College Press.

Gallagher, Winifred. 2001. *Spiritual Genius: The Mastery of Life's Meaning.* New York: Random House.

Galtung, Johan. 1969. "Violence, Peace, and Peace Research." *Journal of Peace Research* 6, no. 3: 167–91.

Garrison, Jim. 1997. "The Crossroads of Poetry and Prophecy." *Philosophy of Education Journal,* 57–60. https://ojs.education.illinois.edu/index.php/pes/article/download/2170/865.

Garrow, David J. 2004. *Bearing the Cross: Martin Luther King, Jr., and the Southern Christian Leadership Conference.* New York: HarperCollins.

Geuss, Raymond. 2008. *Philosophy and Real Politics.* Princeton, N.J.: Princeton University Press.

Giles, Mark S. 2006. "Howard Thurman: The Making of a Morehouse Man, 1919–1923." *Journal of Educational Foundations* 20, nos. 1–2: 105–22.

———. 2010. "Howard Thurman, Black Spirituality, and Critical Race Theory." *Journal of Negro Education* 79, no. 3: 354–65.

Glaude, Eddie S., Jr. 2007. *In a Shade of Blue: Pragmatism and the Politics of Black America.* Chicago: University of Chicago Press.

Goodenow, Ronald K. 1978. "Paradox in Progressive Education Reform: The South and the Education of Blacks in the Depression Years." *Phylon* 39: I:60–74.

Green, Judith M. 2008. *Pragmatism and Social Hope: Deepening Democracy in Global Contexts.* New York: Columbia University Press.

Gyekye, Kwame. 1997. *Tradition and Modernity: Philosophical Reflections on the African Experience.* New York, N.Y.: Oxford University Press.

Hanh, Thich Nhat. 2007. *Teachings of Love.* Berkeley: Parallax Press.

Harding, Vincent. 1974. "The Vocation of the Black Scholar and the Struggles of the Black Community." In *Education and the Black Struggle: Notes from the Colonized World.* Harvard Educational Review Monograph no. 2. Cambridge: Harvard Educational Review.

———. 1999. "Dangerous Spirituality." *Sojourners* 28: 1–11.

———. 2008. *Martin Luther King: An Inconvenient Hero.* Maryknoll, N.Y.: Orbis Books.

———. 2010a. *Hope and History: Why We Must Share the Story of the Movement.* Maryknoll, N.Y.: Orbis Books.

Harris, Leonard. 2000. *Philosophy Born of Struggle: Anthology of Afro-American Philosophy from 1917.* 2nd ed. Dubuque, Iowa: Kendall/Hunt.

Heltzel, Peter Goodwin. 2015. "The Morehouse Gospel: Howard Thurman, Martin Luther King, Jr., and Prophetic Black Christianity." *In the Beginning: The Martin Luther King, Jr. International Chapel at Morehouse College; a Festschrift in Honor of Lawrence Edward Carter, Sr.*. Edited by Echol Lee Nix and Hugh M Gloster. Macon, Ga.: Mercer University Press.

Heschel, Abraham Joshua. 1962. *The Prophets.* [1St ed.]. New York: Harper & Row.

Herstein, Gary L. 2009. "The Roycean Roots of the Beloved Community." *Pluralist* 4, no. 2: 91–107.

Hollenback, Jess Byron. 1996. *Mysticism: Experience, Response, and Empowerment.* University Park: Pennsylvania State University Press.

Hord, Fred L. (Mzee Lasana Okpara), and Jonathan Scott Lee. 1995. *I Am Because We Are: Readings in Black Philosophy.* Amherst: University of Massachusetts Press.

Jackson, Lawrence. 2008. "Richard Wright." CHOP Research Institute Summer Scholars Program.

———. 2013. "Richard Wright and Black Radical Discourse: The Advocacy of Violence."

In *Black Leaders and Ideologies in the South: Resistance and Non-Violence*. Edited by Preston King and Walter Earl Fluker. Hoboken, N.J.: Taylor and Francis.

James, William. 1911. *Memories and Studies*. New York: Longmans, Green.

———. 1985. *The Varieties of Religious Experience*. Cambridge, Mass.: Harvard University Press.

———. 1987. *Writings, 1902–1910*. Edited by Bruce Kuklick. Library of America 38. New York: Literary Classics of the United States.

———. 2011. *The Essential William James*. Edited by John R. Shook. Amherst, N.Y.: Prometheus Books.

Jantzen, Grace. 1995. *Power, Gender, and Christian Mysticism*. Cambridge Studies in Ideology and Religion 8. Cambridge: Cambridge University Press.

Jelks, Randel Maurice. 2012. *Benjamin Elijah Mays: Schoolmaster of the Movement*. Chapel Hill: University of North Carolina Press.

Jensen, Kipton E. 2012. "William James and the Anti-War Campaign: 'On the Moral Equivalent of War' and a 'Certain Blindness in Human Beings.'" *William James Studies* 8: 132–51.

———. 2017. "Pedagogical Personalism at Morehouse College." *Studies in Philosophy and Education* 36, no. 2 (March): 147–65.

Johnson, Alonzo. 1997. *Good News for the Disinherited: Howard Thurman on Jesus of Nazareth and Human Liberation*. Lanham, Md.: University Press of America.

Johnson, James Weldon. 1928."The Dilemma of the Negro Author." *American Mercury*, December, 477–81.

Jones, Edward A. 1967. *A Candle in the Dark: A History of Morehouse College*. Valley Forge, Pa.: Judson.

Jones, Lawrence N. 1981. "Black Christians Antebellum America: In Quest of Beloved Community." *Journal of Religious Thought* 38, no. 1 (Spring–Summer): 12–19.

Jones, Rufus M. 1909. *Studies in Mystical Religion*. Repr. London: Macmillan.

———. 1915. "Mysticism in Present-Day Religion." *Harvard Theological Review* 8, no. 2: 155–65.

———. 1919. *Studies in Mystical Religion*. London: Macmillan.

———. 1930. *Some Exponents of Mystical Religion*. New York: Abingdon Press.

———, and Charles A. Bennett. 1931. *A Philosophical Study of Mysticism, an Essay by Charles a. Bennet, . . . Reprinted with a Preface by Rufus M. Jones*. New Haven: Conn., Yale University Press.

Jones, William R. 1978. "The Legitimacy and Necessity of Black Philosophy: Some Preliminary Considerations." *Philosophical Forum* 9, nos. 2–3: 149–60.

Kant, Immanuel. 1996. *Religion and Rational Theology*. Translated and edited by Allen W. Wood, and George Di Giovanni. Cambridge: Cambridge University Press.

———. 2007. *Perpetual Peace and Other Essays on Politics, History, and Morals*. Edited by Ted Humphrey. Indianapolis: Hackett Publications.

Kaplan, Edward K. 2010. 1982. “Howard Thurman: Meditation, Mysticism, and Life's Contradictions.” In *Debate and Understanding: Simmering on the Calm Presence and Profound Wisdom of Howard Thurman*, 19–26. Edited by Ricardo A. Millett and Conly H. Hughes, Jr. Special Edition.

———. “A Jewish Dialogue with Howard Thurman: Mysticism, Compassion, and Community.” *Cross Currents* 60, no. 4: 515–25.

Katz, Steven T. 1978. *Mysticism and Philosophical Analysis*. New York: Oxford University Press.

———. 1989. “On Mysticism,” *Journal of the American Academy of Religion* 56, no. 4: 751–57.

Kierkegaard, Søren. 1956. *Purity of Heart Is to Will One Thing: Spiritual Preparation for the Office of Confession*. Translated by Douglas V. Steere. New York: Harper.

———. 1978. *Parables of Kierkegaard*. Edited by Thomas C. Oden, and L. S. Johnson. Princeton, N.J.: Princeton University Press.

King, Martin Luther, Jr., 1958. “My Pilgrimage to Nonviolence.” *Fellowship* 24, no. 17: 4–9.

———. 2000. *The Papers of Martin Luther King, Jr: January 1957–December 1958*. Vol. IV, *Symbol of the Movement*. Edited by Clayborne Carson. Berkeley: University of California Press.

———. 1970. “Honoring Du Bois.” In *W. E. B. Du Bois Speaks: Speeches and Addresses, 1890–1919*. Edited by Philip S. Foner, with a tribute by Martin Luther King, Jr. New York: Pathfinder Press.

———. 1991. *Testament of Hope: Essential Writings and Speeches of Martin Luther King Jr.* Edited by James M. Washington. San Francisco: Harper Collins.

———. (1963) 2010. *Strength to Love*. Minneapolis: Fortress.

———. (1968) 2010. *Where Do We Go from Here: Chaos or Community?* Boston: Beacon.

———. 1998. *A Knock at Midnight: Inspiration from the Great Sermons of Reverend Martin Luther King, Jr.* Edited by Clayborne Carson and Peter Holloran. New York: Intellectual Properties Management in association with Warner Books.

———. 2014. *The Radical King*. Edited and introduced by Cornel West. Boston: Beacon.

Kloppenberg, James T. 1988. *Uncertain Victory: Social Democracy and Progressivism in European and American Thought, 1870–1920*. New York: Oxford University Press.

Knudson, Albert C. 1969. *The Philosophy of Personalism: A Study in the Metaphysics of Religion*. New York: Abingdon.

Kramer, Kenneth. 2003. *Martin Buber's I and Thou: Practicing Living Dialogue*, with Mechthild Gawlick. New York: Paulist.

Larson, Stephen. 1998. *The Shaman's Doorway: Opening Imagination to Power and Myth*. Rochester, Vt.: Inner Traditions.

Lee, Jonathan Scott, and Fred L Hord, eds. 2016. *I Am Because We Are: Readings in Africana Philosophy*. Revised. Amherst: University of Massachusetts Press.

Lewinson, Barbara. 1998. "Mays's Educational Philosophy." In *Walking Integrity: Benjamin Elijah Mays, Mentor to Martin Luther King, Jr.*, ed. Lawrence Edward Carter, 215–32. Macon, Ga.: Mercer University Press.

Makechnie, George K. 1988. *Howard Thurman: His Enduring Dream.* Boston: Boston University Press.

Mantena, Karuna. 2012. "Another Realism: The Politics of Gandhian Nonviolence." *American Political Science Review* 106, no. 2: 455–70.

Marsh, Charles. 2005. *The Beloved Community: How Faith Shapes Social Justice, From the Civil Rights Movement to Today.* New York: Basic Books.

Marty, Martin E. 1998. Foreword to *A Strange Freedom: The Best of Howard Thurman on Religious Experience and Public Life*, ed. Walter E Fluker and Catherine Tumber, xi–xiv. Boston: Beacon.

Mays, Benjamin E. 1938. *The Negro's God as Reflected in His Literature.* New York: Russell and Russell.

———. 1942. "The Role of the Negro Liberal Arts College in Postwar Reconstruction." *Journal of Negro Education*, July.

———. 1942. "Negro Higher Education in the War and Post-War Reconstruction," *Journal of Negro Education* 11, no. 3: 400–411.

———. 1942. "Sermons from Elders." *The African American Pulpit*, vol. 11, 25–27. Judson Press.

———. 1962. "What's Ahead for Our Negro Schools?" *Together*, pp. 32–34.

———. 1964. "Desegregate and Integrate to What End? Livingston Founder's Day Address" (February).

———. 1968. *The Negro's God, as Reflected in His Literature.* New York: Russell and Russell.

———. 1987. *Born to Rebel: An Autobiography.* Athens: University of Georgia Press.

Mills, Charles, 2001. "Prophetic Pragmatism as Political Philosophy." In *Cornel West: A Critical Reader*, edited by George Yancy, 192–333. Malden, MA: Blackwell, 2001.

Mikelson, Thomas J. S. 1990. "Cosmic Companionship: The Place of God in the Moral Reasoning of Martin Luther King, Jr." *Journal of Religious Ethics* 18, no. 2: 1–14.

Mitchell, Mozella G. 1982. "The Shaman's Doorway: Techniques of Myth and Ritual in Thurman." In *Debate and Understanding: Simmering on the Clam Presence and Profound Wisdom of Howard Thurman.* Edited by Richardo A. Millet and Conley H. Hughes, 27–26. Special Edition. Boston: Boston University.

———. Untitled. 1983. In Henry J. Young, ed., *God and Human Freedom: A Festschrift in Honor of Howard Thurman.* Richmond, Ind.: Friends United Press.

———. 1985. *Spiritual Dynamics of Howard Thurman's Theology.* Bristol, Ind.: Wyndham Hall.

———. 1992. *The Human Search: Howard Thurman and the Quest for Freedom.* Proceedings of the Second Annual Thurman Convocation. New York: P. Lang.

Muelder, Walter G. 1947. "Essential Elements in the Christian Conception of Man." Unpublished ms.

———. 1955. *The Idea of the Responsible Society*. Boston: Boston University Press.

———. 1959. *Foundations of the Responsible Society.* New York: Abingdon Press.

———. 1966. *Moral Law in Christian Social Ethics.* Richmond: John Knox Press.

———. 1982. "The Structure of Howard Thurman's Social Ethics." In *Debate and Understanding: Simmering on the Calm Presence and Profound Wisdom of Howard Thurman,* 7–13. Edited by Ricardo A. Millett. Special edition.

———. 1983. *The Ethical Edge of Christian Theology: Forty Years of Communitarian Personalism.* New York: E. Mellen.

Nagl, Ludwig. 2012. "Loyalty: Royce's Post-Kantian, Pragmaticist Conception of Ethics." In *Josiah Royce for the Twenty-First Century: Historical, Ethical, and Religious Interpretations.* Lanham, Md.: Lexington Books.

Neal, Anthony Sean. 2015. *Common Ground: A Comparison of the Ideas of Consciousness in the Writings of Howard W. Thurman and Huey P. Newton.* Trenton, N.J.: Africa World.

Niebuhr, Reinhold. 1932. *Moral Man and Immoral Society.* New York: Charles Scribner's Sons.

Nietzsche, Friedrich Wilhelm. 2006. *Thus Spoke Zarathustra: A Book for All and None.* Edited by Adrian Del Caro and Robert B Pippin. Cambridge Texts in the History of Philosophy. Cambridge: Cambridge University Press.

Nkrumah, Kwame. 1965. *Consciencism: Philosophy and Ideology for Decolonization and Development with Particular Reference to the African Revolution.* New York: Monthly Review Press.

Nussbaum, Martha C. 2016. *Anger and Forgiveness: Resentment, Generosity, Justice.* New York: Oxford University Press.

Nyerere, Julius K. 1974. *Freedom and Socialism: Uhuru Na Ujamaa: A Selection from Writings and Speeches, 1965–1967.* London: Oxford University Press.

Penner, Hans H. 1983. "The Mysticism Illusion." In Steven T. Katz, *Mysticism and Religious Traditions.* New York: Oxford University Press.

Pollard, Alton, III. 1992. *Mysticism and Social Change: The Social Witness of Howard Thurman.* New York: P. Lang.

Raboteau, Albert J. 1978. *Slave Religion: The Invisible Institution in the Antebellum South.* New York: Oxford University Press.

———. 2001. "In Search of Common Ground: Howard Thurman and Religious Community." In *Meaning and Modernity: Religion, Polity, and Self.* Edited by Richard Madsen, William M. Sullivan, Ann Swindler, and Steven M. Tipton, 150–62. Berkeley: University of California Press.

Rauschenbusch, Walter, and Charles H. Hopkins. 1950. *A Gospel for the Social Awakening: Selections from the Writings of Walter Rauschenbusch.* Edited by Benjamin E. Mays. New York: Association Press.

Reed, Adolph. 1995. "What Are the Drums Saying, Booker? The Current Crisis of the Black Intellectual." *Village Voice*, April 11, pp. 31–36.

Richard Rorty. 1991. "The Professor and the Prophet." *Transition,* no. 52: 70–78.

Richardson, Robert D. 2006. *William James: In the Maelstrom of American Modernism: A Biography.* Boston: Houghton Mifflin.

Rockefeller, Steven C. 1991. *John Dewey: Religious Faith and Democratic Humanism.* New York: Columbia University Press.

Rodney, Walter. 2014. *The Groundings with My Brothers.* East Point, Ga.: Walter Rodney Press.

Royce, Josiah. (1913) 2001. *Problem of Christianity.* Washington, D.C.: Catholic University Press.

———. 2005. *The Basic Writings of Josiah Royce: Culture, Philosophy, and Religion.* Edited by Ignas K. Skrupskelis. Fordham University Press.

———. 2005. *The Basic Writings of Josiah Royce*, vol. 2: *Logic, Loyalty, and Community.* Edited by Clayton Crockett. New York: Fordham University Press.

Santayana, George. 1922. *Interpretations of Poetry and Religion.* New York: Scribner's.

Savage, Barbara Dianne. 2007. "Benjamin Mays, Global Ecumenicalism, and Local Religious Segregation." *American Quarterly Journal* 59, no. 3 (September): 785–806.

Schmidt, Leigh Eric. 2003. "The Making of Modern Mysticism." *Journal of the American Academy of Religion,* 71, no. 2: 273–302.

———. 2012. *Restless Souls: The Making of American Spirituality.* Second edition with a new preface. Berkeley: University of California Press.

Shinault, Carley M. 2014. "Fractal Complexity of The Education of Black People: Ten Critiques, 1906–1960 by W. E. B. Du Bois." *Phylon* 51, no. 1 (Fall): 1–17.

Shook, John R., James A. Good, and John Dewey. 2010. *John Dewey's Philosophy of Spirit: With the 1897 Lecture on Hegel.* American Philosophy. New York: Fordham University Press.

Smith, John E. (1950). *Royce's Social Infinite.* New York: The Liberal Arts Press.

Smith, Kenneth L., and Ira G. Zepp, Jr. 1998. *Search for the Beloved Community: The Thinking of Martin Luther King.* Valley Forge, Pa.: Judson.

Smith, Luther E. 1988. "Intimate Mystery: Howard Thurman's Search for Ultimate Meaning (1900–1981)." *Ultimate Reality and Meaning* 11 (2): 85–101.

———. 2006. *Howard Thurman: Essential Writings.* Maryknoll, N.Y.: Orbis Books.

———. (1981) 2007. *Howard Thurman: The Mystic as Prophet.* Richmond, Ind.: Friends United.

———. 2007. *Howard Thurman: The Mystic as Prophet.* 3rd ed. Richmond, Ind.: Friends United.

Snyder, Jeffrey. 2015. "Progressive Education in Black and White: Rereading Carter G. Woodson's Miseducation of the Negro." *History of Education Quarterly* 55, no. 3 (August): 273–93.

Stace, W. T. 1960. *Mysticism and Philosophy.* Philadelphia: J. B. Lippincott.

Steinkraus, Warren E. 1973. "Martin Luther King's Personalism and Non-Violence." *Journal of the History of Ideas* 34, no. 1 (January–March): 97–110.

Thich Nhat Hanh. 2008. *Teachings on Love.* N.p.: ReadHowYouWant.

Thurman, Howard. 1945. *Deep River: An Interpretation of Negro Spirituals.* Mills College, Calif.: Eucalyptus Press.

———. 1951a. *Deep Is the Hunger: Meditations for Apostles of Sensitiveness.* New York: Harper & Bros.

———. 1951b. "The Meaning of the Philosophy of Loyalty," audio. http://hgar-srv3.bu.edu/web/howard-thurman/virtual-listening-room/detail?id=341418.

———. 1953. *Meditations of the Heart.* New York: Harper & Row.

———. 1954. "Love Your Enemies," sermon, April 25. Available from Expanding Common Ground, the Howard Thurman & Sue Bailey Thurman Collections at Boston University, http://archives.bu.edu/web/howard-thurman/virtual-listening-room/detail?id=344230.

———. 1956a. "Freedom." Unpublished sermon (12/09/1956). Howard Gotlieb Archival Research Center. Boston University. Box 11, File 152.

———. 1956b. *The Growing Edge.* Richmond, Ind.: Friends United.

———. 1959. *Footprints of a Dream: The Story of The Church for the Fellowship of All Peoples.* New York: Harper.

———. (1961) 1973. *Mysticism and the Experience of Love.* Pendle Hill Pamphlet 115. Wallingford, Pa.: Pendle Hill.

———. 1961. *The Inward Journey: Meditations on the Spiritual Quest.* New York: Harper & Row.

———. 1962. "Quests of the Human Spirit: The Quest for Identity." Audio recording.

———. 1963. *Disciplines of the Spirit.* New York: Harper & Row.

———. 1965a. *Luminous Darkness: A Personal Interpretation of the Anatomy of Segregation and the Ground of Hope.* New York: Harper & Row.

———. "Jesus and the Disinherited: The Conquest of Hate and Violence," July 21, 1968, Box 13, Folder 53. http://archives.bu.edu/web/howard-thurman/search/detail?id=352742.

———. 1970. "Mysticism and Ethics." *Journal of Religious Thought.* Summer Supplement: 23–30.

———. 1971. *The Search for Common Ground: An Inquiry into the Basis of Man's Experience of Community.* New York: Harper & Row.

———. (1954) 1972. *The Creative Encounter: An Interpretation of Religion and the Social Witness.* Richmond, Ind.: Friends United.

———. 1973. *The Mood of Christmas.* [1St ed.]. New York: Harper & Row.

———, ed. 1973. *A Track to the Water's Edge: The Oliver Schreiner Reader.* New York: Harper & Row.

———. 1975. *Deep River and the Negro Spiritual Speaks of Life and Death.* Richmond, Ind.: Friends United Press.

———. 1978. *Temptations of Jesus: Five Sermons.* Richmond, Ind.: Friends United Press.

———. 1979. *With Head and Heart: The Autobiography of Howard Thurman.* New York: Harcourt Brace Jovanovich.

———. 1980. "The Sound of the Genuine." *Spelman Messenger* 96, no. 4: 14–15.

———. 1984. *For the Inward Journey: The Writings of Howard Thurman.* Selected by Anne Spencer Thurman. San Diego: Harcourt Brace Jovanovich.

———. (1949) 1996. *Jesus and the Disinherited.* Boston: Beacon.

———. 1998. *A Strange Freedom: The Best of Howard Thurman on Religious Experience and Public Life.* Edited by Walter E Fluker and Catherine Tumber. Boston: Beacon.

———. 2009. *The Papers of Howard Washington Thurman*, vol. 1: *My People Need Me.* Edited by Walter E. Fluker. Columbia: University of South Carolina Press.

———. (1966) 2009. "Desegregation, Integration, and the Beloved Community." In *Benjamin E. Mays: His Life, Contributions, and Legacy*. Edited by Samuel D. Cook. Franklin, Tenn.: Providence House.

———. 2012. *The Papers of Howard Washington Thurman*, vol. 2: *Christian, Who Calls Me Christian?* Edited by Walter E. Fluker. Columbia: University of South Carolina Press.

———. 2015. *Mysticism and Social Action: Lawrence Lecture and Discussions with Dr Howard Thurman, October 13 and 14, 1978.* Edited by Richard Boeke and Patrick Wynne-Jones. United States: International Association for Religious Freedom.

———. 2015. *The Papers of Howard Washington Thurman*, vol. 3: *The Bold Adventure, September 1943–May 1949.* Edited by Walter E. Fluker. Columbia: University of South Carolina Press.

———. 2017. *The Papers of Howard Washington Thurman*, vol. 4: *The Soundless Passion of a Single Mind, June 1949–December 1962.* Edited by Walter E. Fluker. Columbia: University of South Carolina Press.

———. 2018. *Breaking White Supremacy: Martin Luther King Jr. and the Black Social Gospel.* New Haven, Conn.: Yale University Press.

———. 2018. *Sermons on the Parables.* Edited with an introduction by David Gowler and Kipton Jensen. Maryknoll, N.Y.: Orbis Books.

———. 2019. *The Papers of Howard Washington Thurman*, vol. 5: *The Wider Ministry, January 1963–April 1981.* Edited by Walter E. Fluker. Columbia: University of South Carolina Press.

Tunstall, Dwayne A. 2008. "Cornel West, John Dewey, and the Tragicomic Undercurrents of Deweyan Creative Democracy." *Contemporary Pragmatism* 5, no. 2 (December): 109–29.

———. 2009. *Yes, but Not Quite: Encountering Josiah Royce's Ethico-Religious Insight.* New York: Fordham University Press.

Watley, William D. 1985. *Roots of Resistance: The Nonviolent Ethics of Martin Luther King, Jr.* Valley Forge, Pa.: Judson.

Weaver, Harold D., Paul Kriese, and Stephen W. Angell, eds. 2011. *Black Fire: African American Quakers on Spirituality and Human Rights*, with Anne Steere Nash. Philadelphia: Quaker Press of Friends General Conference.

West, Cornel. 1982. *Prophesy Deliverance! An Afro-American Revolutionary Christianity.* Philadelphia: Westminster.

———. 1989. *The American Evasion of Philosophy: A Genealogy of Pragmatism.* Madison: University of Wisconsin Press.

———. 1993. *Prophetic Reflections: Notes on Race and Power in America.* Beyond Eurocentrism and Multiculturalism, vol. 2. Common Courage Press.

———. 1993. *Keeping Faith: Philosophy and Race in America.* New York: Routledge.

———. 1999. *The Cornel West Reader.* New York: Basic Civitas Books.

———. 2001. *Race Matters.* Boston: Beacon Press.

———. 2001. *Cornel West: A Critical Reader.* Edited by George Yancy. Malden, Mass.: Blackwell.

———. 2016. Introduction. In Martin Luther King, Jr. *The Radical King.* Edited by Cornel West. The King Legacy Series. Boston: Beacon Press.

Wood, Mark David. 2000. *Cornel West and the Politics of Prophetic Pragmatism.* Urbana: University of Illinois Press.

Woodson, Carter G. 1931. "The Miseducation of the Negro." *Crisis* 38, no. 8: 266–67.

———. (1933) 2000. *The Mis-Education of the Negro.* Chicago: African-American Images.

Yates, Elizabeth. 1964. *Howard Thurman, Portrait of a Practical Dreamer.* New York: John Day.

Young, Andrew. 1996. *An Easy Burden: The Civil Rights Movement and the Transformation of America.* New York: HarperCollins.

Index

About the Author

KIPTON E. JENSEN is an associate professor of philosophy at Morehouse College, the director of the leadership studies program in the Andrew Young Center for Global Leadership, and the codirector of the International Comparative Labor Studies program. He earned a doctorate in philosophy from Marquette University and was a Fulbright Scholar at Martin-Luther-Universität. Jensen is the author of *Hegel: Hovering* and *Parallel Discourses* and coeditor of Howard Thurman's *Sermons on the Parables.*

CONTENTS

BEYOND THE CITY AND THE BRIDGE

INTRODUCTION

Globalizing Suburbia

The appearance of Asians within suburban pockets of the greater New York area in the 1970s was a novel phenomenon. In 1972, an article appeared in the *New York Times,* concerning a Japanese grocery store that had opened in 1969—"The Far East (in Fort Lee)."[1] It was reported to be the only such store in the New Jersey metropolitan area at the time. During the 1970s and 1980s, the press periodically reported on new communities made up of businessmen from Japan and their families in the suburbs of New York. Their rapid influx into Fort Lee piqued curiosity as the borough became home to the largest Japanese community in the tri-state suburban area. Headlines in the *Times* conveyed a sense of surprise and interest: "Fort Lee: The Suburb of Japan"; "Why Fort Lee Lures Japanese"; "In Jersey, Japanese-Style New Year's."[2] An established resident in Fort Lee, a white female, recalls the seventies: "There used to be a Japanese restaurant on Main Street . . . and [there] was this line of Japanese guys in suits, bowing to a limousine as the limousine pulled away." Besides being the first nonwhite influx in the history of Fort Lee, the newcomers seemed to follow their homeland culture without signs of assimilation.

Some forty years later, the presence of Asians in Fort Lee is ubiquitous and no longer stirs such curiosity. The group that has developed a major ethnic presence, Koreans—and increasingly, the Chinese as well—have replaced the diminishing Japanese. The coresidence of these three groups is visible and audible in the library, church, and school and in the range of languages heard in public spaces. Bulletin boards in local Japanese and Korean supermarkets are covered with flyers in Chinese, Japanese, and Korean, as well as English, advertising apartment rentals, music and art classes, English conversation classes, summer camps, garage sales. Ethnic businesses, restaurants, and cafés—mostly Korean, some Chinese and Japanese—line the thoroughfares and shopping malls of Fort Lee.

Nowadays it is Asians who increasingly deal with local whites as business owners, store clerks, and health care and other service providers.

Passage of the Immigration and Nationality Act (the Hart-Celler Act) in 1965 resulted in a surge of immigration from Asia and Latin America into the United States.[3] From 1980 through 2000, the percentage of Asians and Hispanics doubled in the United States. The percentage of foreign-born immigrants and their U.S.-born offspring is currently at its greatest level since the Second World War—25 percent of the U.S. population.[4] Between 2000 and 2010, the Asian population grew faster than any other racial group in the United States. According to the U.S. census, Asians represented 4.8 percent (14.7 million) of the nation's population in 2010, and this proportion is expected to double by the year 2050.

In recent decades, the American suburbs have become an important site of immigrant settlement. Beginning in the 1960s, large numbers of Asians and Latinos who had become economically and socially established began to move out of central city areas to settle in outlying suburbs. This development was in part due to the rise of a U.S.-born middle class in both groups, but the driving factor was immigration from Asia and Latin America. By the year 2000, the majority of foreign-born persons in the United States were living in the suburbs.[5] Today, some suburban neighborhoods—those of metropolitan New York and Los Angeles, for example—have higher concentrations of ethnic group members than city neighborhoods. Asians are the most suburban of all racial minority groups: in 2010, 62 percent of Asians resided in the suburbs of America's one hundred largest metropolitan areas.[6] Such patterns challenge two enduring social myths—the notion of the American suburbs as homogeneous havens of the white middle class and of immigrants as predominantly the settlers of urban enclaves. The increasing move of immigrants to "new destinations" and "new gateway" suburbs, areas that had previously experienced little migrant flow, has drawn increased scholarly attention to these locations.[7] Unprecedented ethnoracial diversity is now rapidly reconfiguring suburban life and landscapes and is raising questions regarding immigrant incorporation.[8] Although research on immigrant communities has traditionally centered on cities, today the suburbs present a critical locus for the study of immigration.

This book concerns the immigrant communities of a metropolitan suburb of New York and the social transformations that have accompanied the dramatic demographic shifts at this location from the 1970s to the present. The site is Fort Lee, a borough of Bergen County in northern New Jersey. Ten miles from midtown Manhattan, Fort Lee is situated on the waterfront area recently dubbed the New Jersey "Gold Coast." It lies along the Hudson River, stretching between Bergen and Hudson counties. The area has witnessed a real estate boom since the 1980s.[9] Urban economic restructuring and resultant suburban development since 1970 have transformed the borough into a highly urbanized middle-class suburb with modern office buildings in the downtown and high-rise luxury apartments along the Palisades overlooking the Hudson. Despite its suburban location, Fort Lee's proximity to New York City offers a sense, for residents, of being an "extension" or a "borough" of New York.

Fort Lee is a familiar name to New Yorkers: as the first town across the Hudson from Manhattan, many recall "having passed through" the borough en route to elsewhere. Less known is the fact that Fort Lee has now one of the largest concentrations of East Asians (Chinese, Japanese, Koreans) of any suburb on the East Coast. Successive waves of East Asian immigrants have transformed this suburban space through expanding entrepreneurship, the educational system, and political and civic participation. This study aims to shed light on the rise of this contemporary multiethnic suburb, the changing system of social relationships within it, and the conditions under which such transformations have occurred.

ASIAN IMMIGRATION IN FORT LEE AND BERGEN COUNTY

New Jersey is one of the five, major immigrant-receiving states in the United States—after California, New York, Florida, and Texas. The state has been an important destination for Asian immigrant groups and now has the fourth largest Asian population after California, New York, and Texas. The largest group is Asian Indian, followed by Chinese, Filipino, and Korean, all of which have been on the increase to date.[10] East and South Asians were the fastest-growing immigrant groups in New Jersey in the 1990s. During this decade, New Jersey's Asian populations grew by 61 percent—a rate higher than the national growth rate of 40 percent. The number was even higher in Bergen County, at 64 percent.[11]

Bergen is the most populous county in the state of New Jersey (905,116 inhabitants as of 2010). Along with the steady influx of Hispanic immigrants, the county began to attract East Asian immigrants in the 1970s. According to the census of 1970, Bergen already had the largest number of Japanese (1,177) and the second largest number of Chinese (1,372) among the twenty-one counties of New Jersey.[12] During the 1990s and 2000s, Bergen County became the largest and fastest-growing suburban settlement of Korean immigrants in the New York metropolitan area.[13] By contrast, the formerly predominant white population of Bergen County has markedly declined. Today, Asians make up almost half the population of some towns in Bergen County and have a presence in almost every municipality.[14] Thriving immigrant businesses have breathed life into ailing downtowns. Bergen County's low crime rate, its cleanliness, its parks and open areas, the ease of access to the mountains and to recreational areas to the north, and its numerous institutions and establishments serving the general public have all been sources of attraction for newcomers searching for a desirable place of residence.

Fort Lee was largely composed of German, Irish, Italian, and Jewish populations in the postwar period. The census registered 97 percent of the population as white in 1970; Italians constituted the majority of the white population in the same year—27.6 percent of the borough's population.[15] Between 1970 and 2010, the percentage of whites dropped, from 97 to 46.7 percent. Within four decades, the three Asian groups—Chinese, Japanese, and Koreans—have come to constitute 34.7 percent of the borough's population, an increase from 1.7 percent in 1970 (table 1). Hispanics represented 11 percent in 2010. The number of Filipinos and Asian Indians has also increased while the number of blacks has shown a slight increase. As table 2 shows, the decline of white inhabitants has been offset mainly by the increase of Asians but also, more recently, by Hispanics.

The concentration of East Asians in Fort Lee is one of the highest in New Jersey. Over the last forty years, the composition of the East Asian population has, however, shifted (table 3). Japanese were the majority Asian group during the 1970s through the 1980s. Their numbers have rapidly decreased since the 1990s, yet Fort Lee still remains home to the largest number of Japanese in New Jersey. A Korean influx followed the declining number of Japanese around 1990, doubling in size between 1990 and 2000. Currently, Koreans form the largest minority group in the borough and represent the second largest Korean population in New Jersey after the neighboring borough of Palisades Park. While there has been a small proportion of longtime Chinese residents since the 1970s, the significant Chinese influx began in more recent years.[16] Fort Lee now has the largest number of Chinese residents in Bergen County, a population that has grown rapidly since the 1990s. By 2010, the number of Chinese had surpassed that of Japanese. Fort Lee's ethnoracial mix—rather than the predominance of one ethnic group—has produced a uniquely pluralistic, multiethnic suburban community.

The rapid influx of Asian immigrants into Fort Lee further reflects a new facet of the post-1965 immigrant wave—an increased proportion of well-educated, middle-class professionals. In 2015, Asians had the highest annual median household income ($76,679) of all racial groups—including non-Hispanic whites ($67,114)—and had incomes higher than those of the median household for the borough ($70,415).[17] Asians also had the greatest level of education for all racial groups in the borough in 2015: 65.7 percent had gained a bachelor's degree or higher, by comparison with 54.1 percent of non-Hispanic whites.[18]

The proportion of foreign-born residents has increased over the years in Fort Lee. According to the census of 1970, 19 percent of the Fort Lee population was registered as foreign-born. This figure increased every decade, and by

TABLE 1 Racial and ethnic composition, borough of Fort Lee, New Jersey, 1970–2010

Race/ethnicity	1970		1980		1990		2000		2010	
	Number and percentage of borough population									
	N	%	*N*	%	*N*	%	*N*	%	*N*	%
Chinese	115	0.4	285	0.9	844	2.6	1,988	5.6	2,653	7.5
Japanese	385	1.3	1,944	6.0	2,764	8.6	2,091	5.9	1,302	3.7
Korean	n/a	—	388	1.2	2,468	7.7	5,978	16.9	8,318	23.5
Hispanic or Latino	(901)	(2.9)	1,342	4.1	1,779	5.6	2,791	7.9	3,877	11.0
Non-Hispanic black	202	0.7	519	1.6	383	1.2	555	1.6	805	2.3
Non-Hispanic white	29,827	97.3	27,494	84.7	23,361	73.0	20,350	57.3	16,514	46.7
Other	102	0.3	477	1.5	398	1.2	1,708	4.8	1,876	5.3
Total	30,631	100.0	32,449	100.0	31,997	100.0	35,461	100.0	35,345	100.0

SOURCE: U.S. Bureau of the Census, 1973, 1982, 1992a, 2001, 2010.

NOTE: "Other" includes American Indian and Alaska Native, native Hawaiian and other Pacific Islander, Asian Indian, Other Asian (e.g., Filipino, Vietnamese), some other race, and two or more races. The categories included under "Other" vary by the census year. Koreans were not specified in the 1970 census for Fort Lee and may have been included in "Other" for that year. For 1970, the information concerning the race of people of "Spanish origin" ($N = 901$) was unavailable. The numbers reported for "white," "black," and "other" in the census are reproduced in the table.

TABLE 2 Population growth, selected, Fort Lee, 1980–2010

Percentage change from preceding decade	1980	1990	2000	2010
Chinese	147.8	196.1	135.5	33.4
Japanese	404.9	42.2	−24.3	−37.7
Korean*	—	536.1	142.2	39.1
Hispanic or Latino	48.9	32.6	56.9	38.9
White	−5.0	−15.0	−12.7	−18.8
Total	5.9	−1.4	10.8	−0.3

SOURCE: U.S. Bureau of the Census, 1973, 1982, 1992a, 2001, 2010.

* Koreans not specified in 1970 census.

TABLE 3 Changes in East Asian population, Fort Lee, 1970–2010

Groups as percentage of East Asian population	1970	1980	1990	2000	2010
Chinese	23.0	10.9	13.9	19.8	21.6
Japanese	77.0	74.3	45.5	20.8	10.6
Korean*	—	14.8	40.6	59.4	67.8
Total	100.0	100.0	100.0	100.0	100.0

SOURCE: U.S. Bureau of the Census 1973, 1982, 1992a, 2001, 2010.

* Koreans not specified in 1970 census.

2000, nearly 45 percent of the borough's population was foreign-born.[19] In 2015, 53 percent of the borough residents were foreign-born; 64 percent of these were from Asia. Among the foreign-born, 60.9 percent were naturalized citizens.[20] Regardless of place of birth, Fort Lee's population in general has been transient and has included a large portion of new arrivals with short tenures of residency.

THEORIZING IMMIGRANT SUBURBANIZATION IN THE UNITED STATES

Suburbanization as a Sign of Assimilation

Traditionally, immigrants have settled in ethnic "enclaves," defined by national origin, in central cities of the United States. Later immigrants, with limited resources, were drawn to the same communities, as havens of assistance with housing, jobs, and cultural familiarity. An *enclave* can be defined as a "spatially concentrated area in which members of a particular population group, self-defined by ethnicity or religion or otherwise congregate as a means of enhancing their economic, social, political, and/or cultural development."[21] Such enclaves occupy a transitional phase in the incorporation of new groups into society, providing mutual support, orientation to the new land, and a channel for integration. Immigrant enclaves have been viewed as a stepping stone toward integration and upward mobility in the mainstream; eventual departure from the enclave has been regarded as a sign of social success.[22] Those who become economically secure leave the enclave and frequently convert their occupational mobility and economic assimilation into residential gain—in places with greater advantages and amenities, frequently in suburbia.[23]

The "spatial assimilation" model proposed by Douglas Massey—an influential theoretical framework for immigrant suburbanization—holds that the move into white, middle-class suburbs is associated with immigrant acculturation and rising socioeconomic status, indicative of integration into mainstream society.[24] The process of moving out of the urban ethnic enclave entails the geographic dispersion of minority group members, opening the way for increased contact with members of the white majority and thus desegregation and greater assimilation. According to this model, the suburbs promote increased association with members of the majority group, eventually leading to the disappearance of ethnic distinctiveness. Spatial assimilation, closely connected with the idea of residential integration, may be viewed as a form of status attainment through relocation to the suburb.[25]

Spatial assimilation has been used widely to assess the degree of residential segregation of various ethnoracial groups, the significance of suburbanization with regard to the assimilation of immigrants, and patterns of immigrants' residential distribution in the United States and beyond (e.g., in Canada).[26] It has been found that English proficiency (a measure of acculturation) and high socioeconomic status are strongly correlated with the suburbanization of ethnic minority groups. Minority suburbanization can also be viewed as a process driven primarily by the motivation for status attainment rather than ethnic preference.[27] Asian representation in those suburbs with large white populations has increased more than that of African Americans and Hispanics. This has been interpreted by some as indicative of the declining significance of "race" for Asians.[28] That suburbs with large Asian populations tend to be wealthier and more self-sufficient may seem to support the spatial assimilation model. Asians' lesser degree of residential segregation from whites, compared with that of blacks or Hispanics, does not, however, automatically imply greater contact with whites. In fact, scholarship has indicated that depending on the region, an increase in Asian immigration has also led to an increase of Asian–white segregation.[29]

Maintaining Ethnicity in Suburbia

Contrary to previous assumptions of a reduction in the probability of ethnic aggregation, it was found that by 1990, most groups had established ethnic communities in suburbia. Ethnic concentration has not disappeared in the suburban setting. For some groups, "the suburban enclave provides an alternative to assimilation—it is an ethnic community in a relatively high-status setting."[30]

In the last few decades of the twentieth century, Asian ethnic communities began to develop in metropolitan suburban areas to accommodate affluent U.S.- and foreign-born Asians. Many new immigrants from Asia now settle directly into middle-class suburbs, bypassing the urban ethnic enclaves; they position themselves within the middle or upper-middle strata on arrival in the United States. Recent immigrants often arrive with considerable amounts of financial capital, high levels of education, desirable occupational skills, and the social capital necessary for settlement in desirable locations, even while lacking signs of acculturation such as English proficiency. Scholars interpret this recent pattern among Asians as the reflection of greater resources, volitional selection, and a preference for coethnic residency, rather than social constraints such as discrimination in housing.[31] In light of this new trend, the proposed correlation between level of assimilation and residential mobility in the spatial assimilation model appears less tenable. The question arises whether the suburbanization of nonwhites today has the same impact on them that it had on earlier European immigrants.

Recent conceptualizations of emerging suburban ethnic communities have drawn upon the case of Chinese immigration in the Los Angeles suburbs. These "ethnoburbs" are defined by urban geographer Wei Li as "suburban ethnic clusters of residential areas and business districts in large American metropolitan areas," where one ethnic minority group has a significant concentration but may not necessarily be a majority.[32] The ethnoburb is a product of a multitude of factors including economic globalization, geopolitical shifts, and changes in immigration policy. The ethnoburb differs from urban enclaves and, it is argued, is not a "suburban Chinatown."[33] As an expression of the international expansion of fiscal and economic structures, high-waged, highly skilled professionals involved in international trade tend to live in the ethnoburb, with an overrepresentation of those in the finance, insurance, and real estate (FIRE) sector. Yet in Li's example from the environs of Los Angeles, the ethnoburb retains "some features of an ethnic enclave economy," since working-class Chinese follow the professional classes to provide ethnic services and businesses.[34] Ethnoburb residents are thus of diverse socioeconomic status, producing a new class stratification within the ethnic suburb.[35] This combination of global ties and local service jobs gives the ethnoburb the feeling of a "global outpost" with a distinctive ethnic character.

The ethnoburb model describes a framework of resistance to complete assimilation and a propensity for the maintenance of immigrant cultural heritage. The ethnoburb is a voluntary concentration of the ethnic group, created and maintained through deliberate effort, and is self-contained as a place of residence and work. As a result of such sociospatial arrangements, the assimilation process slows down and takes different forms. Despite the ethnic concentration, ethnoburb residents have greater interaction with the host compared to those in urban enclaves and can integrate into mainstream society through economic activities, political involvement, and community life.[36]

Another contemporary form of suburban ethnic community is that of relatively privileged Chinese immigrants residing "without propinquity." In this case, ethnic linkages are retained without clustering in a physically defined community. According to such "heterolocalism," recent immigrants with resources "adopt a dispersed pattern of residential location while maintaining strong social cohesion."[37] Ethnic organizations such as language schools, churches, community organizations, and cultural and political agencies provide for the maintenance of community. The spatial dispersal of ethnic services and institutions allows for such residential patterns while the high socioeconomic status of immigrants obviates the necessity of clustering together for ethnic support.[38] Affluent immigrants may choose to live in dispersed areas solely for practical reasons (e.g., the education of children) without necessarily being assimilated.

Immigrant professionals and upwardly mobile, U.S.-born Chinese Americans who settle in affluent suburbs among diverse ethnic groups tend to blend in with the local scene and are viewed as "generally assimilated" by some scholars.[39] Such "Yacht" Chinese are "not perceived as a threat to Caucasian majorities in life or work, as opposed to the 'boat' people of various backgrounds."[40] It does not seem that these highly educated, affluent Chinese immigrants drawn to the suburbs are concerned with favorably impressing their white neighbors, however. This tendency may instead be ascribed to social origin: coming from developed countries with high standards of living, such immigrants are "confident of their own values when encountering the outside world."[41] Whether dispersed or clustered, Wei Li considers contemporary Chinese communities as a "new ethno-spectrum of multiclustered settlement patterns and multifaceted community forms."[42]

EVERYDAY LIFE IN THE GROWING MULTIETHNIC SUBURB

Metropolitan suburban communities in the United States have evolved into "global neighborhoods" in which native-born groups live side by side with immigrants of different national origins. Emergent multiethnic suburbs have been documented in several ethnographic studies, whose findings underscore the increasing significance of immigration and ethnic relations for suburbia. The majority of studies have focused on the Los Angeles area, including Monterey Park and the San Gabriel Valley.[43] The primary issues considered include intra-ethnic and interethnic political strife, ethnoracial representation, the development of panethnic coalitions, the transnational economy, and the specific local formations of racial identity and ideology. Studies have documented tensions between established residents and newcomers (mainly Chinese with relatively privileged backgrounds), as well as the incorporation of newcomers into civic life through participation in political and social struggles. Incorporation in turn contributes to the transformation of the community and redefinition of the meaning of "American." Suburban space is thus considered a site of immigrant ethnic solidarity, while at the same time offering a way of forging new identities—both ethnic and American.[44]

Despite the growing body of literature on the suburbanization of nonwhite immigrants, there is still a want of knowledge about communities and everyday life in multiethnic suburbs, especially on the East Coast. Existing research focuses on the Angeleno suburban communities, where native-born Asian and Latino American residents had established their middle-class home prior to the post-1965 inflow of Asian immigrants. By 1970, Asian and Latino (primarily Mexican) Americans constituted roughly half the population of Monterey Park. The San Gabriel Valley similarly had begun to receive middle-class Chinese, Japanese, and Mexican Americans who were leaving urban enclaves during the 1950s. Their political power increased during the 1980s through their greater representation in local electoral politics.[45] Today, in the San Gabriel Valley and Monterey Park, the Asian ethnic minority is the numerical majority, with Chinese being the overwhelming majority among Asians.[46] In contrast to the Los Angeles suburbs, detailed scholarly accounts of Asian immigrant communities in the suburbs of New York City, particularly those of New Jersey, have hitherto been few.[47]

The sociohistorical conditions of Fort Lee differ from the Californian suburbs in several important ways. Fort Lee is an older suburb with colonial origins. The proportion of East Asians is lower in Fort Lee, and whites still constituted the numerical majority in the borough through the first decade of the twenty-first century. The majority of the East Asian groups are foreign-born, first-generation immigrants who came to the United States in the latter part of the twentieth century, with very few native-born, later-generation Asian Americans. Non-Asian minority groups were relatively small in size until very recently. The recent influx and concentration of the three East Asian groups are particular to Fort Lee and distinguish it from the Californian suburbs, where a single ethnic group constitutes the numerical majority. These conditions give rise to a different kind of multiethnic suburb and immigrant experience than those found on the West Coast. Fort Lee thus offers a further vantage point for insight into the impact of globalization and immigration in the contemporary American suburb.

The present inquiry considers some of the key aspects that constitute the suburban life of immigrants in the United States today. How have these Asian communities formed, developed, and changed over time in Fort Lee? What are the patterns of social assimilation among Asians, and how are they negotiated? In what ways has Asian immigration influenced the community? How is the ethnoracial identity of Asians in Fort Lee shaped by the conjuncture of the three East Asian communities and the multiracial milieu? How do native white residents perceive Asians, and how have social relationships between immigrants and native whites changed over time? Fort Lee allows for a comparative analysis of the three Asian groups—their differences and similarities as immigrants, racial minorities, and in terms of their social interrelationships. While considering the social forces that shape these patterns, this study explores the everyday practices of social actors and how these are negotiated within the transformation of the suburb.

In the light of contemporary social diversity, it is important to study the relationships of multiple ethnoracial groups and their relations with each other rather than to focus on a single group or on nonwhite minorities alone. Unlike other suburban locations that have exhibited strong nativist opposition and antipathy toward nonwhite immigrants, overt hostility and confrontation have been less apparent in Fort Lee.[48] Understanding immigrant community formation and assimilation requires a consideration of the reception by native residents and the local context. In this respect, our investigation moves beyond the traditional focus on immigrant groups and their characteristics alone to a consideration of their interaction with the host society and the conditions that both newcomers and established residents face.

Minority-majority relationships are changing in certain contemporary contexts—Asian immigrants with high socioeconomic status, for example, may now provide normative standards, challenging the idea of white America as the standard of social aspiration.[49] But the suburbanization of Asians does not mean that they are becoming the white middle class—once a premise of immigrant suburbanization. Rather, the meaning of social boundaries in the middle-class suburbs is subject to change. Asians may be seen as the "other" and confront contradictory designations as both an "oppressed" and yet "privileged" minority.[50] As ethnic transitions take place in "suburban society," Fort Lee offers data for an alternate paradigm of immigrant-native relations.[51] The case tells a story of the local effects of globalization, shedding light on how people are dealing with increasing diversity and contemporary contestation and revision of the meanings of race, ethnicity, and Americanness.

METHODOLOGY AND DATA

Multiple methods were employed for the present study: in-depth interviews, ethnographic fieldwork, analysis of census data, and media and document analysis. The primary method was semistructured interviews with local residents, workers, business owners, and community leaders. Fifty-six interviews were conducted with Chinese, Japanese, Koreans, and native-born whites, recruited through snowball sampling or direct contact.[52] Field observations were conducted at a number of local institutions, facilities, businesses, and community events; institutions included the Jack Alter Fort Lee Community Center, Fort Lee Museum, Fort Lee Public Library, the recreation center, the Richard A. Nest Senior Citizens' Center, and various schools and local parks. I observed local events such as concerts, arts and cultural festivals, plays, film screenings, Independence Day firework displays, and historical reenactments. I also participated in municipal meetings and school-sponsored events, as well as ethnic festivals. Field observations were also conducted in other boroughs in Bergen beyond Fort Lee, including Edgewater, Englewood, Englewood Cliffs, Hackensack, Leonia, Palisades Park, Paramus, and Ridgefield. I visited businesses, cultural events, religious services, and ethnic organizations (e.g., Chinese-language schools) at these locations. Throughout the course of fieldwork, informal conversations and interviews were conducted. Whenever the time and place seemed appropriate, I engaged people in conversation and then posed questions relevant to the study. The primary data collection was undertaken from 2007 through 2008; additional interviews and fieldwork were continued with decreased frequency from 2009 to 2010 and 2016 to 2017. The interviews (tape-recorded with permission) were transcribed, and field observations were recorded in detail as field notes for subsequent analysis.

The qualitative data from interviews and field observations were supplemented by the analysis of secondary data sources. First, an analysis of media accounts of the coverage of East Asian immigration in Fort Lee and Bergen County was undertaken. The *New York Times* was consulted from 1972, when the first coverage on the Japanese in Fort Lee appeared, through 2011. The local daily, the *Record,* was consulted from 1984, the earliest date available in the Fort Lee Public Library database, through 2011. The local weeklies, *Bergen News* and *Fort Lee Suburbanite,* were consulted from 2007 (through 2011) and 2008 (through 2012), respectively, as was *Gold Coast Life* (continuation of *Fort Lee Suburbanite*) from 2016 to present. In addition, online news websites were regularly consulted (e.g., Fort Lee Patch, NJ.com). Second, local archival documents—including those of the Fort Lee Regional Chamber of Commerce (formerly the Greater Fort Lee Chamber of Commerce) and municipal records (e.g., meeting minutes)—were consulted. Finally, decennial census data for the period 1970 to 2010 (and, where pertinent, since 1950), the American Community Survey, and the 5-Percent Public Use Microdata Sample (PUMS) were analyzed.[53]

PLAN OF THE BOOK

Chapter 1 provides the local context through two fundamental frames of reference: time and space. An overview of topography and the significance of local history for the collective identity of the borough is the prelude to this study of Asian suburban settlement. The chapter also discusses postwar suburban development in Fort Lee. Chapter 2 examines the sociohistorical formations and transformations of the Chinese, Japanese, and Korean communities, analyzing the trajectories, forms, and features of each group. This chapter examines the development patterns of each ethnic community and their relationships with each other and the wider community, with a consideration of what kinds of suburban ethnic communities they represent. Chapter 3 concerns how assimilation and the maintenance of ethnicity are enacted through everyday practices and ethnic organizations. These are dialectical and multivalent processes, at once conscious and unconscious and requiring constant negotiation. The trends of assimilation and ethnic retention are posited as strategies used in the search for a place within society. Chapter 4 turns to native white resident perceptions and reactions to East Asian immigration and attendant social shifts in Fort Lee. A consideration of the host society is essential to understanding the process of immigrant assimilation. How has the local community been changed by immigration, and how have native white perceptions shifted over time? Chapter 5 explores ethnoracial identity among East Asians in Fort Lee. How do immigrants and their offspring understand "Asianness," and how do they construct and negotiate the meaning of being "Asian" in a multiethnic suburb? How does residence in a diverse community affect ethnic and panethnic identity? Asians in Fort Lee feel an increasing sense of pride and confidence in their ethnicity as a result of their growing demographic presence and socioeconomic success. Yet "race" continues to play an important role in place-making by Asian immigrants. The book concludes with a consideration of the issues raised in regard to group relations, the organization of the communities, immigrant assimilation, and ethnicity in Fort Lee.

A NOTE ON TERMINOLOGY

Throughout this discussion, the term "East Asian" is used to refer to people of Chinese, Japanese, and Korean descent. Chinese include those originally from Hong Kong, mainland China, Taiwan, and Southeast Asia; whenever relevant, the country of origin is specified. "Korea" and "Korean" are used to refer to South Korea and South Koreans. The terms "Asian" and "East Asian" are used interchangeably. When referring to people of South Asian or Southeast Asian origin (who are not ethnic Chinese), they are specified as such. The term "white" is used to refer to native-born whites whose ancestral origins may vary (e.g., Irish, Italian, and Jewish) as well as those who identified themselves as having multiple white ethnic origins.

1 · A TOWN OF IMMIGRANTS

> This has always been a town of immigrants. We've always valued its multicultural quality.
>
> —Jack Alter, former mayor of Fort Lee, 1996

During a typical weekday evening rush hour, many East Asian passengers can be seen in the cars of the New York City subway's uptown A train. In formal business attire, they make their way home from work in the offices of Manhattan. As the train arrives at the 175th Street station (George Washington Bridge Bus Station), the commuters jostle with the crowds and make toward the exit. Through the dimly lit passageway, they hurry silently to the buses that will ferry them across to New Jersey. One cannot be certain of their ethnonational origin by their appearance, and they are typically alone. Yet occasional signs of ethnic membership are suggested by the paraphernalia of their belongings: translucent, red plastic shopping bags with Chinese characters in black; Korean-language newspapers; Japanese paperbacks, thinner and smaller in size than those found in the United States, protected by a paper cover. In this racially and ethnically diverse scene of everyday transit between Manhattan and northern New Jersey, East Asians play a conspicuous part.

The George Washington Bridge offers spectacular views of the bluffs of the Palisades on the west bank of the Hudson River and the Manhattan skyline to the east. On a clear day, the Statue of Liberty is visible on the horizon at the southern tip of Manhattan. The Palisades flank the massive steel structure of the bridge at the approach to Fort Lee. Within five minutes, the bus is on the New Jersey side, making its first stop at Bridge Plaza, the main disembarkation point for many Asian passengers. Today's diversity makes it hard to believe that only forty years ago, Fort Lee's population was almost entirely ethnically white.

History and social background are important for the consideration of contemporary East Asian migration and to the development of the borough as a whole. Preexisting ethnic and cultural diversity in Fort Lee has been an obvious source

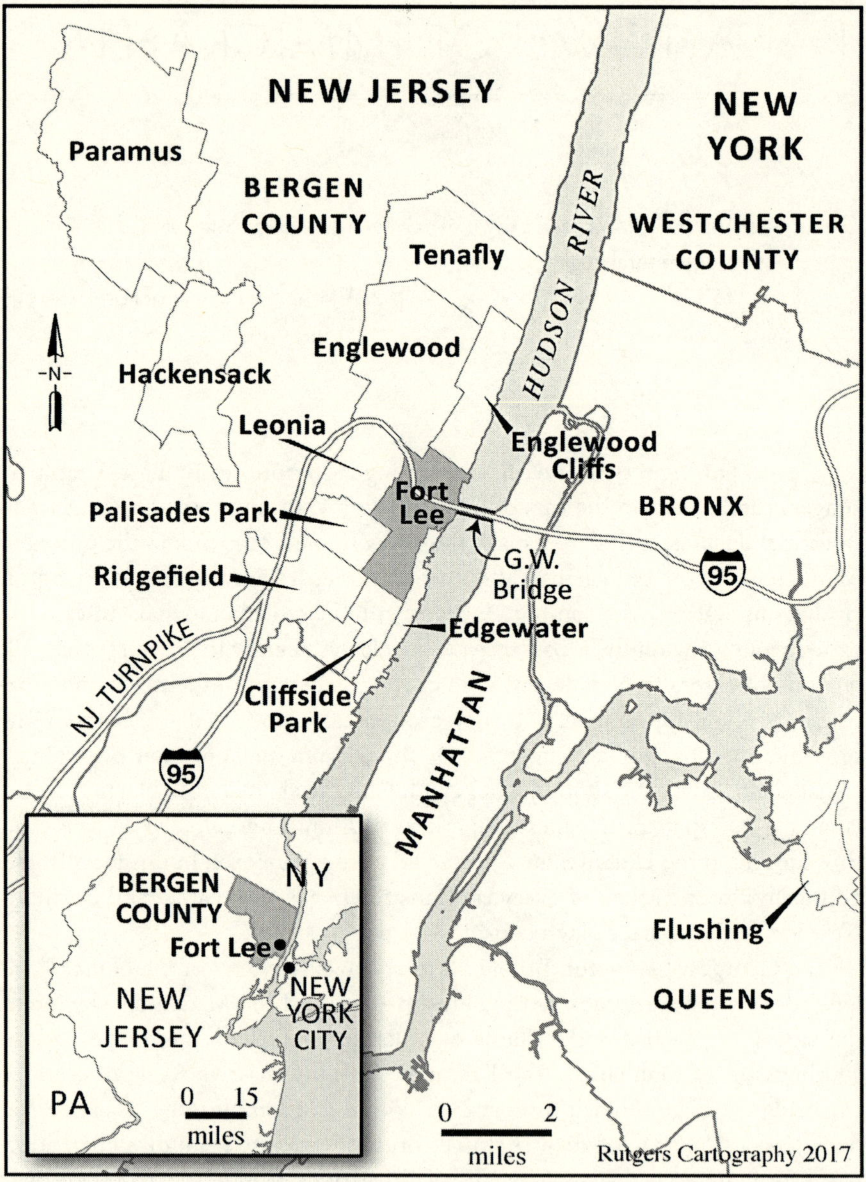

FIGURE 1. Map of Fort Lee and environs, Bergen County, New Jersey, and New York City. Prepared by Michael Siegel, Geography Department, Rutgers University.

of attraction for more recent immigrants. Diversity was a social by-product of the George Washington Bridge, which established a direct link with New York from the 1930s on. The bridge offered a pathway for various ethnic groups from New York into the suburbs of New Jersey.

This chapter focuses on the two fundamental frames of reference: time and space. After introducing the topography of Fort Lee, the chapter discusses the local historical narratives that have been instrumental in the construction of the identity of the borough. This discussion is followed by a consideration of postwar development. Today, in general, Bergen County is increasingly diverse, but residents in the vicinity still view Fort Lee as the epitome of diversity. The cultural context and spatial disposition of the town—particularly its geographic relationship with New York City—are essential in understanding how and why East Asians have made Fort Lee their suburban home.

TOPOGRAPHY

Ten miles from midtown Manhattan, Fort Lee is situated on the Palisades overlooking the Hudson River (figure 1). The borough covers 2.5 square miles and had 35,345 residents in 2010.[1] Fort Lee's history has been tied to the heights on which it stands and to the river, where it narrows and where the cliffs are closest to the river's edge.[2] The prominent headlands on both sides of the Hudson led to the choice of Fort Lee as the western terminus of the George Washington Bridge. The bridge also joins the site of one Revolutionary-era fort to another—Fort Washington on Manhattan island and Fort Lee on the New Jersey side (figure 2).

The entry point into Fort Lee from New York is George Washington Bridge Plaza, where several major highways intersect (figure 3). "Cars, trucks, and

FIGURE 2. Hudson River and George Washington Bridge, looking toward Fort Lee, seen from Upper Manhattan, 2017. Author photo.

FIGURE 3. New Jersey Turnpike, Fort Lee, looking west from Bridge Plaza, 2017. Author photo.

buses, in a seemingly endless stream, carry people and goods through Fort Lee," connecting northern New Jersey to Manhattan and providing access to the state and beyond.[3] The bridge carries Interstate 95, the main artery connecting Maine to Florida, one of America's busiest highways. The fourteen lanes of the interstate receive 300,000 vehicles per day—2.1 million per week.[4] The sheer scale of this ceaseless circulation impresses the first-time visitor. For the inhabitants of Fort Lee, the bridge is both a cherished cultural symbol and the root cause of a perennial local problem—traffic. The bridge, as one informant put it, "is both a blessing and nemesis."[5]

The modern office complexes visible from Bridge Plaza, rising against a background of high-rise apartment buildings, give a highly urbanized impression. To the south lies Main Street, Fort Lee's political and commercial center, originally a colonial road, running east-west. Business districts have traditionally grown along older arterial road systems in many suburban communities. The borough's municipal institutions stand close together on Main—the post office, borough hall, senior center, and public library. Next to the library is the Church of the Madonna (established in 1858), the oldest Catholic church in Bergen County.[6] Lemoine Avenue, running north-south across Main Street, has also developed business and commercial areas. Most of Fort Lee's stores have grown in a linear manner along Main and Lemoine. The businesses in the central commercial areas are within walking distance of each other. Retail stores, restaurants, real estate agencies, banks, travel agencies, insurance agencies, and doctors' and dentists' offices are grouped closely together.

Main Street, with its row of small businesses, has remained structurally the same for the past forty years.[7] A white male in his fifties, a native of Fort Lee and a local real estate agent, told me that the types of local business on Main Street and Lemoine Avenue before Asian immigration in the 1970s included food stores (delis, grocery stores, restaurants, bakeries, luncheonettes, etc.), clothing stores, dry cleaners, repair stores, barbershops, beauty parlors, and insurance and real estate agencies. Some still exist today, but these have frequently been replaced by Korean businesses. Established hardware outlets, the cigar store, the pizzeria, and bagel store—all of which might be classified as "American"—are now interspersed with Korean stores along Main Street. Some of the long-time "fixtures" have been replaced by new businesses: for example, Callahan's, a hot-dog restaurant, was replaced by the Bank of New Jersey in 2007, and the Fort Lee Diner, which was in business for several decades, is now a Korean restaurant.[8]

The impact of Asian immigration is visible throughout Fort Lee's downtown with Korean stores and restaurants lending an ethnic character to the appearance of its streets. On all the major thoroughfares in Fort Lee, there are numerous signs for businesses and stores in *Hangul* (Korean characters) with some in Chinese and Japanese. In 2006, the local press reported on an "Asian-American entrepreneurial explosion" in the United States, with New Jersey being one example of the trend.[9] Bergen County had the largest number of Asian-owned firms in New Jersey in 2002. The spread of Chinese, Japanese, and Korean-owned businesses was especially evident in the downtown business districts in Fort Lee and the neighboring boroughs of Palisades Park and Leonia. Multilingual signs in Japanese and Korean, or Chinese and Korean, along with English, have also appeared.[10] Once past the commercial areas, businesses along the streets become sparse. Nevertheless, those at a distance from Main Street frequently have bilingual signs in English and *Hangul* advertising medical offices, accounting and law firms, SAT and TOEFL preparatory schools, restaurants, dry cleaners, and hair salons.

Fort Lee's center has a couple of small-scale shopping malls that are typically composed of a variety of mainstream and Asian businesses—for example, Chinese restaurants, Asian bakeries, and a tae kwon do school along with chain drugstores and delicatessens. In a few other malls the businesses are entirely Korean-run, signaled by the predominance of bilingual signs in English and Korean. Asian-style bakeries are popular with local residents of varied ethnicities, some of which represent pan-Asian enterprise. One such bakery, originally

Japanese, is franchised in Taiwan. At the time of my field observation, the owner of this bakery was Chinese and the store manager Korean. One Japanese informant told me the owner used to be Japanese. These bakeries are influenced by European-style patisserie but also reflect Asian-style confectionery—a curious fusion of West and East.

Main Street businesses do not in general appear to be bustling, although the roads are always busy with traffic. In the commercial area, the majority of pedestrians are Asians—generally younger age groups, including children. Senior citizens tend to be white—often seen in cafés and bakeries, in groups or alone. On weekdays, young and middle-aged Korean men and women in business suits and formal office attire are a common sight in the commercial areas—evidence of the numerous Korean white-collar businesses in Fort Lee—sometimes speaking Korean, sometimes English. Pedestrian traffic is limited, especially on the weekend. One reason for these quiet downtown streets is the prevalence of banks and business offices. By ten at night, apart from a few restaurants, all the businesses on Main Street are closed. Starbucks and the former Borders bookstore café are usually filled with Asian customers until the late hours. Asian restaurants and food stores appear to be thriving. Economic recession has led to the closing of some Korean retail stores since late 2009, but newly opening businesses since then tend to be Korean owned.

Residents, however, expressed the feeling that Fort Lee's offerings for consumers were inadequate: they claimed that they have to go to other boroughs (e.g., Edgewater, Hackensack), whether to shop or for movies. The president of the Greater Fort Lee Chamber of Commerce (now the Fort Lee Regional Chamber of Commerce) remarked that the biggest complaint he heard from residents was the lack of variety in Main Street businesses.[11] My informants nevertheless did not seem particularly frustrated; they found it easy to reach alternatives by car. Without traffic, one can get "anywhere" within five to ten minutes—a convenience frequently noted as one advantage of living in Fort Lee.

Fort Lee's social geography is varied, despite its small size. From the latter half of the nineteenth century until well into the postwar period, the town was divided into four sections—Coytesville, Fort Lee proper, West Fort Lee, and Palisade. These sections were separated by extensive wooded tracts even into the 1930s, but the area was gradually filled in with the construction of residential apartments after the Second World War.[12] During this process, the sectional divides receded. Defined by religious affiliation, social class, ethnic group, and accompanying ethnic rivalry, each section was distinct in physical appearance. Vestiges of that legacy are still discernible today. The northern part of the town, Coytesville, was a predominantly working-class Irish settlement, where the house and lot sizes were small—it was also home to a number of film studios in the early decades of the twentieth century. Today, newer, bigger, single-family houses and duplexes have replaced the older wooden houses. These new houses line the streets immediately adjacent to each other, since the lot sizes remain small. By contrast, to the south (formerly "Palisade") there were professional, upper-middle-class, primarily German and Jewish residents. Today, grander houses and mansions, conveying the wealth of the residents, remain visible in this area. The central part of town, near Main Street and other commercial areas, was once predominantly Italian. There are still signs of an Italian concentration—plaster statuettes of the Virgin Mary are found in many of the gardens of the single-family houses, which generally look small and relatively old.

High-rise apartments are a dominating presence, but low-rise apartments, mostly built prior to the 1950s, are also common.[13] Many of the high-rises were built along the Palisades. Because high-rise zoning was extended to the center of town, regular residential houses adjacent to towering blocks are now a common sight in most parts of Fort Lee (figure 4). By contrast with the luxury high-rises, there are several low-rent and rent-subsidized housing developments. Compared with neighboring boroughs such as Englewood Cliffs (north) or Leonia (west), which are largely residential without high-rises, Fort Lee is more built-up and more diverse and eclectic in age and type of building. Old and new coexist in the architecture of Fort Lee.

A few minutes' drive from the central commercial district leads to tranquil residential areas with two-story, single-family houses, well maintained with gardens and garages—although not "typical" suburban homes with a "white picket fence," as one white male informant put it. During field observations there were almost always new residential schemes under construction in some part of town. Larger brand-new, pale-pink, brick-and-stucco houses continued to appear throughout the period of this study. Unlike Main Street and the business and commercial district, people are rarely seen on the sidewalks in the residential areas; driving along these streets, the ethnic composition of the neighborhood is not always immediately visible. Occasionally, one might see East Asian residents who happen to be outside—sitting on a terrace on a summer evening or at a garage sale. The ninety-minute-long procession of San Rocco, an Italian-Catholic annual event held in August, offers an opportunity to observe the ethnic composition of neighborhoods in the center of town. During the event, onlookers follow the procession at street level and from the windows of their apartments. The bystanders are racially and ethnically mixed—whites, Hispanics, and South Asians. In the high-rises, the spectators at windows and on verandas are largely East Asian.

Religious establishments are dispersed. Some are located in quiet residential areas, although most are built along major thoroughfares: Main Street and Anderson, Center, Lemoine, and Palisade avenues. There are six public schools:

FIGURE 4. High-rise apartment buildings (Century Tower and The Colony) from Parker Avenue, Fort Lee, 2017. Author photo.

four elementary schools (Numbers 1–4), one middle school (Lewis F. Cole Middle School), and one high school (Fort Lee High School). These are also dispersed throughout the town. Civic amenities are conveniently located for residents: the recreation center is in William T. Birch Park to the west of Fort Lee, the Fort Lee Community Center on Anderson Avenue, and there is a youth center on Lemoine Avenue.[14] There are also several parks that are used for open-air community events. Some native white informants recalled that there were once three movie theaters in Fort Lee, although none were extant during this field research.

THREE HISTORICAL NARRATIVES

Collectively remembered history typically consists of eventful moments and periods that are interspersed with long stretches of seemingly empty time. The way the past is remembered and memorialized amplifies the momentous while compressing or ignoring what is considered uneventful—hence, some periods are "marked," while others are essentially "unmarked."[15] History and meaning are inevitably partial: regions, periods, groups of people, and individuals from these groups are selected for the historical discourse to make them stand out.[16]

Three historical periods and events have received emphasis in the local media and community activities of contemporary Fort Lee: George Washington's retreat into New Jersey during the American War of Independence in 1776, the early development of the film industry in the first decades of the twentieth century, and the opening of the George Washington Bridge in 1931. Apart from these, Fort Lee's history remains largely undocumented. The parks and their monuments memorialize the War of Independence. Fort Lee Historic Park (part of the Palisades Interstate Park system, founded 1900) houses the Visitor Center that provides information regarding Fort Lee during the Revolutionary War. Monument Park is a few blocks away from Main Street, adjacent to the Fort Lee Museum, staffed by volunteer members of the Fort Lee Historical Society.[17] To the north of Main Street lies Constitution Park.

The figure of George Washington and events related to the American Revolution constitute one of the privileged historical narratives of Fort Lee.[18] Initially called Fort Constitution, the town was renamed after Charles Lee, one of Washington's generals. A fort to protect the North River was constructed on Washington's orders, and several streets were laid out. Washington and the Continental Army occupied the fort in the summer of 1776. When Fort Washington on the opposite shore of the river was captured by the British, the colonial force was evacuated and began the retreat across New Jersey on November 20, 1776. Thomas Paine was stationed in Fort Lee as an aide-de-camp to General Nathanael Greene and wrote *The American Crisis* during the retreat. Fort Lee has been claimed as "the birthplace of *The American Crisis*."[19]

The advent of the film industry in the early twentieth century made Fort Lee into a boomtown. Motion-picture companies from New York City, in search of rural settings, found Fort Lee a convenient location for outdoor shooting. Filmmakers began to arrive by 1908 and found the town filled with hotels, saloons, and livery stables—businesses that had been developed to serve the summer tourist trade.[20] During the second decade of the century, a dozen or so studios and film laboratories were built and many residents found employment in the industry as extras or working in labs.[21] The movie industry flourished for about a decade, and so did local business. Fort Lee was noted by a contemporary in the first decade of the twentieth century as "the scene . . . of a continuous performance of extremely animated, open-air theatricals. . . . [where] the native population has become accustomed to bands of Indians yelling and dashing about the roads and by-paths, to troops landing on the river bank, to dancing villagers, and every variety of battle, murder, and sudden death at their very doors."[22]

The boom was short-lived. By the 1920s, the majority of studios and businesses were leaving for the brighter prospects of California. Problems of transportation from New York, harsh weather, lack of natural light during winter (prohibitive for outdoor shooting) and a wartime shortage of coal drew producers away to Hollywood for its temperate climate, low taxes, sunlight, and access to outdoor sites.[23] By 1935, unable to recover from its loss, Fort Lee seemed "a scene of ruin and desolation."[24] This historic episode nevertheless offers justification for local claims of Fort Lee as the "birthplace" of the American motion-picture industry.[25]

The opening of the George Washington Bridge in 1931 was a decisive factor in Fort Lee's transformation from small rural town to cosmopolitan suburb of New York City. An architectural tour de force, the bridge was twice as long as any suspension bridge in the world (4,760 feet between anchorages).[26] The rapid rise of the automobile starting in the 1920s, the prospect of a crossing to Bergen County, and a new direct link to Manhattan led to real estate speculation of unprecedented dimensions in Bergen and Fort Lee. Completion of the bridge, however, coincided with the Great Depression.[27] The anticipated building boom did not materialize, and Fort Lee was plunged into bankruptcy.

Although the full effects did not make themselves felt until after the war years, the bridge nevertheless salvaged the economy, which had collapsed when the movie industry left for the West Coast. Opening up Fort Lee and a sleepy hinterland of truck farms, farming centers, and early railroad suburbs, the George Washington Bridge is the only bridge connecting Manhattan with New Jersey and the continent beyond. Reproduced widely in official publications and websites that reinforce its symbolic meanings for the borough, the George Washington Bridge has an aesthetic value in addition to its commercial and economic role.[28] On a symbolic level, the bridge and its name provide an anchor for collective memory.

The local history of the Revolutionary War is an important stake in contemporary narratives concerning the identity of Fort Lee. The memory of the struggle for independence and of George Washington, the founding father of the nation, is manifest today in civic nomenclature—monuments, exhibits, and various community-wide events. These include the following:

The monument *Soldiers of the American Revolution*, a bronze sculpture dedicated in Monument Park in 1908[29]

Murals and paintings in public facilities, including the Borough Hall and Post Office[30]

The annual reenactment of the retreat of the Continental Army[31]

The Visitor Center (opened 1976) in Fort Lee Historic Park, devoted to the history of Washington's retreat

Fort Lee Historic Park's programs for schools, which offer the experience of living in an eighteenth-century military encampment

The Common Sense Society, a local nonprofit group, initiated a fund-raising campaign in 2008 for the erection of a statue of Thomas Paine—the third statue of Paine in the United States. The statue is being planned to face the Monument in Monument Park. Storytelling of the American Revolution in Korean was offered at the Public Library in 2009. Pride in the town's revolutionary origins is evident. Whether newcomers or old timers, residents often remarked, "This is where the American Revolution started."

That Fort Lee was once a center of the motion-picture industry is also of increasing significance for the borough's collective consciousness. Current attention to the history of film—including the establishment of the Fort Lee Film Commission in 2000—is a product of the interest of local leaders and devotees of the medium. Interest is reinforced by borough-sponsored events: for example, the annual Historic Jitney Tour, offering free visits to historic film sites of Fort Lee. Film festivals screening both classic American and foreign films are held throughout the year. The film commission has also worked toward incorporating the Asian constituency in the area by reaching out to them to participate in film programming.

In the minds of local leaders, history has rendered Fort Lee "unique" through its association with wider issues of national identity and values—the American Revolution, patriotism, and film and culture. In 2004, the centennial of the borough's incorporation, Richard Koszarski's work on the motion-picture industry in Fort Lee was published. In a statement commending the publication, one former mayor of Fort Lee concluded his open letter with the phrase "Our story is America's story." The "story," however, is subject to interpretation and reinforcement by present-day actors—as comments by the executive director of Fort Lee Film Commission make clear:

> Fort Lee has a great history . . . I don't see a town in America with this rich history as Fort Lee across the board. Other towns would kill for our history in terms of history of the American Revolution. If it was just the American Revolution, that was it, no bridge, no anything else, that would be a great history. My God, how many towns were founded by George Washington? Not only did he sleep here, he laid out our streets, and he successfully got out of town and saved the cause of the American Revolution . . . *The American Crisis* . . . Look at the first few paragraphs, he [Paine] writes about Fort Lee. Now, if that was it, wow, OK, I'm happy. Then we have the George Washington Bridge. Forget the American Revolution, if it was just the bridge. We've got the prettiest bridge in the world next to the most vibrant city in the world. Structurally and aesthetically, there's not a bridge that looks better than that. I love that bridge. I love the Brooklyn Bridge, and I walked across many times there, but that bridge is special. So if it was just the George Washington Bridge, what a history we have. Forget about the bridge, forget about

> the American Revolution. Now we have film. This is where the American film industry was born, Universal, Fox, everything started here. The whole Barrymore [clan] lived in Fort Lee. So now, just talk about film, we have a great history. Now put that together—the Revolution, the bridge, and film. No town has a better history than that. No town.[32]

The collective memory of Fort Lee is further perceived as having a universal aspect—by living in Fort Lee and thereby sharing its historical past, assimilation as an American is open to all:

> It's an amazing history, and it's a history that appeals to any ethnic group that comes in a hundred years from now. A hundred years from now, people—I don't care what their background is in Fort Lee—they're going to be talking about what we're talking about now. The history of film, they're going to talk about the history of the American Revolution and the George Washington Bridge. They are the things they'd be proud of as Americans who live in Fort Lee, regardless of their backgrounds. So I'm very confident because of our rich history, we appeal to any ethnic group that comes in. And that history and quid pro quo becomes their history. So all these kids who are in the school system, that's their history, they are as much American as I am. They have as much claim to the American Revolution as I do, that's their history. And that's going to be the kids' history.[33]

Creating a local identity is on the agenda of community leaders in Fort Lee. The historical record is being reconsidered in a way that recalls the construction of symbolic life in America in the early twentieth century, documented in the study of social anthropologist W. Lloyd Warner. Historical events or places for community celebration are chosen—for what the people consider to be *their* history. These "symbols," as part of the cultural system, ultimately function to affirm present-day beliefs and values of the community. In contemporary Fort Lee, in parallel fashion, "the knowledge of past greatness makes the [modern] city important to itself and to the whole society."[34]

POSTWAR SUBURBAN GROWTH SINCE THE 1950S

Today, half the population of America lives in the suburbs of metropolitan areas—urban areas outside central cities, as defined by the census bureau.[35] Suburbs have increasingly gained social, political, and economic significance in the post–World War II era. According to some scholars, suburbs, rather than cities, may be considered the "transformer" of America.[36] Mass-scale suburbanization of residences during the 1950s and 1960s was followed by the suburbanization of jobs from the 1970s through the 1990s, as the suburbs began to offer sites for employment. Suburban growth is attributed to retail and industrial development, which has accelerated since the early 1960s in tandem with decentralization and economic restructuring in the cities.[37]

Contrary to the social myth of the suburb—the locus of white, middle-class families governed by conformism—the contemporary suburb appears heterogeneous in terms of race, ethnicity, class, homeownership, lifestyles, and cultural milieu. Contemporary suburbanization is characterized by distinctive labor markets, demographic differentiation, and economic specialization. The large-scale forces that have affected cities in the postwar period—notably, globalization—have similarly affected the suburbs. One indication of such impact is the growing presence of foreign enterprise in the suburb. Increasing heterogeneity—according to economic function, class, and ethnic and racial characteristics—suggests that the suburb is becoming more "classically urban."[38] Suburbs are no longer merely the peripheries of cities; the contrast between city and suburb is less marked than might at first be thought.[39]

Fort Lee was committed to economic expansion before the Second World War. This commitment was linked to plans to increase municipal revenues in the face of mounting deficits and unpaid taxes caused by failure in land speculation, premature subdivisions, and overdevelopment of the infrastructure connected with anticipated income from the opening of the George Washington Bridge. Faced with bankruptcy, the borough was placed under the supervision of the State Municipal Finance Commission. Fort Lee's activities were monitored by the state from 1933 until early 1955, when control over finances was finally relinquished to the municipality.[40]

As with the American suburbs in general, home building in Fort Lee accelerated during the 1950s. Postwar housing shortages led to the conversion of single-family homes to two-family houses and the building of apartment projects (e.g., garden apartments) beginning in the late forties. Officials supported virtually unlimited development: the borough imposed no restrictions on the building of high-rise apartments, which seemed to be the ultimate answer to the question of growth. The first luxury high-rise complex was built between 1964 and 1968—a total of six buildings on thirty-two acres—ushering in an era of upward social mobility. The municipality continued to adapt its zoning restrictions to accommodate such development, despite objections from certain residents. Fifteen high-rise apartments were built between 1965 and 1975.[41]

Between 1950 and 1975, Fort Lee was rapidly transforming from a suburban community of predominantly single-family homes into a cosmopolitan mix dominated by high-rise apartments that were occupied by upper-middle-income families. The population burgeoned during the 1950s—well before the influx of the East Asian populations. Between 1950 and 1960, the population of Fort

Lee increased at a rate of 87.3 percent (from 11,647 to 21,815)—approximately double that of Bergen County during the same period (44.7 percent). The population increase continued during the following decade of the 1960s at 40.4 percent.[42] The majority of those who moved to Fort Lee between 1950 and 1970 were Italian, followed by Germans and Irish. By 1970, newcomers of Polish and Russian origin had increased also.[43]

State-wide phenomena also help in understanding Fort Lee's development in the postwar period. Proximity to New York City and Philadelphia shaped New Jersey's economy and its population distribution—given an extensive highway system linking city to suburb and suburb to suburb.[44] The decades following the end of the war witnessed growth in New Jersey associated with the widespread ownership of automobiles and the rapid construction of superhighways. State Routes 4 and 17 begin at the George Washington Bridge and run through Bergen County. The perceived need for large-scale "through routes" expedited the construction of the Garden State Parkway (1946–1957) and the New Jersey Turnpike (1951), which have become the most densely utilized toll roads in the Northeast.[45] Bergen County thus had two major periods of growth. The first was during the 1920s, as the automobile began to make home ownership beyond the city a reality. The second was during the suburban building boom of the postwar years, when home ownership itself fell within reach of most of the population.[46]

The surge of high-rise apartment houses brought a change in the social characteristics of the population. In 1950, the census recorded about 40 percent of Fort Lee resident occupations as blue collar. Over time, the most commonly held occupations have shifted from blue to white collar (administrative, managerial, and professional).[47] The census data agree with the account of a retired white schoolteacher who taught in the Fort Lee school system for fifty years—she reminisced that Fort Lee was a "blue-collar community" consisting mainly of Italians when she first arrived there. The rise to middle-class suburb occurred in the 1970s and continued well into the 1980s.

While many suburban communities were committed to exclusionary zoning, others were more than willing to accommodate development. Such pro-development communities either were dominated by landowner and developer interests or had started out poor enough that middle-income housing and apartments looked fiscally attractive.[48] Fort Lee was certainly pro-development and appears to fit the latter scenario. The experience of bankruptcy and insolvency in the 1920s drove the borough's determination to increase revenue sources, primarily through real estate development. Unlike nearby towns, zoning in Fort Lee accommodated prospective developers—the borough was almost always open to commercial development and the building of apartments, despite opposition from homeowners.[49] Although residents of Fort Lee were of mixed socioeconomic status, a focus on developing middle-income housing effectively functioned to inhibit low-income groups from moving in.

By the 1970s, Fort Lee had the reputation of being a high-rise bedroom community for New York City and an affluent metropolitan suburban town.[50] The image of luxury high-rise condominiums lining the Palisades, with Hudson River and Manhattan skyline views, is often used to represent the borough. During this period, the social characteristics of the community altered drastically. By 1975, Fort Lee had a large upper-middle-class segment with many single residents and empty nesters. During the 1970s, the balance of power shifted from the older, predominantly Republican homeowners to younger, overwhelmingly Democratic tenants.[51]

The abundance of rental property has led to a relatively large number of renters in Fort Lee by comparison with other boroughs in Bergen County.[52] Renter-occupied housing increased during the 1960s and 1970s, and so did owner-occupied housing between 1980 and 1990.[53] According to one local real estate agency owner, the majority of Fort Lee's apartments were built as rental properties whose price included utilities. Having properties as rentals subsequently became uneconomic for many property owners due to the unprecedented level of inflation during the 1980s. Most rental properties were converted to cooperatives or condominiums during this decade.

Convenience for commuters to Manhattan, a good school system, and a safe environment have attracted New Yorkers and those from farther afield to Fort Lee. While functioning as a place of residence, Fort Lee also became a business center by the 1980s.[54] Suburban municipalities in New Jersey routinely welcomed firms bringing jobs.[55] Currently, more than 1,500 business establishments operate in Fort Lee. If the firms not employing staff are included, the number of firms exceeds 5,000.[56] Fort Lee has all the functions of a traditional downtown in a major city, including a place to live, work, and shop.

Interestingly, despite wide acknowledgment of the convenience of travel to New York City, the residents interviewed rarely seem to visit the city unless employed in Manhattan. The everyday activities of residents for the most part seem limited to Bergen County. The trend of increasingly weak ties between New York and the surrounding region was noted in press accounts some twenty years ago.[57] Such trends reflect the shift of retail business and employment into suburbia with a consequential loss of attraction to the city. During interviews, informants often remarked that I was coming to Fort Lee "all the way from New York," as though this were a great distance—a distance that in fact is psychological and social, not actual.

REDEVELOPMENT AREA 5: LONG-STANDING COMMITMENT TO GROWTH

For nearly forty years, sixteen acres of wasteland just off the approach to the George Washington Bridge have remained dormant—unused since the time of their initial leveling in 1972. The site was the last vacant tract of land in Fort Lee. Formerly the site of an Italian community—with residences, retail stores, and a movie theater—the land had been designated for large-scale redevelopment, but none of the proposed projects were realized.[58] A local developer originally purchased the land in the seventies but due to financial need turned to the Investors Funding Corporation for financing. In 1975, the latter was convicted of bribery of municipal officials to gain support for the establishment of a shopping center on the site.[59] In the early 1980s, another developer bought the property but resold the land in the late 1990s.[60]

Town and Country Developers purchased the property in 2003. The site plan was approved in April 2005 by the borough and ground was broken the following October. In 2007, the plan, known locally as the "Centuria" project, was ready to be launched. It was reported that the multimillion-dollar project would be "the biggest in Fort Lee history"—a large-scale, high-profile, multiuse complex of retail stores, office space, more than eight hundred luxury condominiums, a first-class hotel, and a conference center.[61]

The euphoria did not last. In May 2008, Fort Lee Borough Council declared the developer in default of its agreement.[62] Despite the extensive plan, only site preparation work had been completed by that time. Town and Country owed the borough $750,000 in back taxes and a contribution for the relocation of utilities at the site. The developer did not pay back the debt by the date set forth by the borough. In June 2008, the Borough Council terminated the agreement. In September, it was reported that the project remained "stagnant," with nothing further on the horizon.[63] Centuria was often tagged as "ill-fated" in the press. The undeveloped space remained an abandoned patch of broken concrete, rubble, and weeds during the course of the present study.

In late 2009, however, the local press reported excitedly on a new mega- and mixed-use redevelopment plan.[64] In the midst of the economic crisis, four developers competed in response to a Request for Proposal (REP) issued by the mayor and council.[65] The Centuria project was renamed "Redevelopment Area 5." Four public-hearing sessions were held in early December 2009, one for each proposal. The two-hour sessions included a presentation by the developer and an audience question-and-answer period.[66] About 250 residents packed the meeting room of the community center for each session, with standing room only. The sessions often overran the scheduled two hours, lasting for nearly three hours. The audience was largely composed of business people, community leaders, and concerned residents and families. There was a noticeable presence of Koreans but few blacks or Hispanics in the audience. During the question-and-answer period, several Koreans, including those with leadership roles in the community, raised issues along with those posed by white residents. The questions from the audience included the traffic flow, the impact of the project on existing retail business, and the project's likely effects on the school system and community as a whole. The Korean residents were clearly integrated into these public forums. The mayor of Fort Lee explained that he had made efforts to invite the leaders of major ethnic and civic organizations in Fort Lee for participation in the meetings to gain "a good selection of our community representation." Support from all groups, the mayor stated, is crucial for a diverse community.[67]

Enthusiasm in the town was running high—the venture was announced as the biggest in Fort Lee since the construction of the George Washington Bridge and welcomed as a much-desired source of increased municipal revenue. In addition, some of the proposals included an arts/cultural component—a film museum and a movie theater. While the role of Korean business in the revitalization of Fort Lee's economy was acknowledged by many residents, the current mayor stated his belief that "Fort Lee has gotten old and tired" in recent years—losing economic ground to neighboring boroughs such as Englewood (north) or Edgewater (south), where redevelopment has successfully regenerated the local economy. Redevelopment Area 5 was deemed essential for Fort Lee's "renaissance" and for "retail and residential revival."[68] Ground was finally broken in 2013. For local leaders, Redevelopment Area 5 promised to be a transformative factor in Fort Lee's thriving urban community.[69]

A TOWN OF IMMIGRANTS IN TRANSFORMATION

Fort Lee embodies several dualities: urban and suburban, cosmopolitan and local, transient and rooted. Such contraries can be an attraction for some residents—while remaining accessible and offering urban amenities, Fort Lee maintains a "small town feel." On the one hand, a large segment of Fort Lee lives in high-rise apartments and condominiums—an affluent, transient population, for whom Fort Lee is mainly a bedroom community. Within twenty years, Fort Lee has become, to quote residents, "semiurban," a "mini-Manhattan." With such shifts, the suburban character has been permanently lost, according to many established residents. Several remarked that Fort Lee had remained a quiet town until the late 1980s, indicative of perceptions of large-scale and rapid development as a relatively recent phenomenon.[70] Yet despite a large transient population and urbanization, Fort Lee retains a core sense of community and a strong native white constituency. Cultural institutions such as the Fort Lee Museum offer a site where established residents organize events and gather together, maintaining tightly knit relations. The heterogeneity of the population, however, is seen by some as contributing to the general lack of neighborly contact and a sense of "division" within the population.

The diversity of Fort Lee is not limited to ethnoracial minorities. The white population is also ethnically diverse. Yet rapid East Asian immigration has been closely linked with Fort Lee's transition from suburban to urban, from homogeneity to heterogeneity. The social construction of place reflects a complex of attitudes and values. A political climate that is "exceptionally receptive to change and economic development" has certainly played a role in the influx of East Asians and capital.[71] Unraveling the social mechanisms that have placed Fort Lee in the vanguard of multicultural development in northern New Jersey may help in the understanding of wider issues of multiethnic community and the patterns and consequences of contemporary migration.

The following chapters undertake an inquiry into such transformations. They explore the forms and organization of ethnic/immigrant communities that have emerged in this particular suburban context over the last forty years. What can Fort Lee teach us regarding contemporary questions of ethnic communities and immigrant assimilation and ethnicity in the American suburb?

2 · COMMUNITY AND COMMUNITIES

Fort Lee is surely America, but it's not really America either.

—Japanese male, expatriate,
Fort Lee resident, forty-four years old

I think this [Fort Lee] is a more . . . Asian place to me.

—Chinese female, first-generation,
Fort Lee resident, forty-two years old

People want to be where they are comfortable . . . it's a very comfortable place for many of the Korean Americans to live.

—Korean female, 1.5-generation,
business owner and community leader

Communities formed by ethnic group members in the United States have been theorized as the key to the retention of ethnic tradition while also smoothing the way for the assimilation of newcomers. Although it might be thought that immigrant groups tend to be insular, Asian immigrant communities have a long history of being part of multiracial and multiethnic neighborhoods in the United States.[1] When immigrants with varied histories, cultures, and needs arrive in cities and neighborhoods, their presence disrupts taken-for-granted categories of social life and urban space as the immigrants struggle to redefine the conditions of their relation to the new society.[2] Urban communities with diverse populations face challenges regarding ideas of belonging.

The creation of community is a universal feature of the human condition.[3] Community and place are wide-ranging thematics, with regard to the development of collective identities and social relationships, and are central to sociological inquiry.[4] "Community" functions conceptually to define the boundary between "us" and "them," creating the dichotomy of inclusion and exclusion. This chapter explores the trajectories, forms, and characteristics of Chinese, Japanese, and Korean communities in Fort Lee. The discussion follows the chronological sequence of the immigrant waves, beginning with the Japanese and followed by the Korean and Chinese. What are the factors and conditions that have contributed to the formation of each community? What form do these ethnic communities take? In what ways have Asian communities reinvented the suburban space of Fort Lee?

JAPANESE IMMIGRATION AND ECONOMIC GROWTH IN THE 1960S: THE FIRST ASIAN WAVE IN FORT LEE

Large-scale Japanese immigration into the New York area began in the 1960s. This migration was based on an outwardly dependent economic policy in postwar Japan, which encouraged Japanese companies to develop export markets for manufactured goods in hard-currency countries such as the United States. This highly successful policy led to Japan's status as the fastest-growing economy in the world during the late 1960s through the 1970s.[5] Japanese banks and trading companies began to venture overseas in the 1950s, followed by manufacturing companies in the 1970s. With the acceleration of Japanese direct investment in the United States in manufacturing, finance, and wholesale trade, corporate job assignments abroad were a crucial element within mainstream Japanese companies.[6] The majority of Japanese immigrants to the United States during this period consisted of male expatriates (*chūzaiin*)—temporary migrants residing abroad on corporate assignment. Expatriates, more "sojourners" than immigrants, have been theorized as a nonintegrative component in the host society, forming a small yet often highly visible and functionally important group.[7]

Beginning in the mid-1960s, Japanese expatriates began to concentrate in the New York borough of Queens, mainly in Flushing and Fresh Meadows, where they found housing they could afford.[8] Notwithstanding their "business elite" status, expatriates faced economic challenges, since limitations on funds taken outside Japan and the considerably weaker yen left them with incomes that were barely sufficient for survival. They tended to live alone in the United States, leaving their families in Japan during their overseas assignments. Expatriates began to suburbanize in the 1970s as the improvement of their financial situation allowed them to settle in what they perceived as better places to live. By 1990, the Japanese were among the most suburbanized minorities in the greater New York area.[9] Expatriates, increasingly with families, began to settle primarily in three suburbs in the tri-state area: Bergen County (New Jersey), Fairfield County (Connecticut), and Westchester County (New York).

During the 1970s, Bergen was attracting Japanese manufacturing firms as the county became one of the thriving business and industrial regions of the New York area. Bergen County shared in the general economic upsurge of the suburbs, following corporate relocations to Essex, Morris, Passaic, and Union counties, as well as the suburbs of Westchester and Connecticut.[10] Containerization—the transformation of the marine transport system in the 1960s—rendered the New York ports obsolete and made the area around Newark and Elizabeth, New Jersey, a new center for international trade.[11] For Japanese manufacturers, it made good business sense to locate their U.S. headquarters in New Jersey, since they customarily transported assembled items to the United States by container. In 1981, the *New York Times* counted approximately seventy Japanese corporations in northern New Jersey.[12] Additional advantages offered by Bergen for multinational corporations were proximity to the Japanese banks of New York City and convenient access to the three major airports (John F. Kennedy International Airport, LaGuardia Airport, Newark Liberty International Airport). The settlement of Japanese in Bergen County was directly related to the increased presence of Japanese companies there.

The first nonwhite minority of significant proportion, Japanese began to settle in Fort Lee in the 1970s, and the overwhelming majority were business expatriates and their families. Today, an estimated 80 to 85 percent of the Japanese in Fort Lee are expatriates; the remainder are U.S. citizens or permanent residents.[13] In the earlier phase of immigration, the Japanese were typically male executives in their fifties with established positions in their companies. Overseas assignments signified honor—the number of opportunities were limited and premium wages were paid for overseas work. During the 1970s, the Japanese of Fort Lee represented an elite group with high prestige.

Fort Lee was attractive to expatriates for several reasons: the convenience of the commute to Manhattan, safety, a lower population density (compared to Queens), and a relatively reasonable cost of living and of real estate. The availability of rental properties in Fort Lee was important in fostering the influx of temporary immigrants who had little inclination to purchase homes. The existence of a Japanese real estate agency seems to have been a key factor as well. Opening for business in 1974, this was the first Japanese (and also first nonwhite) real estate agency and now one of the oldest realtors in Fort Lee. The president of the agency, a Japanese-speaking, third-generation Japanese American male, served as a bridge for expatriates. When he began his business, his clients were 99 percent white, but the growing number of Japanese in the Fort Lee area completely changed the composition of the agency's clientele—by the 1980s, the majority were Japanese expatriates seeking rental properties. The agency has also worked with Chinese, Greek, Italian, Jewish, and Korean landlords, who have customarily rented properties to Japanese expatriate families. Non-Japanese landlords are said to prefer expatriate families whose housing expenses are subsidized by their companies, which offers a guarantee of financial reliability.

Interviews with established Japanese residents indicate that anti-Japanese hostility from natives was a major concern for earlier expatriates and that this was related to their choice of Fort Lee. Japanese settlement in various suburban communities in the New York area during the 1970s triggered tension in both working-class and upper-middle-class communities.[14] Such reception was interpreted by the Japanese as not only racial but also class based. The reputation of Fort Lee's racial and ethnic tolerance circulated among expatriates, and such tolerance was interpreted by expatriates as related to the class status of the borough—neither working class nor upper class. One first-generation Japanese female stressed the relative receptiveness of Fort Lee toward newcomers compared to upper-class suburbs elsewhere in the New York area, including northern Bergen and Westchester, where the Japanese, despite their relatively comfortable means, felt unwelcome. Resentment was less evident in Fort Lee compared with other townships.

THE FORMATION AND DECLINE OF A "JAPANESE VILLAGE"

The majority of Japanese expatriate families arrive in Fort Lee directly from Japan, frequently based on the advice of former expatriates in their companies. Fort Lee is perceived as providing a "foothold" for newcomers to the United States because of its convenience and the availability of ethnic services. Expatriate families in the borough tend to be homogeneous socioeconomically and are typically well educated and middle class. The majority return to Japan on completion of their temporary corporate assignment. Others continue to assume overseas assignments in other locations in the United States or in other countries and lead transnational lives.

In the 1970s, the Japanese population was growing faster in Fort Lee than in any other town in the greater New York area. Fort Lee represented one of the largest expatriate concentrations in the suburbs of the tri-state area between 1970 and 1990. By the early 1980s, 80 percent of all Japanese in New Jersey were recorded as living in Fort Lee, and their number exceeded five thousand in 1986.[15] During the 1970s and the 1980s, Fort Lee came to be known among Japanese residents throughout the New York Area as the "Japanese Village."[16]

The influx was felt most strongly in the school system. In 1982, one-quarter of Fort Lee's public school children were Japanese. An expatriate wife who had lived in Fort Lee, and later in Tenafly for more than twenty years, recounted scenes from 1986 in School Number 1, where her fourth-grade son was enrolled, following her arrival in Fort Lee: "When I took a look at my child's class, there were three Americans, and the rest were Koreans and Japanese . . . and the cafeteria, they eat lunch there, you know. All of those sitting there were Japanese. Gosh, it was like, is this a school in Japan? [*laughs*]."

Two Japanese weekend schools were formerly located in Fort Lee in rented public school buildings, sponsored by the Fort Lee Board of Education. Nine hundred Japanese students were enrolled in these weekend schools, half of whom were from Fort Lee.[17] These schools are no longer in operation due to the decrease in Japanese students.

From the mid to late 1980s, the economic boom in Fort Lee was largely attributable to the growing Japanese presence. The similarity in socioeconomic status, lifestyle, and consumption patterns of sojourning expatriates led to the opening of new stores and businesses by coethnic town workers who were also immigrants.[18] Ethnic businesses functioned as an environmental bubble—the "village"—where it was possible to live in an almost exclusively Japanese environment. Japanese businesses never became predominant in Fort Lee, however, even at their peak concentration during the 1980s.

The majority of the Japanese-owned businesses documented by previous research and in press reports had long disappeared by the time of my field research—many of them have been replaced by Korean businesses. Nevertheless, the Japanese can still live in Fort Lee "as though they are in Japan." Existing Japanese ethnic businesses continue to provide indispensable services: realtors, doctors, dentists, afterschool programs, bakeries, restaurants, hair salons, and, perhaps most important for expatriate families, a shopping mall complex in Edgewater, a short car ride away. One expatriate wife, a resident of Fort Lee for four years, remarked that her life in the United States is only possible because she is able to communicate in Japanese in her locale of residence. Some Japanese felt, on the other hand, that "too many Japanese" in Fort Lee inhibited exposure to American life and that this was not the ideal place for those who wanted to learn English or about American culture.

Residential concentration is now less marked than in the past. The existing pattern is a result of the tendency of Japanese real estate agencies to refer Japanese sojourners to the same properties. Sometimes, apartments do not even return to the rental market, since word-of-mouth referrals allow a transferred family to move in when others leave. One expatriate wife told me that her Greek American landlord has rented only to Japanese expatriate tenants over the years; as a consequence, her neighbors in the duplex are another Japanese expatriate family. Expatriates do not, however, always reside in a geographically based enclave, even though they may use ethnic institutions for support.[19] According to the principal of a private Japanese school in Englewood Cliffs, "The American media come around and ask where the Japanese are—they assume that there is something like Chinatown. But what is meant by a Japanese concentration in this area is just that there is one Japanese family per block. It's not like everyone on the block is Japanese. By habit, Japanese would not occupy an entire apartment building and things like that—they try to have some distance between themselves, even though it is said that there are so many Japanese around here."

The absence of an enclave formation no doubt owes to the fact that the majority of Japanese in Fort Lee do not stay on permanently in the United States. The transience of individual expatriates, however, does not mean that expatriate communities are necessarily transitory. Increasing international interdependence leads to the perpetuation of such communities, which tend to become a permanent fixture of the social scene in the host society.[20] Linguistic challenges in English and transience nevertheless have resulted in the insulation of the Japanese community in Fort Lee, a subculture that has been reproduced by new, temporary, coethnic immigrants. The expatriate community in Fort Lee has endured over a period of time but with a membership that is in constant flux. The notion of an eventual return to Japan shapes expatriate attitudes regarding their life in the United States. Temporary immigrants do not intend to settle down or assimilate even if they have an interest in American culture. The defining characteristic of such sojourners is their orientation toward the homeland, with a corollary "in-group solidarity."[21] Although their engagement in community life is not entirely absent, for the most part the Japanese remain "guests"—the term frequently used for expatriates by locals.

Expatriates in Fort Lee today are younger than in the past—now in their thirties and forties and, increasingly, in their twenties—as companies aim to cut down on costs, which are especially high for executives.[22] Due to the relatively young age of these families, a significant number of pupils in the elementary schools of Fort Lee have been Japanese, although the proportion has steadily declined since the late 1990s. The meaning of overseas assignment has also changed with time—such postings no longer carry the same cachet they did in the past. Foreign assignments are now common to mainstream middle-class experience.[23] Unlike earlier decades when expatriates in Fort Lee tended to commute to their offices in New York, more expatriates today work in northern New Jersey, reflecting the general trend of job relocation to suburbia (see table 4).

By 2010, the Japanese in Fort Lee numbered fewer than 1,500, down from 5,000 in the mid-1980s. The decrease of expatriates was owed to the economic downturn in Japan beginning in the early 1990s, accompanied by reduced business activity in the United States. Many companies cut back on costly overseas assignments, and the surplus of expatriates returned home. Fort Lee nevertheless still serves as a relocation site for Japanese companies from Manhattan in search of lower rents and thus continues to function as a suburban site for the transnational economy. Although the borough retains the largest Japanese

TABLE 4 Economic and social characteristics (selected) of East Asian populations, Public Use Microdata Area (PUMA) including Fort Lee, Bergen County, New Jersey, 2000a

	Chinese	Japanese	Korean
Place of work (%)b			
New Jersey	56.8	54.5	59.5
New York	43.2	43.1	39.4
Other states and abroad	0	2.4	1.1
Class of worker (%)c			
Employee of private company	84.0	84.8	75.9
Employee of government	8.7	1.1	4.0
Self-employed	7.3	14.1	20.1d
Citizenship status (%)			
U.S.-born	26.6	15.5	18.8
Naturalized citizen	31.3	8.3	22.4
Not a U.S. citizen	42.1	76.2	58.8
English ability (%)e			
Speaks English very well	47.9	39.2	29.2
Speaks English well	29.1	30.5	36.1
Speaks English not well or not at all	23.0	30.3	34.7

SOURCE: 5-Percent Public Use Microdata Sample (PUMS) file, U.S. Bureau of the Census, 2000.

a The PUMA here includes Cliffside Park, Edgewater, Fairview, Fort Lee, Leonia, Palisades Park, and Ridgefield Park (PUMA code 00303).

b Excludes those under age sixteen, the unemployed, those not in labor force, and those who have a job but are not at work.

c Excludes those under age sixteen and those with no work experience since 1995.

d Includes unpaid family workers.

e Excludes those under age five and those who speak only English.

population in New Jersey, the rapid decrease has led to local perceptions that "there are no longer any Japanese in Fort Lee."

KOREAN IMMIGRATION AND SUBURBANIZATION

Major Korean immigration into the United States followed the passage of the Hart-Celler Act of 1965 and peaked in 1987. Newly arriving Koreans in the New York area initially moved into several areas in Queens, including Elmhurst, Flushing, and Jackson Heights. The Korean population increased by 125 percent in the New York–New Jersey area in the decade between 1980 and 1990, with 200 percent growth in New Jersey. Flushing became known as an "overseas Seoul" from the late 1980s onward.[24]

The reasons for such a rapid wave of immigration were contingent on a variety of social, economic, and political factors in Korea and in the United States. A population explosion caused overcrowding in Korea, which emerged as an urgent problem in the 1960s and served as one of the push factors. The dictatorship of the postcolonial period prompted some, especially from the professional middle class, to leave Korea for the United States in the 1970s through the 1980s. Fierce competition in education—and for good jobs among the well educated—was another reason for migration.[25] In describing her parents' decision to emigrate to the United States, one high school student remarked that even with a bachelor's degree, one "cannot get a job as a janitor" in Korea. Korean informants frequently cited "better living" and "better education" as reasons for migration.

The suburbanization of Koreans in the New York area began in the 1980s with the improvement of their economic status. Koreans from Queens began to move to New Jersey and other suburban tri-state areas. For many economically successful Asian immigrant families, Flushing is seen as the first stopping place en route to suburban homes in Long Island, Connecticut, or New Jersey.[26] My Korean informants who had moved to Fort Lee in the late 1980s recalled there were not many Koreans then but that there was still a sizable Japanese population. In the late 1980s, Koreans still had difficulty finding a Korean food market there.[27] The major influx of Koreans to Fort Lee began around 1990.

Before immigration to Fort Lee, beginning in the mid-1960s, Koreans had settled in Palisades Park, a neighboring town to the west. The Korean population in Palisades Park rapidly increased during the 1980s. Though only 5.6 percent of the borough's population in 1980, the number of Asians grew to 20 percent by 1990, the majority of whom were Korean.[28] Palisades Park was on the verge of bankruptcy prior to the Korean influx of the 1980s. Korean immigrants began to buy vacant properties and ultimately revitalized the local economy. Palisades Park now has the largest Korean population in New Jersey, constituting more than half the population of the borough.[29] Locally, it is informally referred to as "Koreatown." Almost all the businesses on Broad Avenue, the main commercial and business strip, are Korean-owned today. During the 1990s, it was reported that Korean entrepreneurs acquired 95 percent of the businesses in Palisades Park.[30] The first Korean American council member in Bergen County was elected there in 2004.

Both Korean and white informants tended to believe Koreans were initially drawn to Palisades Park because of the less expensive property values compared with those of Fort Lee.[31] The subsequent flow to Fort Lee signified the increased economic power and upward mobility of the group. The move into Fort Lee was also related to overcrowding in Palisades Park. Some Korean informants felt that Palisades Park was "too Korean," whereas Fort Lee represented a "nice mix" of Korean and white residents. While a coethnic presence is a consideration for comfortable living, an aversion to too many coethnics is present among Koreans; Koreans feel it is important to be exposed to American culture. Given overcrowding in Palisades Park and the affordability and convenience of travel to New York City, Fort Lee was a "logical choice."[32]

Guided by Korean media coverage, some Korean immigrants arrive in Fort Lee with prior knowledge of the area. Word of mouth also plays a role. According to one Korean bilingual teacher of twenty years, Koreans often learn of the reputation of the Fort Lee school system through social networks. She told me that her school sometimes receives phone inquiries directly from Korea. Korean students would tell her, "We know so and so, who used to be in this school, and they told us that school [X—the informant's school] was the best, so we moved here." Although many of my Korean informants were aware of the earlier presence of Japanese in Fort Lee, they felt this had little bearing on subsequent Korean immigration. The presence of fellow Koreans is, however, considered a crucial factor; roughly half of my Korean informants indicated they had chosen Fort Lee because of their preexisting social network in the area.

CHARACTERISTICS OF KOREANS IN FORT LEE

Unlike the Japanese, Koreans in Fort Lee consist largely of first-generation immigrants, 1.5 and second generation: in 2000, in the Fort Lee area, nearly 60 percent of Korean residents were not citizens of the United States, while roughly 40 percent were citizens by birth or naturalization (table 4). My informants came to Fort Lee directly from Korea or from New York City, Queens, Los Angeles, or neighboring boroughs such as Palisades Park or Cliffside Park. Many Koreans who moved to Fort Lee during the 1990s were not new arrivals to the United States but professionals in their twenties, thirties, and forties who considered themselves part of the 1.5 generation—born in Korea but raised in the United States, hence fluent in English and sharing both Korean and American values. One 1.5-generation Korean female estimated that approximately half of Koreans moving to Fort Lee are 1.5 or second generation and move to the borough in order to raise children and for proximity to their workplaces in New York City. Working-age Korean immigrants also bring aging parents with them, a factor in the increase of Korean tenants in senior housing in Fort Lee.

Koreans in Fort Lee represent a well-educated, middle-class group. All my Korean informants held a bachelor's degree or higher from institutions in Korea or the United States; the majority had white-collar occupations and were homeowners. A first-generation Korean leader who works in the Fort Lee area and is a resident of Flushing, Queens, remarked on the class differences among Koreans in Flushing and Fort Lee: the latter tend to be white collar, whereas the former tend to be more "daily based, hard workers" in small businesses. Korean-owned small businesses do exist in Fort Lee, including dry cleaners, restaurants, and retail stores. Compared to Chinese and Japanese, a higher proportion of Koreans are engaged in self-employment in the Fort Lee area (table 4). Some Koreans run small businesses in Fort Lee while being resident in other boroughs in northern Bergen County. Others own small businesses in New York City while residing in Fort Lee.

Census data indicate some income disparity among Koreans in Fort Lee, indicative of the presence of a low-income group. Immigration among lower-class Koreans to the United States, replacing their middle-class counterparts, became more prevalent starting in the 1980s.[33] The perceived affluence of Koreans, nonetheless, appears frequently in the comments of non-Korean residents—one recurring local anecdote concerned the Korean elderly who arrive at the senior center by Rolls-Royce. The dreams of Korean immigrants were often reductively posed by my non-Korean informants as the desire to attain "a BMW and two houses." The mythic potential of the automobile to indicate wealth among residents is often heard. One second-generation Chinese American male in his twenties offered the following observation:

> If you drive around Fort Lee, just look at the cars. . . . Everybody drives like Mercedes or BMW. I used to compare [other places to] a town like this, because I went to school in Michigan and in California. It's just like cars are really nice here. In Michigan, they are all American cars, very cheap cars. But here, you see Ferraris, right? Or like really expensive cars: Lamborghinis, things like that. We are not like super rich, but there are people that are rich enough to afford that kind of luxury.

Another first-generation Chinese female observed that Korean residents in Fort Lee "always have a good car" and "are more high-class people." This informant commented on the wealth displayed among Fort Lee's school children, which she identified as a source of "peer pressure"—an envious desire for brand clothing or electronic gadgets similar to those owned by Korean students from privileged family backgrounds.

The Korean population in Fort Lee includes a small yet growing segment of expatriates (similar to those from Japan) who are employees of Korean multinational companies located nearby. Another growing group is referred to as the "early study abroad students" in Korea. The trend emerged in the mid-1990s, notably among middle-class Koreans: children are accompanied by one parent, usually the mother, to study in English-speaking countries, including the United States, while the father stays behind in Korea.[34] The goal is for the children to acquire English-speaking ability to better prepare them for college admission in English-speaking countries or to have a competitive advantage in the job market in Korea, where English fluency is desired.[35] Intensification of the already competitive education system in Korea has further promoted this trend. Typically, one parent (usually the mother) obtains a student visa through enrollment in a community college or language school. Based on this status, children are able to obtain a dependent visa relatively easily.[36] The arrangement is supported by money sent from Korea for living expenses by the other parent (typically the father). Such transnational family household arrangements are referred to as *kirŏgi* ("wild geese") families.[37] These recent trends suggest patterns that depart from the typical model, where the entire family migrates for a better life permanently. Contemporary Korean immigration in Fort Lee contains a highly mobile, transient segment.

THE ECONOMIC AND POLITICAL INVOLVEMENT OF THE KOREAN COMMUNITY

Rapid Korean immigration has had a marked influence on local life and in particular on the local economy. Korean-owned businesses in Fort Lee began to emerge in the 1990s and rapidly expanded during the decade. In 2001, approximately three hundred Korean retail stores were documented.[38] At the time of our interview in late 2008, a representative of the Korean American Association of Fort Lee (KAAFL) estimated that more than half of local businesses were Korean owned.[39] Although the listing is likely not exhaustive, according to one Korean business directory, there were close to four hundred Korean businesses in Fort Lee in 2009; in 2016, more than five hundred Korean businesses were listed.[40] Korean membership in the Fort Lee Regional Chamber of Commerce (formerly Greater Fort Lee Chamber of Commerce) rapidly increased during the century's first decade, growing from just a few members to approximately 30 percent of the membership by 2010.

According to the Korean business directory's listing, the main types of Korean businesses in Fort Lee are professional services. The largest concentration has been in real estate, followed by law, accounting, and mortgage and financial services. The real estate business is a particularly favored occupation among Koreans; many acquire licenses on arrival in the United States and begin to work as agents. In the business directory of 2009, nearly two hundred Korean real estate agents were listed as engaged in both Korean and non-Korean real estate agencies.[41] A number of Korean-owned businesses with multiple locations in New York and New Jersey have branch offices in Fort Lee. Cultural centers primarily targeting Koreans offer classes in real estate licensing, language classes in Chinese and Spanish, and cultural classes such as flower arrangement. Medical and health-related services are also prevalent. Korean-owned retail and service businesses in Fort Lee represent more than sixty different types of business activities, including restaurants, supermarkets, bakeries, hair salons, spas, dry cleaners, car services, and movers. Many local businesses originally owned by whites are now run by Korean merchants. In fall of 2009, H Mart (Han Ah Reum supermarket), a major Korean supermarket chain, opened in Fort Lee on the former premises of an American supermarket. A number of multinational corporations of varying industries have headquarters or branch offices in Fort Lee, from apparel and telecommunications to ethnic media. The U.S. headquarters of two major Korean corporations, LG and Samsung, are located in the neighboring boroughs of Englewood Cliffs and Ridgefield Park, respectively.

The thriving private afterschool academies and tutoring institutions in and around Fort Lee are another aspect of local Korean business activity.[42] According to Jamie Lew, tuition-based afterschool academies and educational counseling services are often found in Korean ethnic enclaves. These institutions offer SAT, TOEFL, and other preparatory courses for college admission—catering to Korean parents' desires to provide extracurricular resources for the educational success of their children.[43] One reason for the parental resolve to send children to English-speaking countries is to avoid the extreme competition of education in the home country.[44] Ironically, flourishing private educational businesses in areas with large Korean concentrations in the United States are in some measure reproducing the academic competition found at home.

Perceived business opportunities and the availability of coethnic networks encourage Korean entrepreneurship in Fort Lee. New Korean-owned retail stores continued to open up during field observations for the present study. A variety of Korean businesses appear to be prospering in the suburban environment with a predominantly Korean-speaking clientele. During one interview with a Korean realtor, the agent received several phone calls and responded in Korean to all. Yet what may appear to be an ethnic economy is not entirely exclusive; Korean-owned businesses such as restaurants, supermarkets, and bakeries are also patronized by non-Koreans. Reputed for their authenticity, Korean restaurants in Fort Lee attract non-Korean patrons from New York state. And despite the prevalence of Korean businesses, a large proportion of Korean residents also work in New York—outside what appears as the "ethnic economy" of Fort Lee and its vicinity (table 4).

Korean representation in the borough's political life has also increased since the first decade of the twenty-first century. The planning board and the board of adjustment each elected one member of Korean origin during the period of the beginning of this research (2006–2007). Since then, Korean members have continued to be part of these boards. Koreans are also represented on other municipal boards and committees, including those related to health, the library, beautification, historic sites, structure, culture and landmarks, and sign/façade review.[45] Fort Lee's police department has appointed Korean-speaking officers since 1998.[46] The new and stricter ordinance concerning requirements for shop signs, building façades, and sidewalks went into effect in 2008. The Sign/Façade Review Committee, charged with review of proposals for signage, has two Korean members.[47] Believing the proportion of municipal representation to be inadequate, the Korean American community seeks greater influence in being "fairly represented."[48] The increasing number of registered Korean voters has augmented their voice in general elections. Although previously viewed as nonparticipatory, the political mobilization of the Korean community in recent years has led to a cultivation of Korean support by elected white officials.

RELIGIOUS AND EDUCATIONAL INSTITUTIONS AND THE KOREAN COMMUNITY

Ethnic churches are considered the most important community centers for Korean immigrants and their offspring in the United States. They play a key role in preserving traditional values, ethnic identity, and in-group solidarity.[49] The Korean church provides social ties, networks, and an opportunity to engage in ethnic and cultural practices—including the teaching of Korean language to U.S.-born children. One second-generation Korean American male, in his forties and a resident of Fort Lee, explained that he attends a Korean church in another borough in Bergen because of his close friendship with the pastor. He was probably the most detached from Korean culture of all my Korean informants; he neither eats Korean food, nor celebrates Korean holidays, nor follows the Korean media. He considers church activities his most ethnic activity. In the words of one nonchurchgoing, first-generation Korean female, "If you don't go to church, then you are kind of isolated."

Fort Lee had eight Korean churches in 2008; six providing services in Korean and two in English. The first Korean church emerged in Fort Lee in the 1980s, eventually moving to Teaneck and becoming one of the largest Korean churches of Bergen County. The already congested property situation has forced some Korean congregations to rent space from other congregations. Some Korean churches share the same building with established local churches. While foreign-born Koreans are motivated to join Korean churches, some with English fluency also join American churches. Korean residents in Fort Lee attend churches beyond Fort Lee as well—including in Queens—a choice based on personal networks.

Korean immigration has had an impact on existing local churches. The Church of the Madonna began to offer masses in Korean starting in November 2005. The Irish American pastor that I interviewed recalled that when he arrived at the church in that year, there were only a few Korean members. The pastor explained that local Korean leaders urged that the mass be held in Korean, since Korean Catholics were converting to Protestantism due to the absence of Korean-speaking Catholic churches. A Korean pastor was assigned in June 2006, and the number of Korean members grew dramatically. Within three years, the Church of the Madonna had registered more than three hundred Korean families. The number of masses offered in Korean, or in English and Korean, has increased to accommodate the growing need. In the bilingual masses, the white pastor celebrates mass in English and a Korean youth follows in Korean. The congregation for the bilingual mass sings hymns in Korean—the Irish American pastor has the songs written out in transliterated Korean, phonetically, for his own use. His involvement in the Korean mass aims to resist possible fracture of the church into ethnically separate parishes. In other boroughs in Bergen County, attempts to merge Korean and white congregations have been unsuccessful once official separation has become entrenched. The pastor of the Church of the Madonna serves all the members of the church and to this extent considers himself a part of the Korean American community. The church also has Korean members from Manhattan, since it is their closest Catholic Church with Korean outreach.

Education has been deeply influenced by the immigration from Asia. In Fort Lee's public schools, the numerical predominance of East Asians is more evident here than in any other social domain, due to the relatively youthful population of Asians compared with whites.[50] In 2008, roughly one fourth of the students enrolled in middle school and high school spoke Korean, Japanese, Mandarin, or Cantonese at home as a first language. For students in all of the four elementary schools (Numbers 1–4), the proportion was higher: roughly one third of them spoke one of these languages. The proportion of those who speak Korean, Japanese, Mandarin, or Cantonese at home has continued to increase. By 2015, roughly 30 percent of the students enrolled in public schools spoke the East Asian languages listed here; in one of the elementary schools, the rate reached nearly 50 percent of the student body. In all of the six public schools, the Korean language is the majority minority language spoken at home; this is the case for 20 to more than 30 percent of students.[51] Site visits to school premises give an impression that greatly exceeds the recorded proportions, since there are many English-speaking Asian students who are not counted by the official statistics. The enrollment of Asian American students in each school ranged from 41 percent (high school) to nearly 60 percent (School Number 3) in 2015.

Schoolteachers explained that a roughly equal number of foreign-born and U.S.-born Korean students are enrolled at the elementary school. At the Catholic school, about half the students are Korean.

School personnel consider the presence of Asian students important for the school district's reputation. This can be seen in the repeated comments of educators quoted in the press and in my interviews. Asian students are considered as having enhanced the program by establishing a positive ethos for education and behavior and also by providing an opportunity for American students to gain global perspectives.[52] Indeed, a former mayor became a target of criticism from parents at one point for espousing such a "pro-Asian" stance.[53] Many Asian names appear in the regular honor rolls published in the local newspaper—mostly Korean, followed by Chinese and Japanese. In the view of teachers, Asian students have raised standards in the high school. The public schools of Fort Lee have been consistently ranked as one of the highest performing in the state.[54] Various new programs have been introduced to the high school, including the International Baccalaureate Diploma Programme, since December 2008.[55] Asian students excel in art and music: they are a notable presence in cultural activities in the high school and constitute an overwhelming majority in the high school band and among the technology staff of the school theater. One art teacher proudly pointed out some artwork by Korean students displayed in the classroom. When asked how the presence of Asian students has changed Fort Lee High School, one response from teachers was, "Our band got bigger." Asian students are conspicuous in local press coverage of academic achievement, the arts, and sports.

With time, the Korean community has become preeminent in various domains of local life. Koreans are increasingly visible in both political and nonpolitical arenas. Korean businesses simultaneously compete with and support each other. A number of Korean organizations, including the ethnic churches, provide coethnic support. For those who are connected to Fort Lee through business or civic engagement, the importance of place cannot be overemphasized. One 1.5-generation Korean male resident in his thirties commented on the vibrancy that Korean immigrants brought to Fort Lee: "Korean residents . . . I think, actually brought back vitality to this town. And that is evidenced by all the Korean restaurants that have been opened up and all the newer businesses that are opening up. If you go to the schools, 30 percent of the student population is Korean American . . . I'm not saying that that would be the only reason why this town is so vital as it is now. But they certainly played a major role in that. . . . This town is constantly evolving."

TRENDS IN CONTEMPORARY CHINESE IMMIGRATION

Although Chinese constitute the largest and oldest Asian group in the United States, their growth was limited by the Chinese Exclusion Act of 1882, which remained in effect until 1943. The Hart-Celler Act of 1965 reversed the trend: the influx of Chinese immigrants since 1965 led to a more than tenfold growth in the Chinese American population in the United States. Over 70 percent of all Chinese Americans in the United States are born abroad.[56] In 2010, Chinese were the largest Asian group in the New York metropolitan area; in New Jersey, they were the second largest Asian group after Asian Indians.[57]

Contemporary Chinese immigration to the United States has been characterized as "dual immigration"—to indicate the trend of class bifurcation.[58] The literature has noted the growth in affluent, highly educated professionals from Hong Kong, Taiwan, and mainland China, who settle in suburban locations immediately upon arrival. Chinatowns in major metropolitan cities continue to serve as a "port of entry" for many low-skilled immigrants, but they no longer house the majority of the Chinese population in the United States. The dispersal of Chinese to the outer boroughs of Manhattan was primarily caused by rising rents in Chinatown, pushing the poorer residents into the less expensive suburbs. "Satellite Chinatowns" have appeared in the outer boroughs of New York City as distinct ethnic business centers, in Sunset Park, Brooklyn, and Flushing, Queens.[59]

Both foreign- and U.S.-born Chinese have become spread throughout the New York metropolitan area over the last few decades of the twentieth century, to the east as far as Long Island and as far southwest as central New Jersey. During this period, the greatest relative growth in the Chinese population of metropolitan New York took place in the suburbs. In New Jersey, with fewer than six thousand Chinese in 1970, the population in the northern part of the state grew to more than eighty-three thousand by 2000.[60] Although the Chinese in Bergen County never constituted the largest Asian subgroup (contrary to the trend of the Chinese population in New Jersey as a whole), they are rapidly growing in the area. Fort Lee today has the largest Chinese population in the county.

CHARACTERISTICS OF THE CHINESE IN FORT LEE

A small group of Chinese has lived in Fort Lee since the 1970s. One second-generation Chinese male in his twenties, a native of Fort Lee whose family is originally from Hong Kong, explained that Chinese families from Hong Kong tend to be well-established residents and know each other well because of the small size of this group. Since the beginning of the twenty-first century, the number of Chinese immigrants, primarily from the mainland, has been rising. The president of the Chinese-American Family Coalition (CAFC), a local ethnic organization, estimated that 90 percent of current Chinese immigrants into Fort Lee are Mandarin speakers from northern China.[61] The remaining 10 percent are from Taiwan and Hong Kong.

My Chinese informants, the majority of whom were first-generation immigrants, came to the United States for a variety of reasons: for college education, or marriage with an American spouse, but most often, "for better opportunities." According to the president of CAFC, many recent Chinese immigrants in Fort Lee are moving from other states, mainly New York, rather than arriving directly from abroad. My Chinese informants tended to be middle-class, well-educated, established professionals, working in mainstream American companies with largely white American colleagues rather than in the ethnic economy. Some noted that they were the only Asian employees in their company. The majority worked outside Fort Lee, either in other boroughs of New Jersey or in New York City. The president of Huaxia Chinese School (Paramus, Bergen County), when asked about the occupations of parents coming to the school, responded that they are largely "professionals," although "some work in restaurants." My informants typically had relationships with those of similar middle-class backgrounds and seemed unaware of the economically less successful Chinese in the area.

The majority of Chinese informants chose Fort Lee for convenience for work—in Manhattan, Westchester, or other towns in New Jersey. Table 4 shows that around 43 percent of the Chinese residents in the Fort Lee area worked in New York in 2000. The good reputation of the school district and an environment with more green spaces for children were also considerations for some, while for others the decision was based on social networks or personal contacts. Although no Chinese informant indicated a choice of Fort Lee based on coethnic presence, several agreed that the "Asian" milieu had played a role in their decision, since this signified the availability of "Asian" services and shops, though not necessarily those of coethnics. The president of the Chinese-American Family Coalition gave a different story, however. She suggested that the Chinese moving to Fort Lee are aware of a Chinese presence beforehand, through information spread by social networks and the ethnic press. Though prior knowledge of the Chinese in Fort Lee was not mentioned by my Chinese informants, this seems to serve as an underlying reason for settlement. My informants tended to have Japanese or Korean neighbors, not coethnics: generally, the Chinese have not formed a coethnic residential cluster.

CHINESE AS THE "INVISIBLE" MINORITY

Other than several real estate agencies, medical and financial services, restaurants, and a few branch offices of Chinese companies, Chinese businesses and associations are scarce in Fort Lee.[62] In the absence of Chinese supermarkets, advertising flyers in Chinese are frequently found on bulletin boards in local Japanese and Korean ones, indicating Chinese patronage. This is in stark contrast with the concentrated Chinese populations in the suburbs of Los Angeles or in Brooklyn and Queens in New York, where the Chinese have profoundly altered the local landscape; the Chinese have not formed a visible concentration that may be considered an "ethnoburb" in Fort Lee or in Bergen County.[63] This may be related to the proximity of Fort Lee to New York City and the ethnic enclaves there. One first-generation Chinese female remarked, "Maybe it's too close to Flushing . . . People would rather go to Flushing than stay here" for dining or shopping. Chinese companies are fewer in Bergen County compared with Japanese or Korean businesses, although this may change in the future. One portent may be the sister city agreement of 2011 between Fort Lee and the city of Fushun in the northeast province of Liaoning, China. Delegates of the Foreign Affairs Office of Fushun hope to "create more 'roads' for Chinese businesses abroad through business projects" and consider the sister city arrangement to be "a bridge for businesses between America and China."[64]

Surprisingly, some Chinese informants seemed unaware of a coethnic presence in Fort Lee. At the Golden Moon Festival in 2008, I spoke with one first-generation Taiwanese male, a resident of Fort Lee for three years. In the presence of large numbers of Chinese in the audience, he remarked he had never guessed there were so many Chinese in Fort Lee. In some cases, the reported impression was based on daily observation. For example, one Chinese female, whose child was attending an elementary school in Fort Lee, did not feel the population of Chinese was increasing because she had not observed any growth in the number of Chinese parents making donations to the school in recent years. The local press has not reported on Chinese immigration as widely as that of Japanese and Koreans, except for the coverage of ethnic celebrations such as the Chinese New Year. Yet my non-Chinese informants indicated the presence of Chinese in their congregations and in their neighborhoods. Often, after some probing, residents would say, "Oh, yes, there are also a few Chinese."

That the Chinese in Fort Lee have not formed a dense ethnic community has rendered them "invisible" in the minds of many residents. Instead, Chinese seem to be living with members of various ethnicities without attracting attention. The resources of professional, suburban Chinese obviate the need for local coethnic support. In some cases, lack of knowledge about coethnics was ascribed to their general lack of neighborly contact within Fort Lee. For many informants of Chinese descent, their closest coethnic relationships—familial, friends, or religious—existed outside the borough. One first-generation Chinese female, originally from Hong Kong, remarked that she did not socialize with the Chinese parents she met at Fort Lee High School, which her daughter attended, and that she considered them "acquaintances." She explained that her best friends (Chinese) were in New York City. Her other friends were from her congregation in Englewood, where she was the only Asian member.

The majority of Chinese informants nevertheless spoke of the importance of ethnic heritage in their lives—for example, the celebration of the Chinese New Year and the retention of Chinese language for offspring. As will be discussed in the following chapter, the vibrancy of the two Chinese schools in Bergen, in which hundreds of Chinese parents and children participate, attests to this. Middle-class Chinese in Fort Lee represent a "heterolocal" "cultural community," held together by cultural and community institutions that provide opportunities for coethnic cohesion and solidarity.[65]

While appreciating the "Asian" environment of Fort Lee, the Chinese in Fort Lee feel that too great a concentration of Asians is not necessarily desirable. One first-generation female from mainland China, in her forties with two children in the public school system, described her future plans for leaving Fort Lee: "I like some Asian activities for my children because I don't want them to forget where they came from. But I don't want to go somewhere where there are too many Asians as well, because, after all, this is America." While the Chinese may not be inclined to discard their home country's values and identities, they are also intent on assimilation. Such tendencies were more clearly articulated by Chinese than by Japanese or Korean informants.[66]

OVERLAPS AND SEPARATION: THE CONFIGURATION OF SUBURBAN ASIAN COMMUNITIES

Asians tend to live in ethnically and racially mixed neighborhoods in this small borough: the majority of my informants had non-coethnic neighbors. A report in the local press, for example, noted the development of multiethnic neighborhoods in northern Fort Lee—during the 1990s, Korean families joined the Japanese families who had moved there in the 1980s. By the end of the decade, the same neighborhood was receiving Chinese and Russian families.[67]

There remains a small pocket of Japanese concentration in the north of Fort Lee today where abundant duplex rentals, the most popular type of rental properties among expatriate families, can be found. Real estate agents and residents remarked that developers had demolished old houses and built "numerous oversized, brick duplexes" starting in the early 1980s because of their popularity among Japanese families.[68] This area is also a preferred choice for the Japanese due to the proximity of a private Japanese school in Englewood Cliffs, to the north of Fort Lee.

Koreans live in both ethnically mixed and ethnically homogeneous neighborhoods. Several areas of Korean residential density were remarked on by my informants—for example, near the Fort Lee Community Center. The Korean concentration in this area can be noted from the several Korean businesses that comprise a small strip mall across the street from the community center—a bakery, restaurant, barbershop, dry cleaner, and supermarket. A 1.5-generation Korean female in her twenties told me that approximately 70 percent of her apartment building was occupied by Koreans. Another Korean female in her thirties told me that although she grew up in ethnically mixed neighborhoods, the block on which she and her family currently reside is predominantly Asian. A number of Korean informants also resided in areas where the majority of their neighbors were established white residents. In fact, many of my non-Korean informants, including native whites, indicated that they have Korean neighbors. Except for a few cases, Chinese informants did not have coethnic neighbors, while many had Japanese or Korean neighbors.

Such mixed residential patterns, however, do not automatically lead to the development of social relationships between residents of different ethnic origin. Residents' evaluations of their neighborhood relations were strikingly similar—good, pleasant, but ultimately perfunctory and shallow.[69] "Basically a 'hello' relationship," where even the pleasantries seem superficial, was how a few informants put it. One Japanese female in her fifties, who had been living in Fort Lee for twenty-seven years, remarked on the changes she had perceived over time: "I have a lot of friends who live in Fort Lee. They'll say hello to the neighbors, but that's it. It's not like years ago, you know, 'You wanna have coffee over at my house?' I don't think there's stuff like that. I think they are all just busy."

Given that the informants generally lived in racially and ethnically diverse neighborhoods, they implicitly referred to non-coethnic neighbors in describing their neighbor relationships. Such relationships generally appear detached, which relates to the increasingly semiurban environment of Fort Lee—residents tend to "keep to themselves." One second-generation Chinese male in his early twenties remarked, "I think a lot of people that live in Fort Lee, actually, they don't work in Fort Lee, they are not part of the community, they just live here, you know. Like most of them work in the city, and they commute here. And that's it . . . they are not part of the community. That's one big problem I actually see. There is no sense of community in Fort Lee. You know, everybody is just here, living here, not to be part of the community." Though posed in general terms, this view suggests there is little mixing of different ethnic groups, coupled with a general sense of detachment among residents of the borough. A few Asians reported having close friendships with their Asian neighbors (whether coethnic or not), but none mentioned having a white neighbor as a close friend. One Japanese female, the wife of an expatriate and a former resident of Fort Lee, lived in a neighborhood that had few Japanese, in order to blend in. She had a good relationship with her white neighbors, sharing food, but never invitations into each other's homes.

As social actors, group members draw, maintain, and redraw ethnoracial boundaries. Although the three East Asian groups coexist in a shared space, they generally remain socially separate from each other. One 1.5-generation Korean American female, a museum staffer in Newark, was involved in outreach to Asian communities in Bergen County. After visits to various East Asian organizations, such as Korean churches, Japanese schools, and Chinese centers in Fort Lee and nearby boroughs, she felt that each group served coethnics and was "not looking at themselves as part of a bigger community."

The boundaries that sustain ethnic distinction are, however, not immutable. The convergence of East Asians in Fort Lee can ease the crossing of ethnic boundaries. "Boundary crossing" refers to the moves by individuals from one group to another without any real change to the boundary itself.[70] In Fort Lee, Asians move across ethnic divides while the ethnic boundary remains unaltered. Asians of different ethnic origins form business partnerships—for example, Kumon Learning Center in Fort Lee (opened 1987) is a franchised Japanese afterschool math and reading enrichment program. The Fort Lee branch is owned jointly by a Japanese and a Korean. The Japanese owner indicated that knowledge of the program among Korean parents was owed to her Korean partner.

Ethnic businesses and services do not serve coethnics exclusively but cater to non-coethnic clients as well. A second-generation Korean American male in mortgage financing in his thirties explained that even though local business is predominantly Korean, Fort Lee provides a "very open business climate." While acknowledging that for business owners and managers who do not speak English, it is practically appealing to have Korean-speaking customers, the informant continued, "It really is [an open climate] I can tell from a Korean American perspective, you know, we just like doing business, period. You know, whether it's with another Korean or whether it's with another American, whether it's with another Japanese, whether it's with anybody."

Asian parental devotion to education for their children also leads to the possibility of boundary crossing. The presence of Asian students (not necessarily coethnic) was perceived as a benefit for children's education. Some Japanese and Korean parents have their children attend the Chinese-language school to learn Chinese, believing in the advantages of knowing Chinese in the global economy. Chinese and Korean students also attend the Japanese afterschool program mentioned previously. The program enrolls students of diverse ethnic backgrounds, including Chinese, Hispanics, Indians, Japanese, and Koreans. An instructor in this program explained that non-Japanese parents gain information about the program by word of mouth at public schools. These examples suggest that parental choices, based on the benefits for children, promote the crossing of ethnic boundaries.

Mention should be made of another trend among members of the three East Asian groups in Fort Lee: moving northward in Bergen County. The primary reason is the search for a better school district, such as Tenafly or Ridgewood. For example, Korean media coverage reporting Tenafly High School as one of the best schools in the United States resulted in a rapid increase of Korean students there.[71] Another reason for the move north is the preference for locations with fewer coethnics, for quicker integration into the United States for their children. Still another reason is the desire for residence in a locale with less congestion than Fort Lee. According to one Korean male resident in Fort Lee, Koreans used to move to Fort Lee and Palisades Park from Queens; today, some Koreans run small businesses in Fort Lee or Palisades Park while living in northern Bergen County, in towns such as Tenafly and Norwood. Asian informants frequently mentioned their future plans to move to areas in Bergen with better school systems than those of Fort Lee.

My Chinese informants appeared to be the most ambivalent about Fort Lee among the three East Asian groups, although many considered it a convenient and pleasant place to live. Many Chinese I interviewed were in the process of moving or considering moving out of Fort Lee, with a view to improve their quality of life, such as better schools for children and better housing. Chinese informants did not seem to have the deep attachment to place found among some Koreans or the sense of Fort Lee being "our town." East Asian dispersal to more affluent and less "Asian" suburbs in northern Bergen County, already an established trend, suggests a suburban settlement pattern that is more fluid than static. Observers have noticed that recent immigrants settle in suburban ethnic centers and reproduce the ethnic environment there as their "final desired destination."[72] But there is a flexibility in actors' decisions and expectations. Some first-generation Asians are ready to leave their suburban ethnic community, which they had initially thought desirable, for what they perceive to be "better" places.

TOWARD A NEW FRAMEWORK FOR THE MULTIETHNIC SUBURB

Unlike comparable suburbs of Los Angeles that have a longer history of Asian immigration and established American-born Asian populations, Fort Lee had limited experience of an Asian presence until the postwar period. The borough has been predominantly white for most of its history. In the relatively short period since the 1970s, however, continuous immigration from East Asia has led to the formation of a highly multiethnic suburban community. The community contains a large proportion of foreign-born Asians, which reinforces the reproduction of an ethnic milieu. Fort Lee's geographic position and environment, which offer both urban convenience and suburban amenities, have been attractive for middle-class Asian immigrant families with children. The factors that were essential to the making of these ethnic communities—proximity to New York, the quality of the school system, and safety, to name a few—are also a reflection of similarities in class status, life stage, aspirations, and outlook among East Asian group members.

At first glance, the case of Fort Lee may seem to resemble the "ethnoburb." Closer examination, however, demonstrates that the case of three coexisting Asian communities offers a more syncretic picture. The formation of the Japanese community in Fort Lee hinged on the international mobility of capital and human resources, based largely on strategic business decisions by multinational corporations. The global economy was clearly a determining factor, but the transience of expatriates renders their community distinct from the ethnoburb.

The Korean community appears to offer a closer fit to the ethnoburb model. The majority of immigrants from Korea have financial resources and are highly educated professionals. The Korean community demonstrates characteristics that are more open compared to urban ethnic enclaves and has a proliferation of professional enterprises—which follows the conceptual framework of the ethnoburb.[73] Economic globalization has certainly played a major role in the formation of the Korean community in Fort Lee, as for the Japanese. Lacking visible ethnic clustering, the community of Chinese, on the other hand, exemplify "heterolocalism" rather than the "ethnoburb." Their social networks tend to extend beyond the borough, and they maintain coethnic ties through them.

Recent trends in immigrant concentration in the suburbs have problematized some of the premises of spatial assimilation; the ethnoburb model, for example, rejects the spatial assimilation model entirely.[74] In light of the findings from Fort Lee, however, the spatial assimilation model still holds for the experience of some Asians, to the extent that suburban settlement has signified upward mobility for them. For Japanese and Korean immigrants, the move from ethnic concentrations in Queens to Fort Lee during the 1970s and 1980s, for what was deemed a "better" environment, was contingent on their increased economic power. More recently, Chinese residents of Fort Lee make a distinction between themselves and the coethnics in Flushing as one of "professionals" versus "immigrants"—suggestive of a sense of status accorded by place of residence. For some East Asians, therefore, settlement in Fort Lee is associated with an awareness of occupational hierarchy, social class, and their own upward mobility.

Assumptions regarding sociocultural integration in the spatial assimilation model, however, require some reconsideration. For some of these Asian groups, the experience in Fort Lee runs counter to the premise of assimilation as the precondition for their suburbanization. Their suburban residence has been based primarily on the possession of economic capital. First-generation Asians in general did not choose to move to Fort Lee because of sociocultural integration; rather, possession of the means of living in the suburb allowed for residence there without prior assimilation into American society. At the same time, informants indicated a desire for assimilation and exposure to American culture—which they felt the ethnic environment of Fort Lee might inhibit.

The local space that has become "Asian" helps promote a sense of comfort among Asian residents. But while this ethnic milieu is enjoyed and appreciated, the three Asian communities generally remain separate. The relative autonomy of each group stems from their middle-class status and the availability of coethnic support. Regardless of the sense of comfort expressed by members of the three Asian groups, the degree of rootedness to Fort Lee varies by group: Koreans seemed far more attached to Fort Lee than either the Chinese or Japanese.

A community is neither monolithic nor always physically demarcated. Diversity, heterogeneity, and transience characterize the East Asian communities in Fort Lee. Such characteristics problematize assumptions of uniformity and homogeneity among these immigrant communities, which do not entirely fit with existing models. One way or another, however, the Asian communities necessarily work on negotiation of the notion of "belonging" in the United States. Their separate and yet overlapping ethnic communities help sustain their particular cultures and practices while facilitating boundary crossing in everyday life.

3 · STRATEGIES OF ASSIMILATION AND DISTINCTION

With the lengthening of daylight in late spring, a warm evening in May provides the occasion for people to gather together and relax on the great lawn of the Fort Lee Community Center, where a free annual concert is about to be performed by students of Fort Lee High School. The performers of the honor choirs, the chamber and wind ensembles, and the symphonic band, all in formal attire, are predominantly East Asian, with a handful of black, Latino, and white students. The audience seems to be mainly family and friends of the performers; Asians, blacks, whites, Latinos, and women with headscarves are among the crowd, with conversation in Japanese and Korean audible. Among those assembled, there are white senior citizens without apparent ties to the students. The master of ceremonies asks the audience at one point whether there are any veterans in the audience, as a way of introducing a tune—a few among the white, senior members of the audience raise their hands in response. At a distance, across the lawn, one group picnics on Korean food. The choirs perform jazz and popular standards such as "Take Five" and "What a Wonderful World," sung by the Asian performers. The symphonic band then performs several arrangements from the work of Gustav Holst, and "The Olympic Spirit," written by John Williams for the Seoul Olympics in 1988.

The scene of this local event, with its ethnoracial mix and little interaction between the different ethnic groups, suggests how diversity is lived in Fort Lee. Two high school students, Asian males, assisting with the concert stopped to answer some questions about the event. A sense of excitement could be discerned from their report that the symphonic band was made up almost entirely of Asian students. Hearing that I was engaged in writing about East Asians in

Fort Lee, they gave a thumbs up with a smile and assured me they would read the book. These Asian youths appeared to be at once comfortable and self-conscious of their presence in the locale.

As a minority group that has been consistently viewed as "forever foreign," the question of assimilation has been problematic for Asians. Despite socioeconomic achievement and success as a group, Asian Americans are still viewed as "culturally distinct and suspect" by mainstream society because of their nonwhite status.[1] While the suburbanization of a minority group is posited as a sign of integration, according to the spatial assimilation model, recent scholars have argued that Asian suburbanization is not necessarily indicative of assimilation.[2] Alternatively, the compatibility of assimilation and ethnic retention has been suggested. For example, Vietnamese immigrants engage in reconstructing their ethnicity in suburban contexts, and this practice serves as a precondition for their Americanization.[3] Generally assumed to be contradictory processes, assimilation and ethnic retention are, in reality, complex and suggest a symbiosis shaped by social relationships within and across groups.[4]

The concepts of assimilation and integration have been criticized by some scholars for their normative implications—as "achieved" or "desirable" states. They are taken to focus on "outcomes" while ignoring the compromise and conflict inherent in the process of integration and assimilation. Here, I argue that the concept of assimilation—and that of ethnic retention—should be considered *processual*. It is precisely the processes of negotiation that are integral to an understanding of both. Assimilation and ethnic retention signify a social "practice"—routine actions produced and reproduced in everyday life by social actors. Though habitualized and taken for granted, human practice is also spontaneous and creative.[5] Enacted consciously and unconsciously, assimilation stems from both purposive action and the unintended consequences of myriad actions, decisions, and choices.[6]

Reflecting on the scene of the open-air concert that began this chapter, American-born Asian youth in Fort Lee seem assimilated. They possess a confident fluency in English and a familiarity with American youth culture, and they form friendships with non-Asians. Yet Asians inhabit an ethnic (and multiethnic) space that contains a high portion of foreign-born residents, which promotes ethnic continuity. The ethnoburb model argues that a highly ethnic suburban environment "resists" assimilation.[7] Yet little in-depth research of assimilation and ethnic retention among suburban Asians has been undertaken. How does the multiethnic context of Fort Lee affect these processes?

The following explores patterns of assimilation and ethnic retention among East Asians in Fort Lee, focusing on individual and institutional practices. Ethnic organizations function to "help the immigrant to 'adjust' to the conditions of life and cultural habits in the country of adoption."[8] Institutions such as churches and language schools offer an important nexus where immigrants socialize, rebuild networks, and make their communal life more comfortable in their adopted land. While promoting integration into the interpersonal networks of the coethnic group, such organizations facilitate acculturation. East Asian groups in Fort Lee have established a number of ethnic organizations, the major among these being the following: the Japanese-American Society of New Jersey (founded 1974), the Korean American Association of Fort Lee (founded 1999), and the Chinese-American Family Coalition of New Jersey (founded 2006).[9] These have primarily served coethnic members and have helped maintain group cohesion. Organizations initially established for a specific ethnic group, however, may offer the possibility for boundary crossing by those from different ethnic backgrounds. Various individuals and groups within East Asian communities have also actively reached out to the Fort Lee community in search of recognition. After discussion of examples of grassroots organizational practices, this chapter then considers individual-level practices and the perceptions of assimilation and ethnic retention.

JAPANESE COMMUNITY INVOLVEMENT: GUEST STATUS AND RECIPROCITY

Expatriate status has profoundly defined the attitudes and community involvement of the Japanese in Fort Lee. During the height of the influx in the 1970s and 1980s, there was some local hostility, although this dissipated over time.[10] As temporary residents, the Japanese never felt a sense of "rootedness"; instead, they had a strong desire to "give back to the community" that had provided them with a place to live. *Giving back* largely took the form of fund-raising events for local public institutions.

Grassroots activities were instrumental to this exchange.[11] The Japanese Women's Organization (JWO) played an active role in promoting interaction between the locals and Japanese. Founded in 1975 by a first-generation Japanese woman married to a white man, the group's members were mostly expatriate wives. JWO at its peak counted 120 members, but by 1997, this had dwindled to 15. The organization provided help for Japanese wives in a "foreign" land, but its activities were explicitly targeted at the local community. The organization's primary goal, according to the founder, was "to contribute to the community."[12] JWO organized a program called Japan Open House at the Fort Lee Public Library in the mid-1970s, which continued into the 1980s. The members demonstrated aspects of Japanese culture, including food, crafts, kimono (traditional women's dress), flower arrangements, koto (stringed musical instrument) concerts, and calligraphy. The director of the library recalled that the events were successful, with high attendance by both local whites and Japanese. Proceeds were donated to the library. JWO also donated a large number of Japanese books; as a result, Fort Lee Public Library became the only library in Bergen County with a considerable collection of volumes in Japanese.[13] JWO made further donations to the ambulance corps and to the high school as well as underwriting a scholarship "only for Americans" in gratitude to the host country.[14]

Fund-raising events were common for towns in Bergen County with Japanese populations. A Japanese female who has lived in both Fort Lee and Tenafly for more than twenty years as the wife of an expatriate remarked that the bazaars organized by Japanese residents in Tenafly were so well attended that lines formed to get in. She recalls raising seven to eight thousand dollars at each bazaar, including corporate donations. The funds raised were donated to public institutions in Tenafly. The Japanese business community was also supportive. The director of the Fort Lee library recalled the CEO of Minolta, Sam Kusumoto, then a Fort Lee resident, who played a significant role in fund-raising efforts for the public library's extension project:

> I remember we had a reception at one point. And he [Kusumoto] invited all his contacts from the Japanese Chamber of Commerce and so forth, and they all came. And he gave a talk in English and Japanese. And in English, he more or less said, "This town and this country, but especially the town of Fort Lee, have been very good to you. They have welcomed you into their midst and they've done a lot for you. Now it's time for you to give back." And everyone, all Japanese businessmen, you know, they were all signing their checks [*laughs*] . . . Having him on the fund-raising board was, it was just magnificent, it was just wonderful.

The activities of the Japanese expatriate community, including events and donations to local institutions, were perceived by locals as gestures worthy of reciprocation, thereby easing tension between Japanese and native-born residents.[15] To a certain degree, these grassroots events helped promote cultural understanding. Still, the question remains how widespread hospitable feelings toward the Japanese actually were. Public institutions may have fostered amicable relations but there is no direct evidence that Fort Lee residents felt positively as a result of donations to the community. The act of giving back appears, in fact, to have helped reinforce the position of the Japanese as "guests"—that is, outsiders who, ultimately, do not belong.

With the dissolution of grassroots organizations, Japanese involvement in the local community has diminished. The tradition of volunteerism (for American philanthropies such as orphanages or relief efforts for the victims of natural disasters), though small-scale and informal, continues and remains the primary venue for Japanese participation in the community. A choral group founded in 1987 by women from Fort Lee has performed in nursing homes, churches, and public schools since its formation and has continued the tradition of an annual concert performance since 1989. Illustrated articles covering the group's activities appear in the local press.[16] Japanese volunteer involvement in the community is clearly defined by gender—primarily involving expatriate wives, who tend to stay home.

Other than these limited venues, the Japanese are not generally involved in the civic life of Fort Lee. As expatriates, their lack of American citizenship precludes participation in local politics. They tend not to become involved in community activities even when these do not require citizenship, nor are they seen at many of the public events in the borough. One first-generation Japanese male in his early seventies (a naturalized U.S. citizen) who was involved in volunteer activities in multiple municipal institutions considered the Japanese to be generally nonparticipatory. This, he observed, was in contrast with Koreans, for example, who are active at the senior center. Japanese volunteer activities are undertaken with coethnics and "for America" but not at American institutions with Americans. Detachment from local life is influenced by transience, which reduces readiness and opportunity for integration into the host environment. Expatriates are "largely cut off from the social reality of the country of their sojourn, and often oblivious to it."[17]

Japanese self-perceptions and the native view of them as "guests" reinforce the notion of "giving back" to the community. Japanese have tended to view residence and access to services such as the school system as an obligation to reciprocate. In turn, local acceptance of the Japanese in Fort Lee has hinged largely on their expatriate status—signifying "transience" and "privilege"—bringing white-collar corporate culture into the town. The social involvement of Japanese residents has been ultimately conditioned by such characteristics—their orientation to the home country and concrete plans of return. For the most part, the notion of assimilation has had little bearing on expatriate families.

BRIDGING THE KOREAN AND WHITE COMMUNITIES

Several Korean ethnic organizations, including alumni associations and cultural organizations, exist in Fort Lee. The Korean American Association of Fort Lee (KAAFL) is the most significant in terms of visibility and influence in the local community.[18] KAAFL was established by a group of first-generation Korean business owners in 1999 to represent their voices in the local community because they felt they were outside of the American mainstream and that their views and interests were not being well represented. They needed resources for information and networking opportunities with other Korean American merchants. The fact that a large number of Korean residents in Fort Lee were business owners facilitated the development of such an organization. Initiated primarily to promote Korean merchant interests, KAAFL evolved into a community service organization during the first decade of the twenty-first century. Though it continues to provide support for business owners, the organization has also become a resource for Koreans new to Fort Lee or residents who require information and assistance. KAAFL is staffed by volunteers, mainly business owners.

KAAFL cooperates with other Korean organizations in ethnic events such as the celebration of *Chuseok* in Leonia, the Korean Day parade in Manhattan, or other local events where support is needed.[19] KAAFL has collaborated with another local group, Korean American Civic Empowerment (KACE)—formerly Korean American Voters' Council (KAVC)—at election time, encouraging Korean voters to participate. KACE has conducted voter registration drives and undertaken community education and advocacy. They have also helped immigrants with translation services for voter registration forms and naturalization procedures. Both KAAFL and KACE are active participants in the Korean American Census Task Force, which campaigns to maximize Korean participation.[20] KAAFL has a strong place-based identity: a representative from KAAFL noted that it is important not to "overstep other people's boundaries" and to maintain focus on the Korean community in Fort Lee.

Scholarship suggests that Korean immigrants in the United States belong to tightly knit communities that have maintained stronger ethnic attachments than other Asian groups.[21] In Fort Lee, this tendency is linked to an in-group orientation among many Koreans. Some Koreans characterized their coethnics as a "highly closed community" where "cultural conservatism" prevails.

Interviews and observation indicate, on the other hand, that Koreans in Fort Lee have increasingly come to participate in broader community activities. KAAFL plays an active role and has become highly visible in the borough's public sphere—a transformation that has been developing gradually over time. The involvement with the local community includes donations and voluntary support for various events and institutions. For example, the association provides support for the activities of the Fort Lee senior center and is also involved with the Fort Lee Education Foundation—a scholarship fund that supports public schools in Fort Lee, especially in the fields of art and culture. When the Fort Lee Education Foundation runs the annual "bikeathon" fund-raiser (known locally as the "Tour de Fort Lee"), KAAFL participates in the event and contributes to sponsorship. When the local chapter of Veterans of Foreign Wars mounts events for Memorial or Independence Day, KAAFL volunteers to help. Such participation by the Korean community is widely acknowledged by whites in local politics and public services. KAAFL is the only Asian sponsor of the multiethnic annual "Brotherhood Luncheon"—an event supported by a number of ethnic and local organizations, including B'nai B'rith, the Hellenic Society, and Unico International. This annual luncheon has been held in Fort Lee since

1984, and KAAFL's participation as a sponsoring organization began around 2001, according to one Korean American civic leader.[22]

Such involvements reflect a conscious effort by Korean American leaders to create a bridge with the local white community—a metaphor frequently used among Korean civic leaders to describe their role. In 2008, the Greater Fort Lee Chamber of Commerce made a Korean civic leader of Fort Lee their "Person of the Year," in recognition of extensive community service, for his decade-long work to bring together various ethnic communities in the borough. The importance of "bridging the gap between the Korean and Fort Lee communities" was emphasized by the honoree: "The Korean community should try not to be separate but rather mingle with the rest of the community by getting more involved in functions and issues related to the borough's government and chamber . . . everyone needs to come together to work hard as one community."[23]

"Community" denotes a supposed mainstream, defined against the "other," and immigrant civic leaders demonstrate their intent to become part of this general trend in social life.[24] Many Koreans in leadership positions who I interviewed concurred with such views. According to another Korean community leader, in contrast to earlier Korean immigrants, who "did not know how [to become involved]," Koreans today "are trying to assimilate and integrate." That is, the Korean community is trying to serve the "bigger community" beyond their own. Leaders of KAAFL have articulated that their role is not to create "a new Seoul" but to promote and improve community values for both Korean and non-Korean residents—indicative of a willingness to integrate and to achieve cultural openness.[25] With leaders actively involved in local life and consciously making efforts to communicate with white leaders, KAAFL appears to have contributed to the development of constructive relationships with the local community. KAAFL's community involvement is regularly reported with photographs in *Fort Lee Today*, the municipal quarterly newsletter, which signifies the official recognition of this grassroots organization. In the assessment of some Koreans, the community engagement of KAAFL has rendered the social experience in Fort Lee distinct from those of other boroughs in Bergen County with high Korean concentrations.

For Koreans, another way of serving the local community is through involvement in the administrations in schools. By 2002, Korean students made up nearly one-quarter of Fort Lee's school-age population. But although Koreans had previously run for office, voters had not yet elected one Korean member to the school board. Fort Lee's thriving Korean community and the academic success of Korean students were adduced as the reason for political complacency. The local media quoted one Korean leader who remarked that because of their economic success and contentment, Koreans "do not believe they have to change the status quo"—the community was, in effect, "a victim of its own success."[26]

Such attitudes have changed. The change seems "slow" for some, but nevertheless the gradual increase of Korean representation in public office is manifest. Korean Americans were in fact the first to achieve political representation as a nonwhite group in the history of Fort Lee. KAAFL has been active in this transformation. An article from the local daily, the *Record*, reported in 2001 that one major focus of KAAFL was "to build political power for Koreans with the goal of one day having representation on the Borough Council and school board."[27] The breakthrough came in 2007 with the election of a Korean American to the board of education—this was considered a major step by many Koreans that I interviewed. Another Korean American member was elected to the board of education in 2008, and another in the following year. The Korean member elected in 2009 specifically attributed the success of his campaign to the organizational network of KAAFL.[28] That most recent victory was understood by Korean informants as owing to the candidate's credentials, which gained him votes from both Koreans and non-Koreans. Since 2007, Korean members have consistently served on the board of education.

In making progress in the public sphere of Fort Lee, the process has not always been entirely smooth. The entry of Koreans into the realm of the public school system led to what was perceived locally as a racially motivated incident. During the board of education election in 2007, a former white board member lost his seat after the count of absentee ballots. The majority of these were cast by voters with Korean names. The losing candidate countered that these were invalid, on the alleged grounds that the Korean absentee voters were neither Fort Lee residents nor U.S. citizens, or had filed false applications. The candidate filed a lawsuit requesting a new election; those named in the legal action were served with subpoenas. The action was stopped, however, by a state appellate division court, and the lawsuit was eventually withdrawn by the plaintiff.[29] The experience nevertheless was said to have "intimidated" Korean electors, some of whom were first-time voters.[30] Despite the outcome, the incident was interpreted by some as evidence of a pervasive local resistance to Korean civic involvement.

Koreans, unlike the Japanese, actively participate as volunteers at local institutions such as the ambulance corps and the Greater Fort Lee Chamber of Commerce. Koreans are active volunteers in local elections: for example, they help type up letters in Korean and mail them to members of the local party. Korean American youth volunteers help solicit voters at election time. Growing youth volunteerism and community involvement is one cause for a sense of optimism among Korean community leaders for greater social integration in the future.

Those at the leadership level noted a narrowing of the distance between the Korean and wider Fort Lee communities from around 2006. Both Koreans and whites believed their relationships were improving. In the view of a representative of KAAFL, Korean leaders felt that their increasing participation was being accepted on both the American and Korean sides:

> You actually see the changing of the guard, so to speak. It's tough—that transitional period is tough. I think we are in that transitional period right now. Because before, although we were in this town, we weren't really in this town. And that means that we weren't really participating in the community events. We weren't active in many aspects of what was going on in this town. But I think the Korean community has evolved, and it's grown to the level that [those in it] look around and reach out and explore other cultures and other people. Actually, we have reached the point where we can work together and listen to each other. There was that growing pain in the last year and a half.

One 1.5-generation female civic leader remarked that the Korean community today is in the process of assimilation through greater community participation: "As we have more people that are involved in the community, I think it would be just natural for the community to assimilate, just like Italians and Greeks. When they first came here, it was the same way. I think the Koreans are probably the new kid on the block."

Korean community consciousness is exemplified by a strong and organized leadership. Herbert Gans has recorded how ethnic group leaders may lead public lives in the ethnic community while devoting part of their private lives to assimilatory activities. Because ethnic leadership requires association with those from other dominant groups, ethnic leaders "may even be participating in some on-the-job assimilation, voluntary and involuntary, if only in order to be able to work with leaders of the dominant group."[31] Korean leaders recognize that their interests—the growth and stability of the Korean community—are better served by joining with the mainstream white community. This goal is aligned with the town's efforts to reinforce a distinct identity for Fort Lee through programs such as town beautification, improvement of the school district, economic growth, and promotion of the borough's culture and history. Korean leaders expressed the need to move forward with other ethnic groups—especially whites—in the preservation and development of the Fort Lee community.

CULTURAL ORGANIZATIONS: ETHNIC MAINTENANCE AND ASSIMILATION

Immigrant-initiated cultural institutions are prevalent in the Fort Lee area and operate to promote ethnic culture and local outreach. They also fulfill an important role in serving the pragmatic needs of coethnic members. Such organizations formed by the three East Asian groups, discussed next, are similar in their goals and activities while having little contact with each other.

Established in 1974, the Japanese-American Society of New Jersey (JAS of NJ) is the only formal Japanese organization based in Fort Lee. The society was founded to provide services to Japanese residents in response to their increased presence during the 1970s. The organization aims to promote understanding between Japanese and Americans and offers programs in culture and language, including classes in English, Japanese, the tea ceremony, traditional flower arrangement, calligraphy, the kimono, and arts and crafts. The society's Japanese-language library holdings—composed of more than twenty-five thousand books, magazines, newspapers, comics, films, and television programs—are the largest in the tri-state area. New publications and DVDs of Japanese television programs are added to the library every month and loaned free of charge to members who wish to remain informed of trends in Japan. As the only cultural and social resource in the area, the society attracts Japanese beyond Fort Lee.

The overwhelming majority of members of JAS have been expatriate families, and this has shaped the programs and offerings of the organization. Central to their activities are the English classes for expatriates and their families. Visitors come to the organization to attend classes, browse magazines, borrow books and DVDs, or chat with each other. The office provides space for the exchange of information on various issues related to living abroad. Its members are predominantly Japanese, but there are also non-Japanese visitors—including Chinese, Koreans, and whites—who take Japanese classes or rent DVDs. Japanese membership in the society has declined sharply since its heyday in the 1980s. However, non-Japanese membership—and the number of non-Japanese taking Japanese classes—has increased in recent years. Aiming to expand beyond the expatriate clientele, the society has sought to create more opportunities for sharing Japanese culture with English-speaking Americans. One initiative is represented by language exchange workshops, where English-speaking Japanese learners and Japanese-speaking English learners gather to practice each other's language and exchange cultural knowledge. Financial survival has inspired outreach to other non-Japanese minorities to offset the reduced number of Japanese members. Another strategy has been to offer SAT or TOEIC (Test of English for International Communication) preparation courses (taught by native English speakers) to non-Japanese, non-native English speakers—for example, Koreans and Hispanics.[32]

Koreans have initiated a similar cultural organization in the area: Donghwa Cultural Foundation, a nonprofit Korean cultural organization located in Englewood, established in 2003. The stated aim of the foundation is to promote "Korean heritage and culture to American society through education, including programs on most aspects of traditional Korean culture, arts, manners, food, etc."[33] Donghwa's goal of promoting Korean culture in the United States is similar to that of JAS of NJ. In addition to sponsoring cultural events, the foundation offers arts and educational programs in subjects such as calligraphy, traditional painting, music, dance, traditional knotting, pottery, *baduk* (Korean chess), cuisine, tea ceremonies, and Korean language. The membership is largely Korean, both first and second generation, with some Americans but no Chinese or Japanese. White American parents with Korean adoptees utilize the center for their children to learn about their cultural roots. The foundation receives both local residents and those from Connecticut or upstate New York regularly. Donghwa Cultural Foundation considers itself a part of the wider community and aims to be recognized as a local cultural resource.

Most recently, the growing Chinese presence has led to the establishment of their own cultural organization. Originally begun as the Chinese Cultural Club of Fort Lee, the Chinese-American Family Coalition (CAFC) was founded in 2006 in Fort Lee. Staffed entirely by volunteers, CAFC is composed of nine staff members and some high-school and middle-school student volunteers. Membership has grown over the years: beginning with about forty members, it reached more than three hundred within a few years, with members representing approximately one hundred Chinese families. CAFC has been involved in the coordination and sponsorship of recreational and cultural activities that promote traditional heritage among Chinese American families. The coalition operates as a community service organization: it offers help for newcomers with language problems and has raised funds for natural disasters, such as the earthquake in Sichuan in 2008. The aims of the coalition are "to improve the well being and the quality of life of Chinese-American individuals and families in New Jersey by providing advocacy and access to immigrant assistance, social/recreational services, and resources toward the goal of facilitating family function and stability, economic self sufficiency and assimilation into the American mainstream."[34] *Assimilation* is explicitly stated as an organizational objective. The Japanese or Korean cultural organizations, by comparison, tend to express their aims in terms of achieving "cultural understanding" between the United States and Japan or Korea.

The Chinese-American Family Coalition has sponsored cultural and recreational activities for members, including traditional Chinese dance classes, arts and crafts, Chinese singing, chess, and karaoke parties, as well as tai chi. The organization also helps support tai chi classes held at the Fort Lee Community Center. At the same time, CAFC has created channels of communication with the local community. The coalition has hosted the Golden Moon Festival at the Fort Lee Community Center and Chinese New Year celebrations in Fort Lee schools. Overall, leaders of these organizations do not present ethnic culture as a sign of separateness from the mainstream but as something to be promoted and shared.

Notwithstanding the expressed aim of integration, ethnic organizations serve to foster an appreciation of ethnic roots for coethnics. Joane Nagel suggests that for an ethnic parent, raising children represents a kind of "reverse cultural transmission," as he or she is motivated to reconnect with an ethnic ancestral identity; as a result, the parent may develop a new ethnic self-awareness.[35] Such individuals reinforce this new identity by seeking out others from the same ethnic group, joining ethnic organizations, and participating in ethnic community activities. Donghwa, for example, is used by U.S.-born Koreans to rediscover and reclaim Korean ethnic heritage. The experience of rejection or marginalization by the mainstream prompts some second-generation Korean Americans to return to their cultural and ethnic heritage. They encourage their children (third generation) to learn about their cultural roots—a knowledge that they themselves lacked. This trend was remarked on by the director of Donghwa:

> People of Korean descent, I think, have started to recognize . . . they are the ones who really didn't have an opportunity to learn about Korean culture or arts, because their parents were so busy making money. The way they thought was to study hard so that you can go to a good school, and that kind of secures your future. But that kind of thinking really changed because they realized that once you get into companies or wherever they end up working, they [the mainstream] still see you as Asian. Right? Once they see you're Asian, there's a limit. You can't be promoted or get yourself into the position you want. So in that case, people will say, "OK, how come you look Asian but you don't know about anything [Asia]?" I think [second-generation Koreans] realize that, so, it's a bit too late for them, but they don't want it to happen to their own children. That's why they bring their children [to the foundation].

The need to sustain ethnic heritage may thus be a response to impediments within the mainstream. Unable to be fully accepted as "American," Asian Americans feel a need to socially construct their ethnicity and culture to adapt to a restrictive environment.[36]

ANCESTRAL LANGUAGES

The retention of ancestral languages by U.S.-born children is of major concern for Asian immigrant parents. Some parents deliberately avoid speaking English in front of their children in order to encourage communication in the ancestral language. The majority of Asian parents of elementary school age children that I interviewed indicated their eagerness and efforts to maintain their mother language in the domestic environment, to counteract its rapid loss among children. Few foreign-born Asian parents encouraged their U.S.-born children to converse in English with them, although Chinese parents reported they had to resort to speaking English with their children because the children do not understand or refuse to speak Chinese. This bilingual milieu may also be confirmed by the census data. The majority of each East Asian group in 2000 in the Fort Lee area reported that they speak English "well" or "very well" (table 4). The tendency to speak the ancestral language at home, therefore, may be purposeful in some cases and not the reflection of a lack of English linguistic ability among immigrant parents.

Asian parents aspire to bilingualism for their children. Parents with children who did not grow up bilingual express admiration for those parents who have succeeded in raising their children to be so. Among my informants, loss of the ancestral language was considered a "failure" on the parents' part—they had "mistakenly" shown their English ability in front of their children, which should have been avoided at all costs. The retention of the ancestral language is considered useful for pragmatic reasons: for example, for communication with relatives in the home country. The growing importance of Chinese-speaking countries in Asia also motivates Chinese parents to reinforce the language among children. Similarly, parental enthusiasm for Korean-language schools is related to the awareness that English acquisition is not a problem for children but losing Korean is. Korean parents are also aware of the advantage of bilingualism for college admission and employment. The maintenance of the mother language is of less concern for expatriate Japanese parents—even when their children attend public schools, their Japanese ability does not seem to diminish. Their concern is to ensure that children learn some rudiments of English, which serves as an advantage in school entrance exams after returning to Japan.

Enthusiasm for ethnic-language schools is high among Chinese and Korean parents in Fort Lee because of this parental commitment to bilingualism for their offspring. Korean-language schools operating on the weekend are prevalent in the area (e.g., Englewood, Saddle Brook, Tenafly). Many Korean parents in Fort Lee send their children to these schools. They offer Korean-language classes as well as extracurricular classes on Korean art and culture, including calligraphy, folk dance, and martial arts. Korean-language schools are often affiliated with churches.[37] One 1.5-generation Korean female with children attending a local Korean-language school explained that these schools receive free textbooks, supplied by the Korean government and designed for Koreans abroad. Second-generation Koreans recounted a wide range of topics they learned at the Korean school when they were younger—art, culture, and the history of Korea—in addition to the language. Ethnic schools function to socialize suburban youth into their ethnic heritage despite being distant from the ancestral land.

Two Chinese-language schools exist in Bergen County: Bergen Chinese School in Hackensack and Huaxia Chinese School in Paramus.[38] Both schools take place on Sunday in rented local school facilities.[39] Teaching instruction at each school follows the homeland style—Bergen Chinese School, predominantly Taiwanese, teaches traditional Chinese; Huaxia Chinese School, primarily mainland Chinese, teaches simplified Chinese. Attracting Chinese families from towns in Bergen County, including Fort Lee, parents tend to choose between schools based on their country of origin.

Bergen Chinese School, established in 1972, has had various locations in different boroughs.[40] About 170 students were enrolled at the time of the field observation in 2009, although the school had three hundred pupils in the past. An administrator explained that the decline of students of Taiwanese origin is attributable to the growing number of Taiwanese families moving to other states. However, the relative stability of student registration at Bergen Chinese School is in part due to the increasing popularity of Chinese as a foreign language: the school offers college preparation Chinese courses.[41]

Huaxia Chinese School was founded as a Saturday school by immigrants from mainland China in the early 1990s.[42] With the growth of student enrollment between 1995 and 2010, the school branched out, and there are now nearly twenty schools in Connecticut, New Jersey, New York, and Pennsylvania. The school is the largest of its kind in the United States. Since its foundation, the number of students has increased from seventy to more than seven thousand. The Bergen branch of Huaxia Chinese School has been in operation since the mid-1990s and was originally located in Fort Lee. In 2010, several hundred students were enrolled at the Bergen branch in Paramus, largely attracting Chinese from the mainland, along with those from Hong Kong, Malaysia, Singapore, and Taiwan.

With the aim of promoting Chinese culture, both schools offer a variety of cultural classes (e.g., calligraphy, chess, craft, folk dance, painting, poetry, song) as well as sports programs such as basketball, soccer, and tennis. Both schools rely on the voluntary efforts of parents who organize and lead classes and activities for the children and who influence the content of the offerings of the school. The Chinese schools have been described as a "marketplace," bringing together a wide range of Chinese families.[43] They fulfill a need for networks and connectedness for suburban Chinese. While children attend classes, adults perform administrative duties, pay fees, prepare for events, and socialize in the school cafeteria, discussing education, the economy, and jobs. Grandparents of pupils are also visible in the cafeteria, reading Chinese newspapers or playing games.

The school cafeteria turns into a temporary market, where several vendors create makeshift storefronts selling Chinese foods and books. Despite limited success in inculcating language skills among U.S.-born youth, the strong parental commitment to the transmission of ethnic heritage and language, coupled with networking opportunities for the dispersed Chinese, likely ensures continued growth for these schools.

For Japanese, several full-time Japanese schools and weekend supplementary schools in the area serve to keep the children of expatriates on schedule with the Japanese school system they will eventually need to reintegrate into. These schools are organized to follow the school calendar and curriculum of schools in Japan as closely as possible. Some U.S.-born children of Japanese immigrants attend these schools because parents wish to inculcate language skills among children and supplement their studies at public school. But unlike the schools for Chinese and Koreans, Japanese schools in the Fort Lee area function primarily to serve the needs of expatriate families.

ETHNIC FOOD

As with the use of the ancestral language, ethnic cuisine, and the taste for it, become markers of cultural continuity within immigrant communities. Indeed, the preference for ethnic food, especially among first-generation Asians, seems universal. Asian immigrants and their children shop at Asian supermarkets and eat ethnic food at home regularly. One 1.5-generation Korean female in her twenties indicated a desire to raise her own family in Fort Lee in the future: "I feel like a little bit of Korea is here" because "there're so many Korean things, like Korean supermarkets, which is important, 'cause it's what you eat." U.S.-born children may identify themselves as "American," but their parents find relief in their children's continued preference for Asian food. Many second-generation members told me they grew up eating ethnic food at home. One second-generation Chinese male explained that his mother only cooks Chinese food at home because his father would never eat "hamburgers and stuff." Food serves as a way to help preserve Asian culture and signal a chosen identity: the choice of where and what to eat communicates this to others.[44]

One second-generation Korean female in her twenties, a resident of Palisades Park for four years, gives the appearance of being an assimilated Korean American. Yet she maintains close ties with her relatives and Korean friends and neighbors. Despite her ease with American mainstream culture, she remarked that one reason she feels comfortable in Palisades Park is the sense of being at home:

> If you are pretty much a Korean family, you know this area . . . It kind of gives you a sense of home, like, when I cook my food—I know a lot of people feel

> uncomfortable interacting with [non-coethnic] neighbors; it's a very . . . pungent kind of . . . very distinct kind of smell that our food makes. So when I have one of those moments where I want to make a home-cooked meal, I can make it. If I don't know [how], I can go downstairs—there's actually a [Korean] family that just moved in. They can help me out and give me the recipes [and] ingredients as well.

Palisades Park is "very comfortable" for this informant, where she feels as though "English is the second language" (although she is more fluent in English than Korean). Her statement that the distinct flavor of ethnic food may meet with disapproval from non-Korean American neighbors—and that there is no need to worry what neighbors might think in a coethnic environment—suggests a desire to avoid potential intolerance from the mainstream.

The growth of ethnic grocery stores, supermarkets, and restaurants in Fort Lee and the surrounding area is indicative of the demand for ethnic food among Asians. The abundant offerings attract dispersed Asians from northern Bergen County to shops in the Fort Lee area. The wide availability of Asian foods has been co-opted in the local celebration of "diversity"—extensive coverage of such business establishments appears regularly in the local press. Asian shopping malls reflect Asian American suburbanites' sense of identity, sense of place, and common cultural practices.[45] Such malls serve the needs of residents for a sense of community, culture, and place. Mitsuwa Marketplace, formerly Yaohan Plaza, is a major shopping complex located in Edgewater, an adjacent borough, to the south of Fort Lee. The mall contains more than twenty Japanese stores and restaurants—including a bookstore, cosmetic stores, stationers, video stores, hair salons, a dry cleaner, a dentist, a travel agent, and a real estate agency. First opened in 1988, Yaohan was the largest Japanese supermarket complex on the East Coast. After its bankruptcy in 1997, the complex was taken over by a new owner and renamed. In the early 1990s, the press reported an average of thirty-five thousand customers per week: 40 percent Japanese, 30 percent non-Japanese Asians, and 30 percent whites.[46]

Ethnic supermarkets are increasingly patronized by non-coethnic clients, including local whites who shop at Asian supermarkets regularly. Mitsuwa has begun to attract a new customer base, replacing the diminishing number of Japanese. According to the estimate provided by Mitsuwa, today, about one third of the customers are Japanese, while the rest are non-Japanese—Chinese, Koreans, whites, Hispanics, and Russians. Chinese and Korean, along with Japanese, are frequently heard inside the supermarket. In the food court, which offers a wide range of relatively inexpensive Japanese foods, customers are of various ethnicities, including non-Asians. Mitsuwa exemplifies ethnic transformation: it has evolved from an ethnic place primarily for Japanese expatriate families into a multiethnic site, a place where different ethnic group members come together. One first-generation Japanese male in his sixties commented, "Mitsuwa has become all mixed up," with a hint of loss connected with the declining Japanese population.

Not surprisingly, Korean supermarket chains have expanded in the area. In 2009, a Korean supermarket, Han Ah Reum Mart (H Mart) opened in Fort Lee and in Little Ferry, following the store previously established in Ridgefield. The opening of this supermarket was enthusiastically anticipated by Korean residents in Fort Lee. Advertisements for H Mart and Mitsuwa appear in local weeklies regularly, appealing to a wide public that includes non-coethnic customers.[47] Non-Korean Asians, Latinos, and whites patronize H Mart in the area, and non-Korean staff members are employed in the store. These ethnic supermarkets offer a site for ethnic mixing and intergroup contact while providing a cultural resource for immigrant identity.

Ethnic supermarkets play a role in reaching out to the ethnic communities for participation in response to requests from the Census Bureau. During 2010, the U.S. Census Department and a Japanese organization placed volunteers at Mitsuwa for two weekends. Inside H Mart, television monitors and posters promoted the census to raise awareness about the importance of the decennial count.[48]

ETHNIC FESTIVALS: SPACES FOR ETHNIC RETENTION AND INTEGRATION

The concept of the festival joins both ideational and material elements of culture. The expressive components—rituals, food, art, music—are used to revitalize ethnic tradition. Ethnic festivals function to bring group members together, temporarily constructing a "symbolic community," creating cohesion and a sense of solidarity for coethnic participants.[49] At the same time, the symbolic material provides "compelling imagery" for non-coethnic observers. "Exotic" and "foreign" elements are emphasized—for instance, traditional music and dance with performers in ethnic costumes.[50] Regardless of commercial and economic motives—and the possible reinforcement of racial stereotypes—ethnic festivals allow revivification of the cultural practices of immigrants.[51]

Festivals organized periodically by the Chinese, Japanese, and Koreans add ethnic flavor to the local scene in the Fort Lee area. Since 2002, *Chuseok*, the annual Korean festival held in the autumn (the date follows the lunar calendar), has been celebrated in Overpeck County Park in Leonia as one of the largest ethnic festivals in the Fort Lee area.[52] In its first year, the festival drew an estimated twenty-five thousand people from New York and New Jersey. Six years later, the number of participants was estimated at one hundred thousand. Since 2009, the festival has been a three-day event.[53] The festival has received wide coverage in the local press (e.g., front-page display images of the event in the *Fort Lee Suburbanite*) in the spirit of "celebrating" diversity. In spacious grass meadows, close to the New Jersey Turnpike, participants set up food stands and corporate and vendor booths for local Korean businesses—insurance and cable TV companies and fur, clothing, and foodstuffs stores. The pungent aromas of Korean barbecue drift through the air. The event is open to the public, but the overwhelming majority is Korean.

During my observation in 2009, the event featured outdoor stage performances, including Korean folk dance, music, drums, tae kwon do, and contemporary popular cultural performance such as hip-hop dancing. Each performance was introduced in Korean by a female host in *hanbok*, traditional dress. The audience, accommodated in around two hundred folding chairs in front of the stage, was largely Korean. Many in the audience stood while watching the performances. Noticeable groups of attendees were Korean teenagers, socializing with friends. The hip-hop performance by a group of young Korean males was intently observed by them. The tae kwon do demonstration included both Korean and white practitioners. One of the festival's goals was announced as the acclimatization of New Jersey to Korean culture.[54]

Speeches by local politicians followed the performances. The forty-three dignitaries included the governor of New Jersey; one U.S. senator, congressmen, state senators, assemblymen and assemblywomen, freeholders, mayors of boroughs in Bergen (including Fort Lee), the Korean consul general, local Korean council members, and the presidents of several Korean companies.[55] The American officials began by saying "hello" in Korean, and a few included the Korean words for "thank you." Speakers offered thanks for their invitation to the event, congratulated the organizers on its success, praised the beauty of Korean tradition, and emphasized the similarities between American and Korean culture—in particular, the values of family and hard work. Speakers placed stress on the fact that Korean culture is part of a diverse American culture and addressed the audience by emphatically stating, "You are American." Politicians articulated their appreciation for the Korean presence in the area. One local white male politician remarked that Korean immigrants in Fort Lee, Leonia, and Palisades Park were making America a richer place: "Will you make me part of your family?" he appealed enthusiastically. The audience responded with resounding applause. Within the context of the festivity, the emphasis was on the positive values of coexistence—a sense of "your culture," which is different from "ours," yet constitutive of the American fabric. The incorporation of local white politicians indicated the balance of ethnic preservation and integration signified by the event.

The Chinese-American Family Coalition has hosted the annual Golden Moon festival in October at the Fort Lee Community Center since 2008. During the festival that I attended, among the events and activities, there were fund-raising sales of Chinese books, DVDs, drawings, tea, and food, as well as demonstrations of puppetry and tai chi. Calligraphic works by pupils were displayed in the auditorium. The main attractions were the outdoor performances, which lasted for four hours, including the lion dance, traditional Chinese music, folk songs and dances, and Peking opera. Performers included children from Fort Lee elementary schools along with professionals from a local troupe. Each performance was accompanied by an introduction in Chinese and in English. Of the three hundred or so audience members, about 80 percent seemed to be Chinese; the rest were largely white, with very few blacks and Hispanics. When the Chinese American hostess in a traditional dress asked the audience how many were from Fort Lee, more than half raised their hand, indicating that the event had drawn crowds from other boroughs as well. By comparison with *Chuseok*, whites were more noticeable in the audience, including some with children, possibly Chinese adoptees. The incorporation of local politicians as invited guests was again an integral part of the festivity. Several council members of Fort Lee were in attendance, and the mayor of Fort Lee gave a speech in praise of the beauty and cultural richness of the borough's ethnic diversity.

Chinese-language schools also sponsor seasonal celebrations, and the Chinese New Year is an important annual event. In Bergen Chinese School in Hackensack, the celebration of the Chinese New Year lasted for five hours on a Sunday afternoon and featured a Chinese food fair, an exhibit of student works, and stage performances by students and parents from participating Chinese schools.[56] Open to the public, the festivity attracted a large crowd, mostly Chinese but also with some non-Chinese. The school auditorium (which has approximately five hundred to six hundred seats) was fully packed, with standing room only. A variety of performances included student linguistic demonstrations (e.g., skits, tongue twisters in Chinese), traditional dances (e.g., the lion dance, feather dance, long sleeves dance) and songs in Chinese by students from dance, theater, or singing groups. The students on stage included non-Chinese children—whether these children were of mixed origin, with one Chinese parent, was not clear. The hallways were decorated with student works: cards and notes in Chinese written by students—the fruits of their learning in the school. The event is at once a cultural celebration and an opportunity to demonstrate student competence in Chinese language and traditional arts and crafts.

The celebration of International Children's Day, held in Fort Lee since 1983, was initiated by a local white resident in memory of her son's friendship with the son of a neighboring Japanese expatriate family. The event was inspired by Children's Day, a Japanese holiday on which colorful carp streamers are displayed as a symbol of healthy growth. The resident asked the mayor of Fort Lee to allow the display of the carp streamers using the flagpoles of the borough hall on the day of the annual celebration; the mayor agreed. Every year, a small event with about fifty participants, now organized by the resident and her Japanese friends, is held quietly one Sunday in May. The event begins with the raising of carp streamers and the singing of a Japanese song, "Flying Carp," translated into English. After this ceremony, the children and parents parade to Monument Park, where various Japanese outdoor games, American dances for children, and a demonstration by children from the local karate school are performed. The resident organizer's son, now a grown man, also helps with the event. The term *international* was added to the name of the event because the Japanese organizers wanted to be more inclusive in recognizing the ethnic diversity of the area. The majority of participants nevertheless appeared to be Japanese when I observed the event. Others included Chinese, Hispanics, Koreans, and Russians. A Filipino mother, intermarried with a Korean, told me that she participated in the event because her daughter was eager to dress in an ethnic costume, which the organizers encourage. At one point, children were prompted by one of the organizers to introduce themselves to the group in turn, including their national origin—the intent of the organizer being to showcase the diverse origins of the participants. A Japanese festival is thus being "reinvented" in multiethnic America: an ethnic tradition is incorporated within the context of an ideology of diversity.[57] As with *Chuseok* and the Chinese New Year, this event was covered by the local press with photographs.

As well as providing a locus for immigrant groups to reinforce ethnic heritage, these festivals serve as an occasion for integration into the host society—the inclusion of local white politicians at *Chuseok* and the Golden Moon festival is indicative in this regard. The immigrant promotion of ethnic culture may thus be understood as a mode of assimilation. Display of ethnicity by immigrant groups may come to be used as a display of diversity by American officials. The assertion of immigrant heritage through festive demonstrations is not independent of the context of the host culture but exists in relation to the milieu in which it takes place.

BOUNDARIES BETWEEN "ETHNIC" AND "AMERICAN"

To consider assimilation and ethnic retention as relational does not assume the absence of negotiation. Such processes are frequently accompanied by tension and conflict, resulting in internal division within each East Asian group. These tensions reflect processes of assimilation that occur at different rates within an ethnic group. Since individual members of an ethnic group may assimilate at different speeds, a certain tension becomes unavoidable.[58]

The theme of a perceived divide within the school system between immigrants and those born in the United States recurred in my interviews with Korean informants. One Korean bilingual teacher at Fort Lee High School expressed her concern regarding first-generation students' unwillingness to integrate into the mainstream and tendency to stick to their own group:

> I realize my students from Korea or Japan—I mean, from anywhere—they are, like, all Americanized. It doesn't matter where [or] what part of the world they live in, because Western culture, I think, is dominant, especially in Korea. They are very familiar with American culture. So when they come here, I don't think it takes a big adjustment to American culture itself. My concern is more the other way, because they don't try to integrate. They try to get together only with Korean students. That's my bigger concern, because they don't make friends with the other students, like Caucasian students . . . They always hang out with their Korean friends. So it also is a big obstacle for them in learning English, because they never get to speak English to each other. They always hang out with each other, and they take the same classes all day. They hang out after school together. I wish they were more aggressive in making friends with people from other countries . . . they have their excuses, always. They say they don't speak English, and white students don't wanna talk to them. But I don't think that's true.

These tendencies relate to the formation of a group boundary between first-generation (recently arrived immigrants) and second- (and 1.5-) generation Koreans. Such self-sorting leads to the cliques that are found in the public schools. One Korean female student at Fort Lee High School spoke of a noticeable separation among Korean students: "There are divisions between the Koreans: like the Koreans who really don't want to be Americanized, and then there are Koreans who are trying to get somewhere here, trying to work hard and, you know, [thinking,] 'I should learn English' and do that kind of stuff. And the ones who don't wanna be Americanized, they form their own little group, they act like they live in Korea, they eat just like [they're] living in Korea; it's kind of stupid."

The same student described the Korean population in Fort Lee as having "a good ratio of FOBs and Twinkies." In her words, *FOBs* are "fresh off the boat; it's usually for kids who just came to this country and don't speak much English. They all stick together." On the other hand, there are *Twinkies*—that is, "yellow, and if you break it, it's white inside. It's like a whitewashed Asian." From the point of view of first-generation Korean youth, the assimilated coethnics are "not really Korean." One U.S.-born Korean female in her early thirties, a resident of Fort Lee for twenty-four years, recounted that when she was in high school, she was viewed by first-generation Korean students as "not Korean enough." That she did not speak Korean and had non-Korean friends delegitimized her as a Korean in the eyes of her peers from Korea.

A social divide also exists between expatriate and immigrant Japanese. Expatriate Japanese tend to look down on immigrant Japanese, because the former are generally better educated and have occupations with greater prestige and higher incomes than the immigrants who tend to be engaged in services and small businesses such as restaurants. On the other hand, Japanese immigrants see expatriates as less open to American life and culture, isolated from the mainstream, and certainly different from them. In the words of one first-generation Japanese female (a permanent immigrant), "Expatriates are like tourists"—they take advantage of living in the United States and opportunities for travel at every holiday yet rarely spend time with Americans to get to know American culture. A couple of Japanese real estate agents (permanent residents and U.S. citizens) complained of the demanding attitude of expatriates toward coethnics: they are fastidious ("the property has to be new") and file complaints about their housing with the Japanese realtor rather than with their non-Japanese landlords. Permanent immigrant Japanese claim they prefer to maintain a distance from the "Japanese community"—meaning "the expatriate community."

Tensions within Asian immigrant families between first-generation parents and second-generation offspring surrounding assimilation are well documented in the literature.[59] In Fort Lee, a similar tension between foreign-born parents and U.S.-born offspring is noticeable. For example, Chinese parents with elementary school–age children often remarked how their children resist the idea of "Chinese." The first-generation Chinese mothers I interviewed had sent their elementary school–age children to Chinese-language schools, but the children rebelled against learning Chinese and eventually quit. Their children thought of themselves as "American," in denial of their Chinese heritage. One Chinese mother explained that despite her daughter's excellent academic performance in public school, she was not interested in studying Chinese: "I don't know why, the Chinese thing, she's so against. I have no idea why she's like, 'No, I'm American.' I say, 'No, you were born here. Your look, your face, you are Chinese; your mom, your parents are Chinese. You cannot change yourself.' You know, she doesn't understand. But hopefully one day she'll understand that. She doesn't know—[she says,] 'I speak English.'" Language retention may be "involuntary" for the majority of Chinese children whose first language is English because the decision for retention is made by parents.[60] Though disappointed by their child's resistance, Chinese parents nevertheless maintain hopes for their children's future recognition of the importance of their ancestral culture as they mature.

Tensions observed among my informants reflect the presumed contrariety of being "ethnic" and "American." In everyday life, assimilation and ethnic retention may be experienced by social actors as entailing conflicts and contestations, as though they are incompatible. At the same time, however, such contestation among social actors often accompanies learning and adapting to American life—for example, while Korean mothers are puzzled by the Americanized behavior of their children (e.g., demand for attention, assertiveness) they also learn how such behavior stems from American practices in which their children are immersed at school.[61] Regardless of the multiethnic social environment, many of the tensions are described as existing within the coethnic group. This may be attributable to the relative separateness of these groups from each other, as discussed in the previous chapter. The practices of assimilation and ethnic retention are enacted, then, not only in relation to the mainstream but also in relation to coethnics.

UNINTENDED ACCULTURATION

Assimilation has different meanings for temporary immigrants who undergo the process of repatriation than for immigrants who settle in the host society. Although Japanese expatriates do not follow the socialization pattern found among Chinese or Korean immigrants and their offspring in adaptation to the life in the United States, some expressed concern that being away from Japan may lead to maladjustment when they return. The average length of expatriate service—three to five years—is considered insufficient to fully adapt to the host culture yet long enough to lose the sense of being Japanese.[62] Despite relative insularity and a seeming distance from assimilation, expatriate families observe American lifestyles and become used to them. On being asked whether she would prefer to return to Japan or remain in the United States, an expatriate wife in her forties (living in the United States for more than thirteen years) responded,

> Now it's very complicated. If I were asked that question five years ago, I think I would have answered, "I would definitely want to go back to Japan." I was ready to return the following day. But now when I think about returning, I feel very mixed. Not just because I am psychologically unprepared, but also—because I have been away from Japan for such a long time—I feel I won't be able to adjust so quickly. My child attends Japanese school here, and I feel they care about children much better than the schools in Japan do. Teachers are very caring. So I'm hoping we could extend our stay little by little.

Comparing their experiences in the United States with those in Japan, expatriate families feel life is more relaxed in the United States, and they value what they perceive to be a more family-oriented lifestyle in suburban America. For expatriate wives, being back in Japan means that family life will have to be sacrificed not only for the husband's job but also for other numerous family and social obligations (e.g., care for aging parents). Expatriate wives characterize their temporary residence abroad as a "long vacation" devoid of the mundane responsibilities they associate with life in Japan.[63]

Failed experiences of readjustment after returning to Japan prompt some expatriates to return to the United States permanently.[64] Some expatriates quit their companies and return for permanent residency for the sake of their children, for example, who are unable to adapt to Japanese schools. Such a change of life course reflects the degree to which expatriate families become acculturated—sometimes to the extent that readjustment to Japan is considered insurmountable.[65] Despite their homeland orientation, temporary immigrants cannot remain completely insular; they undergo transformation even though this seems mostly unintended.

ETHNIC DISTINCTION AND ASSIMILATION

The social practices of individuals of Asian descent and ethnic organizations show mixed tendencies of assimilation and an attempt to maintain and reproduce ethnicity. Such assimilation and ethnic retention involve countless quotidian decisions and actions that are at once conscious and unconscious, routine and spontaneous.

Assimilation and ethnic retention are also part of the social actors' "practical strategies." This is evident in Asian parents' interest in ensuring their children are exposed to both ethnic and American cultures. Extracurricular activities, much in evidence among children of East Asian origin in Fort Lee, suggest parental orientation toward both assimilation and ethnic retention. Children are frequently involved in both American and ethnically specific activities. Asian mothers reported having their children participate in a wide range of programs in arts, music, dance, and sports that are considered "American" (e.g., ballet, basketball, ice-skating) while making sure that children are also engaged in "ethnic" activities. Asian parents universally favored the idea of bilingualism for their children based on pragmatic necessity—they saw it as helpful for their children's future careers—and this strategy is reflective of a wider ethos of pluralism. The class status of the immigrant groups must also be considered, since immigrants with resources and positive socioeconomic prospects are likely to have greater control over whether to assimilate.[66]

Ethnic organizations are undergoing transition in Fort Lee: they are opening to wider constituencies beyond coethnic members. None of the representatives of the organizations I interviewed viewed themselves as insular but rather demonstrated a will to integrate with and be accepted by the local community.

It has been argued that financial need is one of the factors for the formation of panethnic organizations.[67] Economic necessity certainly motivates changes, in orientation and goals, in ethnic organizations in Fort Lee. Nevertheless, this has not yet led to the formation of a "pan-Asian" organization. More notable in Fort Lee is the trend of ethnic organizational leadership intent on the integration of the group into the established mainstream community.

Some scholars have argued that recent immigrants deliberately seek to produce an ethnic milieu in suburbia for ethnic continuity.[68] This synchronic view ignores that assimilation is a process subject to fluctuations and social change over time. Assimilation and ethnic retention are conditioned by social context. Richard Alba and Victor Nee argue that the retention of ethnicity is promoted when immigrants perceive little social cost in doing so.[69] Furthermore, assimilation into the mainstream is eased "insofar as the individuals undergoing it do not sense a rupture between participation in mainstream institutions and familiar social and cultural practices and identities" and when immigrants "do not feel forced to choose between the mainstream and their group of origin."[70] According to such conceptualizations, assimilation and ethnic retention are necessarily linked. They are concurrent processes and presuppose one another.

Ethnicity can be conducive to social involvement and, ultimately, to integration, as seen in ethnic festivals and celebrations, which provide immigrant groups a forum for connection with the local community. Assimilation, in other words, may be developed through ethnic specificity within the cultural apparatus. It should be recognized, however, that ethnicity is used as an instrument by the immigrants themselves. Integration through a focus on ethnicity does not happen naturally. Ethnic and cultural specificity is a form of symbolic capital—a source of power—to achieve the group goals of creating a space in the local community. Ethnic retention does not concern solely the preservation of an old identity; the ethnic group is also a "central agent of assimilation," where the new rules and behaviors necessary for the immigrants to fulfill their aspirations are transmitted.[71] Assimilation and ethnic retention thus appear as relational rather than expressing contradictory, mutually exclusive processes.

4 · ACCOMMODATING "OTHERS"

The Japanese were more of the global economy thing, before anybody talked about the global economy, in the '70s. They would come here for business purposes. I think the Japanese brought the dynamic to the town. I think they got Fort Lee's feet wet, so to speak.

—white male, Fort Lee resident, forty-seven years old

The way the Korean population has been dealing with stores and businesses has been a mistake. It's not welcoming. It's very divisive.

—white female, Fort Lee resident, sixty-years old

Just as a resident I've seen that change. I guess, over time, they say, "Okay, you're in the neighborhood, one of us. It doesn't matter whether you're Korean anymore." All these things, I guess, soften with time.

—white female, Leonia resident,
working in Fort Lee, forty-seven years old

Previous research into the relationship of nonwhite immigrants with native-born white residents has documented a variety of social dynamics: segregation, conflict, accommodation, and cooperation.[1] Everyday social relations in communities, neighborhoods, institutions, and families play a role in altering the boundaries between ethnoracial groups and the way in which groups are defined and perceived. People establish relations through work, worship, or play and through living together when they make their homes in the same locality.[2] Migration and demographic inflow, however, have an immense impact on the sense of attachment to place and to the perception of who "belongs": "Feeling at home" in an immigrant society is "not only a challenge for new arrivals, but also for the native-born who see their world changing every day."[3] For those who are well established, such changes are often not of their choice.

The reception of newcomers is modified by the particular characteristics of immigrant receiving areas. One widely studied case—Monterey Park, California—reveals conflict and tension between native-born residents and immigrants, with widespread anti-Asian feeling among the established population.[4] Caroline Brettell, on the other hand, has documented a variety of local responses to the rapid wave of immigration at two suburban locations in Texas, indicative that local reception can be accommodating.[5]

Unlike other suburban locations in the United States that have demonstrated strong nativist opposition and antipathy toward newcomers, overt hostility and confrontation have been largely absent in Fort Lee. This may be inferred from the scarcity of coverage of conflict in the local media over time. Certainly, the impact of East Asian immigration on local life has been widely reported—in education, ethnic business, demographic change, immigrant cultures, and transnational ties. From the 1980s to the present, the coverage in the local daily, the *Record,* conveys a tone of peaceful coexistence. Statements appear frequently in the media on the role of immigrants in the revitalization of the local economy and school systems.[6] The *Fort Lee Suburbanite,* a fully illustrated local weekly, regularly features events that celebrate the diverse ethnic heritages of the area; the openings of new Asian restaurants and retail stores are also reported prominently. To be sure, tensions have been recorded in Fort Lee and other municipalities in Bergen County.[7] Overall, however, the local media has reported on immigration in terms of diversity and cultural richness rather than as an "issue."

Given the absence of reported intergroup conflict and interviews that suggest resident ignorance of any ethnic conflict, the situation in Fort Lee might be considered harmonious and the integration of the newcomers successful. The situation should not, however, be oversimplified. The day-to-day negotiation of accommodation is frequently accompanied by ambiguity and even antagonism. The absence of open ethnic conflict does not necessarily indicate a lack of resentment among the native-born. This chapter examines perceptions and responses among established whites. How have white residents responded to the East Asian influx and the changes brought by immigration? In what ways have the cognitive and social boundaries of the host been transformed as a result of East Asian immigration? What factors account for the relative absence of overt intergroup conflict in Fort Lee?

DISCERNING DIFFERENCE: LOCAL WHITE VIEWS OF ASIANS

Social actors define each other constantly by drawing and sustaining cognitive boundaries. During the data collection for this study, native-born white residents in Fort Lee consistently referred to East Asians as "them"—a blunt indication of their view of East Asians as "different." This sense of essentialized difference is pervasive among whites—and marginalizes the Asians as "other." Rather than designation by use of the category "Asians," white residents tended to identify subgroup differences among Chinese, Japanese, and Koreans and specified references to ethnonational groups: for example, "There used to be many Japanese, but now it's all Korean." Locals felt that Japanese and Koreans differed greatly in attitude and in their relation to the local community. From the point of view of whites, these attitudinal differences stem from varying consciousness regarding the goals of settlement. The commitment to lay down roots in Fort Lee by Koreans was generally understood to lead to greater social involvement. A former mayor of Fort Lee observed that Koreans are "more into the community" by comparison with the Japanese; lack of involvement in community life among the Japanese was attributed to their transience. The Japanese would never come to council meetings, the former mayor explained, whereas Koreans did—a difference he felt was contingent on their "different purposes." Compared to Japanese and Koreans, Chinese were rarely mentioned by white residents, although some were aware of the growing number of Chinese in the area.

Coupled with their experiences of traveling in Asia, white informants were often well informed about the modern history of East Asia and of lingering antagonisms, which in their view resulted in a lack of rapport between Japanese and Koreans in Fort Lee. One white female in her late forties who worked for both Korean and Japanese companies in the area recounted her personal experience of rivalry among her employers:

> When I left [the Korean company], I understood it was very insulting for the comptroller: "We hired you, we brought you in, we offered you travel opportunities, we trained you, and you betray us. Not only by leaving, but by going to a Japanese company!? Oh!" You know, because I know that there is no love lost between the Koreans and the Japanese. On the other hand, when I came to the Japanese company, the manager who hired me would say periodically, "Well, I bet we compare very favorably with your last employer, don't we?" with a [sense] of pride, you know.

That the majority of East Asian immigrants are middle-class professionals with advanced degrees is also widely recognized by white residents. This knowledge was frequently underscored in my interviews. In 1976, the *New York Times* quoted the Fort Lee assistant superintendent of schools on Japanese students: "Socioeconomically, they come from a select group of parents with an especially high regard for education . . . they are the sons and daughters of the cream of the Japanese corporate structure. They are not run-of-the-mill immigrants."[8] Despite the general perception that Asian immigrants in Fort Lee are of middle-class status, some whites also observed class disparities among them. For example, some mentioned class stratification among Koreans. Teachers also remarked on class differences among Chinese students—some were from privileged families while others received free lunch in school. Thus although the view of "Asians of privileged status" prevails, native whites also seem sensitive to the varied class positions among Asians.

Such distinctions discernible among the Asian subgroups have a bearing on the perceptions of white residents. Koreans, rather than "Asians," were often singled out as a cause of feelings of alienation or resentment. Whites recognized, however, that Koreans, not Japanese, were at the same time becoming part of the wider community and more broadly "American."

ASIAN "TAKEOVER": ALIENATION AND RESENTMENT

Commonly expressed feelings among established white residents in Fort Lee indicate a sense of "threat" and "alienation." As a comparison, in their case study of a small suburban community in the United Kingdom, Norbert Elias and John L. Scotson found that old-time residents established "a common mode of living and a set of norms," which they both observed and were proud of.[9] "Emotional barriers" among established residents occur when faced by outsider groups. The influx of newcomers is experienced as a threat to their way of life. As mentioned above, white residents of Fort Lee are conscious of the privileged class backgrounds of Asians. Perceived privilege may also play a role in some residents' feelings of being threatened.[10] This sense of social difference was expressed by one white male in his forties:

> What I find to be fascinating, examining the Asian influx, is that for the first time, in what I know of, in our history, we had an immigrant group come in that can compete for white-collar jobs. And I think that intimidated a lot of people. People come with educations, with, you know, computer backgrounds. They weren't coming here to drive cabs. They weren't coming over to pick up garbage. They weren't coming over to do the jobs that maybe other groups did. These people were coming over to start businesses.

In her theorization of the "middleman minority," Edna Bonacich has argued that such groups develop great economic power in a community to which they feel fundamentally alien. Their economic power appears devastating to host members, who believe their space is being "taken over" by an alien group.[11] In the present case, the idea of being "taken over" is considered a cause of alienation by established residents, who feel that Fort Lee is "their" town. The term *alienation*—used frequently among white residents in reference to the Korean presence—connotes a psychosocial fear characterized by a sense of displacement and estrangement from the familiar.[12] The changing appearance of Main Street and the emergence of flourishing immigrant businesses have resulted in a sense of rupture for some white residents. One white female put it this way: "There was a lot of alienation in the town from the white residents against the Koreans. Not against the Japanese, not against the Chinese, but against the Koreans, 'cause they were so much more visible, I guess."

The feeling of being "taken over" and of an "Asian invasion" were most prevalent among white senior citizens. They found the changes accompanied by Asian immigration more unsettling than other age groups. Outright hostility from white residents at the senior center was not uncommon. According to the director, white seniors would say "all the time" that "Koreans are taking over." One white female in her forties told me that seniors, including her grandmother, openly speak about how the "Koreans have invaded." The signs in Korean in many storefronts on Main Street create discomfort among established senior citizens—they no longer recognize the Fort Lee they once used to know. The sense of being "taken over," however, may not be limited to the predominance of Korean businesses but to a generalized perception regarding "Asians" as a whole. One white female related the following episode: "I've heard things like, 'Oh, they're taking over.' I remember once, in the elevator . . . I was teaching [English to] somebody in that [apartment] building. And there was this little old grandmotherly type on the elevator, and some Japanese or Asian kid got on, and she was, 'Hi, dear.' As soon as they got off, she said to somebody, 'They are taking over.'"

Transformations in Fort Lee—demographic shifts, town development, and urbanization—signified for some established residents the demise of a small, "beautiful," and "nurturing" community. Expression of the "loss" of this community relates to resentment, for example, against the continued appearance, across town, of "bigger houses that take up space"—implicitly built by nonwhite newcomers. Established white residents often conveyed a nostalgic sense that Fort Lee used to be a "better" place. They recounted how there were "American-type" businesses including "mom-and-pop" stores or "five- and ten-cent stores," now long gone. In their view, the increase in immigrants has coincided with other dramatic economic and social changes, including deterioration of the environment.[13] The visibility of immigrants tends to be conflated with broader community issues such as overcrowding.

A recurring comment heard during interviews with established white residents was that now "there are only banks and nail salons in Fort Lee." To be sure, any observer cannot fail to notice the prevalence of banks in town.[14] One white female informant remarked, "My son always used to kibitz when he was a child, 'The only thing we have here in Fort Lee are banks and nail salons.' [*laughs*] If you look on every corner, there is a bank." As a result, for some residents, "there is nothing" in Fort Lee. Here, there is an implicit assumption that banks are also Korean owned: informants' frequent conjunction of banks with nail salons, the latter typically an Asian occupational niche, reveals such assumptions. In reality, however, ethnic banks are far smaller in number by comparison with mainstream American banks. Still, lack of variety in businesses, which is a community problem, has become conflated with Asian immigration. The types of business that have replaced the old stores are viewed disapprovingly by some white residents. One white female in her sixties recalled there used to be a variety of stores on Main Street and that she could buy everything in Fort Lee but that this is no longer true: "There's nothing anymore. Nail salons and banks. I mean, banks—how many banks do you need? I mean, if you walk down Main Street, there are two nail salons, and one street over, there are two more . . . I mean, I frequent one of the nail places, but there are so many. There's no reason to walk on Main Street." Perceived lack of variety among businesses on Main Street connotes the decline of "American" businesses. In turn, the density of Korean business has resulted in growing local resentment. On the negative reactions of residents toward Korean businesses, one white female resident of Leonia observed, "Even talking about me and my little town Leonia, which is very tiny, we have a little tiny Main Street. You should see how many Korean businesses are even here. And a large appliance store, maybe the largest store in this little town, closed. Everybody said, 'Oh, god, it's going to be another nail salon.' Even among us [in Leonia]."

Such feelings are mainly held privately. Several white informants remarked that native feelings are not openly demonstrated but that people hold them "under their breath"—this "undercurrent" of resentment is hidden beneath a general politeness. Lack of public conflict is thus not an accurate indicator of the inner feelings of native residents. The resistance from established residents against East Asian newcomers has been received by town officials in the form of statements such as, "What are you going to do with all these foreigners?" Moreover, silence does not mean that Asians do not sense native hostility. According to one second-generation Chinese American male, a native of Fort Lee, "My neighbors are very old, and they are all white people. They never said anything. But I know they are thinking something. . . . They've been here for so long and seen such a shift. I'm just guessing. They never actually said anything to me, but my educated guess would be that they might be a little pissed off, like we are taking over their houses or what not."

Although no white residents expressed resentment against the Chinese or Japanese in interviews, some did remark on the resentment felt during the time of the first Japanese influx, provoked by memories of the Second World War, or the feeling that the Japanese were "pushing up prices" in housing. Resentment toward Asians is not always limited to older age groups. A white male cab driver in his forties related the following episode: "I had a woman say to me one time . . . this was interesting. She had [had] a few drinks, and I don't think she was all there. I was taking her across the bridge. And she was trying to make it sound like, I've got a bum deal, or we've got a bum deal, because, you know, like, 'Oh, look, you are driving a cab, and this guy, this Asian guy, is driving a BMW.' I said, 'Because, well, it's a free country.' . . . You might hear it once in a while. It's almost like there is maybe a level of resentment." Among residents, the resistance to change is generally contained. At the official level, possible intergroup conflict is also mediated. The following discussion concerns one public example where local government has worked to diffuse the possibility of divisive social tension.

THE POLITICS OF AESTHETICS: ETHNIC SIGNAGE

One factor in established residents' feelings of "alienation" in Fort Lee relates to the use of commercial and business signage in Korean. For some white residents, the use of immigrant ancestral language signifies a source of division within the community. One white female resident told me that because of such signage in the business district, the non-Korean population "doesn't feel comfortable even walking in" stores or businesses. The resistance against non-English signage is both linguistic and symbolic and concerns the establishment of cognitive territory and boundaries connected with the sense of space.

Signage in downtown Fort Lee was a cause of heated debate during the 1990s.[15] Several towns in Bergen County, including Fort Lee, moved to require the display of shop signs in English alongside non-English signage. The source of contention was principally Korean signage, which, by the end of the 1990s, was highly visible. The local ordinances were, in effect, aimed at Korean business advertising. A federal court ruling in California had struck down a similar law as unconstitutional, and this led to a reconsideration of the situation in New Jersey.[16] In Ridgefield Park, a Korean American businessman filed a lawsuit against such ordinances on the grounds of violation of freedom of speech. The ordinances, it was claimed, could be interpreted as xenophobic or racist. After all, there had been signs in the borough in Greek, Hebrew, and Italian prior to the English-translation requirement. The former mayor explained that "when this law came along, Korean merchants felt it was directed at them."[17] English requirements were subsequently changed, since to adopt such a policy was contrary to the first amendment. The storefronts on the major commercial strips in Fort Lee continued to display Korean signage.

Here, the comparison with the suburbs of Los Angeles is of interest. In Monterey Park, California, where Chinese constitute half the population, Chinese business signage met with vehement opposition and was connected with the "growth control" movement and English-only resolutions of the late 1980s and early 1990s.[18] In 1986, the city council of Monterey Park passed Resolution 9004, declaring English the city's official language. Business signs in Chinese characters were cited as "evidence that the immigrants do not want to become a part of the United States."[19] The resolution was rescinded but then reinstituted as a state constitutional amendment. The attempt to legally control Chinese business signage resurfaced in July 2013. As part of a general revision of the law, the city council of Monterey Park unanimously voted to require some words in the "modern Latin alphabet" on the storefronts.[20] This measure was received by the overwhelmingly Asian resident population, civil rights groups, and the media as the revival of the racially charged atmosphere of the 1980s. Ultimately, the city council dropped the proposal in light of mounting opposition from activists and the anticipation of possible litigation.[21]

In Fort Lee, no proposal for mandating English signage has been raised since the controversy of the 1990s. The presence of Korean signage was not ignored by the local government but took a different direction. In 2008, Fort Lee adopted a revised, comprehensive ordinance concerning requirements for shop signs, building façades, and sidewalks that had been unanimously approved by the governing body.[22] Rather than mandate bilingualism, the municipal government promoted the concept of town "beautification"—with the stated aim, in the words of the mayor, of having "one unified, homogeneous approach" to the streetscape. The ordinance stipulates the size and style for acceptable signage, detailing the proportion of signage on the awnings, windows, and the exterior of buildings. No stipulation regarding language appears in the fifty-two-page ordinance.

A business sign must be reviewed by the Sign/Façade Review Committee, instituted in 2008 to ensure, according to the mayor, that the sign is "aesthetically pleasing" and that there is "uniformity in the building." Then chairman of the Sign/Façade Review Committee, a former councilman, was quoted as saying, "I've lived in Fort Lee all my life . . . When I walk through town, I've been disgusted. There are signs covering every inch of the windows."[23] Signage displays were thus reformulated as a matter of aesthetics within the official discourse of town planning. Despite the absence of reference to ethnicity in these narratives and an explicit focus on "beautification," the sign and façade ordinance had an impact on Asian language signage, in particular Korean, given its prevalence in the locale. The official discourse in effect framed ethnic signage as an element contrary to the "suburban" standards of a clean and quiet environment. Behind the discourse lay the issue of an implicit ethnic divide.

Two bilingual Korean members were appointed by the mayor to the five-member Sign/Façade Review Committee to facilitate communication with Korean merchants. Business owners themselves, these members were known to local officials prior to their appointment for their activity as civic leaders. The mayor noted that the inclusion of two members of Korean descent on the committee confirmed that the ordinance requirements were "not about Caucasian versus Korean American."[24] Nevertheless, the mayor indicated that "with folks of Asian descent, the culture dictates that each storefront be very busy with multiple signs"—and thus, implicitly, "inappropriate," in view of the stated goal of beautification.

One of the Korean members of the Sign/Façade Review Committee commented in our interview that the reason for the control of business signage by ordinance was that the municipal authority did not want Fort Lee to be "like Flushing or some other very busy town." Here, the counterexample is a highly urbanized locale that has undergone rapid demographic transformation through Asian immigration, with a resultant proliferation of non-English signage.

In middle-class suburbs, the normative taste for "aesthetic" landscapes becomes hegemonic, operating to maintain class exclusivity.[25] This mechanism finds a parallel in cases where different racial groups are involved. Such residential values are shared not only by the native-born but also by those of immigrant origin in Fort Lee. Rather than resisting the suburban normativity that reflects white middle-class values, Korean American leaders endorsed and supported official attempts at town beautification. As discussed in chapter 3, such attitudes are tied to the investment in being part of the local community. Adherence to municipal recommendations for business signage among Koreans may be interpreted as strategic acquiescence, with the aim of gaining security and rootedness in the locale.

The committee recommends that at least 50 percent of the sign or awnings be in English, although this is not stated in the ordinance. The language recommendation is justified for safety concerns—to ensure that police, fire, and ambulance services will recognize the name of the store in case of emergency.[26] Over the years, signs for the majority of storefronts have begun to look more unified and discreet, whether in Korean, English, or other Asian languages (figure 5). Many newly opened, Asian-owned stores displayed bilingual signs where English was more prominent than the Asian language or English was given alone. The mayor believed the ordinance had made a great difference and that, in general, "folks are cooperating" with the policy.

FIGURE 5. Multilingual signs, Fort Lee, 2017. All signs are bilingual (English/Korean), with the exception of the lowest (Japanese/English). Author photo.

Economic growth is integral to the debate on signage. The new regulations were intended to promote growth by creating a "distinctive commercial environment which attracts business because of a heightened visual quality and image"[27] The mayor wanted to rejuvenate Fort Lee's economy, which he described as "suffering" from a lack of variety among businesses through which to attract customers (see chapter 1). To counter this, a visually cleaner commercial area would entice shoppers, the mayor believed.[28] Yet in my interview, the mayor further registered white residents' complaints about businesses on Main Street because the signs were in a "different language." He felt there seemed to be a "wall" on Main Street creating "two communities" within Fort Lee, which in his view operated as a brake on economic growth.

The aim of achieving an "aesthetically pleasing" appearance is more complex and delicate than it seems on the surface. The implementation of the ordinance with a view to town beautification represented an official effort to govern public space through the control of signage. Although the mayor stated clearly that the ordinance was not about race, a sense of exclusion was expressed during the same interview—"The [Korean] culture does not invite everybody from our town to come and patronize these businesses." While acknowledging the value of Fort Lee's diversity, the mayor emphasized the importance of "not having one particular group dominate the area." In this municipal intervention on space in Fort Lee, compromise rather than confrontation has characterized the relationship between established whites and Koreans, where the signage ordinance worked not to exclude immigrants but toward co-optation.

TOWARD ACCOMMODATION: CHANGE AND RESISTANCE

Fort Lee is not just a story of social tension. The white community of Fort Lee has responded and made accommodations to the changes brought by Asian immigration. Social integration is not unidirectional; the established majority group is also deeply touched by the change. The relations of locals and immigrants work dialectically: for example, the more host institutions become accommodating, the more immigrants are attracted to the locale. Fort Lee's adjustments to growing ethnic diversity may also be understood as an indication of how newcomers have the power to influence native attitudes.

Conflicting Assessments of Asian Students: Schools and White Parents

Since the immigration of Japanese to the area during the 1970s, Fort Lee schools have made concerted efforts to accommodate newcomers. A noteworthy feature of the public school system in Fort Lee is its long tradition of bilingual teaching. New Jersey state law mandates the implementation of bilingual education programs in school districts with twenty or more Limited English Proficiency (LEP) students.[29] School districts with ten or more LEP students but no more than twenty from any single language group are required to implement English as a Second Language (ESL) programs by the state board of education.[30] ESL and Japanese bilingual programs were initiated in 1976 in Fort Lee, the first of their kind in New Jersey. The availability of bilingual teachers in Fort Lee public schools has been attractive for Japanese expatriate families without facility in English. Initiatives for bilingual programs were motivated by the goal of a "more comprehensive care of ethnic differences, a healthier juxtaposition between Asian students and the total student population."[31] The presence of bilingual students in the school district is also beneficial to schools in gaining federal funding, which can be used for any aspect of school business.

Earlier efforts of accommodation included sensitivity training for teachers, where teachers were placed in a Japanese class and addressed only in Japanese to help understand how the students felt. Another program to promote mutual understanding was the annual "study tour" to Japan and Korea. Begun in 1989 with other educators in the New York metropolitan area, the expressed aim was to deepen knowledge of Japanese and Korean education.[32] Research was conducted on bilingual students and how to make them feel comfortable in Fort Lee.

The implementation of various programs to accommodate newcomers owes much to one former superintendent—often referred to as an exceptional leader—who strongly supported the bilingual program and Japanese immigration to Fort Lee.[33] Emphasis on cultural exchange continues today. Teachers of English from Korea are invited to Fort Lee for several months to coteach with American teachers, to learn about each other's pedagogical methods and educational systems.[34] In 2011, the school superintendent of Fort Lee visited Korea to solicit partnerships with educators for Fort Lee's school system.

Schools have also organized "International Tea" and "International Dinner" days: students of different ethnic backgrounds are invited to talk about their cultures, and parents bring homemade foods that represent their cultures. End-of-semester luncheons are held, during which the mothers of students bring food from their own cultures to share with the teachers. Fort Lee schools have also provided channels for foreign-born parents to become more involved in school affairs. For example, working with PTA volunteers, ESL lessons for foreign-born parents have been arranged, sometimes at volunteers' houses, to provide an opportunity to get together and help make parents feel comfortable. In the late 1980s, a bilingual Parent Advisory Council (PAC) was established to provide opportunities for non-English-speaking parents to get together with other members of their group.[35] This aimed to encourage Asian parents who were not participating in school activities, especially PTA activities, due to the language barrier. Originally there were four PACs—Chinese, Japanese, Korean, and Spanish. According to the president of the Korean Parent Advisory Council (KPAC), theirs and the Spanish PAC were the only remaining PACs at the time of interview in 2010. The KPAC functions as a support group for the PTAs; their major involvement is with volunteer activities requested by the PTAs as well as fundraising for scholarships for high school students and cultural events. The Chinese and Japanese PACs were ultimately dissolved due to the decreased need for linguistic assistance among parents and a decline in membership, respectively.

From the perspectives of educators, Asian students are a benefit to Fort Lee's academic community. A white female former schoolteacher who taught in the Fort Lee school system for forty years recalls,

> After World War II, after the Korean War, there was a period of peace and prosperity. Everybody was just happy, happy, happy . . . and it wasn't until the late 1950s, when the Russians put up Sputnik, that all of a sudden, everybody said, "Hey, we have to educate our children better." And so more emphasis was put on math and science. And of course when the Japanese students came, they were

> so far ahead of us in terms of their [math and science] . . . first of all, you have to understand that all the children that came were children from privileged families that had great emphasis on education. So they really revitalized everybody's ideas about education.

Today, the academic achievements of Asian students—mainly Korean—are similarly regarded positively by white parents. One white male told me that he is glad his two children have Asian friends at school: "We like the fact that most Asian cultures value education and expect their kids to do well at their studies. And that becomes a good environment for my children to grow up in, for my children to pursue academic excellence as well."

School initiatives toward inclusiveness and accommodations for Asian students have not always met with community approval. For example, in 2006, the proposed bilingual schooling known as "dual-language immersion," with Korean as the target language along with English, was met with resistance from non-Korean parents.[36] Skepticism exists among white informants as to whether hosting events such as "International Day" would help foster a genuine appreciation for diversity in the community or if the demonstration of ethnic culture might merely become an "obligatory" representation of diversity in public settings.[37]

White parents have not always welcomed the increase of students who were not fluent in English. When Japanese students began to enroll in public schools in large numbers, strong objections from white parents erupted into community-level opposition. The resistance claimed that Japanese lack of English fluency lowered the school district's test scores. White residents (allegedly) resisted the foreign-born student influx into local schools because they might lower the averages for annual achievement examinations—which would adversely affect school reputations and, by extension, real estate values.[38] Moreover, the cost of educating one Japanese child far exceeded the amount of property tax paid by each Japanese family; there were times when the school budgets for ESL programs became a target of attack from local residents: "Why do they [schools] have to use taxes for those who are to return to their country in a few years?"[39] Disapproval regarding Asian student enrollment continues today. Senior residents reportedly believe that immigrants are taking advantage of American services. On the other hand, Asian parents are aware that many decisions concerning the schools (e.g., improvement of aging school facilities) are rejected by established white residents.[40] Lack of U.S. citizenship, however, inhibits the participation of recently arrived Asian parents with school-age children in such decision-making processes.

The numerical dominance of Asian students has produced a situation where white students may be in a minority position. A *New York Times* article from 1982 quoted an Italian American resident commenting that one drawback of the large presence of Japanese was the prejudice her daughter suffered at nursery school, where she was the only non-Japanese student in a class of thirteen.[41] Nobody played with her until she learned to say some things in Japanese. A white informant in her forties recalled how her daughter in kindergarten had made efforts to become "Korean" in order to be accepted by fellow Korean pupils. As a minority in classes, the experience of exclusion by white pupils is not an isolated experience in Fort Lee.

Moreover, the schools' appreciation of Asian students may not necessarily be shared by white parents. A white female in her forties recalled that when her child was in elementary school the presence of Asian students changed the nature of school events around Christmas. Rather than students singing together, the performance turned into a series of concert solos:

> The Christmas show used to be just everybody singing. And now, because Korean kids are so into the music and they are very good musicians, it's sort of just become violin solos, where it's not an American-style Christmas show anymore. It's more like a show-off session, according to how Americans feel. . . . We just wanna hear our kids singing some happy winter songs or whatever, but it becomes this solo, or one kid playing for twenty minutes, solo. . . . I could remember complaining about that, saying, "I take off time to come, I wanna hear my daughter sing, not just one song and then all these individual solos." I don't wanna see that. No offense, but, I don't want to see that.

Such solo performances were considered part of the privileged backgrounds of immigrant families and related to the school's interest in reaping benefits from this cultural capital. The informant felt this reflected the school's use of student excellence to leverage its reputation, when, in fact, "it's coming from this kid's hours of private lessons."

Local Institutions

The growing number of Korean businesses has stimulated a response from the wider business community in Fort Lee. A separation between Korean and native white business communities emerged with the expansion of immigrant-owned businesses. One white board member of the chamber of commerce told me of his efforts to encourage Korean business owners to work together with other local businesses:

> They don't hire any English-speaking people. What they call "white people" don't feel comfortable going in the stores or restaurants. They never made it feel comfortable. So they're kind of divided. There was a big division; there still is. I told them, "You got to change, you need to hire people who speak English." And both

> ways. American businesses need to hire Korean-speaking people . . . I said that "you know, you need to work with the community you are in." So I tried. I put them on the board of the chamber. I always felt it was important. If we worked together—'cause there are so many Korean businesses—so that when there are issues that come up, I'm sure they have the same problems we have. If we did it together, we would get around it or make it work. That hasn't worked out as well as I expected, but we are making headway.

The increased collaboration between white and Korean business community leaders is owed in part to the active involvement of the latter (see chapter 3). Korean businesses demonstrate a shifting desire to serve both a Korean and a non-Korean customer base.[42] Furthermore, Asian-owned businesses are becoming more mainstream American than Asian oriented.[43] The white business community considers Korean businesses an important and integral part of the local economy rather than competitors. A growing number of local American businesses noticeably employ bilingual Korean staff.

The annual awards for the Fort Lee Regional Chamber of Commerce "Persons of the Year" are for "those who have distinguished themselves through service benefiting both the business and civil communities in the greater Fort Lee area."[44] In 2000, the chamber of commerce, along with the State of New Jersey senate, honored a Japanese American realtor and his wife for their community service and contributions.[45] This was the first recorded nonwhite business owner to receive such recognition in Fort Lee. A Korean community leader received the award in 2008, along with the Fort Lee police chief.[46] In 2009, Chinese American realtors were named "Persons of the Year." Numerous display advertisements and congratulatory messages in the chamber's annual directory for those who have received the award signify local business recognition of awardees as legitimate, honored members within the Fort Lee community.

Whites use medical services offered by Asian doctors: "If anything," one white female stated, "Asian doctors study harder and go to better schools, so I would prefer an Asian doctor," a view informed by the "model minority" stereotype but telling nonetheless. Whites dine at local Chinese, Japanese, and Korean restaurants and shop at local Asian supermarkets. One 1.5-generation Korean female in her twenties related an episode to illustrate how the mainstream is changing as a result of the presence of Korean culture. Her father runs a karaoke restaurant in Palisades Park that is frequented by various age groups, from high school students to those in their forties and fifties. Although the majority of their customers are Korean, the restaurant has begun to attract whites as well. One day, schoolteachers from Palisades Park came to the restaurant—they explained that they wanted to see "what this place is that the kids are talking about."

Michael Jones-Correa's study on suburbs in metropolitan Washington, D.C., found that local responses by public agencies to immigration varied by agency type.[47] In contrast to regulatory agencies, service agencies, whose mission is to serve a local clientele, are more adaptive to demographic change. For example, libraries keep track of population shifts, actively seeking foreign language–speaking staff and increasing holdings in foreign languages and media. Similarly, efforts toward accommodation in municipal service agencies in Fort Lee are evident. Along with hiring multilingual staff, the Fort Lee Public Library has developed a significant foreign language book collection. As noted previously (in chapter 3), the library had the largest Japanese-language book collection in Bergen County for a number of years. The largest foreign language collection in the library at the time of the field observation was Korean. Library brochures were printed in Korean and Chinese. The library posted multilingual flyers on the bulletin board in Chinese and in Korean, advertising library holdings in each language—a trend unseen prior to 2009. The library has also added an increasing number of foreign language periodicals, including Chinese, Japanese, Korean, Russian, and Spanish titles. Foreign films, including Asian films, were regularly screened at the facility to the public for free.

The senior center was another institution that has made accommodations, even though it was considered the locus of a high degree of native resistance. The center's membership at the time of the field observation reflected the demographic composition of Fort Lee—25 to 30 percent Asian, of which the overwhelming majority were Korean but which also included some Chinese and a few Japanese. The number of Korean elderly who immigrate to join adult children residents of Fort Lee has grown rapidly.[48] Korean seniors actively participated in the center's programs, attending classes, doing exercises, and working at crafts alongside white seniors. The senior center offered English classes where a bilingual Korean instructor taught a group of Korean seniors. The quality meals that the center provided for a small fee brought in more than one hundred seniors at lunchtimes—with a long waiting list.[49] Quite a few seniors—white and Asian—could be found in the dining room, talking with friends over coffee or reading newspapers as lunchtime neared. Around lunchtime, the dining room would quickly become full. People would be seated at tables with friends of the same ethnic group. Rarely did Asian and white seniors communicate, indicative of the divide between groups that do not otherwise interact on a daily basis.

Diversity in Everyday Life

While the fear of "takeover" and psychological resistance may persist, some white residents appreciated the ethnic mix and being part of a multiethnic community. They viewed the ethnoracial mix—not just East Asians but also growing numbers of Hispanics, Middle Easterners, and Russians, among others—as a positive community value. One white female teacher reported with pride that there were at least seventy different nationalities of students in the high school. She remarked that in the foreign language office of her school, "You open up the cabinet and look at all the different dictionaries we have for testing, [and] you can see how many different languages we get"—testimony that Fort Lee is "like the U.N." and "a microcosm of America."

Potential benefits of an ethnically mixed environment for children were frequently mentioned by white parents. One white female commented on the diversity of her neighborhood and its benefits for her children's development: her children would grow up without experiencing residential segregation, since growing up in a multiethnic neighborhood would be normal for them. Parents of mixed race children considered Fort Lee's diverse environment an essential part of the socialization of their children. In their view, growing up in a multiethnic suburb among people of varied backgrounds produces values that are not superficially multicultural but that genuinely transcend racial and ethnic boundaries. Observing that her children's dating partners have consistently been of different ethnoracial origin, one white female in her fifties, intermarried with a Japanese person and a resident of Fort Lee for more than sixteen years, considered this as an indication that a person's race or ethnicity did not matter to her children and that this was what growing up in Fort Lee had given them. During the interview, the informant shared photographs of her daughter (attending a college on the East Coast) with her college friends, pointing out the various ethnoracial backgrounds, "just like Fort Lee."

Social actors may search for common reference points in order to reach the ideal of social harmony. One white congresswoman, in citing the example of the *Chuseok* festival, suggested how such local ethnic events might help toward a better understanding of cultural similarities rather than differences. The celebration of the *Chuseok* festival can convey to local residents that Koreans have an autumnal holiday "just like we have Thanksgiving." The universal value and meaning of this ethnic harvest festival were also emphasized by Korean institutions. Cultural referents can be used by both sides, immigrant and host, with a view toward achieving mutual understanding and the negotiation of difference.

The process of accommodation is not always smooth, but Fort Lee has increasingly come to regard cultural diversity as "natural." Asian groups received much less pressure to discard their own ways of living than in other towns.[50] Diversity became such a mundane experience that residents were unaware of it until they experienced a contrary reference point elsewhere. For example, one white mother commented that the racial and ethnic diversity of Fort Lee did not occur to her until her daughter's track team in Fort Lee High School visited other communities with teams that offered a sharp contrast. Those white residents who were acclimated to the diverse environment of Fort Lee expressed how they felt relaxed when they returned from predominantly white regions of the United States. One white female recalled, "I remember going down to Virginia to visit relatives and coming back. And I just went into a Korean store to get some groceries, and I was just, 'Phew . . . [*laughs*] I'm home.'" Another white female recounted how local whites used to stumble over the pronunciation of Japanese names in the 1970s but that Asian names were no longer alien to native ears. Daily life is the nexus where gradual yet decisive changes are registered and take place.

Art and Immigrant Incorporation

Art has been instrumental in immigrant incorporation in Fort Lee. Native white leaders believed that Asians value and appreciate art. Such perceived empathy for cultural programs has coincided with initiatives to transform Fort Lee into a "cultural center" for Bergen County and beyond. Fort Lee's historical identity as the "birthplace of the motion picture industry" offers significant opportunities for such efforts. The town aims to deploy its historical cachet in reinventing itself as a center for the arts (see chapter 1). The Fort Lee Film Commission and Office of Cultural Heritage Affairs host a number of local events. These activities include concerts, outdoor film screenings held in parks, outdoor Shakespeare theatrical performances, and the Arts and Music Festival, to name a few examples. The film commission has also organized a program of classic, independent, and foreign films that would rarely be screened, if at all, in regular movie theaters. The events are organized with a view to "spur an arts community" in Fort Lee.

Between 2003 and 2007, the film commission organized an Asian film festival in Bergen County. This event was made possible due to the presence of Asians in the area and with the help and support of key Asian cultural figures. The event was well received, with attendance by a mix of Asians and non-Asians. The executive director of the commission felt that showing Asian films as well as films made by Asian American filmmakers not only would help diversify the content of what they offer to the community but would also help diversify the audience—Asian American directors, for example, would help stimulate the interest of new immigrant groups in the community. "Asians," according to the executive director of the Fort Lee Film Commission, have brought "a new vibrancy" and "a chance to build an arts community." In his view, "Asians offer Fort Lee the ability to do different things."

To make such initiatives financially sustainable, not only is support from the municipality essential, but outreach to the entire community is also necessary. In the view of the film commission, the immigrant population "once tapped correctly, would be very supportive of the arts, very supportive of the film programs" and "would be open to new ideas." Outreach in turn paves a way for new immigrant groups to get involved in the borough's affairs.

Film is treated as a medium through which to socialize youth into Fort Lee's history and culture. One screening event illustrates this role of socialization by film. In June of 2009, toward the end of the school year, a documentary film made by fifth graders and entitled *Fort Lee: A Walk through Time* premiered in the auditorium of Fort Lee High School. A local photographer and film director had tutored the students on film production, from the use of the camera to editing processes. Some twenty students were involved in making the film, during which they interviewed local leaders. The interviews were edited into a thirty-minute film. Six of the eight pupils appearing in the film were of Asian origin—the majority Korean, with a few Japanese, all of whom spoke English fluently. The evening highlighted the conspicuous presence of Asian students in the Fort Lee school system—the students appeared on the stage, introducing the film, and giving "Oscar" awards to the adults who had helped them create the film. It was also noticeable that compared to other community-wide cultural programs, there was a much higher percentage of Asian adults in the audience for this event.[51]

A community agenda for the creation of an "art district" (providing tax incentives) is aimed at attracting potential investors in the art field—artists and gallery owners—"regardless of their background." In the past, borough help has been provided to art galleries in town, mainly Korean owned. As John Logan and Harvey Molotch have argued, the "arts" have become a conscious strategy for growth by which municipal officials and developers attempt to generate rent and revenues.[52] The anticipated economic growth to which art and culture might lend support is evident in the film center and museum that have been built as part of the town redevelopment project.[53] The incorporation of Asians in the artistic and cultural expansion of the borough is conceived in connection within the general goal of growth of the borough.

THE RELATIVE ABSENCE OF OPEN INTERGROUP CONFRONTATION

As the foregoing discussion demonstrates, reactions toward Asian immigration among white residents in Fort Lee have been mixed. Resistance and hostility have never taken the form of overt, collective anti-immigration action. Frequent remarks by residents that "people would never openly protest or demonstrate resentment" acknowledge the existence of hostility but at the same time indicate an understanding that potential conflict is under control. What are the factors that account for the relative absence of open confrontation?

Previous studies have demonstrated the role of class in shaping native attitudes toward newcomers. A case study of Twin Rivers, East Windsor Township, New Jersey, a racially homogeneous community, has shown that perceived economic parity—middle-class status—is connected with the formation of affinity among residents and that this factor can override race, ethnicity, or religion.[54] Similarly, in Monterey Park, California, relative economic equality between newcomers and established residents was found to be a major precondition for the accommodation of nonwhite minority members. Even though class was rarely mentioned in popular discourse, socioeconomic equivalence eventually facilitated interethnic alliances.[55] A comparative study of two suburban locations in Texas has found diverging local reactions: one highly anti-immigration, the other demonstrating greater tolerance and accommodation.[56] One of the differences between the two communities was income level—the more accommodating community was found to have the higher income, leading to the conclusion that "tax base may be an important factor shaping how local communities respond to immigrants in their midst."[57]

Similarly, in Fort Lee, local acceptance of East Asians appears to have been contingent on the largely middle-class status of both immigrants and locals. In the case of the Japanese, their transience also played a role in this aspect of local reception. Local recognition of their transience led to the feeling that Japanese were not a long-term threat. White residents in Fort Lee tended to interpret the lack of interethnic conflict as attributable to relative affluence—although this is not always a premise for lack of resentment. It may be recalled that in more affluent suburban communities in Bergen County and in Westchester, with higher income levels than Fort Lee, the Japanese experienced native opposition (see chapter 2). Thus additional factors, along with class parity, may account for the case of Fort Lee.

The relative lack of tension or open conflict may be explained at least in part by the kind of "civility" and indifference that characterize urban social relationships. Middle-class metropolitan suburbs tend to lack social cohesion, and residents tend to form fluid social relations with each other, due to heterogeneity, transience, fragmentation, and anonymity.[58] These traits—lack of social integration and relative indifference—foster the avoidance of confrontation among neighbors and a preference for a "peaceable way of life." It is not difficult to imagine that such attitudes among middle-class suburbanites are pronounced when dealing with the racialized "other." One white male in his forties stated that if a native white resident had an Asian neighbor, there would definitely be "a level of civility," even if there was resentment. In this view, lack of social cohesion, not intimacy and connectedness, produces an order of civility that is characteristic of middle-class suburban relationships.

Geographical and cultural proximity to New York City also renders Fort Lee relatively tolerant of difference. The borough continues to attract new white residents—transient, younger, working-age groups who choose Fort Lee mainly for its convenience to work. They do not spend much time in town during the weekday and care little about the appearance of Main Street or the town in general. Such newcomers do not view Asians as trespassing on their space; they lack the emotional attachment felt by established native residents of Fort Lee. Reactions and perceptions regarding the presence of Asians thus vary based on length of residence in the community and the life stage of individual residents. Myriad factors have operated to reduce or diffuse the potential for open ethnic conflict. Native acceptance of the newcomers has also been contingent on a further factor: the rationalization by natives of the "Americanization" of Asians.

CROSSING THE BOUNDARIES OF AMERICANNESS

After decades of living together, established white residents have observed changes in attitudes among Asian immigrants. Such perceived change seems to be an important consideration for whites. Neither native views of newcomers nor immigrant-native relations are unchanging. Some white residents felt that Korean integration is happening much faster than that of European immigrants in the early twentieth century. For example, one informant remarked that it had taken Italians a long period of time to get involved in local politics—the first Italian American mayor assumed office in Fort Lee only in the 1980s. By contrast, Koreans have become involved in the school board and other municipal committees within twenty years of their initial settlement.

An example of change among Asian immigrants can be seen in Korean-owned stores where adult whites interact with Koreans. Decades ago, white customers found Korean merchants unwelcoming and felt they were not interested in serving non-Korean customers—a sentiment still heard among some. Yet many others observe a tremendous change over the years, seen as a result of acclimation to the United States. Korean business owners have become more welcoming—even "overfriendly," at times. According to one white female resident of Leonia:

> There is a big difference from those who moved into Leonia thirteen years ago. You walked into a Korean business, they would turn their back on you. But today, "Happy to help you, how can I help you?" So I think . . . thirteen years ago, they were acting like any Korean would act: "I don't know who you are, I don't recognize your face, so I don't want to talk to you." But now, I think that they have become a little bit more Westernized, to say, "Why am I turning away money?

> [*laughs*] It's a silly thing to do." It's a much more of a welcoming environment now if you do shop in Palisades Park.

The attitudinal change remarked by whites is explained as immigrants having "learned how things are here" through the experience of business practices in the United States.

The perceived "Americanization" of immigrants serves as a precondition for native whites' acceptance of the new diversity. White residents tended to see Asians, especially U.S.-born youth, as becoming "American." One white male in his forties, who was raised in Fort Lee, stated that the students of Asian origin in high school today are "as much American as we were when we were in high school." To white residents, the boundaries of Americanness are defined according to certain conditions. For example, they considered the increasing intermixing of Asian and white youth as one such indication. Many white informants repeated the idea that immigrant familiarity with America, the acquisition of English fluency, and participation in the American educational system are prerequisites for acceptance as an "American." In this regard, there is a tacit understanding among whites of the necessity for immigrants and their children to become part of the "mainstream" in order to be considered part of "us." Inclusion as "American," then, depends on the labor of newcomers to assimilate and on their adaptation of white mainstream normativity.

The second generation is viewed as the driving force of change and regarded as the promise of a future, ethnically tolerant Fort Lee—one that will see the disappearance of any lingering resentment and perceived divide. The integration of English-speaking Asian youth into American culture facilitates boundary crossing. The U.S.-born second generation can also provide a vehicle for first-generation parents to adapt to America. One white male remarked, "People become American through their kids." For some white informants, "they [Koreans] are Americans"; *they are us* is an expression never used to describe the Japanese. Japanese residents in Fort Lee were seen as "Japanese" and never as "Japanese Americans." Such comments indicate assumptions—about who is an American and who is not—among local whites. How and when does the designation of *them* become *us*? One white female, a resident of Leonia remarked,

> There are more Koreans getting into the local government, so it's changing. It's changing from that side. Are they Korean? No, they are Korean American. I had some printing done by the [Korean] printer . . . I had new business cards made . . . When I went to them before, the person that I dealt with, she couldn't speak any English, and she always had to get the manager to talk to me. But now, the person I talk to on the phone is Korean American, and she speaks perfectly to me.

> That's who the Koreans are becoming. They're just like the Italian Americans or Greek Americans in Fort Lee, who looked the same. Koreans continue to look like Koreans, but they are not the same. You know, they are us. They are us. So by living here, we just get a chance to see what the world is turning into a little bit quicker.

Whites see the younger generation cope with difference better than their parents' generation. A white female resident of Fort Lee told me that while one of her white neighbors is "angry" with the Asian influx, the child of this neighbor and the child of a Korean family in the neighborhood are nevertheless good friends. The generational shift can be directly observed at work also. A white female who used to work for a Korean company observed that U.S.-born Korean employees had a different set of expectations from those of first-generation Koreans:

> The expectations of the younger Korean managers were frequently less Teutonic or less intense than those of their older, more experienced entrepreneurs . . . I mean, I would have to tell the older Korean manager, "You can't discipline the employee in a public place, you have to take them into private." They didn't understand—"Why not? They did something wrong." "Well, because we don't do it that way in the United States, it's humiliating." [*laughs*] "Oh, OK"—you know, kind of wondering why, but they would do that. But the younger ones, they got it, they understood it a lot better, I think.

One white male chamber of commerce board member remarked that working together with Korean merchants has become easier because "we are dealing now with the second generation. First generation, they were tough. You know, they have their certain ways, they don't speak English that well and all that. So they weren't comfortable. But now, with the second generation, it's getting better. We have a very good relationship."

White residents anticipate attitudinal changes and shifts in social relationships with the rise of the new generation and their Americanization. The tendency among whites to view such change as contingent on immigrant assimilation ironically ignores the reality of the changes occurring to whites. One white female bilingual teacher told me that twenty years ago, the integration of Japanese students was a challenge—until people got used to them. She explained that many Japanese students suffered since they felt unwelcome in Fort Lee. Yet, in her opinion, "having Japanese here has changed the attitudes of people in town, and they take on a much more global perspective." This statement indicates an awareness of the immigrant impact on a locality. As has been remarked in the literature, while immigrants are changed by the suburban context, they themselves are also changing the suburb.[59] Residents often underscored their understanding that achieving integration does not happen overnight but takes "time," for both newcomers and natives.

The Americanization of second-generation Asians that native whites observed in Fort Lee should be considered in light of the wider sociohistorical context. The transformations of American society have made cultural differences easier to maintain and overcome now than in the past: "Ethnicity is not only tolerated, but often celebrated as cultural traditions collide, merge, and co-exist."[60] As observed among second-generation youth in New York City, ethnic homogeneity in the residential environment need not obstruct exchanges with others elsewhere in the city: for example, in schools, in public spaces, or at work.

COPING WITH CHANGES

Native responses and attitudes toward Asians who share the social spaces of residence and work in Fort Lee are often ambivalent and contradictory. Despite an undercurrent of antagonism among white residents, shifts toward collaboration and accommodation are an unmistakable development. As seen in the epigraphs at the beginning of this chapter, in Fort Lee, ethnic coexistence and social distance are maintained synchronously. The local tendency to distinguish between East Asian groups is of interest in light of the general tendency to "lump" Asian subgroups together in the United States. At the same time, the consistent use of "we" to refer to whites and "they" for Asians among white residents reveals the persistence of a view of Asians as "other."

This perception of Asian "otherness" is in fact integral to the official ideology of "diversity." During the research, inside the Jack Alter Fort Lee Community Center, vertical scroll banners with colored images that speak to Fort Lee's civic priorities hung from the high ceilings. One showed Korean children in ethnic costume performing traditional drum ceremonies (*Janggu* and *Buk*). At the head of the banner was inscribed the word "diversity"—incorporating Korean culture into the contemporary ideology of pluralism.[61] Asians were seen as representing the "diversity" of the community, yet this ideology hinges on the notion of the "non-American" other.

Interracial relationships in Fort Lee also suggest the importance of a consideration of class and social status in immigrant suburbanization. The relative absence of intergroup conflict depends, in part, on the behavioral patterns of middle-class suburbanites in public space. The semiurban milieu of Fort Lee diffuses the possibility of open conflict. At the same time, such codes of conduct in middle-class suburbia present a challenge for the adequate assessment of intergroup relationships; these behavioral codes, governed by the principle of "civility," may serve as a veneer to hide the true feelings of residents.

Native resistance and resentment toward newcomers are not part of the concern in the spatial assimilation model since those who settle in suburbs are presumed to be acculturated, having already achieved upward mobility. Premised on social and cultural integration, the model overlooks how the host may be changed by immigration. The present findings suggest that immigrant groups can significantly influence both the cognition and local life of white Americans. Whites observe and recognize the gradual "assimilation" of Asians and rationalize the trend as a long-term undertaking comparable with the process that occurred for earlier European immigrants.

The ethnoburb model, on the other hand, suggests "misunderstandings, distrust, and tensions between the new ethnic minorities and longtime residents of various ethnic groups" because the ethnoburb alters the local residential landscape and business environment of the traditionally white American suburb.[62] The emergence of an ethnoburb is "likely to reinforce the ethnicity for all groups and to reinforce existing division."[63] In Fort Lee, while native resentment against the Asian influx exists, the reception has not been unilaterally hostile but more complex and multifaceted. As discussed in this chapter, whites negotiate with their changing reality, and part of this process is the rationalization of acceptance contingent on the perceived and projected "Americanization" of newcomers.

The case of Fort Lee calls for nuanced reflection on integration, including the perceptions of native whites and practices within the specific local context. The findings are suggestive of the ways in which the transformation of a community takes place, both consciously and unconsciously, "on an incremental basis through compromise and accommodation in the pragmatic process of getting things done."[64] Native white responses are shaped by the local context and in dialectical relation with Asians—white responses in turn influence Asian views of and relations with whites. East Asian communities in Fort Lee do not exist in isolation but in relation to the host community. Within this changing context, the notions of contemporary ethnicity and race are shaped.

5 · REMAKING ASIAN ETHNICITY IN SUBURBIA

As Max Weber has argued, ethnoracial categories play a central role in the construction of social and political groups. *Race*, as an ascriptive status defined and imposed by society, at once assigns and denies our identity. Ethnicity and race are forms of collective identity premised on the binary distinction of "us" and "them." Ethnicity—a social grouping based on imputed common descent or culture—is assumed, as with race, to be permanent and unchanging.[1]

The social category "Asian," which designates groups of diverse national origin as a single entity, has been "racialized" as an identity in the United States.[2] But neither race nor ethnicity is immutable. Different identities can be activated at different times. As social constructs, the meanings of race and ethnicity are in constant flux, subject to transformation, and remade over time. Members of ethnic groups are not passive subjects. The development of ethnoracial identity is relational and dialectical—a negotiation between external ascription and an internal sense that varies according to context. Identity is not simply imposed: it is actively used by individuals, albeit under social constraints. Individuals carry a "portfolio of ethnic identities," selection from which depends on various social settings and constituencies that are "shuffled in and out of prominence depending on the situation."[3]

The ambiguities and multiplicities that surround the notion of "Asian," or "Asian American," are indicative of the malleability of ethnoracial boundaries. Under certain conditions, group members may forge new identities with a view to political mobilization. The concept of "panethnicity," for example, has been defined as a "politico-cultural collectivity made up of peoples of several, hitherto distinct, tribal or national origins."[4] The term "Asian American" was taken up and utilized as a panethnic identity by U.S.-born Asians in the late 1960s as a strategy against racism.[5] David Lopez and Yen Espiritu have proposed that panethnicity may be supplanting both assimilation and ethnic particularlism in the United States with, in the case of pan-Asian identity, the erosion and fusion of varied ethnic identities.[6] Others have argued that pan-Asian and ethnic identity are actually interdependent and that the emergence of panethnicity does not diminish the particular ethnic identities of Asian groups.[7]

This chapter considers the implications of ethnic diversity in relation to "Asianness" in Fort Lee. The importance of place in shaping ethnoracial identity has been discussed in the scholarship.[8] Based on her research of West San Gabriel Valley, California, where Asians and Latinos constitute the overwhelming majority, Wendy Cheng argues that specific regional conditions can shape regional racial order and the identities of residents.[9] Cheng also suggests that a national ideology of racial hierarchy still plays a role for residents in the multiracial and multiethnic suburb. Fort Lee, however, presents a different suburban condition. How do East Asian immigrants and their offspring identify themselves in Fort Lee? How does residence in this multicultural suburban community affect Asian identity and social relations? Does the geographical convergence of Asian immigrant groups lead to the formation of pan-Asian affinities? How are the meanings of "Asian" and "American" constructed in this multiethnic suburb?

UNSETTLED IDENTITIES: CHOICES AND CONSTRAINTS

The patterns of ethnoracial identification among East Asian informants in Fort Lee were varied, and immigrant status played a key role. The majority of first-generation informants identified themselves according to national origin. Being "Chinese," "Japanese," or "Korean" was an important part of their identity, and a strong identification with national origin made them resistant to the label of "Asian," though for some, identification as "Asian" can be compatible with ethnonational identity. A few other first-generation interviewees were dismissive of ethnicity: aspects of their lives such as religious affiliation or parenthood were the primary sources for their identities.

Identification as "American" increases among the U.S.-born. For those born in America or who arrived when very young, being "American" is taken for granted as a part of their identity. In such cases, members of the 1.5 and second generation generally chose the joint designation: "Chinese American," "Japanese American," or "Korean American." "Asian American" was rarely used by U.S.-born informants to define themselves. A second-generation male in his twenties, for example, who identified himself as "Taiwanese American," questioned the notion of "Asian American": "I know that in America, it's like we are so small a population it's detrimental to try to distinguish yourself from other Asian Americans, so let's call us 'Asian American,' because, otherwise, we don't have pulling power, blah-blah-blah, whatever. I don't know, it's just I consider myself as more Taiwanese American than Asian American, because that's where my loyalty lies, I guess."

Few first-generation informants identified themselves as "American," and many showed reluctance in doing so. One first-generation Chinese female in her forties, originally from Malaysia, previously married to a Chinese and engaged to a white American at the time of the interview, was firm on this point: "I consider myself as Chinese. Even though I'm naturalized, I never say I'm American. My fiancé, he always says, 'You're American.' . . . I always say, 'I'm going home [when traveling to Malaysia].' He says, 'Here is your home.' [*laughs*] You see, until somebody's telling you—like all these years, I'm here for thirteen years, but it's like temporary . . . It seems like I treat myself like I'm here just temporarily. I'm a [U.S.] citizen and I never say, 'I'm American.'" When first-generation informants do identify as "American," however, this is clearly a result of negotiation and a conscious decision. First-generation Korean informants more readily identified as "Korean American" than did first-generation Chinese or Japanese. They rarely considered themselves "Asian" or "Asian American." One Korean community leader and resident of Fort Lee was quoted in the local press as stating that "we have to find our identity, not only as Koreans, but as American . . . We are Korean Americans."[10]

On the other hand, some foreign-born informants consider themselves nothing but "American" and, by naturalization, consciously choose to be so. In the words of one 1.5-generation Korean American in his thirties, "This is the only country where you, as an individual, have a choice. You actually choose to become an American. In other countries, you can't do that." One first-generation Korean male and civic leader emphasized that Koreans who immigrate to the United States should try to "become American" to avoid social marginalization. Although no Korean person can change the fact that they are Korean, the same informant felt that immigrants have to become American, because this will be more beneficial to them both in daily life and in work.

One important consideration concerns the sense of entitlement in claiming Americanness. "Asian" and/or "American" appeared antithetical to my Asian informants' perceptions—although the opposition may be susceptible to synthesis by some. The greatest hindrance to identifying as "American" is physical appearance—a factor that permeates perceptions of Asians as "foreigners" or as "the symbolic alien."[11] Nicholas De Genova has argued that Asian national origins are refashioned in the United States as a racialized identity that is rendered "inimical to the 'American'-ness of white supremacy."[12] My first-generation informants maintained a tacit understanding that those who are entitled to be "American" are "white."[13] For foreign-born East Asians, "Americanness" is contingent on possession of symbolic power—that which institutes, names, or defines who is what and who is ultimately to be recognized as a legitimate part of the mainstream.

Identity is a continual process of self-questioning. Racialized and ethnicized notions that shape identity are indicative of the degree of acclimation to America. The absence of racial and ethnic consciousness among temporary Japanese immigrants is revealing. When asked, "How do you identify yourself?," expatriate wives were slow to understand the meaning of the question—they had not considered the issue since they never questioned their Japaneseness and, lacking immersion in American society, seemed unaffected by such thoughts. Japanese expatriates who work with American colleagues, on the other hand, have seen racial division in America and realize that they are classified as "Asian." Greater contact and involvement in American life seem to promote a racialized identification even for temporary immigrants. Korean immigrants, on the other hand, having established contact with whites through business, political participation, schooling, and other institutions, develop notions about Koreanness, "who" they themselves are and, to a certain extent, what they aspire to be. Growing up in the United States sensitizes ethnoracial consciousness among 1.5- and second-generation Asian Americans regarding the importance of race in American society despite their cultural, linguistic, and social assimilation. A Korean female in her forties (who has lived in the United States since high school) put it this way:

> This is something that I've experienced growing up. I speak English, and I may enjoy and do the things the others—let's say, non-Asian people, maybe Caucasians or white Americans—do. But I'll always *look* different. And I think I went through a stage where I didn't even want to speak Korean and, you know, like, pretend that . . . right? But as I get older, it is fairly important, because no matter how fluent we speak the language, and no matter what kind of food we eat—I may only like hamburgers and French fries, and not the Korean food—we are always looked upon as "You are Korean, right?," "Where are you from?" So I tell my children, "We are Korean first. And the United States is just built with people from all over the world. So it's important that you feel good about yourself as Korean first."

Although the issue concerns race ("I'll always *look* different"), the informant does not resort to the notion of "Asianness" but centers her belief in ethnic identity as Korean.

Being ethnic and American can be conflictual but not irreconcilable. One first-generation Korean male in his fifties explained at length how he considers his identity to be made up of both Korean and American elements. His account suggests that such an identity may be negotiated over time:

> Some people think they are still Koreans. They are still Korean immigrants who live in the United States but . . . with a strong ethnic identity as Korean. Also, there's another group who think they are Korean Americans. A long time ago, when my kids were growing up, they were little kids, I always told them—their names are [I] and [J]—"[I] and [J] you are not Koreans, you are not Americans, you are Korean Americans." I used to say that. But these days, my mind-set has changed. These days, I don't think they are Korean Americans. I think they are Americans . . . with Korean heritage. My kids are Americans because they were born here and they grew up here in the States. Their main language is English. They are culturally Korean but still more American than Korean because they grew up here in the States. So I think they are Americans *with* Korean heritage. But even though I'm a first-generation Korean immigrant, I try to think I should be an American with Korean heritage. If I don't think so, I will always live on the margin of the whole community, you know, American society. I do not really like it . . . I should go into the mainstream society. But still, I want to maintain my Korean ethnic background, you know, Korean culture and everything. But I try to learn American culture and society at the same time. So those kinds of conceptual words are very important. I used to be a Korean American. I tried to be a Korean American. But right now, I don't think I'm a Korean American or that I should be a Korean American. I should be an American with Korean heritage.

The same informant's rationale regarding why he should consider himself American is suggestive of the social role of "race" in the definition of being "American": "Being an American does not mean being a white person . . . There are already many ethnic people in the States . . . As far as I remember, already one fourth of Americans are Latinos and Asian. It's growing. African Americans are also growing, compared to Caucasians. So this nation is not white American already. There are many ethnic groups, so, being American means that. Being American does not mean becoming white American." When first-generation Asian informants aspire to be part of the mainstream, although there is a tacit consensus among them that "Americanness" equates with "whiteness," there is also the recognition that America's demographic shift is contributing to a change in the meaning of Americanness.

Ethnic identity is at times contingent on expediency. For example, some first-generation Chinese informants suggested that whether they use "Chinese" or "Asian" depends on the social context. Although many expressed strong attachment to their identity as Chinese, they also considered themselves, at least in part, American—through civic participation and voting, for example. In a similar vein, one second-generation Korean American female in her twenties remarked that having several roles due to her multiple identities can help make life "less boring." Attending a private school in a New York suburb, predominantly Irish and Italian, the informant remembers racial discrimination at school. At the time of this interview, she lived in Palisades Park with her U.S.-born Korean friends from university while working for a mainstream financial firm in New York City. This informant considers herself "unique" by having "cultural roots" as a Korean, a uniqueness related to the facility she has developed through living in bicultural worlds: "When I'm at work, I guess I could put on my white personality, but then at the same time, I can come home or visit my parents and do this, be the Korean daughter they want me to be." This informant was comfortable with an "American" setting and finds herself capable of "switching" whenever she speaks with white friends or with her Korean friends and relatives. Moreover, being a Korean American provides a "unique opportunity":

> It breaks stereotypes, I guess, because, people are saying that "oh, Asians are great at math, great at school," you know, "smart, quiet," whatever. A lot of times, even now, actually, people, when they see me—maybe not New York City, when I go down to South Jersey . . . they automatically assume I don't know English. So when I help out at my dad's store sometimes, it's not that they are not in a great neighborhood, but they try to take advantage of my parents because they can't speak English, and they argue with them. But if I help out, they try to argue with me, they automatically assume I can't speak English. So when they argue with me, they say something to me, I *speak* [with emphasis]. And I have fairly good pronunciation, you know. They get shocked . . . I think it's kind of like trying to break the stereotypes, kind of like an opportunity to prove people wrong.

The narrative points to the complex intertwining of racial and American identities. Having an Asian appearance is associated with foreignness in people's mind, but being born and growing up as American in the United States (indicated by, for example, possession of English fluency) allows her to defy the racial stereotype. This informant's symbolic struggle is premised on two social aspects: visual appearance as an Asian and formation as an American.

Taken together, the accounts of East Asian informants suggest relative autonomy and agency in their choice of ethnic identity, although racialization has imposed limits on the ways they can conceive of themselves as American. It is also evident that ethnic and pan-Asian identities frequently overlap, are interchangeable and flexible, or loosely used. Patterns of identification are malleable among East Asians in Fort Lee.

The role of social class in self-identification is crucial. The middle-class status of the majority of my East Asian informants conditioned their life experience and provided greater options and leverage in their identification.[14] "Symbolic" identification has been considered most likely to occur among those of the highest class, those who have achieved socioeconomic success. The members of this stratum have the greatest interest in their sociocultural heritage and the freedom to assume an ethnic identity without incurring discrimination. In "selective" identification, agents choose to be more ethnic on certain occasions than on others—a strategy related to the goals of economic achievement. In Fort Lee, the example of "symbolic identification" is suggested by the case of Chinese and Taiwanese professionals who are socioeconomically assimilated but at the same time maintain ethnic heritage. The second-generation Korean woman who consciously "switches" her identity, quoted previously, may be considered a case of "selective" identification—being more "white" in the workplace, more "Korean" with her parents. Ethnicity cannot be reduced to class position, but middle-class identity and class experience can give form to ethnic identity. It has been remarked that "flexibility in deciding when and to what degree one is ethnic is a suburban luxury."[15]

Immigrants and their children deal with the choices in identification that are available to them, but generational differences do exist. The second generation more readily upholds its identity as "American" than their immigrant parents do. For first-generation immigrants, identity as an American is based on a conscious decision—and may even be expressed as an imperative ("we should be American"). Frequently this decision seems to be based on a felt need to gain social legitimation in the United States for socioeconomic attainment and the comfort of a sense of belonging. Another overall pattern is the absence of identification as "Asian" or "Asian American," although the degree of adaptation of this panethnic label increases among the U.S.-born. Which factors promote or inhibit the choice of identity as "Asian"?

IDENTITIES AND PATTERNS IN SOCIAL RELATIONSHIPS

The meanings and definitions of self are conditioned by relations with others. Awareness as an "ethnic" actor is gained through relationships with others, both coethnic and non-coethnic. Ethnic identities are sustained by the maintenance of "boundaries"—the lines marking off one group from another.[16] It is important, therefore, for us to examine the types of social relationships that Asian residents form in Fort Lee to understand how identities are shaped. To what extent do racial and ethnic categories matter in the social relationships of East Asians? In turn, how do social relations inform identity?

In general, members of the three East Asian groups tended to have coethnics as best friends. This tendency was pronounced among the first generation, for whom friendships with non-coethnics were inhibited linguistically. For example, Japanese expatriate wives would arrive in the United States with the intention of learning English and of making non-Japanese friends, but this would be hindered by the temporary character of their residency and the fact that they could get by without speaking English.[17] The president of the Japanese-American Society of New Jersey (JAS of NJ) remarked that there are many Japanese who say their English conversation classes provide the only opportunity to speak with a native English speaker no matter how many years they have been resident in the United States.

First-generation East Asians with English fluency have non-coethnic friends, but their closest friends tend to be coethnic. Even in the absence of the linguistic barrier and possession of apparent indicators of assimilation—for example, a job in a mainstream American company or an interracial marriage—a felt cultural gap between themselves and Americans or non-coethnic Asians was mentioned as a reason for not forming interethnic friendships. For example, some first-generation Chinese informants attributed a lack of non-coethnic friends to "cultural difference," which they continue to feel regardless of the length of their residence in the United States. Even though they mingle with various ethnic group members, these first-generation Chinese remarked that they cannot have deep relationships with Americans and that there are topics of conversation they can share only with Chinese. The idea of "difference" between themselves and Americans was recurrent among first-generation Asians who are fluent in English and who work in the mainstream labor market.

On the other hand, U.S.-born Asians have both coethnic and non-coethnic friends. They are generally comfortable in coethnic and non-coethnic worlds. Korean informants who grew up and attended public schools in Fort Lee remembered having white friends at school. One 1.5-generation Korean American female in her twenties recalled that when she was at Fort Lee High School, she never "hung out" with Korean students: her first best friend was white and all of her current best friends since high school have been non-Korean and of different ethnic origins.

Still, those 1.5- and second-generation Korean American informants who had non-coethnic friends considered themselves an exception in high school, where the majority of Korean students associated only with Koreans. Even those who are U.S.-born and fluent in English tend to associate with coethnics. A first-generation Korean father of two U.S.-born sons observed that they only had Asian friends, mainly Korean, in school. A 1.5-generation Korean female in her twenties described her U.S.-born younger brother, who is more comfortable in English than Korean although his friends are Korean and speak "Konglish" among themselves.[18] The tendency to socialize with coethnics was observed during fieldwork—in the public library, in the streets after school, groups of East Asian students, typically made up of several members, were a common sight.[19] Bilingual Korean informants suggested that their coethnic friendships were based on linguistic facility. They told me their Korean-speaking friends did not overlap with their English-speaking friends and that they met with linguistically defined groups separately.

The sense of a boundary that distinguishes coethnic members from others prevails. Asian informants widely shared a sense of separation according to ethnic group. Generally, they believed that the ethnic groups remained separate from each other, even if they seemed to get along on the surface. A first-generation Chinese female in her forties noted how coethnics tend to treat their in-group members differently from those of the out-group:

> I have best friends, Korean, but you still see the difference. They treat their Korean friends and you—you can see the difference. If you call the company for . . . a Korean taxi, they give a special discount for Korean people only, but they don't give it to you. Even if you go to the bank . . . you see how they serve. There are Koreans working there. And you see how they treat them [Koreans] different than when you're not Korean. They do. You see that. I think everywhere in the world you see that.

This informant had also observed a Korean teacher at her daughter's elementary school who, it was claimed, gave preference to Korean students in a class where 75 to 80 percent of the students were Korean. In the morning, the teacher greeted students in Korean, as they did not yet speak English. According to the informant, the teacher was "more on the side of the Korean kids," and this could be sensed by non-Korean students. Although preferential treatment by ethnic belonging is acknowledged as a universal trend, such practices in everyday life reinforce group separateness. Coethnic solidarity overrides potential pan-Asian cohesion.

Ethnic difference can be a source of personal antagonism or of simply not getting along. A second-generation Chinese American male in his twenties who had socialized with Koreans in middle school told me that he eventually fell out with his Korean friends because "sometimes they were doing Korean things; they talked in Korean that I didn't understand." How do such social relations affect the notion of ethnic identity? Coethnic relationships appear to deepen distinction between ethnic groups and seem to further reinforce ethnic rather than "Asian" identity. Asian panethnic affinity can also be strained by contemporary tensions in Asia or the historical memory of Japanese colonialism and imperial aggression in the Pacific during the Second World War.[20] In the past and to a lesser degree today (due to the declining number of Japanese), separation between Japanese and Korean students has been observed.[21] Although very few informants discussed them, historical legacies (considered a taboo subject) continue to have some bearing on interethnic relations among residents.

Supranational relationships are not entirely absent, however. As discussed in preceding chapters, there have been long-term and recent professional partnerships among East Asians, through business relations and employment—newly opened local businesses run jointly by Japanese and Koreans, for example, or the expansion of existing Korean food businesses as a pan-Asian enterprise. Interviews and field observations revealed interethnic friendships of various age groups as well as interethnic marriages between members of the three Asian groups. The various groups cross the ethnonational boundary through popular culture—Asians enjoy each other's food, learn each other's languages (e.g., the interest in the Korean language among Japanese expatriate wives, coincidental with the "Korean Wave" in Asia), and show interest in each other's popular culture (e.g., the taste for Japanese popular culture among Korean youth).[22]

The concept of "panethnicity" concerns shifts in-group identification from smaller- to larger-level groupings, entailing transformation in the constitution of the ethnic group. As Yen Le Espiritu has argued, panethnicity is an emergent, situated identity that is mutable and serves as a political resource to mobilize members of internally diverse subgroups.[23] The civil rights movement of the 1960s and subsequent incidents involving anti-Asian racism stimulated racial consciousness and inspired a struggle for self-determination among U.S.-born Asian Americans.[24] Panethnicity, however, does not necessarily attenuate ethnic distinction. Despite the growth of panethnic affiliations and organizations, ethnonational identity remains important for many Asian Americans.[25]

East Asian communities in Fort Lee have not developed formal pan-Asian organizations. The existing ethnic associations discussed previously (in chapter 3) are mainly run by first-generation immigrants rather than second or later generations. The absence of interdependent links does not appear to be contingent solely on the comparatively small numbers of Chinese and Japanese. There was no pan-Asian organization even when there were roughly equal numbers of Japanese and Koreans in the 1990s—although this lack may be explained partly by the transience of Japanese immigrants. The absence of associative relationships suggests that formal alliances to protect minority interests are perceived as unnecessary or even divergent from the goals of each organization. For example, although the Korean American Association of Fort Lee (KAAFL) has worked with Korean organizations in other townships, the association has not developed connections with other Asian ethnic organizations, whether in Fort Lee or elsewhere.[26] The absence of interaction with other East Asian organizations is attributable to the lack of specific causes on which to take a stand. Other Asian organizations in Fort Lee are more interested in cultural promotion, which diverges from the mission of KAAFL.

The absence of panethnic organization stems from several local conditions. Espiritu has argued that pan-Asian affiliation is formed in reaction to anti-Asian violence and racism or where there are political and economic conditions that favor inclusive panethnic identity. Pan-Asianism is found among second and later generations, who tend to feel alienated from both traditional ethnic communities and the mainstream.[27] None of these conditions hold for Fort Lee. There has been little overt threat of anti-Asian violence. In addition, the overwhelming majority of East Asians are first generation. Many among the first generation, by and large, feel sufficiently supported by the coethnic community, and the three East Asian groups lack a common political agenda that might promote affiliation. The material self-sufficiency of each group has precluded the formation of an overarching Asian American association.

Asian American panethnic identity, however, is not just political but also symbolic and cultural: for example, in pan-Asian church congregations. Such congregations led by ministers of second and later generations are documented elsewhere in the country but have not emerged in Fort Lee.[28] There are congregations that offer bilingual services (Chinese and Korean, or Japanese and Korean), but an "Asian American" church per se has not yet developed.[29] Different religious groups and congregations may share the same building, but without contact. This is due to the significant presence of first-generation Asians in Fort Lee, whose shared language is not English and who are more concerned with coethnic solidarity than with collective Asian identity.

The absence of panethnicity in Fort Lee supports the premise that pan-Asian identity develops neither "naturally" nor "automatically" when different Asian groups inhabit the same social space. As Dina Okamoto suggests, categories such as "Asian American" depend on "structural conditions that encourage group formation" and "narratives that are used and reproduced by leaders and organizations."[30] Panethnic group formation is more likely when ethnic groups are positioned to develop shared interests, relations, and ties.[31] At this point, pan-Asian, supranational connections are limited to informal, individual-level social relationships in Fort Lee.

RACE AND RESIDENCE

Even though few East Asian informants readily identified themselves as "Asian," the idea of "Asian" implicitly plays a role in their decision regarding residential location. The overwhelming majority of Asian informants saw Fort Lee as a "comfortable" place to live. This sense of comfort stems from two factors: perceived racial tolerance in ("Asian-friendly") Fort Lee and the "generalized" presence of Asians. The first is often contrasted with the experience of feeling "uncomfortable" in other parts of the United States where there are only small numbers of Asians. Experiences described by my informants were neither overtly discriminatory nor racist but were silently registered—for example, being scowled at for no reason, curious stares, or the absence of knowledge of and expression of bias against things "Asian." Such social interactions led some Asians to recognize the importance of residence with natives who are seen as more tolerant. One first-generation Japanese female felt comfortable that white Americans in the Fort Lee area were "open toward different cultures" and did not mind ethnic practices.

Informants also mentioned "feeling comfortable" in a place where many residents had similar physical features, even if they lacked personal association. "Race" is a social construct, but a felt, somatic affinity indicates the persistence of a latent ideology of connection through appearance. One Korean male informant in his fifties in the real estate business hypothesized that Koreans choose Fort Lee because they see "Asian" faces there. A Korean female ESL teacher at one elementary school, referring to Asian students, remarked, "There is comfort in knowing somebody who looks like you, who is in a similar situation. Learning English at the same time . . . the Korean, the Japanese will interact better than, maybe, Russian students. They find comfort, that's how I see [it]; they find comfort in just having the same look: 'we are together,' that kind of thing."

Location of residence was equally a concern for the second generation. Throughout their socialization in America, immigrant offspring were made conscious of their being "Asian." One second-generation Korean woman in her thirties, intermarried with a white, expressed her appreciation of "place": "Fort Lee provides a good mix where I feel comfortable, you know, as an Asian person. Sometimes my husband is like, 'Oh, if you move all the way to the other side of New Jersey, near Pennsylvania, houses are bigger and cheaper.' But I can't, it's too white. [*laughs*] So for me, as an Asian person, even though I grew up in this country and everything else, I am aware of that." The informant was considering moving out of Fort Lee for her children's schooling. Although having too many Koreans around her makes her feel uncomfortable, she still prefers to find somewhere that is similar to Fort Lee in terms of ethnic composition—definitely preferring a location where some Asians live. Feeling comfortable in Fort Lee is ultimately related to issues of "race" that Asians have to come to terms with in the United States.

The sense of "comfort" is also specifically derived from the presence of coethnics. One 1.5-generation Korean female remarked that her two children are American-born but she felt it important for them to not be the only Koreans in school. A female high school student (whose family immigrated to Fort Lee directly from Korea) remarked that she feels comfortable in Fort Lee since there are many Koreans and she does not feel as though she is in a "foreign country." Another Korean female senior at Fort Lee High School, who came to the United States when she was in seventh grade, explained, "I came to Fort Lee 'cause there are a lot of Koreans. I heard that there are a lot of Koreans, but not so much that, like, the whole school's like Korean. I wanted to learn English too, but then, as much as I want to learn English, I wanted to adapt easily, and I thought that if there are some Koreans here, they could help me do that. So I moved here." The idea that the presence of coethnics makes adjustment easier was recurrent among informants of Korean origin and was also true for the Japanese to a certain degree. It was never mentioned by the Chinese as a factor in their decision regarding residence. At the same time, as discussed in chapter 2, it is common across East Asian groups to view the presence of too many coethnics as undesirable, since this reduces the opportunity for making contact with "Americans."

Not only first-generation but also U.S.-born Asians seem to stay within ethnic neighborhoods, countering the assumption that a greater degree of assimilation leads to offspring dispersion. According to data provided by Fort Lee High School, the majority of Asian graduates of the school remained in the New Jersey area to pursue postsecondary education in 2009.[32] This tendency was stronger when compared with the preceding two years (2007–2008), when there were significantly more Asian students who moved on to out-of-state public universities.[33]

Interviews with second-generation informants suggest that Asian youth are not necessarily eager to leave the coethnic environment of the Fort Lee area. A second-generation Taiwanese American male in his twenties related that his Taiwanese American friends, including those in college, have remained in New Jersey, near home. Some 1.5- and second-generation Koreans in their twenties and thirties expressed a desire to eventually own a house in the Fort Lee area to raise a family. Although the data are insufficient to be conclusive, many Asian youths appear to remain in the area where they grew up. Contrary to the trend of relocation to more white suburbs in Bergen County discussed in chapter 2, some young U.S.-born Asian Americans prefer a coethnic neighborhood as a place of residence. Philip Kasinitz and his colleagues have observed a similar trend among second-generation youth in New York, indicating that they seem at ease living between different worlds—that of their parents and of mainstream America. Because of the ethos of multiculturalism and ethnoracial diversity in New York, the children of immigrants today do not feel "undue pressure to reject the languages, beliefs, and behaviors of [their] immigrant forebears."[34]

In a similar vein, East Asian youth in Fort Lee, even if they are socioculturally assimilated in America, do not find it necessary to reject residence in the coethnic neighborhood. These immigrant children do not feel inhibited by their ethnic environment.

Very few Asian informants reported direct or indirect experiences of ethnoracial tension or conflict in Fort Lee. Even established residents of East Asian origin of more than twenty years recalled very few negative encounters with native white residents. Such accounts, however, should not necessarily be taken as proof of their absence. Asians are aware that there is a possibility of native hostility against "people who are immigrants or who look different," especially at a time of national crisis, such as the terrorist attacks in 2001. It was noted previously (in chapter 4) that one native white reaction was expressed in terms of a fear of the threat of "invasion." Although hostility may not be openly expressed, Asians are aware of the possibility that their presence may not be fully accepted. One first-generation Korean leader expressed her concerns: "I really hope this area doesn't really mind ethnics. Once we cross the bridge, especially around Fort Lee and Edgewater, a lot of Koreans and Japanese live there. I hope that the American community who lives here don't feel like we as Asians, invaded their territory . . . I think it might feel really bad with so much influence or the effects from Asian culture on their daily lives." Established Asian residents who said that they never experienced ethnic tension prefaced their comments by saying that they may have been "lucky" or "ignorant" about the issue, or that the problems were "hidden" from them. One Chinese female informant in her forties related to me that her white American neighbors complain about the habits of their Korean neighbors—they do not recycle, they are dirty, they make noise. This informant felt her white neighbors complained to her about Koreans because they knew she was Chinese. This made her concerned about "what they say in front of others about me" because "I'm also Asian." Regardless of their ethnic origin, Asians ultimately share the position of "other" relative to non-Asians.

On the other hand, Asian residents understood that whites are not entirely negative about their presence. Another first-generation Chinese female in her forties recounted her experiences with senior residents:

> You go to a park and sit with the older people. They say, "It used to be that this was an all-white place, and now all you Oriental people come, so many of you." They like to say that. But they say, "You guys are very nice people, you don't make a lot of crime here," they do say that to you. They say, "Your kids are doing very well in school, you send your kids to afterschool programs, like tutor[ing in] math, science—that's why you guys are so strong in education." But other than that, maybe there's something they don't tell me, but they always praise you; they like you.

Similar views and experiences regarding native whites were expressed by other Asian informants. They felt that, on balance, white Americans in Fort Lee are racially tolerant. Yet covert fear of a wider racial antagonism continues to be a factor in the aggregation of Asians in Fort Lee. In this way, social space continues to be racialized. The logic of exclusion based on difference prompts ethnic group members to choose a diverse residential location as a point of convergence even where, in reality, Asians are often viewed as "other" by natives (as shown in chapter 4).

RENEWAL OF ETHNORACIAL IDENTITY AND ETHNIC PRIDE

In her analysis of the resurgence of ethnic identity among Native Americans, Joane Nagel defines "ethnic renewal" as "the process whereby new ethnic identities, communities, and cultures are built or rebuilt out of historical social and symbolic systems." Using cultures imported from immigrant homelands, ethnicity is revitalized and constantly renewed "through common identification, group formation and reformation, and cultural production and reproduction."[35] Parallel to the concept of "invented" traditions, such cultures serve the purpose of establishing or symbolizing social cohesion or group membership. According to Nagel, the construction of tradition is a major task facing all ethnic groups. Tradition is a "resource" and is used by groups toward "the collective quest for meaning and community."[36]

While playing a vital function in group cohesion, the reinvention of ethnic tradition may also be a product of assimilation. According to Stephen Steinberg, this surge in ethnic revival and interest in ethnicity is a "symptom of decline, a dying gasp of ethnic consciousness"[37]—that is, people may cling to and emphasize ethnicity when they realize they are losing it. This trend can be heard in the comment of a first-generation Korean resident: "As more Koreans assimilate in Fort Lee and elsewhere, there is a need to remember their roots."[38] As discussed in preceding chapters, my Asian informants generally viewed the maintenance of ethnic heritage as a necessity. The need appears to be associated with length of residence in America and degree of assimilation, which produce a greater feeling of need for the invocation of ethnic heritage. Asian ethnicity in America—whether Chinese, Japanese, or Korean—is, to a certain degree, a product of reinvention, a preference cultivated through life in America by immigrants. In the process, the cultures of national origin transmute into something "foreign" and "exotic," even for the immigrants themselves.

The esteem for tradition was evident in those ethnic organizations that focus on cultural exchange and promotion.[39] The Japanese-American Society of New Jersey offers classes in traditional cultures, in part, in response to the emerging desire of Japanese immigrants to "relearn" traditional arts and practices.

According to the president of the society, the interest in "good old things about Japan" among immigrants resurfaces after living in the United States for many years. Similarly, the Donghwa Cultural Foundation, a Korean organization, arranges the annual celebration of *Chuseok,* the Korean harvest festival.[40] During my observation in October 2009, the director led a culinary demonstration of *songpyeon* (traditional crescent-shaped rice cakes), largely attended by Koreans. The director later told me that, in Korea, people would neither know how to make *songpyeon* nor go to the trouble of making them. Today, they are rarely handmade since people prefer to purchase premade items from stores. The director half-jokingly related how her mother, living in Korea, teases her that Koreans living in the United States are more "old fashioned" than those in Korea. Being distant from the ancestral land reinforces the need to reinvent ethnic tradition in the adopted home precisely because of the distance from the homeland. Rebuilding a cultural basis for a new community revitalizes ethnic boundaries, redefining the meaning of ethnicity.

Efforts to revivify and extend ancestral language usage are major cultural reconstruction projects. Chapter 3 discussed the language demonstrations by youth during performances for the Chinese New Year festival at a Chinese school. Here, the ancestral language is no longer taken for granted among immigrant families but is treated as something that requires special reinforcement. The language of the immigrant group becomes "foreign" with time and hence must be learned through conscious effort by the U.S.-born offspring. Chinese mothers I spoke to at the Chinese school said they enroll their children to learn to speak Chinese without an accent, "like we do." The emphasis on speaking fluent Chinese signifies the belief among the first generation that ethnic linguistic traditions must be maintained through effort, at both the individual and community levels.

The practice of ethnic tradition and heritage may reflect the emergence of pride among ethnic group members. Ethnic pride is considered a product of the political and cultural consciousness of the civil rights era.[41] An alternative trend emerged in the 1970s, however, among Asian Americans who identified with the majority group, denying their minority identity. Their goal was to be known as "American" rather than "Asian."[42] Rejection of the "Asian American" identity, choosing not to stand out, and being accommodating and acceptable to the majority group became a way of survival. Rejection of "Asianness" also relates to a sense of shame and stigma as a result of marginalization and "othering," which in turn renders Asianness a source of possible self-hatred. Since the 1970s, some fifty years on, Asians appear to feel less concern about their Asianness. In Fort Lee, Asians often expressed pride in their ethnic roots through their embrace of ethnonational identity. What accounts for such emerging attitudes?

This resurgence of ethnic pride relates to the growing numerical presence of Asians. It is also derived from visible socioeconomic success—especially in the local economy and the school system. Korean contributions to economic growth in Fort Lee are widely noted among residents of both Korean and non-Korean origin. One second-generation Korean male in his forties remarked how local Korean merchants have contributed to overall growth: "There's no question about it. I think, in that respect, Koreans are very cutting-edge . . . successful Koreans are so systematic and so methodical that they bring a new dimension to the creation of wealth, you know. It's a necessary ingredient. I think it bodes well for Koreans to come into Fort Lee. It's almost like new energy."

Social and economic success fuels a sense of pride in being "ethnic." And ethnic success can be extended to mean "Asian" success, in panethnic terms. Ethnic group pride is returned to the racialized category, offering a renewed meaning of "Asian." In a similar fashion, the academic success of students in the school system was expressed as "Asian"—not distinctly as Chinese, Japanese, or Korean. Ethnic pride is derived from the collateral contributions made by each East Asian group. One first-generation Chinese female in her thirties felt that the Asian presence had benefited Fort Lee's development:

> They [Americans] get some advantage, you know. They can see different people and different cultures, and they can taste different kinds of foods, they can shop different stuff. If I were them, I would appreciate it. They should take advantage of this kind of whole different background . . . if there's no Asian population . . . I don't think Fort Lee will be the same town, right? It's gonna be a different town.
>
> NM: How do you think it would be without Asians?
>
> They're probably gonna be a boring small town. With little stores here and there, like old stores. . . . I was driving the other day in a town . . . It's in west New Jersey. It's an old township . . . there's no Asian people. . . . It's just so different. It's so simple, [such an] old-fashioned town. So that's why I really think if Korean people, or Chinese people, or Japanese people are not here, the town will be completely different in Fort Lee. You can see on Main Street there's lots of business, shops, owned by Koreans and Chinese, mainly Koreans. . . . They are building a different fashion, they have their own style, they have their own kind of business style. I think it's really lovely; I mean, you can see all different kinds of stuff. And that will bring competitors in to compete. That's how the town starts booming, right? If you don't have competition, who cares? I can sell bagels every day, [and] people come here and drop by and buy my bagels because there's no other place to go. Here you have a Korean coffee shop, they have bread in the Japanese

> bakery, they have different bread, cakes, and that's competition, you know? And that's ideas. If there's no competition, people don't think about new ideas. So I think it's a good thing for the whole town.

The meaning of Asianness becomes a factor in both individual and group pride. Positive traits such as business or scholastic achievements were evaluated as "Asian" rather than "ethnic" by informants. Place is important in this development. Being part of a multiethnic suburban community to which they have made a major contribution has brought confidence to Asians of different national origins in Fort Lee.

NORMALIZING ETHNIC DIFFERENCE IN A MULTIETHNIC SUBURB

The shared meaning of ethnicity reflects a given social milieu. The conditions under which the meanings of ethnicity develop in Fort Lee are those of a multiethnic suburb. How does such a demographic configuration influence ethnicity and "Asianness"?

In the view of East Asian residents, Fort Lee is diverse, through and through. The ways in which this is handled at the community level is positively evaluated by East Asians. One Korean American male in his thirties remarked, "This town is actually mature enough race relations-wise, at this point. On the individual level, you never know. But on the community level, we understand that diversity is not a disadvantage." Although Koreans are by far the largest ethnic minority group in Fort Lee, "it's not just that it's all Korean," as one second-generation Chinese male put it. Asian residents acknowledge not only the presence of East Asians but also the increasing number of non-East Asian ethnic groups in Fort Lee—including Hispanics, Middle Easterners, Russians, and South Asians.[43] The ethnic and racial diversity of Fort Lee has produced a milieu that can be considered a "cosmopolitan canopy"—a "pluralistic space" promoting peaceful relations, where people feel at ease with "difference" and where they gain from the experience of encounters with racial and ethnic "others."[44] For instance, customers of diverse races (Asians, Hispanics, and whites) are a common sight at Asian-owned bakeries—having coffee, reading papers, chatting with friends—characterized by civility and urban indifference to "difference."

School is the nexus where diversity is most salient.[45] One 1.5-generation Korean female, who belonged to a cheerleading squad in high school (1999–2003) recalled the multicultural characteristics of her group—"We weren't like typical blonde-haired, blue-eyed cheerleaders." A Chinese mother with a daughter in the high school recalled her daughter's exaggerated comment that "you cannot find a white person at Fort Lee High School" to emphasize the overwhelming presence of nonwhite students. A Chinese father whose child is enrolled in Fort Lee's public school remarked that he was happy with the diversity of Fort Lee, because his child "does not feel he's a minority." "Difference" as a premise within social space helps ethnic minorities become legitimate members of the community. A 1.5-generation Korean female whose daughter was attending Fort Lee High School at the time of our interview related the following anecdote:

> We were talking one day, you know, "So-and-so moved from Wyckoff," and I said, "The person is doing so well here [, better] than while that person was in Wyckoff." And she says, "Mom, in Fort Lee school, you can have three eyes and nobody would care." You know? [*laughs*] So it doesn't matter who you are, because they are so used to so many different ethnicities and different groups of people in and out . . . that's how she put it: You could have three eyes and nobody will really care. They'll accept you as you are. So that's Fort Lee.

Being "atypical" is validated in the context of Fort Lee. Being ethnic and being different is normalized where existing differences are rarely questioned but are taken for granted in everyday life.

While Asians generally appreciate and find comfort in diversity, plurality has produced unintended consequences for some. At Fort Lee elementary schools, children pick up languages other than English from friends with diverse backgrounds. Although this may be viewed as a unique by-product of diversity, foreign-born parents who are struggling to inculcate the ancestral language at home feel challenged by such a trend. Several Asian parents with elementary school–aged children commented on how their children come home and speak the Korean they have picked up from friends at school. One Chinese mother expressed her dismay: "Sometimes my children would get confused. When they come home, they speak Korean to me. They learn from Koreans [friends]. Sometimes I would say, 'Oh, I wish you spoke some Chinese.' And my son would say to me, 'I'd rather die.' You know, I'm not happy about that."

For youth in particular, the case of Fort Lee resembles New York City, where immigrant children do not regularly encounter a white majority but instead coethnic or other ethnic minority groups. How do such conditions influence processes of identity formation? Studies of second-generation youth in New York have found that self-formation cannot be fully explained by concepts of subordination or resistance to the mainstream white majority.[46] Second-generation youth encounter ethnic and racial minorities having only limited encounters with native whites in the city. Race and ethnicity are shaped by majority minority youth—the cultures they bring and re-create.[47] Immigrant children growing up in a multiethnic community develop their identity in relation not only to the mainstream but also to ethnic minority members. The integration of the second generation is occurring in environments where ethnic retention remains possible.

Under these conditions, Asians may not necessarily follow the notion of whiteness as the social norm of aspiration. Tomás Jiménez and Adam Horowitz argue that recent Asian immigrant populations, when they exist in large and concentrated numbers and are of high socioeconomic status, have changed the meanings of existing ethnoracial categories, because they provide the social norm for the native population.[48] The white superordinate position remains firm in American society, and Asians have not overturned this structural position in Fort Lee, yet this does not automatically signify subordinate status for Asians. The case of Fort Lee problematizes characterization based on the "majority-minority paradigm" and offers a vantage point for the reconsideration of group relations. East Asians with relative privilege defy the conventional notion of a minority group being necessarily disadvantaged.[49] Asians in Fort Lee have contributed to redefining and remaking the local context. While doing so, they have challenged the meaning of "Asianness." As Linda Võ has argued, Asians today are in a unique position in facing contradictory designations as at once an "oppressed" and a "privileged" minority.[50] While Asians are unable to avoid racialization, they have nevertheless attempted to self-define what it means to be Asian, defending their own identity of choice.

ASIAN IDENTITY AND IDENTITY OF PLACE

Ethnic identity is continuously negotiated among Asian group members and represents a dynamic process. Different identities can overlap, and social actors do shift the ways they identify themselves. For East Asians in Fort Lee, being "Asian" is inseparable from comparative perceptions regarding what it is to be "American"—the latter perceived as an identity that is antithetical for East Asians, who are not "white." Among many individuals of East Asian origin in Fort Lee, ethnicity remains dominant in self-identification, even among established residents who have been living in the United States for many years. At the same time, in some cases, ethnonational identity and "Asian" identity are compatible. While the importance of ethnic identification remains, U.S.-born immigrant children increasingly identify themselves as "American." The strong tendency to identify with ethnonational origin among informants relates to the absence of pan-Asian associative relations. In Fort Lee, a residential concentration of different immigrant groups has not produced a formal panethnic coalition due to the absence of shared political goals.

Despite the general absence of self-identification as "Asian" among my informants, the idea of race tacitly plays a role in their choice of residence. East Asian residents have selected their "place" in the United States guided by the notion of race: being in proximity to "Asians" is important—even if these may not be coethnics. Perceived native tolerance toward diversity has also been a factor. Although the choice of residence appears to be volitional and contingent on resources, it has been based on a fear of racial tension, antagonism, and the awareness of possible exclusion. Even though East Asians may be socioeconomically "assimilated," they feel they are not fully accepted as Americans. In distinction to the mainstream, the racialized notion of self remains.

At the same time, however, being "Asian" can be a source of pride and confidence. For Asians, Fort Lee is a place where "Asianness" is normalized. The specific local conditions—in this case, the growing presence of Asians—render the notion of "difference" and being "ethnic" a normal part of everyday experience. This appears compatible with the prevailing view of Asians as the "other" among established whites.

Dolores Hayden has argued for the centrality of "place" for minority identity and solidarity. Investment in place can empower marginalized ethnoracial groups.[51] The Vietnamese in the suburbs of California, for example, use place as an anchor of identity through which to strengthen community.[52] Similarly, East Asians are creating and reshaping the suburban landscape of Fort Lee—materially and socially. Through this process of place-making, Asians are becoming "American."[53] The multiethnic suburb offers a way of forging new identities—both ethnic and American. Place, in other words, helps affirm identity for minority groups, and demographic and cultural diversity plays a significant role in such affirmation.

Identity is provisional and negotiable—never secured permanently nor carved in stone. East Asians are assimilating in some ways, maintaining ethnicity in other ways, and creating panethnicity in yet others. Ethnoracial identity, particularly among the first generation, remains firm, but this does not mean that actors do not shift the ways they identify themselves. Individuals may also choose from an array of identities depending on perceived strategic utility. Identity is dialectical and structured in relation to others. To understand the meaning of "Asianness" in the contemporary multiethnic suburb, it is necessary to consider the local context. And this context is increasingly diverse and pluralist.

CONCLUSION

Reconsidering Assimilation and Ethnicity in the American Suburb

During the several years that have elapsed since the completion of this research, the rapid pace of social and economic transformation has continued in Fort Lee. The view of the borough from Manhattan has changed dramatically. The redevelopment discussed previously (chapter 1) has been under way since 2012 (figure 6). The smooth, dark-blue reflective tower of "The Modern"—a luxury apartment building, forty-seven stories high—now stands adjacent to the George Washington Bridge, soaring above the existing high-rise buildings atop the Palisades. The redevelopment site on the eastern half of the sixteen-acre plot, is being developed by SJP Properties in partnership with the Northwestern Mutual Life Insurance Company and Prudential Real Estate Investors. The residential tower opened to prospective tenants in September 2014. As of this writing, a second, identical glass tower is being constructed adjacently. Together, the two towers will contain nine hundred rental units. The site will have a two-acre public park, including a restaurant, a public theater, and a museum devoted to the history of film in Fort Lee.[1]

On the other eight-acre western parcel, an upscale, multiuse complex named "Hudson Lights" is being developed by Illinois-based Tucker Development Corporation, in partnership with the Kushner Real Estate Group. Hudson Lights, "a mixed-use development in excess of one million square feet," features 276 residential units, a 175-room hotel, and roughly two hundred thousand square feet of retail and restaurant space.[2] Where once was an empty tract of wild grass and rubble, there now stands a surface of fresh concrete, with brand-new street furnishings—benches and planters with flowers and trees around a spacious, fresh green lawn. Sidewalks have been renovated—widened and finished. A movie theater, the first in Fort Lee in sixty years—part of the Hudson Lights complex—was opened in August 2016.[3]

FIGURE 6. Redevelopment Area 5, Fort Lee, from Lemoine Avenue, 2017. Author photo.

Main Street has gained many new stores and restaurants, some having replaced older ones. The downtown area has acquired a new brightness and elegance, owed to the fresh appearance of the many recent establishments and renovated sidewalks with trees and potted plants (figure 7). The Business District Alliance was formed early in 2014 as part of the ongoing municipal projects, to revitalize and enhance the Main Street shopping corridor. The initiative was implemented in anticipation of increased customer traffic due to Redevelopment Area 5, which occupies the land between the bridge and Main Street. The Alliance expects that the redevelopment will help revitalize businesses on Main Street and that Main will be part of the resurgence of Fort Lee.[4] Off Main Street, the construction of a twenty-million-dollar parking deck is planned, with more than five hundred parking spaces and a refurbished post office. A fifteen-story rental building with 140 units, half of which are for low-income residents, will also be built off Main. Such developments have involved consideration of demolition and rebuilding projects for several existing buildings.[5] Notwithstanding concerns among some residents regarding the likely aggravation of existing traffic congestion, the pace of urbanization seems to be hastening.

On Main Street and elsewhere, Korean business continues to emerge. The new Asian-owned stores in the downtown area display bilingual signage in which English is prominent. South Asians, Latinos, and African Americans are

FIGURE 7. Main Street, looking west, 2017. Author photo.

more noticeable in pedestrian traffic in the town. Photographs accompanying community and school events reported in the local weekly, the *Fort Lee Suburbanite* (renamed *Gold Coast Life* in November 2016) include Latino children along with Asians more frequently than before. As discussed in foregoing chapters, ethnoracial diversity in the school system has continued to grow. Reflecting the growth of the minority populations, young Asians are more frequently seen interacting with their black or Latino friends. In the political sphere, one Korean American male was elected borough council member in 2014, the first Asian American to serve on Fort Lee's council—a hard-won achievement for the Korean community, which has long sought representation on the central political body of the borough. As of this writing, there are two Korean American council members. The image of Fort Lee today reinforces contemporary notions of the American suburb as a "work-in-progress."

The case opens onto a wider critical consideration of the meanings of assimilation and ethnicity during a period of significant change in the American suburb. This book has considered key sociological questions raised by the formation of a multiethnic place—the construction of immigrant communities, group relations, how the specific local context may affect assimilation, and the meaning of ethnicity and race for Asian immigrants and their offspring. The suburbanization of immigrants in the United States has traditionally been considered the way in which newcomers become "American." More recently, ethnic continuity in the suburbs has problematized this assumption. Metropolitan suburbs in the United States are increasingly homes to nonwhite ethnic groups. Rather than dissolving ethnicity, the spatial dispersion beyond the city has been accompanied by new ethnic concentrations at suburban locations of immigrant choice.

The numerous ethnic businesses, services, and organizations that have been established in Fort Lee serve to fulfill the practical needs of immigrants—they provide for the sustenance of ethnic heritage and offer coethnic support. They also play a crucial role in cultural transmission for newer generations through the maintenance of ethnic-based activities, events, and festivals. Urban sociologist Jan Lin has described how immigrant flows have resulted in a renewal of the urban economy and cultural spaces in the United States. Such transformations, largely since the 1980s, have in some cases involved the revalorization of social space by transnational capital investment. Ethnic enterprise has played a role in revivifying retail districts, not only in central cities, but also in suburban community corridors.[6] Lin refers to such spatial development as that of "ethnic places"—where ethnic actors play a significant part.[7] As can be seen in Fort Lee, a suburban "ethnic place" has grown from the accumulation of successive waves of Asian, predominantly Korean, immigration.

Settlements of professional, middle-class immigrants in the suburbs are a reflection of the global transformations of our time, including world economic restructuring, the demand for highly skilled labor in the American market, and structures of opportunity in the urban and suburban economy. In effect, Fort Lee has come to represent the kind of transnational space that, according to one contemporary scholar, "constitute[s] and convey[s] broader processes of economic and cultural globalization."[8] The Chinese, Japanese, and Korean communities of Fort Lee that have emerged through these processes have remained distinct in form, organization, and structure. Coethnic networks remain important for many residents of East Asian origin in Fort Lee who are largely foreign-born and without need for the aid of a formal pan-Asian grouping. But at the same time, these "communities" are coterminous, multiple, ethnic bodies that fuse, mix, and intersect. In actuality, ethnic suburban communities are in flux. The fluidity and conjunctures of the Asian communities of Fort Lee suggest a suburb composed of complex, novel ethnic interconnections in ways that differ, for example, from the monolithic model of the "ethnoburb."

East Asian groups have reached out to the local white community in Fort Lee rather than remaining entirely insular. Asian organizations and grassroots groups with the mission of ethnic maintenance have been communicating with native whites, even if on a limited basis. Both Japanese and Korean communities have volunteered and raised funds for the local community. In particular, recent self-identification of the Korean American community as part of the wider Fort

Lee community (rather than as a "new Seoul"), along with practices of increasing community involvement, are manifestations, by Koreans, of willingness for integration.

At our present juncture, how are the processes of assimilation and ethnic retention being negotiated? Both processes are integral to the everyday practices of social actors. On the one hand, East Asians indicate a desire for recognition by the mainstream. The second generation's immersion in American suburban experience—the English language, the education system, work, and social relationships—is evident. On the other hand, Asians engage in ethnic practices to maintain ethnic identity and to inculcate cultural heritage among U.S.-born offspring. In the multiethnic environment of Fort Lee, Asian immigrants are oriented neither solely toward ethnic retention nor toward resistance to assimilation. Ethnic practice does not rule out the process of assimilation. Conscious preservation of ethnicity, paradoxically, may function as a channel for contact with the mainstream and the attainment of local recognition. The intention to assimilate and yet to retain ethnicity was not viewed by informants as contradictory. Asians in Fort Lee engage in both practices with flexibility and creativeness.

The consideration of the everyday practices of social actors in a multiethnic suburban community is crucial for gauging the adaptation, intergroup relations, and influence of immigration on the host society. These are the products of processes that are neither entirely conscious nor unconscious but are rooted in an ongoing dialectic of learning.[9] For the most part, a practice is developed without conscious deliberation—but it is not without purpose. Social actors have goals and interests in locating the sources of their practices in their own experiences of reality. Social situations are infinitely varied, never completely identical, and require that actors have a "strategy"—a "permanent capacity for invention."[10] Assimilation is effectively promoted "when it has resulted from the choices of the individuals undergoing it, as part of a strategy intended to improve their own life chances or those of their children."[11]

This study has argued for the understanding that immigrant assimilation, ethnic retention, and community belonging need to be considered in relation to native responses to immigration. As the local economy, politics, school system, and other institutions have been transformed by the influx of East Asians and significant demographic shifts, so have the experiences of native whites. Encounters with East Asian immigrants in various domains of everyday life have often produced ambivalent attitudes, ranging from resistance to acceptance.[12] Local white leaders have shown a willingness to accommodate and work together with immigrant communities. Such acceptance is based in part on the perceived benefits that Asian immigrants bring: improvement of the school district and development of the local economy rendered possible by the influx and growth of

Asian business capital. Ethnic entrepreneurship has clearly served the economic aims of municipal governance.[13]

Apparent native tolerance and acceptance, however, should be interpreted with caution. While borough leaders may espouse an ethos of diversity, East Asians have not always been received favorably by the locals. Asians remain "others" in the eyes of native white residents. And after more than forty years of coresidence, Asians are still viewed by some as insular and even in hostile terms, as an "Asian invasion." Native perceptions of an Asian "takeover" are indicative of a sense of threat to comfort within the local space, toward which whites maintain a strong proprietary sense. And while immigrant entrepreneurship has buoyed up the local economy, such ethnic businesses are simultaneously seen by established whites as a source of divisiveness within the community. A general lack of patronage of Korean retail business by established whites expresses vestiges of the resistance toward the "unfamiliar." Such resistance still divides Fort Lee along ethnic boundaries.

Serious intergroup confrontation has not, however, occurred in Fort Lee. The seeming harmony is a product of local proclivity for avoidance of open confrontation, without interference in other residents' lives—a tendency among residents to "keep to themselves." The relationships between immigrants and natives, however, are neither unilateral nor static. The large and concentrated Korean presence may meet stronger opposition from natives than that displayed toward the Chinese (more geographically dispersed) or the Japanese (transient and smaller in number than Koreans). Even so, Koreans are ultimately viewed by whites as "becoming American."

Fort Lee's ethnoracial diversity has become a normalized feature of social life. As urban space becomes multiethnic and cross-ethnic interaction becomes common, ethnic difference becomes unremarkable and taken for granted. In contemporary urban settings, such "conviviality" relates to the lived experience of multiculture, where racial difference is legitimated. *Conviviality* and the concept of *cosmopolitan canopy*, while they do not claim "the absence of racism or the triumph of tolerance," nevertheless point to "processes of cohabitation and interaction" that make diversity and "living with difference" an ordinary feature of social life.[14] As diversity becomes part of the normalized life of the community, residents develop habitual familiarity with difference through the "civil virtues" of multiethnic life.[15]

Social milieu is of crucial importance for the present discussion. The history and the contemporary characteristics of the locality affect attitudes toward immigrants and immigrant outcomes. Proximity to New York City—one of the most racially diverse metropolitan regions in the United States—the preexisting diversity of Fort Lee, the propensity to economic growth, its urban character, its function as a bedroom community for commuters, and the transience of its population have shaped this locale's susceptibility to the formation of multiethnic communities. And for Asians, the perception of racial tolerance and receptiveness in Fort Lee, even where mythic, has been an important consideration in their choice of residence. Similarly, the social class positions of both immigrant and host are significant for relations between the various ethnoracial groups. Relative class parity between established residents and newcomers has helped ease the accommodation of the latter. On the other hand, perceived affluence among Asians may remain a source of hostility and resentment for some native residents.

The meanings of "ethnic" and/or "American" are constantly negotiated over time and remain in flux for many East Asians in Fort Lee. The meaning of "Asianness" is undergoing transformation. Being Asian in Fort Lee today provides a renewed sense of pride in ethnic roots. At the same time, viewing themselves as "nonwhite," Asians tend to feel restricted in identifying themselves as unhyphenated "Americans." Relative freedom and autonomy in the selection of ethnic identity among middle-class Asian immigrants and their children do not preclude the possibility of racialization. Privileged class status may serve to ease acceptance by the white community, but this does not entirely override race.

Indeed, although tacit, "race" has been a significant factor in the choice of residence for Asians and their convergence in Fort Lee. Notwithstanding the absence of pan-Asian affinity, East Asian residents generally find "comfort" in this borough, which is in itself indicative of the continuing relevance of "race." Residence in Fort Lee is a purposeful and pragmatic achievement, overdetermined by the possibility of negative social reactions that may exist elsewhere.

Race and ethnicity play an essential role in the social definition of space. Ethnoracial minorities in the United States have made and remade ethnic places by endowing them with social and cultural meanings, which in turn have empowered minorities.[16] Landscapes are linked with ideological formations, with systems of power, and sets of social relations. The suburban landscape offers an important source of identity and a sense of security for its inhabitants. As has been observed in California among the Vietnamese of Orange County, the size and affluence of an ethnic group can provide the basis for the maintenance of ethnicity, which, at the same time, transforms social space.[17] Suburban society is not a given but is constructed and reconstructed through material and discursive operations—processes in which ethnoracial minorities increasingly participate.

Ethnic pride among many East Asian residents of Fort Lee has been gained through their participation in the creation of an ethnic suburb and their sense of belonging to this "place." With resources, Asians have exercised leverage in the social space. Although considered, from the established residents' view, as a threat to collective norms and identities, immigrants, within the context of their remaking of the suburb, are unquestionably becoming "American."[18]

As will have been apparent throughout this study, assimilation, together with ethnic retention, stands in need of reconsideration from multiple perspectives as social processes that are relational and concurrent. Through their lived experiences, both immigrants and natives engage in processes of adjustment to changing cultural contexts. In Fort Lee, Asian immigrants and their offspring—especially Koreans—feel at home, and the community is moving in the general direction of accommodation. Such relations are contingent on flexible social power (modulated by social class and resources) as opposed to fixity within a dominant-subordinate paradigm. Assimilation, in this sense, is a dialectical process between immigrant and host and involves the negotiation of group inclusion and exclusion.

It seems that in light of the anticipated "resurgence" and urbanization of Fort Lee, the borough's diversity will continue to flourish, including the Asian communities along with other minority groups such as Latinos. Expanding Korean business portends the continuity of the Korean American community and its rootedness in Fort Lee. Korean business owners are actively involved in the redevelopment as tenants and in opening new retail stores in the project of Hudson Lights. Unlike other ethnic suburbs, however, Asian or foreign investment has been absent from Redevelopment Area 5. Capital has been provided entirely by mainstream American corporate enterprises. On the other hand, Chinese investment in American suburban development has been observed at other locations in New Jersey.[19] Fort Lee may yet witness increased Asian investment in the future. One such sign is a hotel project in Fort Lee (separate from Redevelopment Area 5) proposed by a local Korean American investor with the aim of soliciting at least forty million dollars from foreign investors, primarily Chinese.[20] Future investments in Redevelopment Area 5 by Asian developers, both within and outside Fort Lee, are considered a highly likely possibility.[21] Growing diversity in the borough will also likely lead to greater minority visibility and representation in the political sphere.

It has been stated that one of the foremost purposes of sociology is "to explain a present reality that is near to us and thus capable of affecting our ideas and actions."[22] In our present study, the social reality at issue is human mobility. As an essential component of social change, international migration is one of the keys to the contemporary flux in American society. Examination of the East Asian immigrant communities of Fort Lee reveals the interdependence of local contexts and global transformations. Attempts to understand contemporary social life need to be rooted also in attention to historicity. During a time of major global change, the case of Fort Lee helps in our understanding of the growing multiethnic suburbs and the social responses attendant on these transformations. Our understanding of social processes is predicated on a constant modification of knowledge and changing social realities. The present research is but one case study within wider patterns of social organization and reflects the specific conditions of a New York metropolitan suburb in its spatial and historical development. As such, our analysis does not presuppose inevitable or easily predicted outcomes. Fort Lee today is nevertheless indicative, for all its specificity, of a contemporary suburban dynamism—a social development that embodies continuous re-creation and heterogeneity.

ACKNOWLEDGMENTS

During the course of research and writing, I have depended on the assistance and cooperation of many individuals and institutions. I should like to extend thanks, through an expression of general gratitude, to all those who have aided me in this work.

Although confidentiality precludes mention of names, I warmly thank my informants, who generously provided their time and helped in this research in myriad ways. I am deeply grateful for the cooperation I have received from several institutions and their respective staffs, in particular the Fort Lee Film Commission, Fort Lee Museum, Fort Lee Public Library, Fort Lee Regional Chamber of Commerce, the mayor's office of the Borough of Fort Lee, and the Richard A. Nest Senior Citizens' Center. Special thanks also to Mina Yoshigaki, president of the Japanese-American Society of New Jersey and to my Korean teacher, Seung Mee Yoo.

This work began as a doctoral thesis in sociology at the Graduate School and University Center, City University of New York. My greatest debt is to my dissertation advisor, Philip Kasinitz. Paul Attewell and Nancy Foner have offered many useful comments and suggestions. The dissertation committee has remained a source of continuous support, guidance, and encouragement for which I am most grateful.

Vilna Bashi-Treitler inspired my interest in the sociology of race during the early phase of my graduate studies at Rutgers University, for which I am deeply appreciative. I warmly thank Vilna, Richard Alba, and members of the Immigration Working Group at the Graduate Center for their valuable feedback on an earlier version of one of the chapters. Tarry Hum has been generous and has offered invaluable suggestions. I thank Joseph Pereira, director of CUNY Data Service of the Center for Urban Research at the Graduate Center, for advice regarding PUMS data. Keumjae Park kindly gave her time to discuss the project with me and offered encouragement. I am grateful for her advice on immigration and the Korean population of Bergen County.

Encouragement and criticism from friends and colleagues in graduate school and beyond have been of great help. I thank Yi Chen, Paoyi Huang, Naoko Kumagai, Yoko Ikeda, Youngmi Lim, Wei-Ting Lu, Yoshio Shibata, and Peiti Wang for their feedback and collegiality. Miyuki Akasaka, Jong-Hee Ko, Frances Leu, Michael Sharpe, and Miho Sharpe deserve special thanks; I warmly thank them for their friendship and help.

I offer thanks for the collegiality I have received while teaching at the University of Vermont. Dale Jaffe, chair of sociology, has been a constant source of support and encouragement. I am thankful to Alice Fothergill, Jinny Huh, Kyle Ikeda, Nikki Khana, Beth Mintz, and Tom Streeter, for their collegiality and advice. Warm thanks to Salli Griggs for administrative help and friendly support. I also acknowledge the College of Arts and Sciences at the University of Vermont for the Small Grant Research Award in support of the publication of this book.

I have been fortunate to work with an excellent team of professionals at Rutgers University Press. I thank Peter Mickulas for his guidance in the production of this publication. The anonymous reviewers provided valuable feedback to help refine the manuscript. Many thanks to Sam Martin for her expertise in the copyediting of the manuscript. I am grateful to Michael Siegel for design of the map for this publication.

I thank my friends, both near and far, for their enduring support and inspiration, in particular Mami Yamashita for her unwavering friendship over many years. Warm thanks to Lorraine Beitler, Lewis Kachur, Norman Kleeblatt, and Peter Prescott for their kindness and friendship. My appreciation to my family is warm and deep: to them, I offer profound gratitude. Finally, I acknowledge Stephen Brown, my intellectual and life partner. For his abiding belief, support, and encouragement, I express my deepest thanks. Although my intellectual debts are immeasurable, all errors remain the author's sole responsibility.

NOTES

INTRODUCTION

1. Shavick 1972.

2. Howe 1986; Lynwander 1982; Maitland 1976. The *Record*, the local daily of Bergen County, ran a series during this period based on interviews with Japanese families, corporate executives, and educators in northern New Jersey (Reed 1988a, 1988b, 1988c). See also Chollet 1993.

3. The Hart-Celler Act abolished the restrictive immigration laws based on national origin quota systems, which had been in place since 1924. The Immigration Act of 1924 had banned immigration from Asia and curtailed immigration from Southern and Eastern Europe. Visas for permanent residence were distributed according to the ethnic composition of the U.S. population—thus favoring immigrants of Northern and Western European origin.

4. Waters and Gerstein Pineau 2015.

5. Nicolaides and Wiese 2006.

6. Frey 2011.

7. "New destination" is used by Massey (2008) and "new gateway" suburbs is developed in Singer, Hardwick, and Brettell (2008). The increasing diversity of settlement patterns is "inextricably bound up with the growing volume of immigration" (Massey 2008, 3). Increasing immigrant dispersion into "new destinations"—small and medium size towns throughout the United States—has been attributed to saturation of the traditional gateway cities and large-scale industrial restructuring (Massey 2008). See also Foner 2005; Fong 1994; Li 1998, 2006; Logan 2001; Singer, Hardwick, and Brettell 2008; Water and Jiménez 2005.

8. Archer, Sandul, and Solomonson 2015; Nicolaides and Wiese 2006; Singer, Hardwick, and Brettell 2008.

9. Martin 2001.

10. U.S. Bureau of the Census 2010. Asian Indians accounted for 40.3 percent of the total Asian population in New Jersey in 2010 and are concentrated in Middlesex and Hudson counties. Chinese were the second largest and constituted 18.5 percent of the Asian population in New Jersey; the largest number reside in Middlesex County (Wu 2012). Fort Lee and its vicinity thus show an immigrant demographic pattern that differs from state-wide trends.

11. Most and Kane 1999; U.S. Bureau of the Census 1983, 1992a.

12. U.S. Bureau of the Census 1973.

13. Oh 2007.

14. *Record (Hackensack, N.J.)* 2001.

15. In 2000, Italians continued to make up the largest ethnic group among whites, though at a decreased level compared to previous decades (11.4 percent), followed by Russians (7.8 percent) and Irish (4.8 percent).

16. See Kim (2003) and Hsu (2007) for media reports, although scholarly work on this trend is lacking.

17. U.S. Bureau of the Census 2015. The figures are for the "Asian alone" and "non-Hispanic white alone" groups. The median household incomes reported are in inflation-adjusted 2015 dollars.

18. U.S. Bureau of the Census 2015.

19. U.S. Bureau of the Census 1972, 2000.
20. U.S. Bureau of the Census 2015.
21. Marcus 1997, 242.
22. See also Portes and Zhou (1993) on the argument for the benefits of spatial separation, characteristic of the enclave, for immigrants.
23. Alba and Nee 1997.
24. Massey 1985. The theory is rooted in the Chicago School's ecological tradition (e.g., the work of Robert Park), which considered the spatial distribution of groups a reflection of their human capital and state of assimilation.
25. Massey and Denton 1985.
26. See Alba, Denton, Leung, and Logan 1995; Alba and Logan 1991; Alba, Logan, and Crowder 1997; Alba, Logan, Stults, Marzan, and Zhang 1999; Allen and Turner 1996; Fong and Wilkes 1999; Frey 1995; Hwang and Murdock 1998; Logan, Alba, and Zhang 2002; Myles and Hou 2004; Skop and Li 2005; Waters and Jiménez 2005.
27. Alba and Logan 1991; Hwang and Murdock 1998.
28. Massey and Denton 1987, 1988; Phelan and Schneider 1996.
29. For complexities of residential distribution among Asians, see Frey and Myers 2005; Kim and White 2010; Palen 1995.
30. Logan, Alba, and Zhang 2002, 299.
31. Alba and Logan 1993; Alba, Logan, Stults, Marzan, and Zhang 1999; Allen and Turner 1996; Kwong and Miščević 2005; Le 2007; Li 1998, 2006; Logan, Alba, and Zhang 2002; Min 2006; O'Hare and Frey 1994; Skop and Li 2005; Zhou and Kim 2003.
32. Li 1998, 482. The first ethnoburb to gain national prominence was that of the Chinese community in northeastern Los Angeles County in the San Gabriel Valley (Fong 1994; Li 1997, 1998, 1999, 2006; Mydans 1994). Other suburban Asian communities have also been identified—for example, the "postsuburban" communities of Koreatown and Little Saigon in Orange County, California (Võ and Danico 2004), and the Asian communities of New York/northern New Jersey (Le 2007; Zhou and Kim 2003).
33. The concept of "suburban Chinatown" is developed in Fong (1994).
34. Li 1998, 484.
35. Kwong 2007.
36. Li 1998, 2009; Zhou 2009.
37. Zelinsky and Lee 1998, 293.
38. Ling 2009; Zeng and Li 2009.
39. Zhou and Li 2003.
40. Li 2005, 37.
41. Kwong and Miščević 2005, 356.
42. Li 2005, 38.
43. Cheng 2013; Fong 1994; Horton 1995; Li 2009; Saito 1998.
44. See Aguilar-San Juan (2005) on Vietnamese Americans in Orange County, California.
45. Cheng 2013; Horton 1995. Indeed, Asian Americans, along with Mexican Americans, have a long history of settlement in the area dating back to the early twentieth century.
46. By the late 1990s, Monterey Park was the only city in the United States, except Hawaii, with a majority Asian population (57 percent). In 2010, Asians constituted 67 percent of the population. Chinese were the overwhelming majority among Asians, at 47.9 percent (U.S. Bureau of the Census 2010).
47. Kalita's monograph (2003) is the only published study, and it treats Asian Indians specifically. Previous research on East Asian groups in Fort Lee has focused on the adaptation of

Japanese expatriate wives to life in the United States (Flory 1989; Kawai 2000; Shinkai 1994) and specific social aspects of Korean immigration (Ha 1988, on parental attitudes toward bilingual education in public school). Oh's study (2007) concerning relationships between spatial dispersion and ethnic linkages among Korean immigrants includes Fort Lee within a wider study of Bergen County. Others have mentioned Fort Lee in passing (McGlinn 2002; Min 2001, 2006). On the other hand, several monographs of Asian immigrant settlements in the outer boroughs of New York City exist, including Khandelwal (2002), Hum (2014), Sanjek (2000).

48. For accounts of native opposition to nonwhite newcomers in suburbia, see Horton 1995; Lung-Amam 2017; Mahler 1995. Espenshade (1997) notes the relatively smooth integration of immigrants in New Jersey compared with the nation as a whole—attributed to the fact that immigrants in New Jersey in general have a higher level of educational attainment, include a lower proportion of undocumented immigrants, and represent a more diverse immigrant population.

49. Jiménez and Horowitz 2013.

50. Võ 2004.

51. The phrase "suburban society" is found in Gans ([1967] 1982).

52. The breakdown for each group was as follows: Chinese (10: 4 men, 6 women); Japanese (14: 5 men, 9 women); Korean (15: 7 men, 8 women); whites (17: 8 men, 9 women).

Chinese informants were of various national origin: mainland China, Hong Kong, Malaysia, and Taiwan, as well as U.S.-born. Their ages ranged from early twenties to fifties; they were naturalized citizens, if not U.S.-born. All Chinese informants had received postsecondary education abroad or in the United States.

The majority of Japanese informants were permanent residents or naturalized U.S. citizens, along with several expatriates. Except for one third-generation Japanese American, all the Japanese informants were foreign-born, first-generation immigrants. Their levels of education varied from high school to graduate school (master's degree). Their ages ranged from early thirties to seventies.

The Korean informants were a mix of foreign-born and U.S.-born. While a few Korean informants were permanent residents, the majority were naturalized U.S. citizens. Their ages ranged from early twenties to fifties. Korean informants were typically university-educated, whether in Korea or in the United States, with a few holding an advanced degree (master's and doctorate).

The majority of white informants were natives of Fort Lee or adjoining boroughs or long-time residents of the area. Their ages ranged from early forties to early eighties. Their levels of education ranged from high school to doctorate; the majority had bachelor's degrees.

Interviews were primarily conducted in English. For Japanese-speaking informants, the interviews were conducted in Japanese (with one exception; the interviewee was fluent in English). Translations of the Japanese interviews are by the author unless otherwise specified. The interviews typically lasted from sixty to ninety minutes. Interview questions concerned the interviewees' immigration histories, their reasons for choosing Fort Lee for residence, and their range of everyday experiences—their neighborhoods, daily activities, friendships, political involvement, experiences concerning interracial and interethnic relationships, ethnic practices, and views on Fort Lee.

53. 5-Percent Public Use Microdata Sample (PUMS) from the census data (U.S. Bureau of the Census 2000a) was consulted in order to identify certain detailed characteristics by East Asian subgroup. The results presented in this book are based on weighted data. Since the PUMS data for Fort Lee alone was not extractable, the smallest geographical area was selected from PUMS subsets—Public Use Microdata Area: PUMA code 00303, which includes the boroughs of Cliffside Park, Edgewater, Fairview, Fort Lee, Leonia, Palisades Park, Ridgefield, and Ridgefield Park village. This dataset thus represents the general East Asian concentration in the vicinity. For further detail, see Matsumoto 2012.

CHAPTER 1 A TOWN OF IMMIGRANTS

1. U.S. Bureau of the Census 2010.
2. Mazur 1981.
3. Spehr 2004, 2.
4. Rockland 2008.
5. "Bridgegate," a political scandal that captured national media attention in 2013, may be considered symptomatic in this regard. The incident concerned alleged retribution by former allies of New Jersey's governor Chris Christie (term: 2010–2018) against the mayor of Fort Lee for declining to endorse the governor's reelection. The closure of lanes of the bridge caused major traffic jams in Fort Lee for a period of five days (Zernike 2016a, 2016b).
6. *Bergen News* 2008b.
7. Confirmed by comparison of historic photographs and current views of Fort Lee's downtown area. See also Bertram 2004, 62, 70.
8. *Bergen News* 2007a.
9. Verdon 2006.
10. The appearance of ads for Japanese-speaking assistants for Korean doctors of Fort Lee (in free Japanese papers circulated in the metropolitan New York area) may be indicative of an increase in Japanese clientele or recruitment of such a clientele.
11. Rossi 2008c.
12. Mazur 1981.
13. Mazur 1981.
14. The Jack Alter Fort Lee Community Center was opened in 2004. The center was named for the former mayor of Fort Lee (term: 1992–2007). During this research, the center was still relatively new, and residents spoke about the facility with a degree of excitement.
15. Zerubavel 2003.
16. Lévi-Strauss (1962) 1966.
17. The Museum was installed in the former residence of Judge Jimmy Moore (1886–1972) in 1999. Built in local bluestone in 1922, the building was on the verge of becoming a strip mall until the community banded together to preserve it (Kim 2009b). The museum is supported by donations and staffed by volunteers, often members of the Fort Lee Historical Society. For a brief biography of Judge Moore, see Meyers 2013.
18. On George Washington (1732–1799) and the local history of the American Revolution, see Leiby (1962) 1992.
19. Thomas Paine (1737–1809) published sixteen papers of political commentary between 1776 and 1783, known collectively as *The American Crisis*. See Meyers 2007, esp. 44.
20. Koszarski 2004.
21. Bertram 2004.
22. *New York Times* 1909.
23. Ferries and trolleys provided access to studios in Fort Lee from Manhattan, but increased traffic resulted in delays to filming schedules. Koszarski 2004.
24. Edmund McCormick, *Bergen Evening Record*, July 12, 1935, quoted in Koszarski 2004, 20.

25. Fort Lee Film Commission 2006. Fort Lee was also home to the Palisades Amusement Park (1897–1971) and a nightclub, The Riviera. Initially built in Coytesville, the club reopened in 1937 on the Palisades overlooking the Hudson. The panoramic view of the river, the George Washington Bridge, and the New York skyline attracted celebrities and bands for more than a decade—and also gambling and crime. The club was condemned by the State of New Jersey in 1953 in order to make way for the Palisades Interstate Parkway (Bertram 2004).

26. Construction began in May 1927, and the bridge was opened to traffic on October 25, 1931. The lower deck was added in 1962. The Swiss Othmar Ammann (1879–1965) was appointed master designer and chief engineer with Cass Gilbert (1859–1934) as architect. Ammann's idea for the uptown Hudson crossing was developed between 1923 and 1925, winning support from newly elected New Jersey governor George Silzer (1870–1940, term: 1923–1926). See Port Authority of New York and New Jersey website (http://www.panynj.gov) and Rockland 2008.

27. Due to economic constraints, the original intention to finish the steel towers with concrete and granite was canceled (Rockland 2008). See also Mazur 1981.

28. The celebrated French architect Le Corbusier's appreciation for the structure is often quoted: "The George Washington Bridge over the Hudson is the most beautiful bridge in the world . . . It is blessed. It is the only seat of grace in the disordered city." Le Corbusier (1937) 1947, 75.

29. Monument Park marks the location of the Colonial fort. The sculpture by Carl E. Tefft (1874–1951) shows a Continental soldier and drummer boy scaling the Palisades. See *New York Times* 1908 and Bertram 2004. The borough rededicated the monument for the 225th anniversary of the retreat in 2001 (Meyers 2007).

30. The murals in the post office were completed in 1941 by Henry Schnakenberg (1892–1970) for the Work Projects Administration. One of the murals depicts George Washington on the Palisades (Bertram 2004; author's observation).

31. The reenactment involves an encampment in Monument Park, artillery demonstrations, drill and musket firing, and maneuvers in Fort Lee Historic Park. The events are orchestrated by the Brigade of the American Revolution, a nonprofit, living history association (founded 1962). In Fort Lee, the reenactment is held on the weekend that falls closest to November 20 and receives wide local press coverage. See http://www.brigade.org.

32. Executive director of the Fort Lee Film Commission, personal interview, May 9, 2008.

33. Executive director of the Fort Lee Film Commission, personal interview.

34. Warner 1959, 133. For the discussion of the functions and meanings of symbolic life in a community in New England ("Yankee City"), see Warner 1959.

35. Hobbs and Stoops 2002; Nicolaides and Wiese 2006.

36. Fishman 1987; Muller 1981.

37. Muller 1997; Palen 1995.

38. Dobriner 1963.

39. See Gober 1989 and also Aguilar-San Juan 2005; Dobriner 1963; Gans 1962.

40. Mazur 1981.

41. Mazur 1981.

42. U.S. Bureau of the Census 1973.

43. U.S. Bureau of the Census 1952, 1962, 1973.

44. Friedman 1994.

45. Schwartz and Prosser 1977.

46. Mazur 1981.

47. U.S. Bureau of the Census 1952, 1962, 1983, 1993, 2000. See, for detail, Matsumoto 2012.

48. Fischel 2004.
49. Mazur 1981.
50. Daniels 1983.
51. Mazur 1981.
52. In 2000, Fort Lee's owner-occupied housing units numbered 9,301, or 53.3 percent, while renter-occupied housing units numbered 7,243, or 41.5 percent. By comparison, the proportion of owner-occupied housing units in Bergen County as a whole was 65.4 percent, whereas renter-occupied housing units were 31.9 percent in the same year. The percentage of vacant housing units for Bergen County was 2.6. The percentages computed here include vacant units. U.S. Bureau of the Census 2000b.
53. U.S. Bureau of the Census 1953, 1962, 1972, 1982, 1992b.
54. Oser 1981.
55. Massey, Albright, Casciano, Derickson, and Kinsey 2013.
56. U.S. Bureau of the Census 2012, 2014. The number of all firms in Fort Lee for 2012 was 5,539 (U.S. Bureau of the Census 2012). According to the Census Bureau, this data includes both firms that employ staff and those that do not. Data User Outreach and Education, Economy-Wide Statistics Division, U.S. Census Bureau, personal correspondence, December 5, 2016.
57. Glaberson 1992.
58. The demolished area was referred to as housing an "Italian" community by my informants, rather than "Italian American." It was noticeable throughout the research that white residents of Fort Lee frequently referred simply to ethnic origin—rather than making the conjunction with "American."
59. Collins 1980.
60. The second developer to purchase the property was the Helmsley, the largest real-estate developer in New York. See Firschein 2009.
61. Estimates in the media varied from seven hundred million to one billion dollars. See also Martin 2007.
62. Rossi 2008a, 2008b.
63. *Bergen News* 2008a.
64. Martin 2009.
65. *Bergen News* 2009; Firschein 2009.
66. One of the proposals represented a joint venture of local and Korean developers. Their project was titled "Amerea" (a portmanteau word joining *America* with *Korea.*). One presenter explained that the president of Cheongwon America, the Korean developer, had personally interviewed business owners to gain insight into local needs and expectations.
67. Fort Lee mayor Mark Sokolich, personal interview, December 3, 2009.
68. The theme of "return to a lost status" was recapitulated in various statements by Mayor Sokolich. Quoted in Almenas 2008b; Sokolich, personal interview.
69. See conclusion of this work, below.
70. Garreau ([1991] 1992) has characterized Fort Lee as an "edge city"—a "new mix of urbanity" along with other towns in New Jersey that underwent rapid development in the 1980s.
71. Mazur 1981, 89.

CHAPTER 2 COMMUNITY AND COMMUNITIES

1. Hum 2014.
2. Sandercock 2003.

3. Sandercock 2003.

4. Cohen 1985; Duncan and Duncan 2004; Elias and Scotson 1994; Gans (1967) 1982; Hayden (1995) 1997; Keller 2003. The influence of modernity and its impact on community and social solidarity are central themes of classical sociology and appear in the work of Émile Durkheim, Georg Simmel, Ferdinand Tönnies, and Max Weber, for example.

5. Trevor 1991.

6. Fang 1996.

7. Bonacich 1973; Cohen 1977; Mizukami 2007; Siu 1952.

8. Shepard 1972. See also Kusumoto and Murray 1989.

9. Alba, Logan, and Crowder 1997.

10. Ferretti 1972.

11. By 1970, Newark and Elizabeth represented the "world's largest container complex" (Levinson 2006, 235). Newark offered an ideal hub; its waterfront offered the space to marshal trucks and had access to nearby rail lines, with convenient connections to the New Jersey Turnpike (opened 1951).

12. Geist 1981. Today these include multinational corporations such as Panasonic (Secaucus), Sanyo (Little Ferry, Allendale), Sharp (Mahwah), Sony (Park Ridge), and Toshiba (Wayne).

13. Estimates based on membership of the Japanese-American Society of New Jersey (discussed in chapter 3) and the characteristics of Japanese clientele given by a Japanese realtor in Fort Lee.

14. Experienced, for example, by a government-subsidized Japanese school originally located in Flushing, Queens, from 1976 to 1992. It was in a largely blue-collar neighborhood, and anti-Japanese sentiment was overt, as one Japanese male informant recounted. After 1992, the school was divided and relocated to Greenwich, Connecticut, and Oakland, New Jersey. When the school sought new premises in Fairfield County, Connecticut, tensions continued despite efforts to blend in with the local community, composed largely of upper-class, white-collar residents.

15. Howe 1986. Established residents of Fort Lee whom I interviewed frequently remarked that "it was all Japanese before."

16. Muto 1985; Shinkai 1994.

17. Lynwander 1982.

18. Flory 1989; Hosler 1998; Shinkai 1994.

19. A similar residential pattern has been noted among Japanese expatriates in the suburbs of Melbourne, Australia (Mizukami 2007). Mizukami considers such settlement a new type of ethnic community contingent on globalization and distinct from other types of labor migration.

20. Cohen 1977; White 1998. Citing examples from Japanese expatriate communities in London and Düsseldorf, White (1998) argues for the consideration of such "non-racialized international migration groups" within the context of the theorization of urban ethnicity.

21. Mizukami 2007.

22. Flory 1989; Shinkai 1994.

23. Kurotani 2005.

24. Kim 1981; Min 1996.

25. Kim 1981; Yoon 1997.

26. Min 1996; Smith 1995.

27. Fasbach 2001.

28. U.S. Bureau of the Census 1983, 1992a. See also Martin 2004.

29. U.S. Bureau of the Census 2010. See also Pérez-Peña 2010.

30. Hanley 1999.
31. Those who can afford to buy more expensive homes often move from Palisades Park to places such as Edgewater. Some bring extended families while others move in "alone," as the first Koreans in a building or block (Martin 2004).
32. The comparison with Flushing, Queens, is of interest. Smith (1995) found that Asians were drawn to Flushing because of the presence of Asians and proximity to Manhattan, similar in this to Fort Lee. Asians also reported job availability as one of the advantages of Flushing, a factor never mentioned by my Korean informants in Fort Lee.
33. The period of the 1980s through 1990s saw the flourishing of a "new" urban middle class in Korea. New prosperity led to a decline in the migration of middle-class Koreans—immigration became less rewarding for them than previously. Lower-class Korean immigrants, on the other hand, saw a comparative advantage in immigration to the United States. See Ch'oe, Lee, and de Bary 2000; Kim 1981; Lett 1998; Min 1996; Yoon 1993.
34. Koo 2007; Ly 2005.
35. Sudol 2009.
36. Lee 2010; Ly 2005.
37. For discussion of the consequences of such household arrangements for family life, see Koo 2007; Lee and Koo 2006; Ly 2005.
38. Fasbach 2001.
39. The Korean American Association in Fort Lee is the major Korean ethnic organization in Fort Lee. See chapter 3.
40. Korea Daily 2009, 2016. According to the census, the number of minority-owned firms in Fort Lee, including those that employ staff and those that do not, was 2,216 in 2012—roughly 40 percent of all firms in the borough. See U.S. Bureau of the Census 2012, 2014.
41. Korea Daily 2009. See also Smith (1995) on Flushing for comparison. When Taiwanese immigrants first began to settle in Flushing, they quickly established real estate businesses, dealing in both commercial and residential property.
42. Nine such schools were located in Fort Lee according to Korea Daily (2009, 2016).
43. Lew 2006.
44. Lee and Koo 2006.
45. These boards and committees have members ranging from five to fifteen and include one or two members of Korean origin; in some cases, the same person sits on multiple committees. There were fifteen municipal boards and committees in 2009; Koreans were represented on seven. In 2016, the number of boards and committees remained the same (though some committees were renamed after 2009), and Koreans were represented on six. The boards and committees lists are available on the borough website. See "Borough of Fort Lee Boards and Committee 2009" (http://www.fortleenj.net/clerk/board_and_committee_2009.pdf) for 2009 data, and "Borough of Fort Lee Boards and Committee 2016" (http://www.fortleenj.org/files/boards-committees_2016.pdf) for 2016 data.
46. Nieves 1998a, 1998b, 1999.
47. Firschein 2008b. See chapter 4, below.
48. Moeller 2011.
49. Chong 1998; Kwon 2003; Min 1992, 2010.
50. In Fort Lee, the median ages in 2010 for Asians and non-Hispanic whites were 37.8 and 55.8, respectively. U.S. Bureau of the Census 2010.
51. State of New Jersey, Department of Education 2008, 2015. During this relatively short period of time (2008–2015), the percentage of those speaking Spanish and Russian at home has also increased.

52. Kinney 2000; Llorente 2000.
53. Layton 1991.
54. Almenas 2010a; see also Wander 2011.
55. The International Baccalaureate (IB) is a two-year diploma program for high school juniors and seniors. The IB program fulfills regular high school graduation requirements, providing an alternative to traditional advanced placement courses and opening the doors to college admission.
56. Yin 2007; Zhao 2010.
57. U.S. Bureau of the Census 2010.
58. Kwong and Miščević 2005; McGlinn 2002.
59. Kwong (1987) 1996; Kwong and Miščević 2005. It has been argued, however, that places such as Flushing are generally more prosperous and include middle-class Chinese immigrants who bypass Chinatown entirely, as well as those who are upwardly mobile and have moved out from Chinatown (Lin 1998b).
60. McGlinn 2002.
61. On this organization, see also chapter 3.
62. The Chinese Yellow Pages lists a total of twenty-eight Chinese-owned businesses and services located in Fort Lee, primarily in real estate, medicine, insurance, and accounting. See Chinese Yellow Pages 2011–2012.
63. On the other hand, Edison, with expansive Asian businesses, has been identified as an ethnoburb in McGlinn (2002). Edison is in Middlesex County, which has the largest Chinese population of all counties in New Jersey.
64. Almenas 2011.
65. Ling 2009; Zelinsky and Lee 1998.
66. This emphasis on assimilation is comparable with observations made in Zhao (2010) regarding upwardly mobile, middle-class Chinese.
67. Geller 1999.
68. Geller 1999.
69. Characteristics reminiscent of another, anonymous New York middle-class suburb. See Baumgartner 1988.
70. Alba and Nee 2003, 60.
71. Sudol 2009
72. Zhou, Tseng, and Kim 2008, 76.
73. Li 1997, 1998.
74. Li 2009; Zhou, Tseng, and Kim 2008; see also Oh 2007.

CHAPTER 3 STRATEGIES OF ASSIMILATION AND DISTINCTION

1. Tuan 1998; Zhou 2004, 29.
2. Li 2009; Oh 2007.
3. Aguilar-San Juan 2005; Wood 1997.
4. It has been remarked elsewhere that social intervention by a minority exercises integrative effects. See the case of West Indian political leaders in New York City, where ethnic assertion has been considered as a mode of assimilation into the host political culture (Kasinitz 1992).
5. Bourdieu (1980) 1990b; Giddens 1984.
6. Alba and Nee 2003; Brubaker 2001.
7. Li 2009.
8. Breton 1964, 197.

9. The Chinese-American Family Coalition has a new location in Englewood as of 2016.
10. Shinkai 1994.
11. Besides the Japanese Women's Organization (JWO), which is discussed here, previous research (Shinkai 1994) discusses two other Japanese ethnic organizations in Fort Lee that are no longer extant: the Services to Parents of Exceptional Asian Children (SPEAC), founded in 1984 for children with disabilities and whose activities extended beyond Fort Lee, and the Japanese Cultural Society of New Jersey (JCSN), established 1991. With the exception of the public library director, who recalled contact with the JWO, my informants were not aware of these organizations. Information is scant.
12. Fine 1997.
13. Flory 1989.
14. Fine 1997.
15. Shinkai 1994.
16. For example, Siegel 1993; *Bergen News* 2010.
17. Cohen 1977, 69.
18. Other Korean organizations in municipalities surrounding Fort Lee include: the Korean-American Association of New Jersey (Bogota), Korean American Voters' Council (Hackensack), New Jersey Korean Chamber of Commerce (Palisades Park). The Korean American Voters' Council (KAVC), currently known as the Korean American Civic Empowerment (KACE), was established in Fort Lee in 2000 but was located in Hackensack during the research. As of this writing, it is located in Fort Lee.
19. *Chuseok* (or *Hangawi*) is one of Korea's major holidays, expressing appreciation for the year's harvest and providing the occasion for sharing abundance with family and friends. The spelling varies: this book follows the usage of the Korea Tourism Organization, http://asiaenglish.visitkorea.or.kr/ena/SI/SI_EN_3_6.jsp?cid=613420 (accessed October 30, 2009).
20. Choi 2009.
21. Min 2006.
22. Greater Fort Lee Chamber of Commerce 2004.
23. Almenas 2008a.
24. Tonkiss 2005.
25. Lee 2011a.
26. Fasbach 2002; also Geller 1997a.
27. Fasbach 2001.
28. Almenas 2009a, 2009b.
29. Firschein 2007a, 2007b.
30. Firschein 2008a.
31. Gans 1999, 165.
32. Demographic shifts have prompted ethnic institutions to adapt and to reach out to non-coethnics. For example, one for-profit language school founded in Edgewater in 1989 (relocated to Fort Lee in 2007) by a Japanese female was initially a Japanese-language school for non-Japanese speakers. The school has since then transformed itself into an ESL (English as a Second Language) school. While the school has always enrolled Japanese expatriates and their school-aged children, by 2008, Koreans comprised 90 percent of the students. The availability of Japanese staff fluent in Korean has promoted Korean enrollment in the school.
33. Donghwa Cultural Foundation, brochure, n.d.
34. Chinese-American Family Coalition of New Jersey website, http://www.chineseamericanfamily.org (accessed April 13, 2010).

35. Nagel 1996.
36. Tuan 1998. This tendency may be compared with the case of Muslim Americans, whose "Americanization" experience prompts immersion in the study of their own religious traditions and ancestral faith (Bakalian and Bozorgmehr 2009).
37. On the causes and consequences of the system of supplementary education for Chinese and Korean communities, see Zhou and Kim (2006).
38. Chinese-language schools in the United States have a long history and date back to the late 1880s (Zhou and Li 2003). Faced with discrimination from the mainstream, the Chinese felt that future prospects for youth were limited to returning to China or working in Chinatowns, so both parents and children saw proficiency in Chinese as a necessity. After the repeal of the Chinese Exclusion Act in 1943, however, the Chinese American community "began to reorient itself from sojourning to putting down roots and reinforcing its commitment to socioeconomic integration" (Zhou and Li 2003, 62). After a period of decline between the Second World War and the 1960s, Chinese-language schools began to flourish from the 1970s.
39. The same school facility in Paramus is also used for a Japanese Saturday school.
40. Bergen Chinese School website, http://www.bergenchineseschool.com (accessed May 16, 2010).
41. Shih 2006.
42. Zhou and Li 2003.
43. Jones-Correa 2008.
44. Nash 2009, 8.
45. Lung-Amam 2015.
46. Kalogerakis 1990; Kinney 2002; Myerson 1992.
47. *Bergen News* (Palisades Park, N.J. 2010); *Fort Lee Suburbanite* (Hackensack, N.J., North Jersey Media Group, Inc., 2009, 2010).
48. Kinney 2010; Llorente 2010.
49. Cohen 1985.
50. Nagel 1996.
51. Zeng and Li 2009.
52. The festival is sponsored by the Korean American Association of New Jersey. The first was held in Palisades Park in 2002.
53. Kim 2009a.
54. Beckerman 2008.
55. "2009 New Jersey Chusok Festival 8th Korean American Thanksgiving Festival," Korean American Association of New Jersey, n.d., http://www.yoo-media.com/img/Chusok-NJ.pdf (accessed October 30, 2009).
56. Hosted by the Chinese Service Center U.S.A., Bergen Chinese School, Bo-Hua Chinese School, and Columbia Chinese School in 2009.
57. See Gans 1999.
58. Alba and Nee 2003; Gans 1999.
59. Alba and Nee 2003; Garrod and Kilkenny 2007.
60. Gans 1999.
61. Geller 1997b.
62. Kawai 2000.
63. Kurotani 2005.
64. Tung 1984; White 1988.
65. Kurotani 2005.

66. Bean and Stevens 2003; Brown and Bean 2006.
67. Okamoto 2014.
68. Li 2009; Zhou, Tseng, and Kim 2008.
69. Alba and Nee 2003.
70. Alba 2009, 43.
71. Gerber 2011.

CHAPTER 4 ACCOMMODATING "OTHERS"

1. Foner and Frederickson 2004; Horton 1995; Smith 1995.
2. Elias and Scotson 1994.
3. Duyvendak 2011, 19.
4. Horton 1995; Saito 1998.
5. Brettell 2008.
6. Llorente 1999, 2000.
7. See Yoo (1999) on divisiveness in schools in Old Tappan, and Chen (1996) and Hanley (1996, 1999) on tension between Korean merchants and town officials in Palisades Park during the mid-1990s. In Fort Lee, in 2004, the burning of a Korean flag was reported at the borough's Korean War Memorial shortly after its dedication (*Record [Hackensack, N.J.]* 2004). From June 2007 through 2011, the *Bergen News* (local weekly) had no coverage on immigration except for one article on related legal issues (*Bergen News* 2007b). The article raises burgeoning legal problems for the immigrant population of New Jersey and the necessity of compliance with the law. The article further reports on the "Panel of the Regional Conference on U.S. Immigration Law," an event held at Palisades Park Public Library. Although no immigrant group is specified, the panel was presumably intended for Koreans. Two of the four panelists were Korean—an attorney and the executive director of the New Jersey State Law Enforcement Asian American Association.
8. Maitland 1976.
9. Elias and Scotson 1994, xxii.
10. See also Newman 1993. Newman's study of an unspecified suburban community in northern New Jersey (1988–1990) documents open demonstration of white residents' resentment against "privileged" "Oriental'" newcomers.
11. Bonacich 1973.
12. A parallel situation is documented in a study of Dutch citizens who no longer feel at home in their "own" country as a result of immigration (Duyvendak 2011, 84).
13. See Fennelly (2008) for a parallel example in the Midwest and native beliefs that demographic change due to immigration is a primary cause of the demise of "pristine" rural areas.
14. In 2008, there were forty-four banks in Fort Lee, eight of which were Korean (Planning Board meeting, Fort Lee Borough, New Jersey, September 22, 2008). One informant (Korean American male) pointed out that by his count there are nineteen banks within fifteen minutes' walking distance of the commercial district of Fort Lee.
15. Cowen 1996; Goodnight 1999.
16. Asian American Business Group v. City of Pomona, 716 F. Supp. 1328 (C.D. Cal. 1989). U.S. District Court for the Central District of California. July 14, 1989.
17. Cowen 1996.
18. Saito and Horton 1994.

19. Saito and Horton 1994, 240.
20. Shyong 2013a.
21. Shyong 2013b; Vuong 2013.
22. "An Ordinance Amending Chapter 345 Site Plan Review and Chapter 410 Zoning of the Code of the Borough of Fort Lee," Ordinance #2008-34, adopted August 21, 2008, effective August 26, 2008.
23. Rossi 2008c.
24. Mayor Mark Sokolich, personal interview, December 3, 2009.
25. Duncan and Duncan 2004.
26. Rossi 2008c. The same justification was used for a proposed ordinance in Monterey Park in 2013 (Shyong 2013a). Opponents contended that street numbers were sufficient for the recognition of business establishments, even without English signs.
27. Ordinance #2008-34, 3, August 21, 2008.
28. Firschein 2008b.
29. New Jersey Bilingual Education Act of 1975 and administrative code. In Fort Lee schools, the proportion of Limited English Proficiency (LEP) students ranges between roughly 5 and 15 percent. LEP students are higher in proportion at elementary schools (State of New Jersey, Department of Education 2007, 2008, 2015). LEP students at Fort Lee High School represent fifty different languages according to a document created by the high school and communicated by one informant.
30. Villegas and Young 1997.
31. Shinkai 1994, 81.
32. Shinkai 1994.
33. Alan Sugarman, former superintendent, is noted in previous research and was mentioned in the author's interviews with schoolteachers. Fort Lee schools enrolled among the largest number of sojourning Japanese students in the world in the late 1980s. Sugarman believed that Fort Lee schools could establish themselves as the model for a new, special kind of education. Toward this goal, he organized a committee in 1987 to edit a resource booklet containing fundamental knowledge about Chinese, Japanese, and Korean culture and encouraging inclusion of this knowledge into the curricula for all grades (Shinkai 1994).
34. Firschein 2010.
35. Shinkai 1994.
36. Hsu 2006a, 2006b; Shih 2006.
37. See Horton 1992.
38. Kawai 2000, 87.
39. Shinkai 1994, 80.
40. Almenas 2010b, 2010c, 2010d.
41. Lynwander 1982.
42. Lee 2011a, 2011b.
43. Verdon 2006.
44. Greater Fort Lee Chamber of Commerce, press release, December 3, 2008.
45. Discussed in chapter 2.
46. As discussed in chapter 3.
47. Jones-Correa 2008.
48. The director of the Richard A. Nest Senior Citizens' Center indicated that due to the disproportionately high percentage of Korean residents in senior housing in Fort Lee during the 2000s, investigation into possible impropriety was ongoing. The issue was a cause of friction between Korean and white seniors.

49. Director of the Richard A. Nest Senior Citizens' Center, Fort Lee, personal interview, April 23, 2009.
50. Shinkai 1994.
51. Admission fees for this event were donated to the Thomas Paine statue project discussed in chapter 1.
52. Logan and Molotch (1987) 2007.
53. Pugliese 2016b.
54. Keller 2003.
55. Horton 1995.
56. Brettell 2008.
57. Brettell 2008, 81.
58. Baumgartner 1988.
59. Jiménez and Horowitz 2013.
60. Kasinitz, Mollenkopf, Waters, and Holdaway 2008, 273.
61. Williamson (1978) 2010.
62. Li 2009, 44–45.
63. Li 2009, 45.
64. Horton 1995, 225.

CHAPTER 5 REMAKING ASIAN ETHNICITY IN SUBURBIA

1. Murji and Solomos 2015; Weber (1922) 1978.
2. Omi and Winant 1994.
3. Nagel 1996, 21. See also Barth 1969; Hall 1997.
4. Espiritu 1992, 2.
5. Kibria 1998, 943.
6. Typified as a "general assimilation process" (Lopez and Espiritu 1990, 200).
7. Okamoto 2014; Shinagawa and Pang 1996; Võ 2004.
8. Aguilar-San Juan 2005; Cheng 2013; Hayden (1995) 1997.
9. Cheng 2013.
10. Fasbach 2001.
11. De Genova 2006; Tuan 1998.
12. De Genova 2006, 11.
13. The tendency to define "American" as "white" by Asian informants for this study supports other research findings, where "white" appears as the frame of reference for Asians. See Lee 1996; Tuan 1998; Zhou 2004.
14. Bean and Stevens 2003; Brown and Bean 2006.
15. Horton 1995, 229. See also Brown and Bean 2006; Fenton (2003) 2010; Hall 1986.
16. Barth 1969.
17. See Flory 1989; Kawai 2000. Flory indicated a widespread feeling among Americans that the Japanese were intentionally avoiding participation in the American community—an impression quite the contrary of what the Japanese wished to convey.
18. "Konglish" is a hybrid speech, used by Korean speakers, characterized by the use of loanwords and appropriations from English.
19. The prevalent pattern of coethnic friendships conforms with findings in the study of Hong and Min (1999).
20. Okamoto 2014; Shinagawa and Pang 1996.

21. Shinkai 1994.
22. The "Korean Wave" refers to an upsurge of interest in Korean popular culture throughout Asia beginning in the late 1990s. The popularity peaked in the period 2003–2005 in Japan (Hanaki, Singhal, Han, Kim, and Chitnis 2007).
23. Espiritu 1992.
24. See, for example, the case of Vincent Chin (Zia 2000). See also Wong 1972.
25. Okamoto 2014. See also Pew Research Center 2013. The study of the Pew Research Center on patterns of self-identification among Asian Americans found that the majority of those of Asian descent in the United States chose an identity based on their national origin.
26. On the Korean American Association of Fort Lee, see chapter 3.
27. Espiritu 1992.
28. Jeung 2002.
29. For example, there has been report of Korean ministers recruiting Japanese to provide for worship in the Japanese language in the New York–New Jersey area (Ku 2009).
30. Okamoto 2014, 13.
31. Okamoto 2014, 83.
32. "Fort Lee High School Student Outcomes" (2007, 2008, 2009), Fort Lee High School, June 8, 2010. Seventy percent of graduating Asian students moved on to four-year college in 2009; 56 percent of these to in-state universities, 44 percent to out-of-state universities. About 20 percent of Asian students in the same year moved on to two-year colleges; 95 percent of these went to in-state public two-year colleges. I thank Ms. Marcia Leon, guidance secretary at Fort Lee High School for assistance with data on student trajectories.
33. One reason for this was the recession, leading to a tighter economic situation for student families.
34. Kasinitz, Mollenkopf, Waters, and Holdaway 2008, 357.
35. Nagel 1996, 10.
36. Nagel 1994, 163. The assertion of transhistorical links has traditionally played an important role in the cohesion of groups in political-economic struggles. See Wallerstein 1983.
37. Steinberg 2004, 237.
38. Fasbach 2001. See also Moore (1981) regarding the suburban experience of middle-class, second-generation Jews in New York in the 1920s. For descendants of Jewish immigrants, Jewish identity developed through assimilation to America—contact with the mainstream reinforced consciousness of ethnic belonging. Adaptation to American life (suburbanization and upward mobility) did not entail the abandonment of Jewish identity.
39. See chapter 3.
40. See chapter 3.
41. Nagel 1996.
42. Lott 1976.
43. The diversity of the locale is reflected in discourse. The tendency to specify the ethnicity of native whites was noticeable among Asians—they said "German American," "Italian American," and so on rather than "American." This echoes the manner in which whites specify ethnonational origin for East Asians, as discussed in chapter 4.
44. Anderson 2011.
45. See chapter 2 for student demographics in Fort Lee schools. Nearly half of Bergen County's children aged five and younger were from minorities in 2009 (Llorente and Sheingold 2010).
46. Kasinitz, Mollenkopf, and Waters 2002.

47. "Majority minority" designates the case where one or more ethnic or racial minorities make up the majority of the local population.
48. Jiménez and Horowitz 2013.
49. Sakamoto, Goyette, and Kim 2009.
50. Võ 2004.
51. Hayden (1995) 1997.
52. Aguilar-San Juan 2005.
53. Wood 1997.

CONCLUSION

1. Kaysen 2014; Ma 2016. See also the SJP Properties website, http://www.sjpproperties.com/#properties (accessed May 23, 2017).
2. Tucker Development Corporation website, http://www.tuckerdevelopment.com/portfolio_items/15 (accessed May 23, 2017).
3. "Open for Business," *Fort Lee Suburbanite*, August 19, 2016.
4. Pugliese 2016a.
5. Bonislawski 2015.
6. Lin 1998a.
7. Lin 2011.
8. Lin 1998a, 313.
9. Bourdieu 1990a.
10. Bourdieu 1990a, 63.
11. Alba and Nee 2003, 281–283.
12. Mixed reactions among native whites in Fort Lee are similar to findings from other locales, including Flushing (Smith 1995) and Monterey Park (Horton 1995).
13. Lin 1998a.
14. Gilroy (2005) develops the term *conviviality* for sociological usage. See also the concept of *cosmopolitan canopy* in Anderson (2011).
15. Noble 2013; Valluvan 2016.
16. Hayden (1995) 1997.
17. Aguilar-San Juan 2005.
18. Duncan and Duncan 2004; Ray, Halseth, and Johnson 1997; Wood 1997.
19. For example, about 15 percent of the Jersey City project by Kushner companies will be funded through the EB-5 visa program, the vast majority of visa recipients being Chinese nationals (Alvarado and Adely 2017). The EB-5 Immigrant Investor program, created by Congress under the Immigration Act of 1990, provides a channel for eligible immigrant investors to become lawful permanent residents. They must invest at least one million dollars in commercial enterprises in the United States and employ at least ten qualified American workers.
20. Alvarado and Adely 2017.
21. According to the Korean American member of Fort Lee Council, personal interview, June 30, 2017.
22. Durkheim (1912) 1995, 1.

BIBLIOGRAPHY

Aguilar-San Juan, Karin. 2005. "Staying Vietnamese: Community and Place in Orange County and Boston." *City & Community* 4 (1): 37–65.

Alba, Richard [D.] 2009. *Blurring the Color Line: The New Chance for a More Integrated America.* Cambridge, Mass.: Harvard University Press.

Alba, Richard D., Nancy A. Denton, Shu-yin J. Leung, and John R. Logan. 1995. "Neighborhood Change under Conditions of Mass Immigration: The New York City Region, 1970–1990." *International Migration Review* 29 (3): 625–656.

Alba, Richard D., and John R. Logan. 1991. "Variations on Two Themes: Racial and Ethnic Patterns in the Attainment of Suburban Residence." *Demography* 28 (3): 431–453.

———. 1993. "Minority Proximity to Whites in Suburbs: An Individual-Level Analysis of Segregation." *American Journal of Sociology* 98 (6): 1388–1427.

Alba, Richard D., John R. Logan, and Kyle Crowder. 1997. "White Ethnic Neighborhoods and Assimilation: The Greater New York Region, 1980–1990." *Social Forces* 75 (3): 883–912.

Alba, Richard D., John R. Logan, Brian J. Stults, Gilbert Marzan, and Wenquan Zhang. 1999. "Immigrant Groups in the Suburbs: A Reexamination of Suburbanization and Spatial Assimilation." *American Sociological Review* 64 (3): 446–460.

Alba, Richard, and Victor Nee. 1997. "Rethinking Assimilation Theory for a New Era of Immigration." *International Migration Review* 31 (4): 826–874.

———. 2003. *Remaking the American Mainstream: Assimilation and Contemporary Immigration.* Cambridge, Mass.: Harvard University Press.

Allen, James P., and Eugene Turner. 1996. "Spatial Patterns of Immigrant Assimilation." *Professional Geographer* 48 (2): 140–155.

Almenas, Maxim. 2008a. "Person of the Year: Joh, Chief Ripoli Receive Annual Award." *Fort Lee Suburbanite,* May 16.

———. 2008b. "Centuria Goes On: Bidding Begins for New Developer." *Fort Lee Suburbanite,* October 3.

———. 2009a. "Race End with a Bang: Newcomer Joins Two Incumbents on School Board." *Fort Lee Suburbanite,* April 24.

———. 2009b. "Election Brings New Faces to Board." *Fort Lee Suburbanite,* May 1.

———. 2010a. "School District Scores High despite Recent Bumpy Past." *Fort Lee Suburbanite,* January 15.

———. 2010b. "Referendum: After Defeat District Seeks New Solutions." *Fort Lee Suburbanite,* October 8.

———. 2010c. "School's Facilities Project: Voters, Again, to Determine Fate of New School." *Fort Lee Suburbanite,* December 10.

———. 2010d. "Grassroots, Economy Key Factors in Defeat." *Fort Lee Suburbanite,* December 24.

———. 2011. "Foreign Exchange: Borough Connects with Chinese Sister City." *Fort Lee Suburbanite,* April 8.

Alvarado, Monsy, and Hannan Adely. 2017. "Visas a Source of Controversy as Kushner Companies Look to Chinese Investors." NorthJersey.com, May 9.

Anderson, Elijah. 2011. *The Cosmopolitan Canopy: Race and Civility in Everyday Life*. New York: Norton.

Archer, John, Paul J. Sandul, and Katherine Solomonson, eds. 2015. *Making Suburbia: New Histories of Everyday America*. Minneapolis: University of Minnesota Press.

Bakalian, Anny, and Mehdi Bozorgmehr. 2009. *Backlash 9/11: Middle Eastern and Muslim Americans Respond*. Berkeley and Los Angeles: University of California Press.

Barth, Fredrik, ed. 1969. *Ethnic Groups and Boundaries: The Social Organization of Culture Difference*. Boston, Mass.: Little, Brown.

Baumgartner, M. P. 1988. *The Moral Order of a Suburb*. New York: Oxford University Press.

Bean, Frank, and Jennifer Lee. 2004. "America's Changing Color Lines: Immigration, Race/Ethnicity, and Multicultural Identification." *Annual Review of Sociology* 30:221–242.

Bean, Frank D., and Gillian Stevens. 2003. *America's Newcomers and the Dynamics of Diversity*. New York: Russell Sage.

Beckerman, Jim. 2008. "Tae Kwon Do Festival's Big Draw: Martial Arts Competition Popular as Koreans Celebrate Harvest Moon." *Record*, September 28.

Bergen News. 2007a. "Bank of NJ Opens New Headquarters." July 4.

———. 2007b. "Immigration Concerns Discussed." August 8.

———. 2008a. "Higher Taxes, Centuria 'Stagnant.'" September 17.

———. 2008b. "FL's Madonna Church Marks 150 Years." October 29.

———. 2009. "Fort Lee Seeks Proposals for Centuria Development." February 18.

———. 2010. "Valentine's Day Celebrated at Gallen." February 24.

Bertram, Lucille. 2004. *Images of America: Fort Lee*. Charleston, S.C.: Arcadia.

Bischoff, Henry. 2010. *A New Wave of Immigration in New Jersey: Diversity and Vitality 1940–2009*. n.p. New Jersey Historical Commission.

Bonacich, Edna. 1973. "A Theory of Middleman Minorities." *American Sociological Review* 38:583–594.

Bonislawski, Adam. 2015. "Fort Lee Is the New New Jersey." *New York Post*, January 7.

Bourdieu, Pierre. 1990a. *In Other Words: Essays towards a Reflexive Sociology*. Trans. Matthew Adamson. Stanford, Calif.: Stanford University Press.

———. (1980) 1990b. *The Logic of Practice*. Trans. Richard Nice. Stanford, Calif.: Stanford University Press.

Breton, Raymond. 1964. "Institutional Completeness of Ethnic Communities and the Personal Relations of Immigrants." *American Journal of Sociology* 70 (2): 193–205.

Brettell, Caroline B. 2008. "'Big D': Incorporating New Immigrants in a Sunbelt Suburban Metropolis." In Singer, Hardwick, and Brettell 2008.

Brown, Susan K., and Frank D. Bean. 2006. "New Immigrants, New Models of Assimilation." Center for Research on Immigration, Population and Public Policy, University of California, Irvine. Prepared for a Special Issue on "The Second Generation," *Migration Information Source*, Migration Policy Institute, Washington, D.C. (August). http://www.cri.uci.edu/pdf/NewImmigrantsNewModelsOfAssimilation_082306.pdf.

Brubaker, Rogers. 2001. "The Return of Assimilation? Changing Perspectives on Immigration and Its Sequels in France, Germany, and the United States." *Ethnic and Racial Studies* 24 (4): 531–548.

Chen, David W. 1996. "Karaoke Crackdown Stirs Ethnic Anger in Palisades Park." *New York Times*, September 8.

Cheng, Wendy. 2013. *The Changs Next Door to the Díazes: Remapping Race in Suburban California*. Minneapolis: University of Minnesota Press.

Chinese Yellow Pages. 2011–2012. New York, New Jersey, Washington D.C., Philadelphia Edition.

Ch'oe, Yong-ho, Peter H. Lee, and Wm. Theodore de Bary, eds. 2000. *Sources of Korean Tradition. Volume II: From the Sixteenth to the Twentieth Centuries*. New York: Columbia University Press.

Choi, Hee-eun. 2009. "2010 Census Will Aid Korean Community's Political Power." *Korea Times*, July 29. Trans. Sun-Yong Reinish.

Chollet, Laurence. 1993. "Hot Dogs and Miso: Japanese Families Look Homeward." *Record*, June 17.

Chong, Kelly H. 1998. "What It Means to Be Christian: The Role of Religion in the Construction of Ethnic Identity and Boundary among Second-Generation Korean Americans." *Sociology of Religion* 59 (3): 259–286.

Cohen, Anthony P[aul]. 1985. *The Symbolic Construction of Community*. London: Tavistock.

Cohen, Erik. 1977. *Expatriate Communities*. London: Sage.

Collins, Gail. 1980. "Fort Lee Awaits Developer's Visit." *New York Times*, October 5.

Cowen, Richard. 1996. "4 Towns Rethink English on Signs: Court Overturns California Rule." *Record*, December 6.

Daniels, Lee A. 1983. "About Real Estate: Fort Lee's New Identity: Suburban Office Center." *New York Times*, January 12.

De Genova, Nicholas. 2006. "Introduction: Latino and Asian Racial Formations at the Frontiers of U.S. Nationalism." In *Racial Transformations: Latinos and Asians Remaking the United States*. Edited by Nicholas De Genova. Durham, N.C.: Duke University Press.

Denton, Nancy A., and Douglas S. Massey. 1991. "Patterns of Neighborhood Transition in a Multiethnic World: U.S. Metropolitan Areas, 1970–1980." *Demography* 28 (1): 41–63.

Dobriner, William M. 1963. *Class in Suburbia*. Englewood Cliffs, N.J.: Prentice Hall.

Duncan, James S., and Nancy G. Duncan. 2004. *Landscapes of Privilege: The Politics of the Aesthetic in an American Suburb*. New York: Routledge.

Durkheim, Émile. (1912) 1995. *The Elementary Forms of Religious Life*. Trans. Karen E. Fields. New York: Free Press.

Duyvendak, Jan Willem. 2011. *The Politics of Home: Belonging and Nostalgia in Western Europe and the United States*. London: Palgrave Macmillan.

Egan, Timothy. 2011. "Rise of the Ethnoburb." *New York Times*, March 10.

Elias, Norbert, and John L. Scotson. 1994. *The Established and the Outsiders: A Sociological Enquiry into Community Problems*. 2nd ed. London: Sage.

Espenshade, Tomas, ed. 1997. *Keys to Successful Immigration: Implications of the New Jersey Experience*. Washington, D.C.: Urban Institute Press.

Espiritu, Yen Le. 1992. *Asian American Panethnicity: Bridging Institutions and Identities*. Philadelphia: Temple University Press.

Fang, Di. 1996. "Japan's Growing Economic Activities and the Attainment Patterns of Foreign-Born Japanese Workers in the United States." *International Migration Review* 30 (2): 511–534.

Fasbach, Laura. 2001. "An Evolving Community: Koreans Changing Face of Fort Lee." *Record*, June 10.

———. 2002. "In Fort Lee, a Lament by Koreans: Asians Have Never Won School Board Election." *Record*, March 13.

Fennelly, Katherine. 2008. "Prejudice toward Immigrants in the Midwest." In Massey 2008.

Fenton, Steve. (2003) 2010. *Ethnicity*. 2nd ed. Cambridge, U.K.: Polity.

Ferretti, Fred. 1972. "Bergen County Enjoying Industrial and Retail Boom." *New York Times*, January 31.

Fine, Mary Jane. 1997. "A Welcome in Japanese: Coffee, Tea, and Community; Group Eases Way for Women Coming to N.J." *Record*, May 18.

Firschein, Merry. 2007a. "Absentees Swing Fort Lee Vote." *Record*, April 20.

———. 2007b. "School Election Lawsuit Dropped: But Ousted Member Still Wants Probe." *Record*, June 24.

———. 2008a. "Rights Group Says Korean Voters Were Intimidated." *Record*, April 12.

———. 2008b. "Ft. Lee Adopts Rules on Shop Signs, Facades: Goal Is 'Pleasing Streetscape' to Draw Shoppers, Businesses." *Record*, August 28.

———. 2009. "4 Builders Vie for Tract: Focus on Revitalization." *Record*, August 1.

———. 2010. "Ft. Lee Courts School Ties in Korea." *Record*, November 28.

Fischel, William A. 2004. "An Economic History of Zoning and a Cure for Its Exclusionary Effects." *Urban Studies* 41 (2): 317–340.

Fishman, Robert. 1987. *Bourgeois Utopias: The Rise and Fall of Suburbia*. New York: Basic Books.

Flory, Michael John. 1989. "More Japanese than Japan: Adaptation and Social Network Formation among the Wives of Japanese Businessmen Temporarily Residing in Bergen County, New Jersey." PhD dissertation, Columbia University, New York.

Foner, Nancy. 2005. *In a New Land: A Comparative View of Immigration*. New York: New York University Press.

Foner, Nancy, and George M. Fredrickson, eds. 2004. *Not Just Black and White: Historical and Contemporary Perspectives on Immigration, Race, and Ethnicity in the United States*. New York: Russell Sage.

Fong, Eric, and Rima Wilkes. 1999. "The Spatial Assimilation Model Reexamined: An Assessment by Canadian Data." *International Migration Review* 33 (3): 594–620.

Fong, Timothy P. 1994. *The First Suburban Chinatown: The Reality of Monterey Park, California*. Philadelphia: Temple University Press.

Fort Lee Chamber of Commerce. 1972. *Inside Fort Lee*. Cliffside Park, N.J.: Palisadian.

Fort Lee Film Commission. 2006. *Images of America: Fort Lee, Birthplace of the Motion Picture Industry*. Charleston, S.C.: Arcadia.

Frey, William H. 1995. "Immigration and Internal Migration 'Flight' from US Metropolitan Areas: Toward a New Demographic Balkanisation." *Urban Studies* 32 (4/5): 733–757.

———. 2011. "Melting Pot Cities and Suburbs: Racial and Ethnic Change in Metro America in the 2000s." State of Metropolitan America. Washington, D.C.: Brookings Institution Press.

Frey, William H., and Dowell Myers. 2005. "Racial Segregation in U.S. Metropolitan Areas and Cities, 1990–2000: Patterns, Trends, and Explanations." *Population Studies Center Research Report*. Institute for Social Research, University of Michigan, 05-573 (April). http://www.frey-demographer.org/reports/rr05-573.pdf.

Friedman, Judith J. 1994. "Suburban Variations within Highly Urbanized Regions: The Case of New Jersey." *Research in Community Sociology* 4:97–132.

Gans, Herbert J. 1962. "Urbanism and Suburbanism as Ways of Life: A Re-evaluation of Definitions." In *Human Behavior and Social Processes: An Interactionist Approach*. Edited by Arnold M. Rose. Boston, Mass.: Houghton Mifflin.

———. (1967) 1982. *The Levittowners: Ways of Life and Politics in a New Suburban Community*. Morningside ed. New York: Pantheon.

———. 1979. "Symbolic Ethnicity: The Future of Ethnic Groups and Cultures in America." *Ethnic and Racial Studies* 2 (1): 1–20.

———. 1999. "Toward a Reconciliation of 'Assimilation' and 'Pluralism': The Interplay of Acculturation and Ethnic Retention." In *The Handbook of International Migration: The American Experience.* Edited by Charles Hirschman, Philip Kasinitz, and Josh DeWind. New York: Russell Sage.

Garreau, Joel. (1991) 1992. *Edge City: Life on the New Frontier.* New York: Anchor Books.

Garrod, Andrew, and Robert Kilkenny, eds. 2007. *Balancing Two Worlds: Asian American College Students Tell Their Life Stories.* Ithaca, N.Y.: Cornell University Press.

Geist, William E. 1981. "A Clash at the Club." *New York Times,* October 13.

Geller, Adam. 1997a. "Fort Lee Appeals to Koreans to Back School Budget." *Record,* March 27.

———. 1997b. "Parenting, American Style: Fort Lee Class Is Cultural Bridge for Korean-Born Moms." *Record,* June 12.

———. 1999. "A Wave of New Arrivals Transforms an Old Village." *Record,* March 1.

Gerber, David A. 2011. *American Immigration: A Very Short Introduction.* Oxford: Oxford University Press.

Giddens, Anthony. 1984. *The Constitution of Society: Outline of the Theory of Structuration.* Berkeley and Los Angeles: University of California Press.

Gilroy, Paul. 2005. *Postcolonial Melancholia.* New York: Columbia University Press.

Glaberson, William. 1992. "For Many in the New York Region, the City Is Ignored and Irrelevant." *New York Times,* January 2.

Gober, Patricia. 1989. "The Urbanization of the Suburbs." *Urban Geography* 10 (4): 311–315.

Goodnight, Lisa. 1999. "Sign-Law Shocker: Nobody's Fighting—English-Also Rule Lays Amity Bare." *Record,* July 21.

Gordon, Milton. 1964. *Assimilation in American Life: The Role of Race, Religion, and National Origins.* New York: Oxford University Press.

Greater Fort Lee Chamber of Commerce. 2004. *Greater Fort Lee Chamber of Commerce Business News* (March). Fort Lee, N.J.: Greater Fort Lee Chamber of Commerce.

———. 2008. *Community Directory 2008.* Fort Lee, N.J.: Greater Fort Lee Chamber of Commerce.

Ha, Andrew Kwangho. 1988. "A Study of Selected New Jersey Korean Parents' Attitudes toward Bilingual/Bicultural Education." EdD dissertation, Seton Hall University, South Orange, N.J.

Hall, Stuart. 1986. "Gramsci's Relevance for the Study of Race and Ethnicity." *Journal of Communication Inquiry* 10 (2): 5–27.

———. 1997. "Old and New Identities, Old and New Ethnicities." In *Culture, Globalization and the World-System: Contemporary Conditions for the Representation of Identity.* Edited by Anthony D. King. Minneapolis: University of Minnesota Press.

Hanaki, Toru, Arvind Singhal, Min Wha Han, Do Kyun Kim, and Ketan Chitnis. 2007. "*Hanryu* Sweeps East Asia: How *Winter Sonata* Is Gripping Japan." *International Communication Gazette* 69 (3): 281–294.

Hanley, Robert. 1996. "Debating the Language of Signs: New Jersey Towns Tell Asian-Owned Stores: Advertise in English, Too." *New York Times,* April 6.

———. 1999. "1,000 Rally for Korean-American Merchants Who Fear Backlash of Bias in Palisades Park." *New York Times,* November 24.

Hayden, Dolores. (1995) 1997. *The Power of Place: Urban Landscapes as Public History.* Cambridge, Mass.: MIT Press.

Herbers, John. 1986. "Suburbs Absorb More Immigrants, Mostly the Affluent and Educated." *New York Times*, December 14.

Hobbs, Frank, and Nicole Stoops. 2002. *Demographic Trends in the 20th Century*. U.S. Census Bureau, Census 2000 Special Reports. Series CENSR-4. Washington, D.C.: U.S. Government Printing Office.

Hong, Joann, and Pyong Gap Min. 1999. "Ethnic Attachment among Second Generation Korean Adolescents." *Amerasia Journal* 25 (1): 165–178.

Horton, John. 1992. "The Politics of Diversity in Monterey Park, California." In *Structuring Diversity: Ethnographic Perspectives on the New Immigration*. Edited by Louise Lamphere. Chicago: University of Chicago Press.

———. 1995. *The Politics of Diversity: Immigration, Resistance, and Change in Monterey Park, California*. Philadelphia: Temple University Press.

Hosler, Akiko S. 1998. *Japanese Immigrant Entrepreneurs in New York City: A New Wave of Ethnic Business*. New York: Garland.

Howe, Marvine. 1986. "In Jersey, Japanese-Style New Year's." *New York Times*, December 27.

Hsu, Eric. 2006a. "Bilingual Schooling Is Topic for PTA: Fort Lee's Korean Program Set for Fall Launch." *Record*, June 6.

———. 2006b. "Non-Korean Parents Resist Bilingual Class." *Record*, June 8.

———. 2007. "Ethnic Pendulum Swings: North Jersey's Japanese Population Dips, Disperses." *Record*, March 26.

Hum, Tarry. 2014. *Making a Global Immigrant Neighborhood: Brooklyn's Sunset Park*. Philadelphia: Temple University Press.

Hwang, Sean-Shong, and Steve H. Murdock. 1998. "Racial Attraction or Racial Avoidance in American Suburbs?" *Social Forces* 77 (2): 541–566.

Jeung, Russell. 2002. "Asian American Pan-Ethnic Formation and Congregational Culture." In *Religions in Asian America: Building Faith Communities*. Edited by Pyong Gap Min and Jung Hakim. Walnut Creek, Calif.: Altamira Press.

Jiménez, Tomás R., and Adam L. Horowitz. 2013. "When White Is Just Alright: How Immigrants Redefine Achievement and Reconfigure the Ethnoracial Hierarchy." *American Sociological Review* 78 (5): 849–871.

Jones-Correa, Michael. 2008. "Immigrant Incorporation in Suburbia: Spatial Sorting, Ethnic Mobilization, and Receiving Institutions." In *Immigration and Integration in Urban Communities: Renegotiating the City*. Edited by Lisa M. Hanley, Blair A. Ruble, and Allison M. Garland. Washington, D.C.: Woodrow Wilson Center Press; Baltimore: Johns Hopkins University Press.

Kalita, S. Mitra. 2003. *Suburban Sahibs: Three Immigrant Families and Their Passage from India to America*. New Brunswick, N.J.: Rutgers University Press.

Kalogerakis, George. 1990. "The Talk of the Town: Yaohan." *New Yorker*, August 20.

Kasinitz, Philip. 1992. *Caribbean New York: Black Immigrants and the Politics of Race*. Ithaca, N.Y.: Cornell University Press.

Kasinitz, Philip, John Mollenkopf, and Mary C. Waters, eds. 2004. *Becoming New Yorkers: Ethnographies of the New Second Generation*. New York: Russell Sage.

Kasinitz, Philip, John H. Mollenkopf, Mary C. Waters, and Jennifer Holdaway. 2008. *Inheriting the City: The Children of Immigrants Come of Age*. New York and Cambridge, Mass.: Russell Sage and Harvard University Press.

Kawai, Miho. 2000. "Confronting Japanese Selves: A Case Study of Japanese Expatriate Wives in Fort Lee, New Jersey." PhD dissertation, Syracuse University, Syracuse, New York.

Kaysen, Ronda. 2014. "Transforming a Skyline: Residential Tower in Fort Lee, N.J., Begins Leasing." *New York Times,* October 7.

Keller, Suzanne. 2003. *Community: Pursuing the Dream, Living the Reality.* Princeton: Princeton University Press.

Khandelwal, Madhulika S. 2002. *Becoming American, Being Indian: An Immigrant Community in New York.* Ithaca, N.Y.: Cornell University Press.

Kibria, Nazli. 1998. "The Contested Meanings of 'Asian American': Racial Dilemmas in the Contemporary U.S." *Ethnic and Racial Studies* 21 (5): 939–958.

Kim, Ann H., and Michael J. White. 2010. "Panethnicity, Ethnic Diversity, and Residential Segregation." *American Journal of Sociology* 115 (5): 1158–1196.

Kim, Illsoo. 1981. *New Urban Immigrants: The Korean Community in New York.* Princeton: Princeton University Press.

Kim, Jennifer. 2009a. "Thousands Come Out for Festival: Weekend Continues Thanksgiving Tradition." *Fort Lee Suburbanite,* September 25.

———. 2009b. "Fort Lee Museum Celebrates 10 Years Preserving History." *Fort Lee Suburbanite,* December 11.

Kim, Joo-Chan. 2003. "Influx of Chinese-Americans into New Jersey Neighborhoods with High Korean-American Concentration." *Korea Times* (New York Edition), March 4.

Kim, Yung. 2004. "Asians Become New Focus of Bilingual Education." *Record,* April 28.

Kinney, Pat. 2000. "Ex-Schools Chief Helped to Foster Model of Diversity." *Record,* January 9.

———. 2002. "Japan's Outpost: Thriving Edgewater." *Record,* June 12.

———. 2010. "Opinion: Japanese Thriving in North Jersey." *Record,* September 22.

Kolbert, Elizabeth. 1986. "More Asians, Seeking Strong Schools, Choose the Suburbs." *New York Times,* June 13.

Koo, Hagen. 2007. "The Changing Faces of Inequality in South Korea in the Age of Globalization." *Korea Studies* 31:1–18.

Korea Daily. 2009. *The Korea Daily Business Directory.* Long Island City, N.Y.: Korea Daily.

———. 2016. *The Korea Daily Business Directory.* Long Island City, N.Y.: Korea Daily.

Koszarski, Richard. 2004. *Fort Lee: The Film Town.* Rome: John Libbey.

Ku, Jae-kwan. 2009. "NY Korean Churches Seek Lost Souls among Japanese Americans." *Korea Times* (New York Edition), January 6. Trans. Sun-Yong Reinish.

Kurotani, Sawa. 2005. *Home Away from Home: Japanese Corporate Wives in the United States.* Durham, N.C.: Duke University Press.

Kusumoto, Sam, and Edmund P. Murray. 1989. *My Bridge to America: Discovering the New World for Minolta.* New York: E. P. Dutton.

Kwon, Okyun. 2003. *Buddhist and Protestant Korean Immigrants: Religious Beliefs and Socioeconomic Aspects of Life.* New York: LFB Scholarly Publishing.

Kwong, Peter. (1987) 1996. *The New Chinatown.* Rev. ed. New York: Hill and Wang.

———. 2007. "Moving to the Suburbs." Beyond Enclaves and Ethnoburbs: New Asian Immigrant Communities, New York Immigration Seminar Series Panel, lecture, Graduate Center, City University of New York, October 29.

Kwong, Peter, and Dušanka Miščević. 2005. *Chinese America: The Untold Story of America's Oldest New Community.* New York: New Press.

Lam, Frankie. 1986. "Suburban Residential Segregation of Chinese and Japanese Americans: 1960, 1970, and 1980." *Sociology and Social Research* 70 (4): 263–265.

Layton, Mary Jo. 1991. "Fort Lee Mayor Chastised for Pro-Asian Comments—PTAs Request a Public Apology." *Record,* June 6.

Le, C[uong] N[guyen]. 2007. *Asian American Assimilation: Ethnicity, Immigration, and Socioeconomic Attainment.* New York: LFB Scholarly Publishing.

Le Corbusier [pseud. Charles-Édouard Jeanneret]. (1937) 1947. *When the Cathedrals Were White: A Journey to the Country of Timid People.* Trans. Francis E. Hyslop Jr. New York: Reynal & Hitchcock.

Lee, Hakyoon. 2010. "'I Am a "Kirogi" Mother': Education Exodus and Life Transformation among Korean Transnational Women." *Journal of Language, Identity, and Education* 9:250–264.

Lee, Jae-Hyup. 1998. *Dynamics of Ethnic Identity: Three Asian American Communities in Philadelphia.* New York: Garland.

Lee, Kyung. 2011a. "KAAFL Promotes Diversity and Community, Not 'New Seoul.'" *Fort Lee Patch,* June 17. http://fortlee.patch.com/articles/kaafl-promotes-diversity-and-community-not-new-seoul?n.

———. 2011b. "New Name, Mission: Noah Bank." *Fort Lee Patch,* July 1. http://fortlee.patch.com/articles/noah-bank-strives-for-more-diverse-customer-base-with-new-name-mission.

Lee, Stacey J. 1996. "Perceptions of Panethnicity among Asian American High School Students." *Amerasia Journal* 22 (2): 109–125.

Lee, Yean-Ju, and Hagen Koo. 2006. "'Wild Geese Fathers' and a Globalized Family Strategy for Education in Korea." *International Development Planning Review* 28 (4): 533–553.

Leiby, Adrian C[oulter]. (1962) 1992. *The Revolutionary War in the Hackensack Valley: The Jersey Dutch and the Neutral Ground, 1775–1783.* New Brunswick, N.J.: Rutgers University Press.

Lett, Denise Potrzeba. 1998. *In Pursuit of Status: The Making of South Korea's "New" Urban Middle Class.* Cambridge, Mass.: Harvard University Press.

Levinson, Marc. 2006. *The Box: How the Shipping Container Made the World Smaller and the World Economy Bigger.* Princeton: Princeton University Press.

Lévi-Strauss, Claude. (1962) 1966. *The Savage Mind.* Chicago: University of Chicago Press.

Lew, Jamie. 2006. *Asian Americans in Class: Charting the Achievement Gap among Korean American Youth.* New York: Teachers College Press.

Li, Wei. 1997. "Spatial Transformation of an Urban Ethnic Community: From Chinatown to Chinese *Ethnoburb* in Los Angeles." PhD dissertation, University of Southern California, Los Angeles.

———. 1998. "Anatomy of a New Ethnic Settlement: The Chinese *Ethnoburb* in Los Angeles." *Urban Studies* 35 (3): 479–501.

———. 1999. "Building Ethnoburbia: The Emergence and Manifestation of the Chinese Ethnoburb in Los Angeles' San Gabriel Valley." *Journal of Asian American Studies* 2 (1): 1–28.

———. 2005. "Beyond Chinatown, Beyond Enclave: Reconceptualizing Contemporary Chinese Settlements in the United States." *Geojournal* 64:31–40.

———, ed. 2006. *From Urban Enclaves to Ethnic Suburb: New Asian Communities in Pacific Rim Countries.* Honolulu: University of Hawai'i Press.

———. 2009. *Ethnoburb: The New Ethnic Community in Urban America.* Honolulu: University of Hawai'i Press.

Lim, Gerard. 1992. "Koreans Moving to Jersey Neighborhood." *Asianweek,* April 3.

Lin, Jan. 1998a. "Globalization and the Revalorizing of Ethnic Places in Immigration Gateway Cities." *Urban Affairs Review* 34 (2): 313–339.

———. 1998b. *Reconstructing Chinatown: Ethnic Enclave, Global Change.* Minneapolis: University of Minnesota Press.

———. 2011. *The Power of Urban Ethnic Places: Cultural Heritage and Community Life*. New York: Routledge.

Ling, Huping, ed. 2009. *Asian America: Forming New Communities, Expanding Boundaries*. New Brunswick, N.J.: Rutgers University Press.

Llorente, Elizabeth. 1999. "All of Us: Painting a New Portrait of New Jersey." *Record*, October 24.

———. 2000. "Recent Arrivals Crucial to Clout: Foreign-Born Benefit N.J." *Record*, December 31.

———. 2010. "Food Mart Helps Koreans Get Onboard with Census." *Record*, February 24.

Llorente, Elizabeth, and Dave Sheingold. 2010. "Children of Minorities Find They're the Majority in School." *Record*, September 15.

Logan, John R. 2001. "The New Ethnic Enclaves in America's Suburbs." University at Albany, State University of New York, Lewis Mumford Center for Comparative Urban and Regional Research Report. http://mumford.albany.edu/census/suburban/SuburbanReport/page1.html.

Logan, John R., Richard D. Alba, and Wenquan Zhang. 2002. "Immigrant Enclaves and Ethnic Communities in New York and Los Angeles." *American Sociological Review* 67 (2): 299–322.

Logan, John R., and Harvey L. Molotch. (1987) 2007. *Urban Fortunes: The Political Economy of Place*. 20th anniversary ed. Berkeley and Los Angeles: University of California Press.

Logan, John R., and Charles Zhang. 2010. "Global Neighborhoods: New Pathways to Diversity and Separation." *American Journal of Sociology* 115 (4): 1069–1109.

Lopez, David, and Yen Espiritu. 1990. "Panethnicity in the United States: A Theoretical Framework." *Ethnic and Racial Studies* 13 (2): 198–224.

Lott, Juanita Tamayo. 1976. "The Asian American Concept: In Quest of Identity." *Bridge: An Asian-American Perspective*, November, 30–34.

Lung-Amam, Willow. 2015. "The Vibrant Life of Asian Malls in Silicon Valley." In Archer, Sandul, and Solomonson 2015.

———. 2017. *Trespassers? Asian Americans and the Battle for Suburbia*. Oakland: University of California Press.

Ly, Phuong. 2005. "A Wrenching Choice." *Washington Post*, January 9.

———. 2008. "The Early Study Abroad Trend." *Diverse: Issues in Higher Education* 25 (7): 18–20.

Lynwander, Linda. 1982. "Why Fort Lee Lures Japanese." *New York Times*, January 10.

Ma, Myles. 2016. "Construction Starts on Second Fort Lee Tower." NJ Advance Media for NJ.com. April 26.

Mahler, Sarah J. 1995. *Salvadorans in Suburbia: Symbiosis and Conflict*. Boston, Mass.: Allyn and Bacon.

Maitland, Leslie. 1976. "Fort Lee: Suburb of Japan." *New York Times*, January 25.

Marcuse, Peter. 1997. "The Enclave, the Citadel, and the Ghetto: What Has Changed in the Post-Fordist U.S. City." *Urban Affairs Review* 33 (2): 228–264.

Martin, Antoinette. 2001. "New Jersey: Weighing the Disaster's Impact across the Hudson." *New York Times*, October 7.

———. 2004. "Helping Asians Find Harmonious Locations." *New York Times*, November 28.

———. 2007. "Center Stage in Fort Lee." *New York Times*, April 29.

———. 2009. "Glittering Potential, Shady Past." *New York Times*, August 16.

Massey, Douglas S. 1985. "Ethnic Residential Segregation: A Theoretical Synthesis and Empirical Review." *Sociology and Social Research* 69 (3): 315–350.

———, ed. 2008. *New Faces in New Places: The Changing Geography of American Immigration*. New York: Russell Sage.

Massey, Douglas S., Len Albright, Rebecca Casciano, Elizabeth Derickson, and David N. Kensey. 2013. *Climbing Mount Laurel: The Struggle for Affordable Housing and Social Mobility in an American Suburb*. Princeton: Princeton University Press.

Massey, Douglas S., and Nancy A. Denton. 1985. "Spatial Assimilation as a Socioeconomic Outcome." *American Sociological Review* 50:94–106.

———. 1987. "Trends in the Residential Segregation of Blacks, Hispanics, and Asians: 1970–1980." *American Sociological Review* 52 (6): 802–825.

———. 1988. "Suburbanization and Segregation in U.S. Metropolitan Areas." *American Journal of Sociology* 94 (3): 592–626.

Matsumoto, Noriko. 2012. "Constructing Multiethnic Space: East Asian Immigration in Fort Lee, New Jersey." PhD dissertation, City University of New York, New York.

Mazur, D. Bennett. 1981. "People, Politics and Planning: The Comparative History of Three Suburban Communities." PhD dissertation, Rutgers University, New Brunswick, N.J.

McGlinn, Lawrence A. 2002. "Beyond Chinatown: Dual Immigration and the Chinese Population of Metropolitan New York City, 2000." *Middle States Geographer* 35:110–119.

Meyers, Thomas. 2007. "Thomas Paine and 'The Times That Tried Men's Souls." In *The Revolutionary War in Bergen County: The Times That Tried Men's Souls*. Edited by Carol Karels. Charleston, S.C.: History Press.

———. 2013. "From the Archives: Fort Lee's Hudson River Swimming 'Judge' Jimmy Moore." *Fort Lee Patch*, July 12.

Min, Pyong Gap. 1992. "The Structure and Social Functions of Korean Immigrant Churches in the United States." *International Migration Review* 26 (4): 1370–1394.

———. 1996. *Caught in the Middle: Korean Communities in New York and Los Angeles*. Berkeley and Los Angeles: University of California Press.

———. 2001. "Koreans: An 'Institutionally Complete Community.'" In *New Immigrants in New York*. Edited by Nancy Foner. New York: Columbia University Press.

———, ed. 2006. *Asian Americans: Contemporary Trends and Issues*. 2nd ed. Thousand Oaks, Calif.: Pine Forge Press.

———. 2010. *Preserving Ethnicity through Religion in America: Korean Protestants and Indian Hindus across Generations*. New York: New York University Press.

Mizukami, Tetsuo. 2007. *The Sojourner Community: Japanese Migration and Residency in Australia*. Leiden: Brill.

Moeller, Susan C. 2011. "Korean-American Groups Seeking to Solidify Influence." *Fort Lee Suburbanite*, April 1.

Moore, Deborah Dash. 1981. *At Home in America: Second Generation New York Jews*. New York: Columbia University Press.

Most, Doug, and Paul Kane. 1999. "Ethnic Mix of North Jersey Changes: Numbers of Asians, Hispanics Up Sharply." *Record*, September 15.

Muller, Peter O. 1981. *Contemporary Suburban America*. Englewood Cliffs, N.J.: Prentice Hall.

———. 1997. "The Suburban Transformation of the Globalizing American City." *Annals of the American Academy of Political and Social Science* 551:44–58.

Mumma, Christopher. 1997. "Who We Are: The Changing Face of North Jersey. Population Is Older, Wealthier, More Varied." *Record*, January 1.

Murji, Karim, and John Solomos, eds. 2015. *Theories of Race and Ethnicity: Contemporary Debates and Perspectives*. Cambridge: Cambridge University Press.

Muto, Hiroko. 1985. *Tsumatachi no kaigaichūzai* [Expatriate wives]. Tokyo: Bungeishunjū.

Mydans, Seth. 1994. "Asian Investors Create a Pocket of Prosperity: California Valley Avoids Region's Slide." *New York Times*, October 17.

Myerson, Allen R. 1992. "6,800 Miles from Tokyo, East Meets West at a Shopping Mall." *New York Times*, January 20.

Myles, John, and Feng Hou. 2004. "Changing Colours: Spatial Assimilation and New Racial Minority Immigrants." *Canadian Journal of Sociology* 29 (1): 29–58.

Nagel, Joane. 1994. "Constructing Ethnicity: Creating and Recreating Ethnic Identity and Culture." *Social Problems* 41 (1): 152–176.

———. 1996. *American Indian Ethnic Renewal: Red Power and the Resurgence of Identity and Culture*. New York: Oxford University Press.

Nash, Alan. 2009. "From Spaghetti to Sushi: An Investigation of the Growth of Ethnic Restaurants in Montreal, 1951–2001." *Food, Culture & Society* 12 (1): 5–24.

Newman, Katherine S. 1993. *Declining Fortunes: The Withering of the American Dream*. New York: Basic Books.

New York Times. 1908. "Unveil Monument to Fort Lee Heroes: Quiet Jersey Town Stirred by Marching Troops and Cannon Thundering in Salute. Marks Washington's Camp. Gov. Fort Recalls the Struggles of the Revolution and Tells of a Little-Known Battle at Fort Lee." September 27.

———. 1909. "Woes of the Moving Picture Man: Scenes That Never Come before the Public—an Open Air Performance." December 19.

Nicolaides Becky M., and Andrew Wiese, eds. 2006. *The Suburban Reader*. New York: Routledge.

Nieves, Blanca A. 1998a. "Fort Lee to Add Korean-Speaking Cop: A Response to Demographic Trend." *Record*, June 10.

———. 1998b. "Fort Lee Hiring Cops Who Speak Korean: Seeks Connections to Large Community." *Record*, November 6.

———. 1999. "Fort Lee to Hire 3 Korean Officers: Borough Bypasses Its Eligibility List." *Record*, January 13.

Noble, Greg. 2013. "Cosmopolitan Habits: The Capacities and Habitats of Intercultural Conviviality." *Body & Society* 19 (2/3): 162–185.

Oh, Sookhee. 2007. "Immigrant Communities and Ethnic Linkages: Suburban Koreans in the New York-New Jersey Metropolitan Area." PhD dissertation, New School University, New York.

O'Hare, William P., and William H. Frey. 1994. "Asians in the Suburbs." *American Demographics* 16 (5): 32–39.

Okamoto, Dina G. 2014. *Redefining Race: Asian American Panethnicity and Shifting Ethnic Boundaries*. New York: Russell Sage.

Omi, Michael, and Howard Winant. 1994. *Racial Formation in the United States: From the 1960s to the 1990s*. New York: Routledge.

Oser, Alan S. 1981. "Real Estate: New Office Projects in Fort Lee." *New York Times*, September 9.

Palen, J. John. 1995. *The Suburbs*. New York: McGraw-Hill.

Pérez-Peña, Richard. 2010. "As Koreans Pour In, a Town Is Remade." *New York Times*, December 15.

Pew Research Center. 2013. "The Rise of Asian Americans." http://www.pewsocialtrends.org/files/2013/04/Asian-Americans-new-full-report-04-2013.pdf.

Phelan, Thomas J., and Mark Schneider. 1996. "Race, Ethnicity, and Class in American Suburbs." *Urban Affairs Review* 31:659–680.

Portes, Alejandro, and Rubén G. Rumbaut. 2001. *Legacies: The Story of the Immigrant Second Generation*. Berkeley and Los Angeles: University of California Press.

Portes, Alejandro, and Min Zhou. 1993. "The New Second Generation: Segmented Assimilation and Its Variants." *Annals of the American Academy of Political and Social Science* 530:74–96.

Pugliese, Nicholas. 2016a. "Resurgence in Fort Lee as Long-Empty Lot Developed." NorthJersey.com, May 8.

———. 2016b. "Theater Projects in Fort Lee Put Focus on Town's History as Birthplace of the Modern Movie Industry." NorthJersey.com, June 8.

Ray, Brian K., Greg Halseth, and Benjamin Johnson. 1997. "The Changing 'Face' of the Suburbs: Issues of Ethnicity and Residential Change in Suburban Vancouver." *International Journal of Urban & Regional Research* 21 (1): 75–99.

Record (Hackensack, N.J.). 2001. "Racial and Ethnic Patterns, 1980–2000." Special section, March 9.

———. 2004. "Korean Flag Burned at Fort Lee War Memorial." June 17.

Reed, Leonard. 1988a. "Shall the Twain Ever Meet?—Another World Lives Next Door." *Record*, February 14.

———. 1988b. "Two Cultures: Side by Side, but Not Together." *Record*, February 15.

———. 1988c. "A Quest for Learning: The Japanese Path to Success." *Record*, February 16.

Rockland, Michael Aaron. 2008. *The George Washington Bridge: Poetry in Steel*. New Brunswick, N.J.: Rutgers University Press.

Rossi, Christina. 2008a. "Fort Lee Council Declares Centuria Builder in Default." *Bergen News*, May 7.

———. 2008b. "Fort Lee Ends Agreement with Centuria Developer." *Bergen News*, June 18.

———. 2008c. "Fort Lee OKs Sign, Façade Ordinance." *Bergen News*, September 3.

Saito, Leland. 1998. *Race and Politics: Asian Americans, Latinos, and Whites in a Los Angeles Suburb*. Urbana: University of Illinois Press.

Saito, Leland T., and John Horton. 1994. "The New Chinese Immigration and the Rise of Asian American Politics in Monterey Park, California." In *The New Asian Immigration in Los Angeles and Global Restructuring*. Edited by Paul Ong, Edna Bonacich, and Lucie Cheng. Philadelphia: Temple University Press.

Sakamoto, Arthur, Kimberly A. Goyette, and Chang Hwan Kim. 2009. "Socioeconomic Attainments of Asian Americans." *Annual Review of Sociology* 35:255–276.

Sandercock, Leonie. 2003. *Cosmopolis II: Mongrel Cities of the 21st Century*. London: Continuum.

Sanjek, Roger. 2000. *The Future of Us All: Race and Neighborhood Politics in New York City*. Ithaca and London: Cornell University Press.

Schwartz, Joel, and Daniel Prosser, eds. 1977. *Cities of the Garden State: Essays in the Urban and Suburban History of New Jersey*. Dubuque, Iowa: Kendall/Hunt Publishing.

Shavick, Audrey. 1972. "The Far East (in Fort Lee)." *New York Times*, December 3.

Shepard, Richard F. 1972. "The Ethnic Crackerbarrels of Queens." *New York Times*, February 20.

Shih, Evelyn. 2006. "Why Let Go? Heritage Language Schools Help Bind the Families of Immigrants." *Record*, October 15.

Shinagawa, Larry Hajime, and Gin Yong Pang. 1996. "Asian American Panethnicity and Intermarriage." *Amerasia Journal* 22 (2): 127–152.

Shinkai, Yoshiko. 1994. "Education and Japanese Motherhood in Fort Lee, New Jersey." PhD dissertation, Rutgers, The State University of New Jersey, New Brunswick, N.J.

Shyong, Frank. 2013a. "Monterey Park Sign Ordinance Debate Recalls '80s Ethnic Controversy." *Los Angeles Times*, August 3.

———. 2013b. "Monterey Park Drops Plan for English Signs amid Community Outcry." *Los Angeles Times*, December 5.

Siegel, Jessica. 1993. "Perfect Harmony in Fort Lee: Choir Unites Women of Japan." *Record*, March 3.

Singer, Audrey, Susan W. Hardwick, and Caroline B. Brettell, eds. 2008. *Twenty-First-Century Gateways: Immigrant Incorporation in Suburban America*. Washington, D.C.: Brookings Institution Press.

Siu, Paul C. P. 1952. "The Sojourner." *American Journal of Sociology* 58 (1): 34–44.

Skop, Emily, and Wei Li. 2005. "Asians in America's Suburbs: Patterns and Consequences of Settlement." *Geographical Review* 95 (2): 167–188.

Smith, Christopher J. 1995. "Asian New York: The Geography and Politics of Diversity." *International Migration Review* 29 (1): 59–84.

Smith, Christopher J., and John R. Logan. 2006. "Flushing 2000: Geographic Explorations in Asian New York." In Li 2006.

Spehr, Paul. 2004. "Introduction: City of Intrigue and Mystery." In Koszarski 2004.

State of New Jersey, Department of Education. 2007. "New Jersey School Report Card for 2006." http://www.nj.gov/education/reportcard/2006/index.html.

———. 2008. "New Jersey School Report Card for 2007." http://www.nj.gov/education/reportcard/2007/index.html.

———. 2015. "2014–2015 School Performance Reports." http://www.nj.gov/education/pr/1415/nav/county/03/1550/index.html.

———. n.d. "Report Card Narratives. New Jersey Department of Education. Fort Lee Boro (03-1550)." Kenneth J. Rota, Superintendent of Schools. http://www.nj.gov/education/pr/1415/narrative/03/1550/000.html.

Steinberg, Stephen. 2004. "The Melting Pot and the Color Line." In *Reinventing the Melting Pot*. Edited by Tamar Jacoby. New York: Basic Books.

Sudol, Karen. 2009. "Education Is the Ticket for Koreans: Drawn to Tenafly for Schools." *Record*, April 21.

Tavernise, Sabrina, and Robert Gebeloff. 2010. "Immigrants Make Paths to Suburbia, Not Cities." *New York Times*, December 14.

Tonkiss, Fran. 2005. *Space, the City and Social Theory: Social Relations and Urban Forms*. Cambridge, U.K.: Polity.

Trevor, Malcolm. 1991. "The Overseas Strategies of Japanese Corporations." *Annals of the American Academy of Political and Social Science* 513:90–101.

Tuan, Mia. 1998. *Forever Foreigners or Honorary Whites? The Asian Experience Today*. New Brunswick, N.J.: Rutgers University Press.

Tung, Rosalie L[am]. 1984. *Key to Japan's Economic Strength: Human Power*. Lexington, Mass.: Lexington Books.

U.S. Bureau of the Census. 1952. *U.S. Census of Population: 1950*. Vol. II, *Characteristics of the Population. Part 30, New Jersey*. Washington, D.C.: U.S. Government Printing Office.

———. 1953. *Census of Housing: 1950*. Vol. I, *General Characteristics. Part 4, Michigan–New York*. Washington, D.C.: U.S. Government Printing Office.

———. 1962. *U.S. Census of Population and Housing: 1960. Census Tracts. Final Report. PHC (1)-114*. Washington, D.C.: U.S. Government Printing Office.

———. 1972. *Census of Housing: 1970*. Vol. I, *Housing Characteristics for States, Cities, and Counties. Part 32, New Jersey*. Washington, D.C.: U.S. Government Printing Office.

———. 1973. *Census of Population: 1970*. Vol. I, *Characteristics of the Population. Part 32, New Jersey—Section 1*. Washington, D.C.: U.S. Government Printing Office.

———. 1982. *1980 Census of Housing. Characteristics of Housing Units. Chapter A, General Housing Characteristics. Part 32, New Jersey*. Washington, D.C.: U.S. Government Printing Office.

———. 1983. *1980 Census of Population*. Vol. I, *Characteristics of the Population. Part 32. New Jersey*. Washington, D.C.: U.S. Government Printing Office.

———. 1992a. *1990 Census of Population. General Population Characteristics*. New Jersey. CP-1-32. Washington, D.C.: U.S. Government Printing Office.

———. 1992b. *1990 Census of Housing. General Housing Characteristics*. New Jersey. H-1-32. Washington, D.C.: U.S. Government Printing Office.

———. 1993. *1990 Census of Population. Social and Economic Characteristics*. New Jersey 1990 CP-2-32. Washington, D.C.: U.S. Government Printing Office.

———. 2000a. *Census of Population and Housing: Public Use Microdata Sample (PUMS)*. Washington, D.C.: U.S. Department of Commerce. Bureau of the Census.

———. 2000b. "Profile of General Demographic Characteristics: 2000. Fort Lee Borough, New Jersey." American FactFinder. http://factfinder.census.gov.

———. 2001. *County and City Data Book: 2000*. 13th ed. Washington, D.C.: U.S. Government Printing Office.

———. 2010. "Profile of General Population and Housing Characteristics: 2010 Demographic Profile Data. DP-1." American FactFinder. http://factfinder.census.gov.

———. 2012. "2012 Economic Census: Survey of Business Owners." United States Census QuickFacts, Fort Lee Borough, New Jersey. https://www.census.gov/quickfacts/table/PST045216/3424420,34.

———. 2014. "2014 ZIP Code Business Patterns (NAICS), County Business Patterns." http://censtats.census.gov/cgi-bin/zbpnaic/zbpsect.pl.

———. 2015. "2011–2015 American Community Survey 5-Year Estimates. Fort Lee Borough, New Jersey." American FactFinder. http://factfinder.census.gov.

Valluvan, Sivamohan. 2016. "Conviviality and Multiculture: A Post-integration Sociology of Multi-ethnic Interaction." *Young* 24 (3): 204–221.

Verdon, Joan. 2006. "Tigers on the Rise: Asian-American Business Booming." *Record*, May 17.

Villegas, Ana María, and John W. Young. 1997. "Immigrant Education in New Jersey: Policies and Practices." In Espenshade 1997.

Võ, Linda Trinh. 2004. *Mobilizing an Asian American Community*. Philadelphia: Temple University Press.

Võ, Linda Trinh, and Mary Yu Danico. 2004. "The Formation of Post-suburban Communities: Koreatown and Little Saigon, Orange County." *International Journal of Sociology and Social Policy* 24 (7/8): 15–45.

Vuong, Zen. 2013. "Monterey Park Postpones Decision on 'Modern Latin' Sign Ordinance." *San Gabriel Valley Tribune*, October 4.

Wallerstein, Immanuel. 1983. *Historical Capitalism*. London: Verso.

Wander, Erik. 2011. "Magazine: FLHS Seventh Best High School in State in Demographic Group." *Fort Lee Patch*, August 23.

Warner, William Lloyd. 1959. *The Living and the Dead: A Study of the Symbolic Life of Americans*. New Haven, Conn.: Yale University Press.

Waters, Mary C., and Tomás R. Jiménez. 2005. "Assessing Immigrant Assimilation: New Empirical and Theoretical Challenges." *Annual Review of Sociology* 31:105–125.

Waters, Mary C., and Marisa Gerstein Pineau, eds. 2015. *The Integration of Immigrants into American Society*. Washington, D.C.: National Academies Press.

Waters, Mary C., and Reed Ueda, eds. 2007. *The New Americans: A Guide to Immigration since 1965*. Cambridge, Mass.: Harvard University Press.

Weber, Max. (1922) 1978. *Economy and Society: An Outline of Interpretive Sociology*. Vol. I. Edited by Guenther Roth and Claus Wittich. Berkeley and Los Angeles: University of California Press.

Weil, Lynne. 2000. "The Pacific Rim, a Continent Away: Asians, the State's Fastest-Growing Minority, Are Changing the Face of New Jersey." *New York Times*, October 22.

White, Merry. 1988. *The Japanese Overseas: Can They Go Home Again?* New York: Free Press.

White, Michael J., Ann E. Biddlecom, and Shenyang Guo. 1993. "Immigration, Naturalization, and Residential Assimilation among Asian Americans in 1980." *Social Forces* 72 (1): 93–117.

White, Michael J., Eric Fong, and Qian Cai. 2003. "The Segregation of Asian-Origin Groups in the United States and Canada." *Social Science Research* 32 (1): 148–167.

White, Paul. 1998. "The Settlement Patterns of Developed World Migrants in London." *Urban Studies* 35 (10): 1725–1744.

Williamson, Judith. (1978) 2010. *Decoding Advertisements: Ideology and Meaning in Advertising*. London: Marion Boyars.

Wong, Paul. 1972. "The Emergence of the Asian-American Movement." *Bridge: The Asian-American Magazine* 2:33–39.

Wood, Joseph. 1997. "Vietnamese American Place Making in Northern Virginia." *Geographical Review* 87 (1): 58–72.

Wu, Sen-Yuan. 2012. "New Jersey's Asian Population by Asian Group: 2010." *NJ Labor Market Views* 18 (February 17). State of New Jersey, Department of Labor and Workforce Development. http://www.nj.gov/labor/lpa/pub/lmv/lmv_18.pdf.

Yin, Xiao-huang. 2007. "China: People's Republic in China." In Waters and Ueda 2007.

Yoo, Charles. 1999. "At Separate Tables: High School Longs to Bridge a Racial Divide." *Record*, May 6.

Yoon, In-Jin. 1993. *The Social Origins of Korean Immigration to the United States from 1965 to the Present*. Papers of the Program on Population 121. Honolulu: East-West Center.

———. 1997. *On My Own: Korean Businesses and Race Relations in America*. Chicago: University of Chicago Press.

Zeaman, John. 2004. "Fort Lee's Main Street Mixes It Up." *Record*, December 12.

Zelinsky, Wilbur, and Barrett A. Lee. 1998. "Heterolocalism: An Alternative Model of the Sociospatial Behaviour of Immigrant Ethnic Communities." *International Journal of Population Geography* 4:281–298.

Zeng, Wei, and Wei Li. 2009. "Chinese Week: Building Chinese American Community through Festivity in Metropolitan Phoenix." In Ling 2009.

Zernike, Kate. 2016a. "Chris Christie Knew about Bridge Lane Closings as They Happened, Prosecutors Say." *New York Times*, September 16.

———. 2016b. "2 Ex-Christie Allies Are Convicted in George Washington Bridge Case." *New York Times*, November 4.

Zerubavel, Eviatar. 2003. "Calendars and History: A Comparative Study of the Social Organization of National Memory." In *States of Memory: Continuities, Conflicts, and Transformations in National Retrospection*. Edited by Jeffrey K. Olick. Durham, N.C.: Duke University Press.

Zhao, Xiaojian. 2010. *The New Chinese America: Class, Economy, and Social Hierarchy*. New Brunswick, N.J.: Rutgers University Press.

Zhou, Min. 2004. "Are Asian Americans Becoming 'White'?" *Contexts* 3 (1): 29–37.

———. 2009. *Contemporary Chinese America: Immigration, Ethnicity, and Community Transformation*. Philadelphia: Temple University Press.

Zhou, Min, and Rebecca Kim. 2003. "A Tale of Two Metropolises: New Immigrant Chinese Communities in New York and Los Angeles." In *Los Angeles and New York in the New Millennium*. Edited by David Halle. Chicago: University of Chicago Press.

Zhou, Min, and Susan S. Kim. 2006. "Community Forces, Social Capital, and Educational Achievement: The Case of Supplementary Education in the Chinese and Korean Immigrant Communities." *Harvard Educational Review* 76 (1): 1–29.

Zhou, Min, and Xiyuan Li. 2003. "Ethnic Language Schools and the Development of Supplementary Education in the Immigrant Chinese Community in the United States." *Understanding the Social Worlds of Immigrant Youth, New Directions for Youth Development* (Winter): 57–73.

Zhou, Min, Yen-Fen Tseng, and Rebecca Y. Kim. 2008. "Rethinking Residential Assimilation: The Case of a Chinese Ethnoburb in the San Gabriel Valley, California." *Amerasia Journal* 34 (3): 55–83.

Zia, Helen. 2000. *Asian American Dreams: The Emergence of an American People*. New York: Farrar, Straus and Giroux.

INDEX